TEHILLIM
KING DAVID'S PSALMS

TEHILLIM
KING DAVID'S PSALMS

FROM BIBLICAL HEBREW
TO MODERN ENGLISH

by

Avraham Rand

Tehillim, King David's Psalms:
From Biblical Hebrew to Modern English

Published by Devora Publishing Company
Text Copyright © 2013 Dina Rand

COVER DESIGN: Shani Schmell
TYPESETTING: Ariel Walden
EDITORIAL AND PRODUCTION DIRECTOR: Daniella Barak

Soft Cover ISBN: 978-965-524-132-7

First edition. Printed in Israel

Distributor:
Urim Publications
POB 52287
Jerusalem 91521, Israel
Tel: 02.679.7633
Fax: 02.679.7634
urim_pub@netvision.net.il
www.UrimPublications.com

This translation of sefer Tehillim is dedicated to the millions of Jewish people, who throughout generations have said these sacred words, cry their tears and have spoken from the depths of their hearts to the almighty HASHEM their Father in heaven. May all of their prayers always be answered for good.

With profound emuna to my HASHEM for everything.

To my very dear wife Dina Leah for all her support, companionship and love.

Also to our very dear children:

Blossom and Shaul RABINOWITZ

Bonnie and Aaron Dovid DAVIS

Jeremy and Malka RAND

Aaron and Naomi RAND

Tova Esther and Shlomi RON

Shalom Simcha and Tziona RAND

Moshe Dovid and Karina RAND

Tzipporah Susan and Netanel TUBUL

And to all our dear grandchildren

To my dear and special parents
Reb Moshe Aaron and Chaya Esther RAND z"l

To my dear brother Rabbi Jacob Joseph RAND z"l

To my dear in laws Mr. and Mrs. David SIMON z"l

To my dear brother Dr. Leon RAND

To my dear brother Dr. Shmuel and Debra RAND

To my dear sister Sooge and Yossi AVRAHAMI

FOREWORD

WHILE IT IS TYPICAL FOR AN AUTHOR TO WRITE A foreword to his book, the author, my father Avraham (Abe) Rand z"l was not able to write it. My father passed away on 23 Av, 5769 (2009). This book, this Tehillim was his life's work. It was tremendously important to him to see the sefer completed and published. In fact, the last phone call he made, just a few hours before he passed away, was to Yaacov the publisher, he asked Yaacov to make sure that the book was finished as quickly as possible.

So why sefer Tehillim? Why this book over all the other wonderful books of Torah? As Jews it is the book we turn to for everything in our lives. It is the words we turn to in simcha and sorrow, fear and pain, thankfulness and gratitude to Hashem. Throughout his life Dovid Hamelech experiences many ups and downs. In this beautiful poetic sefer he pours out all of his emotions. It was certainly the sefer my father turned to for everything in his life. My father carried his little white paperback Tehillim in his knapsack. It went with him everywhere. He pulled it out and recited a few prakim whenever he had a free moment. One of my most precious memories with my father took place just eight days before he passed away. My sister and I had met our father at Belinson Hospital where he was having a test done. We talked and laughed for a while and then quietly my father took out his sefer Tehillim. The three of us sat there on the bench, each of us with a Tehillim in our hands, saying Tehillim. Yes it's the sefer you turn to when you are afraid and in pain. But my father was one of the most positive and joyful people that I've ever met. He lived a life in which he served Hashem with simcha. My father believed that Tehillim is the sefer you turn to when you are full of simcha and you want to thank Hashem for all the blessings in your life. He understood that the more Tehillim you say the more bracha and success you bring to your life and to the life of the Jewish people.

The Shlah once said "Blessed is the man that says Tehillim with shira, zimra, simcha and kavanot halev". My father most certainly said Tehillim in this manner. My father knew that in order to say Tehillim with song and joy, and in order to say it in a meaningful way, you needed to understand it. My father commuted for many hours to and from his home and dental practice in Rechovot. He spent many a bus ride saying Tehillim and many times observing others sitting and saying Tehillim. He often wondered if those of us who sit and mumble the words, understood what we were saying or even could appreciate the beautiful poetry of the words they were saying. While there are other books which offer a translation of Tehillim, many of them are written in very biblical words, which are hard for people to understand. My father hoped to write a translation of Tehillim which was written in words that anyone and everyone could understand and appreciate. My father wanted to write a translation in which the beauty and poetry of this masterpiece of David Hamelech would be appreciated by all.

Blossom Rand Rabinowitz

*

We would like to express our hakarat hatov to Yaacov Peterseil who worked as an editor on this book. Our father spent many hours working with Yaacov on this sefer and he greatly respected him. Without his help we would never have been able to complete our father's dream in completing this Sefer Tehillim. We will always be tremendously grateful to him.

The Rand family

INTRODUCTION

There had to be a book of Tehillim in the world. Tehillim – a book of the Torah, a Divinely-inspired book, the Book of King David – is a masterwork about the experience of human life and about the relationship between God and human beings. It speaks to us personally, relating the history of the Jewish people. It is proof that the blessings of Israel are blessings for all humankind, and that Israel has a mission to radiate the light of God every day. The songs of Tehillim are magnificent poetry that contain ideas beyond description. Even as they represent the truest and deepest possible faith, they also depict human hopes and feelings. They sing of prophecies, both those that have already been fulfilled and those that have yet to be fulfilled.

The psalms are the story of human beings appealing to Divine love. They translate unshakable faith in God into song, and prayer for the needs of the people, and the nation.

Where else can one find such great beauty and tender feeling in songs written by human beings?

The psalms contain the ideals of Divine justice, which give our lives happiness and stability. They contain the ideals of Jewish tradition, including our faith in the arrival of Mashiach. They embrace both the Talmud and the Targum.

The psalms show us both individual human suffering and that of the nation of Israel. However, their concluding messages sing of comfort; The triumph of faith and God's ultimate victory in the battle between good and evil.

The five books of Tehillim sing the story of human life and of our striving to walk in the path of God and His Torah. As they sing of our return from the Babylonian exile, they prophesy our return from spiritual exile, praising God for His mercy toward Israel. It was only natural that the psalms' beauty, profound and penetrating imagery, emotions and language would enter the Jewish liturgy, just as they were sung by the Levites in the Beit ha-Mikdash. They are the songs of the angels, the songs of heaven and earth.

The psalms are the conversations of the human heart with God, the Creator.

The Songs of Ascents (Psalms 120–135) have the ability to lift their singers up the steps of life with their expressions of praise and gratitude to God. They speak of the feelings of weary Jewish souls on pilgrimage to Zion and Jerusalem, where they sing of their trust in God despite their painful toil for daily bread.

They sing of suffering, defeat, attacks on Jerusalem, the Babylonian exile and the nation's sins.

The Book of Tehillim crystallizes the yearnings of the human spirit as it speaks to God of His glorious promises, His awesome power, and His control of Israel's history and destiny. They sing of good relationships between siblings and mourn relationships that have gone wrong. They sing of the calm of the Sabbath day, the happiness of husband and wife, parents and children. Even as they sing of the limitations and seeming insignificance of humankind, they assure us of God's call to all human beings and of His loving care.

The psalms tell of God's love, kindness, caring and justice. They sing of His might and constant guidance of the Universe that He created, and of His miracles and victories.

They sing of Israel's mission to call upon every living soul to worship the true God.

What would the world be like without the Book of Tehillim?

The world needs a Book of Tehillim to support the human soul.

TEHILLIM
KING DAVID'S PSALMS

פרק א

א אַשְׁרֵי־הָאִישׁ אֲשֶׁר לֹא הָלַךְ בַּעֲצַת רְשָׁעִים וּבְדֶרֶךְ חַטָּאִים לֹא עָמָד וּבְמוֹשַׁב לֵצִים לֹא יָשָׁב:

ב כִּי אִם־בְּתוֹרַת יְהוָה חֶפְצוֹ וּבְתוֹרָתוֹ יֶהְגֶּה יוֹמָם וָלָיְלָה:

ג וְהָיָה כְּעֵץ שָׁתוּל עַל־פַּלְגֵי מָיִם אֲשֶׁר פִּרְיוֹ יִתֵּן בְּעִתּוֹ וְעָלֵהוּ לֹא יִבּוֹל וְכֹל אֲשֶׁר־יַעֲשֶׂה יַצְלִיחַ:

ד לֹא־כֵן הָרְשָׁעִים כִּי אִם־כַּמֹּץ אֲשֶׁר־תִּדְּפֶנּוּ רוּחַ:

ה עַל־כֵּן לֹא־יָקֻמוּ רְשָׁעִים בַּמִּשְׁפָּט וְחַטָּאִים בַּעֲדַת צַדִּיקִים:

ו כִּי־יוֹדֵעַ יְהוָה דֶּרֶךְ צַדִּיקִים וְדֶרֶךְ רְשָׁעִים תֹּאבֵד:

פרק ב

א לָמָּה רָגְשׁוּ גוֹיִם וּלְאֻמִּים יֶהְגּוּ־רִיק:

ב יִתְיַצְּבוּ מַלְכֵי־אֶרֶץ וְרוֹזְנִים נוֹסְדוּ־יָחַד עַל־יְהוָה וְעַל־מְשִׁיחוֹ:

ג נְנַתְּקָה אֶת־מוֹסְרוֹתֵימוֹ וְנַשְׁלִיכָה מִמֶּנּוּ עֲבֹתֵימוֹ:

ד יוֹשֵׁב בַּשָּׁמַיִם יִשְׂחָק אֲדֹנָי יִלְעַג־לָמוֹ:

ה אָז יְדַבֵּר אֵלֵימוֹ בְאַפּוֹ וּבַחֲרוֹנוֹ יְבַהֲלֵמוֹ:

ו וַאֲנִי נָסַכְתִּי מַלְכִּי עַל־צִיּוֹן הַר־קָדְשִׁי:

ז אֲסַפְּרָה אֶל חֹק יְהוָה אָמַר אֵלַי בְּנִי אַתָּה אֲנִי הַיּוֹם יְלִדְתִּיךָ:

ח שְׁאַל מִמֶּנִּי וְאֶתְּנָה גוֹיִם נַחֲלָתֶךָ וַאֲחֻזָּתְךָ אַפְסֵי־אָרֶץ:

ט תְּרֹעֵם בְּשֵׁבֶט בַּרְזֶל כִּכְלִי יוֹצֵר תְּנַפְּצֵם:

*The way for human beings to find happiness
is to take delight in God's law.*

1 Happy is the man who has not walked in the ways of the wicked, does not act as sinners do and does not keep company with scornful people.

2 Rather, he takes joy in the law of the Lord and meditates upon His law day and night.

3 He will be like a tree planted by streams of water that brings forth its fruit in season and whose leaf does not fade. Whatever he does he will prosper.

4 Not so the wicked. They are like empty husks that the wind blows away.

5 Therefore the wicked and the sinners will not stand in judgment together with the righteous.

6 The Lord knows the way of the righteous – but the way of the sinner will perish.

*Although the nations may plot against God, their
schemes will always fail. God rules the world.*

1 Why are nations astir, and why do the people plot in vain?

2 The leaders of the earth gather, and the rulers conspire together against the Lord and His anointed.

3 "We will remove the bonds that are upon us and throw away our cords".

4 He who sits in heaven laughs; the Lord mocks them.

5 Then He will speak to them in His anger and frighten them in His terrible fury.

6 "It is true I that have established My king upon Zion, My holy mountain".

7 "I will tell you of My decision". The Lord said to me: "You are my son; this day I have created you.

8 Ask of Me, and I will give you nations for your inheritance and the ends of the earth for your possession.

פרק ג

י   וְעַתָּה מְלָכִים הַשְׂכִּילוּ הִוָּסְרוּ שֹׁפְטֵי אָרֶץ:

יא   עִבְדוּ אֶת־יְהוָה בְּיִרְאָה וְגִילוּ בִּרְעָדָה:

יב   נַשְּׁקוּ־בַר פֶּן־יֶאֱנַף וְתֹאבְדוּ דֶרֶךְ כִּי־יִבְעַר כִּמְעַט אַפּוֹ אַשְׁרֵי כָּל־
חוֹסֵי בוֹ:

פרק ג

א   מִזְמוֹר לְדָוִד בְּבָרְחוֹ מִפְּנֵי אַבְשָׁלוֹם בְּנוֹ:

ב   יְהוָה מָה־רַבּוּ צָרָי רַבִּים קָמִים עָלָי:

ג   רַבִּים אֹמְרִים לְנַפְשִׁי אֵין יְשׁוּעָתָה לּוֹ בֵאלֹהִים סֶלָה:

ד   וְאַתָּה יְהוָה מָגֵן בַּעֲדִי כְּבוֹדִי וּמֵרִים רֹאשִׁי:

ה   קוֹלִי אֶל־יְהוָה אֶקְרָא וַיַּעֲנֵנִי מֵהַר קָדְשׁוֹ סֶלָה:

ו   אֲנִי שָׁכַבְתִּי וָאִישָׁנָה הֱקִיצוֹתִי כִּי יְהוָה יִסְמְכֵנִי:

ז   לֹא־אִירָא מֵרִבְבוֹת עָם אֲשֶׁר סָבִיב שָׁתוּ עָלָי:

ח   קוּמָה יְהוָה הוֹשִׁיעֵנִי אֱלֹהַי כִּי־הִכִּיתָ אֶת־כָּל־אֹיְבַי לֶחִי שִׁנֵּי רְשָׁעִים
שִׁבַּרְתָּ:

ט   לַיהוָה הַיְשׁוּעָה עַל־עַמְּךָ בִרְכָתֶךָ סֶּלָה:

פרק ד

א   לַמְנַצֵּחַ בִּנְגִינוֹת מִזְמוֹר לְדָוִד:

ב   בְּקָרְאִי עֲנֵנִי אֱלֹהֵי צִדְקִי בַּצָּר הִרְחַבְתָּ לִּי חָנֵּנִי וּשְׁמַע תְּפִלָּתִי:

ג   בְּנֵי אִישׁ עַד־מֶה כְבוֹדִי לִכְלִמָּה תֶּאֱהָבוּן רִיק תְּבַקְשׁוּ כָזָב סֶלָה:

9　You will break them with a rod of iron" and shatter them to pieces like a potter's dish.

10　Now, you kings, be wise! Be warned, you judges of the earth!

11　Serve the Lord with reverence, and rejoice with trembling.

12　Worship in purity so that God will not be angry and you will not die upon the way when His sudden fury breaks forth. Happy are those who have faith in Him.

TEHILLIM 3

A prayer of trust in God's help when enemies threaten.

1　A psalm by David when he fled from his son Absalom.

2　Lord, how many are my enemies. Many people are attacking me.

3　Many people say of my soul: "There is no help for him from God." Selah.

4　But You, my Lord, are a shield about me. You are my glory and You lift up my head.

5　With my voice I call to the Lord, and He answers me from His holy mountain. Selah.

6　I lay myself down to sleep. I awaken, for the Lord has protected me.

7　I am not afraid of the tens of thousands of people who surround me.

8　Arise, my Lord! Save me, my God! You have struck my enemies on the cheek, and You have broken the teeth of the wicked.

9　Salvation comes from God. May Your blessings be upon Your people. Selah.

TEHILLIM 4

A prayer expressing confidence in God.

1　For chief musician, a psalm by David.

2　Answer me when I call, my righteous God. You protect me when I am troubled. Be gracious to me and hear my prayer.

3　Children of men, how long will you shame me, the king? You love worthless things and are interested in falsehood. Selah.

4　Know that the Lord has separated God fearing men for Himself. The Lord will hear when I call to Him.

פרק ה

ד וּדְעוּ כִּי־הִפְלָה יְהוָה חָסִיד לוֹ יְהוָה יִשְׁמַע בְּקָרְאִי אֵלָיו:

ה רִגְזוּ וְאַל־תֶּחֱטָאוּ אִמְרוּ בִלְבַבְכֶם עַל־מִשְׁכַּבְכֶם וְדֹמּוּ סֶלָה:

ו זִבְחוּ זִבְחֵי־צֶדֶק וּבִטְחוּ אֶל־יְהוָה:

ז רַבִּים אֹמְרִים מִי־יַרְאֵנוּ טוֹב נְסָה־עָלֵינוּ אוֹר פָּנֶיךָ יְהוָה:

ח נָתַתָּה שִׂמְחָה בְלִבִּי מֵעֵת דְּגָנָם וְתִירוֹשָׁם רָבּוּ:

ט בְּשָׁלוֹם יַחְדָּו אֶשְׁכְּבָה וְאִישָׁן כִּי־אַתָּה יְהוָה לְבָדָד לָבֶטַח תּוֹשִׁיבֵנִי:

פרק ה

א לַמְנַצֵּחַ אֶל־הַנְּחִילוֹת מִזְמוֹר לְדָוִד:

ב אֲמָרַי הַאֲזִינָה יְהוָה בִּינָה הֲגִיגִי:

ג הַקְשִׁיבָה לְקוֹל שַׁוְעִי מַלְכִּי וֵאלֹהָי כִּי־אֵלֶיךָ אֶתְפַּלָּל:

ד יְהוָה בֹּקֶר תִּשְׁמַע קוֹלִי בֹּקֶר אֶעֱרָךְ־לְךָ וַאֲצַפֶּה:

ה כִּי לֹא אֵל חָפֵץ רֶשַׁע אָתָּה לֹא יְגֻרְךָ רָע:

ו לֹא־יִתְיַצְּבוּ הוֹלְלִים לְנֶגֶד עֵינֶיךָ שָׂנֵאתָ כָּל־פֹּעֲלֵי אָוֶן:

ז תְּאַבֵּד דֹּבְרֵי כָזָב אִישׁ־דָּמִים וּמִרְמָה יְתָעֵב יְהוָה:

ח וַאֲנִי בְּרֹב חַסְדְּךָ אָבוֹא בֵיתֶךָ אֶשְׁתַּחֲוֶה אֶל־הֵיכַל קָדְשְׁךָ בְּיִרְאָתֶךָ:

ט יְהוָה נְחֵנִי בְצִדְקָתֶךָ לְמַעַן שׁוֹרְרָי הושר [הַיְשַׁר] לְפָנַי דַּרְכֶּךָ:

י כִּי אֵין בְּפִיהוּ נְכוֹנָה קִרְבָּם הַוּוֹת קֶבֶר־פָּתוּחַ גְּרוֹנָם לְשׁוֹנָם יַחֲלִיקוּן:

יא הַאֲשִׁימֵם אֱלֹהִים יִפְּלוּ מִמֹּעֲצוֹתֵיהֶם בְּרֹב פִּשְׁעֵיהֶם הַדִּיחֵמוֹ כִּי
מָרוּ בָךְ:

יב וְיִשְׂמְחוּ כָל־חוֹסֵי בָךְ לְעוֹלָם יְרַנֵּנוּ וְתָסֵךְ עָלֵימוֹ וְיַעְלְצוּ בְךָ אֹהֲבֵי שְׁמֶךָ:

יג כִּי־אַתָּה תְּבָרֵךְ צַדִּיק יְהוָה כַּצִּנָּה רָצוֹן תַּעְטְרֶנּוּ:

5   Tremble and do not sin. Search your heart when you lie down and be calm. Selah.

6   Offer the sacrifices of good and put your trust in the Lord.

7   Many people say, "If only we could see some good!" Lord, shine upon us the brightness of Your face.

8   You have put joy in my heart, much more than when their corn and wine have increased.

9   I will lie down and sleep in peace, for You, Lord, allow me to dwell on my own in safety.

TEHILLIM 5

God accepts no evil, and the righteous may be joyful.

1   For the chief musician on *nehilot,* on wind instruments a psalm by David.

2   Give ear to my words, my Lord, and heed my prayer.

3   Listen to the voice of my cry. My King and My God, to You I pray.

4   My Lord, in the morning You will hear my voice. In the morning I will send my prayer to You, and I look for Your help.

5   You are not a God Who takes pleasure in evil. Evil is not with You.

6   Those who boast will not stand in Your sight. You dislike all evil doers.

7   You destroy those who speak falsehood. The Lord hates men of violence and deceit.

8   As for me, I will enter Your house in the abundance of Your loving kindness. I will bow down toward Your holy Temple with in reverence to You.

9   My Lord, lead me in Your righteousness away from those who want to harm me. Your way lies straight before me.

10   There is no truth in their mouths. Their bodies are a pit and their throats are an open grave. Their tongues are glib.

11   Find them guilty, God. Let them fall by their own counsels. Punish them for their many sins, for they have rebelled against You.

12   Then all who take refuge in You will be joyful. They will always shout for joy, and You will shelter them. Those who love Your name will rejoice in You.

13   You bless the righteous, Lord. As with a shield, You surround him with your favor.

פרק ו

א לַמְנַצֵּחַ בִּנְגִינוֹת עַל־הַשְּׁמִינִית מִזְמוֹר לְדָוִד:

ב יְהוָה אַל־בְּאַפְּךָ תוֹכִיחֵנִי וְאַל־בַּחֲמָתְךָ תְיַסְּרֵנִי:

ג חָנֵּנִי יְהוָה כִּי אֻמְלַל אָנִי רְפָאֵנִי יְהוָה כִּי נִבְהֲלוּ עֲצָמָי:

ד וְנַפְשִׁי נִבְהֲלָה מְאֹד וְאַתְּ [וְאַתָּה] יְהוָה עַד־מָתָי:

ה שׁוּבָה יְהוָה חַלְּצָה נַפְשִׁי הוֹשִׁיעֵנִי לְמַעַן חַסְדֶּךָ:

ו כִּי אֵין בַּמָּוֶת זִכְרֶךָ בִּשְׁאוֹל מִי יוֹדֶה־לָּךְ:

ז יָגַעְתִּי בְּאַנְחָתִי אַשְׂחֶה בְכָל־לַיְלָה מִטָּתִי בְּדִמְעָתִי עַרְשִׂי אַמְסֶה:

ח עָשְׁשָׁה מִכַּעַס עֵינִי עָתְקָה בְּכָל־צוֹרְרָי:

ט סוּרוּ מִמֶּנִּי כָּל־פֹּעֲלֵי אָוֶן כִּי־שָׁמַע יְהוָה קוֹל בִּכְיִי:

י שָׁמַע יְהוָה תְּחִנָּתִי יְהוָה תְּפִלָּתִי יִקָּח:

יא יֵבֹשׁוּ וְיִבָּהֲלוּ מְאֹד כָּל־אֹיְבָי יָשֻׁבוּ יֵבֹשׁוּ רָגַע:

פרק ז

א שִׁגָּיוֹן לְדָוִד אֲשֶׁר־שָׁר לַיהוָה עַל־דִּבְרֵי־כוּשׁ בֶּן־יְמִינִי:

ב יְהוָה אֱלֹהַי בְּךָ חָסִיתִי הוֹשִׁיעֵנִי מִכָּל־רֹדְפַי וְהַצִּילֵנִי:

ג פֶּן־יִטְרֹף כְּאַרְיֵה נַפְשִׁי פֹּרֵק וְאֵין מַצִּיל:

ד יְהוָה אֱלֹהַי אִם־עָשִׂיתִי זֹאת אִם־יֶשׁ־עָוֶל בְּכַפָּי:

ה אִם־גָּמַלְתִּי שׁוֹלְמִי רָע וָאֲחַלְּצָה צוֹרְרִי רֵיקָם:

ו יִרַדֹּף אוֹיֵב נַפְשִׁי וְיַשֵּׂג וְיִרְמֹס לָאָרֶץ חַיָּי וּכְבוֹדִי לֶעָפָר יַשְׁכֵּן סֶלָה:

ז קוּמָה יְהוָה בְּאַפֶּךָ הִנָּשֵׂא בְּעַבְרוֹת צוֹרְרָי וְעוּרָה אֵלַי מִשְׁפָּט צִוִּיתָ:

TEHILLIM 6

A prayer from a troubled soul asking for God's salvation.

1 For the chief musician on an eight stringed instrument. A psalm by David.
2 My Lord, do not punish me in Your anger. Do not chastise me in Your wrath.
3 Be gracious to me, my Lord, for I am suffering. Heal me, my Lord, for my bones ache.
4 My soul is struck with terror. My Lord, how long?
5 Return, my Lord, and deliver me. Save me for Your mercy's sake.
6 In death no one remembers You. In the netherworld, who will give You thanks?
7 I am fatigued with my cries. Every night I make my bed float; I melt my couch away with tears.
8 My vision is dimmed because all my troubles, because of all my enemies.
9 Go away from me, all you evildoers, for the Lord has heard the sound of my weeping.
10 The Lord has heard my cries. The Lord has accepted my prayer.
11 All my enemies will be ashamed and frightened. They will turn away and suddenly be put to shame.

TEHILLIM 7

*A prayer for protection to the Divine Judge
from attacks by hostile people*

1 An error of David, when he sang to the Lord about Cush, a Benjaminite.
2 Lord my God, in You I have taken refuge. Save me from all those who chase and overtake me.
3 They may tear my soul like a lion, tearing it into pieces before I am saved.
4 Lord my God, if I have done this, if I have sin on my hands,
5 if I have sinned against the one who who was a friend, I who freed my injust enemy.
6 Then let the enemy pursue my soul and overtake it and crush my life down to the earth. Let him lay my glory in the dust. Selah.

ח וַעֲדַת לְאֻמִּים תְּסוֹבְבֶךָ וְעָלֶיהָ לַמָּרוֹם שׁוּבָה:

ט יְהוָה יָדִין עַמִּים שָׁפְטֵנִי יְהוָה כְּצִדְקִי וּכְתֻמִּי עָלָי:

י יִגְמָר־נָא רַע רְשָׁעִים וּתְכוֹנֵן צַדִּיק וּבֹחֵן לִבּוֹת וּכְלָיוֹת אֱלֹהִים צַדִּיק:

יא מָגִנִּי עַל־אֱלֹהִים מוֹשִׁיעַ יִשְׁרֵי־לֵב:

יב אֱלֹהִים שׁוֹפֵט צַדִּיק וְאֵל זֹעֵם בְּכָל־יוֹם:

יג אִם־לֹא יָשׁוּב חַרְבּוֹ יִלְטוֹשׁ קַשְׁתּוֹ דָרַךְ וַיְכוֹנְנֶהָ:

יד וְלוֹ הֵכִין כְּלֵי־מָוֶת חִצָּיו לְדֹלְקִים יִפְעָל:

טו הִנֵּה יְחַבֶּל־אָוֶן וְהָרָה עָמָל וְיָלַד שָׁקֶר:

טז בּוֹר כָּרָה וַיַּחְפְּרֵהוּ וַיִּפֹּל בְּשַׁחַת יִפְעָל:

יז יָשׁוּב עֲמָלוֹ בְרֹאשׁוֹ וְעַל־קָדְקֳדוֹ חֲמָסוֹ יֵרֵד:

יח אוֹדֶה יְהוָה כְּצִדְקוֹ וַאֲזַמְּרָה שֵׁם־יְהוָה עֶלְיוֹן:

פרק ח

א לַמְנַצֵּחַ עַל־הַגִּתִּית מִזְמוֹר לְדָוִד:

ב יְהוָה אֲדֹנֵינוּ מָה־אַדִּיר שִׁמְךָ בְּכָל־הָאָרֶץ אֲשֶׁר תְּנָה הוֹדְךָ עַל־הַשָּׁמָיִם:

ג מִפִּי עוֹלְלִים וְיֹנְקִים יִסַּדְתָּ עֹז לְמַעַן צוֹרְרֶיךָ לְהַשְׁבִּית אוֹיֵב וּמִתְנַקֵּם:

ד כִּי־אֶרְאֶה שָׁמֶיךָ מַעֲשֵׂי אֶצְבְּעֹתֶיךָ יָרֵחַ וְכוֹכָבִים אֲשֶׁר כּוֹנָנְתָּה:

ה מָה־אֱנוֹשׁ כִּי־תִזְכְּרֶנּוּ וּבֶן־אָדָם כִּי תִפְקְדֶנּוּ:

7 Arise, Lord, in your anger! Lift up Yourself in wrath against my enemies, and awaken for me the judgment that You have commanded.

8 Let the assembly of nations follow You, and return to Your heavens to rule over them.

9 Lord, who brings judgment to the nations! Judge me, Lord, according to the righteousness and the honesty within me.

10 Let complete judgment come upon the wicked, and may You support the righteous, for You, God of truth, test the heart and the emotions.

11 My protection is with God, Who saves the truthful in heart.

12 God is a righteous judge Who is angered each day.

13 If a man does not repent He will prepare His sword; He has bent His bow and made it ready.

14 He has also prepared for him the weapons of death, His arrows, are swift pursuers.

15 The wicked man labors with evil. He conceives wickedness and gives birth to falsehood.

16 He has dug a pit and cleared the earth from it – and he has fallen into the hole that he made.

17 The evil deeds of a wicked man will return upon his own head, and his violence will come down upon himself.

18 I will give thanks to the Lord for His righteousness, and I will sing praise to the name of the Most High God.

TEHILLIM 8

Although human beings, creations of God, are insignificant,
yet they are valuable partners in Creation.

1 For the chief musician, upon the *gittith*, a psalm by David.

2 Lord our God, how glorious is your name in all the earth! Your majesty is proclaimed above the heavens.

3 Because of Your enemies, You have given power to the voices of babes and infants to turn back foe and avenger.

4 When I look up to Your heavens, the creation of Your fingers, and I see the moon and stars that You have made –

5 What are human beings, that You even consider them? What is the son of man, that You think of him?

פרק ח

ו וַתְּחַסְּרֵהוּ מְּעַט מֵאֱלֹהִים וְכָבוֹד וְהָדָר תְּעַטְּרֵהוּ:

ז תַּמְשִׁילֵהוּ בְּמַעֲשֵׂי יָדֶיךָ כֹּל שַׁתָּה תַחַת־רַגְלָיו:

ח צֹנֶה וַאֲלָפִים כֻּלָּם וְגַם בַּהֲמוֹת שָׂדָי:

ט צִפּוֹר שָׁמַיִם וּדְגֵי הַיָּם עֹבֵר אָרְחוֹת יַמִּים:

י יְהוָה אֲדֹנֵינוּ מָה־אַדִּיר שִׁמְךָ בְּכָל־הָאָרֶץ:

פרק ט

א לַמְנַצֵּחַ עַלְמוּת לַבֵּן מִזְמוֹר לְדָוִד:

ב אוֹדֶה יְהוָה בְּכָל־לִבִּי אֲסַפְּרָה כָּל־נִפְלְאוֹתֶיךָ:

ג אֶשְׂמְחָה וְאֶעֶלְצָה בָךְ אֲזַמְּרָה שִׁמְךָ עֶלְיוֹן:

ד בְּשׁוּב־אוֹיְבַי אָחוֹר יִכָּשְׁלוּ וְיֹאבְדוּ מִפָּנֶיךָ:

ה כִּי־עָשִׂיתָ מִשְׁפָּטִי וְדִינִי יָשַׁבְתָּ לְכִסֵּא שׁוֹפֵט צֶדֶק:

ו גָּעַרְתָּ גוֹיִם אִבַּדְתָּ רָשָׁע שְׁמָם מָחִיתָ לְעוֹלָם וָעֶד:

ז הָאוֹיֵב תַּמּוּ חֳרָבוֹת לָנֶצַח וְעָרִים נָתַשְׁתָּ אָבַד זִכְרָם הֵמָּה:

ח וַיהוָה לְעוֹלָם יֵשֵׁב כּוֹנֵן לַמִּשְׁפָּט כִּסְאוֹ:

ט וְהוּא יִשְׁפֹּט־תֵּבֵל בְּצֶדֶק יָדִין לְאֻמִּים בְּמֵישָׁרִים:

י וִיהִי יְהוָה מִשְׂגָּב לַדָּךְ מִשְׂגָּב לְעִתּוֹת בַּצָּרָה:

יא וְיִבְטְחוּ בְךָ יוֹדְעֵי שְׁמֶךָ כִּי לֹא־עָזַבְתָּ דֹרְשֶׁיךָ יְהוָה:

יב זַמְּרוּ לַיהוָה יֹשֵׁב צִיּוֹן הַגִּידוּ בָעַמִּים עֲלִילוֹתָיו:

יג כִּי־דֹרֵשׁ דָּמִים אוֹתָם זָכָר לֹא־שָׁכַח צַעֲקַת עֲנִיִּים [עֲנָוִים]:

יד חָנְנֵנִי יְהוָה רְאֵה עָנְיִי מִשֹּׂנְאָי מְרוֹמְמִי מִשַּׁעֲרֵי מָוֶת:

טו לְמַעַן אֲסַפְּרָה כָּל־תְּהִלָּתֶיךָ בְּשַׁעֲרֵי בַת־צִיּוֹן אָגִילָה בִּישׁוּעָתֶךָ:

22

6 Yet You have made human beings only a little lower than the angels, and You have crowned them with glory and honor.

7 You have set them over the work of Your hands and placed all things beneath their feet:

8 Sheep and oxen and all the beasts of the field,

9 The birds in the air and the fish of the sea, and everything that lives in the deep sea.

10 Lord our God, how glorious is Your name in all the earth!

TEHILLIM 9

A song of thanksgiving for victory over hostile nations

1 For the chief musician upon the death of king Labin, a psalm by David.

2 I will give thanks to the Lord with my whole heart. I will tell of all Your wonderful works.

3 I will be glad and rejoice in You. I will sing praises to Your name, Most High.

4 My enemies are defeated. They fall and perish before You.

5 You have supported my right and my case. You sit on the throne as a righteous Judge.

6 You warned the nations. You destroyed the wicked and You erased their names for all time.

7 My foe, your ruins are gone forever, and the cities that you destroyed have not even a memory.

8 But the Lord exists forever. He has established His throne for judgment.

9 He will judge the world with truth. He will judge the nations fairly.

10 The Lord will also be a tower for the weak, a high tower in times of trouble.

11 Those who know Your name will put their trust in You, for You, Lord, do not forget those who look to You.

12 Sing praises to the Lord Who dwells in Zion. Tell all the people of His acts.

13 He who avenges spilled blood has remembered them. He does not forget the cry of the humble.

14 Be gracious to me, my Lord. Witness the suffering that my enemies have inflicted upon me, You who lift me up from the gates of death.

פרק י

טז טָבְעוּ גוֹיִם בְּשַׁחַת עָשׂוּ בְּרֶשֶׁת־זוּ טָמָנוּ נִלְכְּדָה רַגְלָם:

יז נוֹדַע יְהֹוָה מִשְׁפָּט עָשָׂה בְּפֹעַל כַּפָּיו נוֹקֵשׁ רָשָׁע הִגָּיוֹן סֶלָה:

יח יָשׁוּבוּ רְשָׁעִים לִשְׁאוֹלָה כָּל־גּוֹיִם שְׁכֵחֵי אֱלֹהִים:

יט כִּי לֹא לָנֶצַח יִשָּׁכַח אֶבְיוֹן תִּקְוַת ענוים [עֲנָיִּים] תֹּאבַד לָעַד:

כ קוּמָה יְהֹוָה אַל־יָעֹז אֱנוֹשׁ יִשָּׁפְטוּ גוֹיִם עַל־פָּנֶיךָ:

כא שִׁיתָה יְהֹוָה מוֹרָה לָהֶם יֵדְעוּ גוֹיִם אֱנוֹשׁ הֵמָּה סֶּלָה:

פרק י

א לָמָה יְהֹוָה תַּעֲמֹד בְּרָחוֹק תַּעְלִים לְעִתּוֹת בַּצָּרָה:

ב בְּגַאֲוַת רָשָׁע יִדְלַק עָנִי יִתָּפְשׂוּ בִּמְזִמּוֹת זוּ חָשָׁבוּ:

ג כִּי־הִלֵּל רָשָׁע עַל־תַּאֲוַת נַפְשׁוֹ וּבֹצֵעַ בֵּרֵךְ נִאֵץ יְהֹוָה:

ד רָשָׁע כְּגֹבַהּ אַפּוֹ בַּל־יִדְרֹשׁ אֵין אֱלֹהִים כָּל־מְזִמּוֹתָיו:

ה יָחִילוּ דרכו [דְרָכָיו] בְּכָל־עֵת מָרוֹם מִשְׁפָּטֶיךָ מִנֶּגְדּוֹ כָּל־צוֹרְרָיו יָפִיחַ
בָּהֶם:

ו אָמַר בְּלִבּוֹ בַּל־אֶמּוֹט לְדֹר וָדֹר אֲשֶׁר לֹא־בְרָע:

ז אָלָה פִּיהוּ מָלֵא וּמִרְמוֹת וָתֹךְ תַּחַת לְשׁוֹנוֹ עָמָל וָאָוֶן:

ח יֵשֵׁב בְּמַאְרַב חֲצֵרִים בַּמִּסְתָּרִים יַהֲרֹג נָקִי עֵינָיו לְחֵלְכָה יִצְפֹּנוּ:

ט יֶאֱרֹב בַּמִּסְתָּר כְּאַרְיֵה בְסֻכֹּה יֶאֱרֹב לַחֲטוֹף עָנִי יַחְטֹף עָנִי בְּמָשְׁכוֹ
בְרִשְׁתּוֹ:

י ודכה [יִדְכֶּה] יָשֹׁחַ וְנָפַל בַּעֲצוּמָיו חלכאים [חֵיל כָּאִים]:

15 So that I may recite all Your praises in the gates of the daughter of
Zion, so that I may rejoice in Your salvation.

16 The nations have fallen into the pit that they made. Their own feet
are caught in the net that they hid.

17 The Lord has revealed Himself and has meted judgment. The wicked
are trapped by the work of their own hands. Think about this. Selah.

18 The wicked will return to the netherworld, as will all the nations that
forget God.

19 The needy will not always be forgotten, nor will the hope of the poor
be lost forever.

20 Arise, Lord! Do not let mortal man have the victory. Let the nations
be judged before You.

21 Place your awesomeness upon them, Lord. Let the nations know that
they are only human beings. Selah.

TEHILLIM 10

A prayer to overcome the suffering caused by wickedness.

1 Why do you stand at a distance, Lord? Why do You hide Yourself in
times of trouble?

2 The poor man is pursued because of the pride of the wicked. Let
them be snared by their own schemes.

3 The wicked man praises his heart's desire, and the greedy man thinks
himself blessed even as he scorns the Lord.

4 In his self-assured heart, the wicked man says, "He will not demand
an accounting." All the time, he thinks: "There is no God."

5 He always prospers. Your judgments are far beyond his sight, and he
lawds it over his enemies.

6 He says in his heart, "I will not be shaken. I will never suffer
affliction."

7 His mouth is full of cursing and lies and hatred. His tongue speaks
evil and falsehood.

8 He sits in hidden places in the courtyards, and kills innocent people
in secret places. His eyes search out those who are helpless.

9 He lurks in hidden places like a lion in his den. He lies in wait to
catch the poor, and indeed he captures the poor by trapping them in
his net.

10 He crouches and sneaks, and the helpless fall into his strong hands.

יא אָמַר בְּלִבּוֹ שָׁכַח אֵל הִסְתִּיר פָּנָיו בַּל־רָאָה לָנֶצַח:

יב קוּמָה יְהֹוָה אֵל נְשָׂא יָדֶךָ אַל־תִּשְׁכַּח עניים [עֲנָוִים]:

יג עַל־מֶה נִאֵץ רָשָׁע אֱלֹהִים אָמַר בְּלִבּוֹ לֹא תִּדְרֹשׁ:

יד רָאִתָה כִּי־אַתָּה עָמָל וָכַעַס תַּבִּיט לָתֵת בְּיָדֶךָ עָלֶיךָ יַעֲזֹב חֵלְכָה יָתוֹם אַתָּה הָיִיתָ עוֹזֵר:

טו שְׁבֹר זְרוֹעַ רָשָׁע וָרָע תִּדְרוֹשׁ־רִשְׁעוֹ בַל־תִּמְצָא:

טז יְהֹוָה מֶלֶךְ עוֹלָם וָעֶד אָבְדוּ גוֹיִם מֵאַרְצוֹ:

יז תַּאֲוַת עֲנָוִים שָׁמַעְתָּ יְהֹוָה תָּכִין לִבָּם תַּקְשִׁיב אָזְנֶךָ:

יח לִשְׁפֹּט יָתוֹם וָדָךְ בַּל־יוֹסִיף עוֹד לַעֲרֹץ אֱנוֹשׁ מִן־הָאָרֶץ:

פרק יא

א לַמְנַצֵּחַ לְדָוִד בַּיהֹוָה חָסִיתִי אֵיךְ תֹּאמְרוּ לְנַפְשִׁי נודו [נוּדִי] הַרְכֶם צִפּוֹר:

ב כִּי הִנֵּה הָרְשָׁעִים יִדְרְכוּן קֶשֶׁת כּוֹנְנוּ חִצָּם עַל־יֶתֶר לִירוֹת בְּמוֹ־אֹפֶל לְיִשְׁרֵי־לֵב:

ג כִּי הַשָּׁתוֹת יֵהָרֵסוּן צַדִּיק מַה־פָּעָל:

ד יְהֹוָה בְּהֵיכַל קָדְשׁוֹ יְהֹוָה בַּשָּׁמַיִם כִּסְאוֹ עֵינָיו יֶחֱזוּ עַפְעַפָּיו יִבְחֲנוּ בְּנֵי אָדָם:

ה יְהֹוָה צַדִּיק יִבְחָן וְרָשָׁע וְאֹהֵב חָמָס שָׂנְאָה נַפְשׁוֹ:

ו יַמְטֵר עַל־רְשָׁעִים פַּחִים אֵשׁ וְגָפְרִית וְרוּחַ זִלְעָפוֹת מְנָת כּוֹסָם:

ז כִּי־צַדִּיק יְהֹוָה צְדָקוֹת אָהֵב יָשָׁר יֶחֱזוּ פָנֵימוֹ:

11 He says in his heart, "God has forgotten. He has hidden His face and He will never see."

12 Arise, Lord God! Lift up Your hand. Do not forget the humble.

13 Why do the wicked scorn God, saying in their hearts, "You will not judge"?

14 You have seen – for You witness trouble and wrath – and allow it. The helpless commit themselves to You. You are the helper of the orphan.

15 Break the arm of the wicked, and search out the evil man's wickedness until none remains.

16 The Lord is King for all time. The nations are lost from His land.

17 Lord, You have heard the desires of the humble. You will direct their hearts and give ear to their prayers.

18 To protect the fatherless and the oppressed so that evil men will no longer terrify the weak of the earth.

TEHILLIM 11

A song of belief in God's protection.

1 For the chief musician, a psalm by David. In the Lord I have taken refuge. How can you say to my soul: "Flee! Go to your mountain, you birds"?

2 The wicked bend their bows. They have aimed the arrow in order to shoot at honest people in the dark.

3 When the foundations of the world are destroyed, what can the righteous do?

4 The Lord is in His holy Temple. The Lord's throne is in heaven. His eyes see and His eyelids search for the children of man.

5 The Lord tests the righteous, but His soul hates the wicked and those who live by violence.

6 He will cause hot coals to rain down upon the wicked. Fire, brimstone and burning wind will be their punishment.

7 The Lord is righteous. He loves righteousness. People of integrity will see His face.

פרק יב

א לַמְנַצֵּחַ עַל־הַשְּׁמִינִית מִזְמוֹר לְדָוִד:

ב הוֹשִׁיעָה יְהוָה כִּי־גָמַר חָסִיד כִּי־פַסּוּ אֱמוּנִים מִבְּנֵי אָדָם:

ג שָׁוְא יְדַבְּרוּ אִישׁ אֶת־רֵעֵהוּ שְׂפַת חֲלָקוֹת בְּלֵב וָלֵב יְדַבֵּרוּ:

ד יַכְרֵת יְהוָה כָּל־שִׂפְתֵי חֲלָקוֹת לָשׁוֹן מְדַבֶּרֶת גְּדֹלוֹת:

ה אֲשֶׁר אָמְרוּ לִלְשֹׁנֵנוּ נַגְבִּיר שְׂפָתֵינוּ אִתָּנוּ מִי אָדוֹן לָנוּ:

ו מִשֹּׁד עֲנִיִּים מֵאַנְקַת אֶבְיוֹנִים עַתָּה אָקוּם יֹאמַר יְהוָה אָשִׁית בְּיֵשַׁע יָפִיחַ לוֹ:

ז אִמֲרוֹת יְהוָה אֲמָרוֹת טְהֹרוֹת כֶּסֶף צָרוּף בַּעֲלִיל לָאָרֶץ מְזֻקָּק שִׁבְעָתָיִם:

ח אַתָּה יְהוָה תִּשְׁמְרֵם תִּצְּרֶנּוּ מִן־הַדּוֹר זוּ לְעוֹלָם:

ט סָבִיב רְשָׁעִים יִתְהַלָּכוּן כְּרֻם זֻלּוּת לִבְנֵי אָדָם:

פרק יג

א לַמְנַצֵּחַ מִזְמוֹר לְדָוִד:

ב עַד־אָנָה יְהוָה תִּשְׁכָּחֵנִי נֶצַח עַד־אָנָה תַּסְתִּיר אֶת־פָּנֶיךָ מִמֶּנִּי:

ג עַד־אָנָה אָשִׁית עֵצוֹת בְּנַפְשִׁי יָגוֹן בִּלְבָבִי יוֹמָם עַד־אָנָה יָרוּם אֹיְבִי עָלָי:

ד הַבִּיטָה עֲנֵנִי יְהוָה אֱלֹהָי הָאִירָה עֵינַי פֶּן־אִישַׁן הַמָּוֶת:

ה פֶּן־יֹאמַר אֹיְבִי יְכָלְתִּיו צָרַי יָגִילוּ כִּי אֶמּוֹט:

ו וַאֲנִי בְּחַסְדְּךָ בָטַחְתִּי יָגֵל לִבִּי בִּישׁוּעָתֶךָ אָשִׁירָה לַיהוָה כִּי גָמַל עָלָי:

TEHILLIM 12

*God answers the prayers of righteous people
who must live in an immoral society.*

1 For the chief musician, on the eight stringed harps, a psalm by David.

2 Help, Lord, for Your faithful people are disappearing, for the faithful are being destroyed from among the children of men.

3 They speak dishonestly with their neighbors; with insincerity and with an untrue heart do they speak.

4 May the Lord silence all lying lips and tongues that speak boastfully.

5 They say: "Our tongues will make us powerful. We have our lips. Who shall be lord over us"?

6 Because of the mistreatment of the poor and the suffering of the needy – "Now I will arise, says the Lord, and I will care for them in safety, they that are oppressed".

7 The words of the Lord are pure, like melted silver poured into a pan and completely refined.

8 You will protect the good, Lord. You will preserve us from this evil generation forever.

9 The wicked walk everywhere, and evil is praised among the sons of men.

TEHILLIM 13

A song of troubles, yet the strong-hearted remain hopeful.

1 For chief musician, a psalm of David.

2 How long, Lord? Will you forget me forever? How long will you hide your face from me?

3 How long will I search in my soul, having sorrow in my heart all day? How long will my enemy be victorious over me?

4 God, look and answer me, Lord my God. Awaken to my eyes before I sleep the sleep of death.

5 Do not let my enemy say: "I have defeated him." Do not let my enemies rejoice when I waver.

6 As for me, I trust in your mercy. My heart will rejoice in your salvation. I will sing to the Lord because He has been good to me.

פרק יד

א לַמְנַצֵּחַ לְדָוִד אָמַר נָבָל בְּלִבּוֹ אֵין אֱלֹהִים הִשְׁחִיתוּ הִתְעִיבוּ עֲלִילָה אֵין עֹשֵׂה־טוֹב:

ב יְהוָה מִשָּׁמַיִם הִשְׁקִיף עַל־בְּנֵי־אָדָם לִרְאוֹת הֲיֵשׁ מַשְׂכִּיל דֹּרֵשׁ אֶת־אֱלֹהִים:

ג הַכֹּל סָר יַחְדָּו נֶאֱלָחוּ אֵין עֹשֵׂה־טוֹב אֵין גַּם־אֶחָד:

ד הֲלֹא יָדְעוּ כָּל־פֹּעֲלֵי אָוֶן אֹכְלֵי עַמִּי אָכְלוּ לֶחֶם יְהוָה לֹא קָרָאוּ:

ה שָׁם פָּחֲדוּ פָחַד כִּי־אֱלֹהִים בְּדוֹר צַדִּיק:

ו עֲצַת־עָנִי תָבִישׁוּ כִּי יְהוָה מַחְסֵהוּ:

ז מִי־יִתֵּן מִצִּיּוֹן יְשׁוּעַת יִשְׂרָאֵל בְּשׁוּב יְהוָה שְׁבוּת עַמּוֹ יָגֵל יַעֲקֹב יִשְׂמַח יִשְׂרָאֵל:

פרק טו

א מִזְמוֹר לְדָוִד יְהוָה מִי־יָגוּר בְּאָהֳלֶךָ מִי־יִשְׁכֹּן בְּהַר קָדְשֶׁךָ:

ב הוֹלֵךְ תָּמִים וּפֹעֵל צֶדֶק וְדֹבֵר אֱמֶת בִּלְבָבוֹ:

ג לֹא־רָגַל עַל־לְשֹׁנוֹ לֹא־עָשָׂה לְרֵעֵהוּ רָעָה וְחֶרְפָּה לֹא־נָשָׂא עַל־קְרֹבוֹ:

ד נִבְזֶה בְּעֵינָיו נִמְאָס וְאֶת־יִרְאֵי יְהוָה יְכַבֵּד נִשְׁבַּע לְהָרַע וְלֹא יָמִר:

ה כַּסְפּוֹ לֹא־נָתַן בְּנֶשֶׁךְ וְשֹׁחַד עַל־נָקִי לֹא־לָקָח עֹשֵׂה אֵלֶּה לֹא יִמּוֹט לְעוֹלָם:

TEHILLIM 14

A song about the ways of an evil society.

1 For the chief musician, a psalm of David. The fool says in his heart, "There is no God." They act corruptly and do evil deeds. There is none who does good.

2 The Lord looks out from heaven upon the children of men to see if there are any men of understanding who desire God.

3 They are all corrupt and they have all become impure. There is none that does good – no, not one.

4 How can all those who sin not know it? They destroy my people like they eat bread, and they do not call upon the Lord?

5 They live in great fear, for God is with the righteous generation.

6 They want to shame the faith of the poor, but the Lord is their refuge.

7 If only Israel's salvation might come from Zion! When the Lord sets His people free from captivity, let Jacob rejoice and let Israel be glad.

TEHILLIM 15

*A song expressing the spiritual beauty of human beings, and
also a summary of the 613 commandments of the Torah.*

1 A psalm of David. Lord, who will dwell in Your house? Who will dwell upon Your holy mountain?

2 He who walks upright and acts righteously, speaks truth in his heart,

3 Who has no slander on his tongue, does no evil to his fellow man, nor disagrees with his neighbor.

4 Who does not favor wicked people, but honors those who fear the Lord, Who keeps his word even though it may mean a loss for him.

5 He takes no interest for his money or bribes against the innocent; He who avoids all these sins will never be shaken, and will remain firmly established.

פרק טז

א מִכְתָּם לְדָוִד שָׁמְרֵנִי אֵל כִּי־חָסִיתִי בָךְ:

ב אָמַרְתְּ לַיהוָה אֲדֹנָי אָתָּה טוֹבָתִי בַּל־עָלֶיךָ:

ג לִקְדוֹשִׁים אֲשֶׁר־בָּאָרֶץ הֵמָּה וְאַדִּירֵי כָּל־חֶפְצִי־בָם:

ד יִרְבּוּ עַצְּבוֹתָם אַחֵר מָהָרוּ בַּל־אַסִּיךְ נִסְכֵּיהֶם מִדָּם וּבַל־אֶשָּׂא אֶת־
שְׁמוֹתָם עַל־שְׂפָתָי:

ה יְהוָה מְנָת־חֶלְקִי וְכוֹסִי אַתָּה תּוֹמִיךְ גּוֹרָלִי:

ו חֲבָלִים נָפְלוּ־לִי בַּנְּעִמִים אַף־נַחֲלָת שָׁפְרָה עָלָי:

ז אֲבָרֵךְ אֶת־יְהוָה אֲשֶׁר יְעָצָנִי אַף־לֵילוֹת יִסְּרוּנִי כִלְיוֹתָי:

ח שִׁוִּיתִי יְהוָה לְנֶגְדִּי תָמִיד כִּי מִימִינִי בַּל־אֶמּוֹט:

ט לָכֵן שָׂמַח לִבִּי וַיָּגֶל כְּבוֹדִי אַף־בְּשָׂרִי יִשְׁכֹּן לָבֶטַח:

י כִּי לֹא־תַעֲזֹב נַפְשִׁי לִשְׁאוֹל לֹא־תִתֵּן חֲסִידְךָ לִרְאוֹת שָׁחַת:

יא תּוֹדִיעֵנִי אֹרַח חַיִּים שֹׂבַע שְׂמָחוֹת אֶת־פָּנֶיךָ נְעִמוֹת בִּימִינְךָ נֶצַח:

פרק יז

א תְּפִלָּה לְדָוִד שִׁמְעָה יְהוָה צֶדֶק הַקְשִׁיבָה רִנָּתִי הַאֲזִינָה תְפִלָּתִי בְּלֹא
שִׂפְתֵי מִרְמָה:

ב מִלְּפָנֶיךָ מִשְׁפָּטִי יֵצֵא עֵינֶיךָ תֶּחֱזֶינָה מֵישָׁרִים:

ג בָּחַנְתָּ לִבִּי פָּקַדְתָּ לַּיְלָה צְרַפְתַּנִי בַל־תִּמְצָא זַמֹּתִי בַּל־יַעֲבָר־פִּי:

ד לִפְעֻלּוֹת אָדָם בִּדְבַר שְׂפָתֶיךָ אֲנִי שָׁמַרְתִּי אָרְחוֹת פָּרִיץ:

ה תָּמֹךְ אֲשֻׁרַי בְּמַעְגְּלוֹתֶיךָ בַּל־נָמוֹטּוּ פְעָמָי:

ו אֲנִי קְרָאתִיךָ כִי־תַעֲנֵנִי אֵל הַט־אָזְנְךָ לִי שְׁמַע אִמְרָתִי:

TEHILLIM 16

A song of joy in being close to God.

1 A memorial by David. Keep me, God, for I have found safety in You.
2 I said to God: You are my Lord. I have no good except in You.
3 As for the holy that are on earth, they are the pure in whom I take all delight.
4 There are those who make many idols. I will never offer their libations of blood. Their names will never cross my lips.
5 Lord, You are the giver of my inheritance and of my good. You guide my fate.
6 My portions are given to me in pleasant places. Truly, I have a good heritage.
7 I will bless the Lord who has given me council. At night, You, God, are with me.
8 I have always set the Lord before me. He remains at my right hand, and I will be faithful.
9 My heart is glad and my soul is happy; my body lives in safety.
10 For You will not give my soul to the netherworld, nor will You force one who follows You to see the pit.
11 You teach me the path of life. In Your presence is complete joy, and in Your right hand is happiness forever.

TEHILLIM 17

A prayer for help

1 A prayer by David. Hear the good, Lord! Listen to my cry. Listen to the truthful prayer from my lips.
2 Let my judgment come from You. Let Your eyes see the truth.
3 You have tested my heart. In the night, You have visited my heart. You tested me and You found no wickedness, no evil thoughts pass my mouth.
4 As for the evil ways of men: according to Your words, I have separated myself from the ways of the violent.
5 My footsteps have followed Your paths, and my feet have not strayed.
6 As for me, I call upon You, for You will answer me, God. Turn to me and hear my speech.

פרק יז

ז הַפְלֵה חֲסָדֶיךָ מוֹשִׁיעַ חוֹסִים מִמִּתְקוֹמְמִים בִּימִינֶךָ:

ח שָׁמְרֵנִי כְּאִישׁוֹן בַּת־עָיִן בְּצֵל כְּנָפֶיךָ תַּסְתִּירֵנִי:

ט מִפְּנֵי רְשָׁעִים זוּ שַׁדּוּנִי אֹיְבַי בְּנֶפֶשׁ יַקִּיפוּ עָלָי:

י חֶלְבָּמוֹ סָגְרוּ פִּימוֹ דִּבְּרוּ בְגֵאוּת:

יא אַשֻּׁרֵינוּ עַתָּה סבבוני [סְבָבוּנוּ] עֵינֵיהֶם יָשִׁיתוּ לִנְטוֹת בָּאָרֶץ:

יב דִּמְיֹנוֹ כְּאַרְיֵה יִכְסוֹף לִטְרוֹף וְכִכְפִיר יֹשֵׁב בְּמִסְתָּרִים:

יג קוּמָה יְהוָה קַדְּמָה פָנָיו הַכְרִיעֵהוּ פַּלְּטָה נַפְשִׁי מֵרָשָׁע חַרְבֶּךָ:

יד מִמְתִים יָדְךָ יְהוָה מִמְתִים מֵחֶלֶד חֶלְקָם בַּחַיִּים וצפינך [וּצְפוּנְךָ] תְּמַלֵּא בִטְנָם יִשְׂבְּעוּ בָנִים וְהִנִּיחוּ יִתְרָם לְעוֹלְלֵיהֶם:

טו אֲנִי בְּצֶדֶק אֶחֱזֶה פָנֶיךָ אֶשְׂבְּעָה בְהָקִיץ תְּמוּנָתֶךָ:

פרק יח

א לַמְנַצֵּחַ לְעֶבֶד יְהוָה לְדָוִד אֲשֶׁר דִּבֶּר לַיהוָה אֶת־דִּבְרֵי הַשִּׁירָה הַזֹּאת בְּיוֹם הִצִּיל־יְהוָה אוֹתוֹ מִכַּף כָּל־אֹיְבָיו וּמִיַּד שָׁאוּל:

ב וַיֹּאמַר אֶרְחָמְךָ יְהוָה חִזְקִי:

ג יְהוָה סַלְעִי וּמְצוּדָתִי וּמְפַלְטִי אֵלִי צוּרִי אֶחֱסֶה־בּוֹ מָגִנִּי וְקֶרֶן יִשְׁעִי מִשְׂגַּבִּי:

ד מְהֻלָּל אֶקְרָא יְהוָה וּמִן־אֹיְבַי אִוָּשֵׁעַ:

ה אֲפָפוּנִי חֶבְלֵי־מָוֶת וְנַחֲלֵי בְלִיַּעַל יְבַעֲתוּנִי:

ו חֶבְלֵי שְׁאוֹל סְבָבוּנִי קִדְּמוּנִי מוֹקְשֵׁי מָוֶת:

ז בַּצַּר־לִי אֶקְרָא יְהוָה וְאֶל־אֱלֹהַי אֲשַׁוֵּעַ יִשְׁמַע מֵהֵיכָלוֹ קוֹלִי וְשַׁוְעָתִי לְפָנָיו תָּבוֹא בְאָזְנָיו:

34

7   Increase Your mercy, You Who hold in Your right hand those who make You their refuge from attackers.

8   Protect me carefully as the apple of Your eye and hide me in the shadow of Your wings

9   From the wicked who attack, from the deadly enemies who surround me.

10   Their evil hearts are closed and with their mouths they speak in pride.

11   Now they have surrounded me and their eyes look out over the earth.

12   The enemy is like a lion eager to make me his prey, like a young lion who lies in wait.

13   Arise, Lord! Attack and bring him to his knees. Deliver my soul from wicked men by Your hand and Your sword, Lord,

14   From men whose interest in life is only this world. In their life in this world you give them good things; they leave their riches to their children.

15   As for me, I see Your face in truth, and be happy in Your likeness.

TEHILLIM 18

A song of thanksgiving from David to God for having saved him.

1   For the chief musician: a psalm of David the servant of the Lord, who spoke the words of this song to the Lord on the day that the Lord delivered him from the hand of all his enemies and from the hand of Saul.

2   He said: I love you, Lord, my strength.

3   The Lord is my rock, my security and my deliverer, My God, my Rock, in Whom I take refuge, my shield, my constant help and my tower of protection.

4   I shout: "Praised be the Lord! I am saved from my enemies".

5   The cords of death encompassed me, and the floods of terrible people alarmed me.

6   The cords of the wicked surrounded me. The snare of death confronted me.

7   In my distress I called upon the Lord. I cried out to my God; from His Temple He heard my voice. My cry came before Him, into His ears.

ח וַתִּגְעַשׁ וַתִּרְעַשׁ הָאָרֶץ וּמוֹסְדֵי הָרִים יִרְגָּזוּ וַיִּתְגָּעֲשׁוּ כִּי חָרָה לוֹ:

ט עָלָה עָשָׁן בְּאַפּוֹ וְאֵשׁ מִפִּיו תֹּאכֵל גֶּחָלִים בָּעֲרוּ מִמֶּנּוּ:

י וַיֵּט שָׁמַיִם וַיֵּרַד וַעֲרָפֶל תַּחַת רַגְלָיו:

יא וַיִּרְכַּב עַל־כְּרוּב וַיָּעֹף וַיֵּדֶא עַל־כַּנְפֵי־רוּחַ:

יב יָשֶׁת חֹשֶׁךְ סִתְרוֹ סְבִיבוֹתָיו סֻכָּתוֹ חֶשְׁכַת־מַיִם עָבֵי שְׁחָקִים:

יג מִנֹּגַהּ נֶגְדּוֹ עָבָיו עָבְרוּ בָּרָד וְגַחֲלֵי־אֵשׁ:

יד וַיַּרְעֵם בַּשָּׁמַיִם יְהוָה וְעֶלְיוֹן יִתֵּן קֹלוֹ בָּרָד וְגַחֲלֵי־אֵשׁ:

טו וַיִּשְׁלַח חִצָּיו וַיְפִיצֵם וּבְרָקִים רָב וַיְהֻמֵּם:

טז וַיֵּרָאוּ אֲפִיקֵי מַיִם וַיִּגָּלוּ מוֹסְדוֹת תֵּבֵל מִגַּעֲרָתְךָ יְהוָה מִנִּשְׁמַת רוּחַ אַפֶּךָ:

יז יִשְׁלַח מִמָּרוֹם יִקָּחֵנִי יַמְשֵׁנִי מִמַּיִם רַבִּים:

יח יַצִּילֵנִי מֵאֹיְבִי עָז וּמִשֹּׂנְאַי כִּי־אָמְצוּ מִמֶּנִּי:

יט יְקַדְּמוּנִי בְיוֹם אֵידִי וַיְהִי יְהוָה לְמִשְׁעָן לִי:

כ וַיּוֹצִיאֵנִי לַמֶּרְחָב יְחַלְּצֵנִי כִּי חָפֵץ בִּי:

כא יִגְמְלֵנִי יְהוָה כְּצִדְקִי כְּבֹר יָדַי יָשִׁיב לִי:

כב כִּי־שָׁמַרְתִּי דַּרְכֵי יְהוָה וְלֹא־רָשַׁעְתִּי מֵאֱלֹהָי:

כג כִּי כָל־מִשְׁפָּטָיו לְנֶגְדִּי וְחֻקֹּתָיו לֹא־אָסִיר מֶנִּי:

כד וָאֱהִי תָמִים עִמּוֹ וָאֶשְׁתַּמֵּר מֵעֲוֹנִי:

כה וַיָּשֶׁב־יְהוָה לִי כְצִדְקִי כְּבֹר יָדַי לְנֶגֶד עֵינָיו:

כו עִם־חָסִיד תִּתְחַסָּד עִם־גְּבַר תָּמִים תִּתַּמָּם:

כז עִם־נָבָר תִּתְבָּרָר וְעִם־עִקֵּשׁ תִּתְפַּתָּל:

כח כִּי־אַתָּה עַם־עָנִי תוֹשִׁיעַ וְעֵינַיִם רָמוֹת תַּשְׁפִּיל:

כט כִּי־אַתָּה תָּאִיר נֵרִי יְהוָה אֱלֹהַי יַגִּיהַּ חָשְׁכִּי:

8 Then the earth began to quake. The foundations of the mountains quaked and trembled from His anger.

9 Smoke rose in His anger and His fury brought a destroying fire. Coals flamed forth from Him.

10 He lowered the heavens and came down, and thick darkness was under His feet.

11 He rode a heavenly cherub and He soared, riding down on the wings of the wind.

12 He made darkness surround Him and His angels were all around Him. In the deep waters and the thick clouds.

13 The light passed before Him through His thick clouds, then came the hailstones and the fiery coals.

14 The Lord also thundered in the heavens; the Most High sent forth His voice with hailstones and the fiery coals.

15 He shot forth His arrows and scattered them; He shot out lightning and made them afraid.

16 The channels of waters appeared, and the foundations of the world were opened when You were angry, when You displayed Your anger.

17 He came from on high and brought me out. He took me out of many waters.

18 He delivered me from my mighty enemy and from those who hated me, for they were too strong for me.

19 They confronted me on the day of my misfortune, but the Lord was my support.

20 He brought me into a spacious place. He saved me because He takes delight in me.

21 God rewarded me according to my righteousness. He has repaid me according to my integrity.

22 For I kept to the Lord's ways, and did not behave wickedly toward my God.

23 I kept His laws in mind, and I did not turn away from His teachings.

24 I behaved honestly toward Him, and I kept away from my sin.

25 Therefore, God repaid me according to my righteousness, and according to the integrity that He saw in me.

26 With the merciful You are merciful, with the upright person You are upright,

27 With the pure You are pure, and with the crooked You are cunning.

28 You save the poor, but humble the eye of the haughty.

29 You light my lamp; the Lord God gives light to my darkness.

ל כִּי־בְךָ אָרֻץ גְּדוּד וּבֵאלֹהַי אֲדַלֶּג־שׁוּר:

לא הָאֵל תָּמִים דַּרְכּוֹ אִמְרַת יְהֹוָה צְרוּפָה מָגֵן הוּא לְכֹל הַחוֹסִים בּוֹ:

לב כִּי מִי אֱלוֹהַּ מִבַּלְעֲדֵי יְהֹוָה וּמִי־צוּר זוּלָתִי אֱלֹהֵינוּ:

לג הָאֵל הַמְאַזְּרֵנִי חָיִל וַיִּתֵּן תָּמִים דַּרְכִּי:

לד מְשַׁוֶּה רַגְלַי כָּאַיָּלוֹת וְעַל בָּמֹתַי יַעֲמִידֵנִי:

לה מְלַמֵּד יָדַי לַמִּלְחָמָה וְנִחֲתָה קֶשֶׁת־נְחוּשָׁה זְרוֹעֹתָי:

לו וַתִּתֶּן־לִי מָגֵן יִשְׁעֶךָ וִימִינְךָ תִסְעָדֵנִי וְעַנְוַתְךָ תַרְבֵּנִי:

לז תַּרְחִיב צַעֲדִי תַחְתָּי וְלֹא מָעֲדוּ קַרְסֻלָּי:

לח אֶרְדּוֹף אוֹיְבַי וְאַשִּׂיגֵם וְלֹא־אָשׁוּב עַד־כַּלּוֹתָם:

לט אֶמְחָצֵם וְלֹא־יֻכְלוּ קוּם יִפְּלוּ תַּחַת רַגְלָי:

מ וַתְּאַזְּרֵנִי חַיִל לַמִּלְחָמָה תַּכְרִיעַ קָמַי תַּחְתָּי:

מא וְאֹיְבַי נָתַתָּה לִּי עֹרֶף וּמְשַׂנְאַי אַצְמִיתֵם:

מב יְשַׁוְּעוּ וְאֵין מוֹשִׁיעַ עַל־יְהֹוָה וְלֹא עָנָם:

מג וְאֶשְׁחָקֵם כְּעָפָר עַל־פְּנֵי־רוּחַ כְּטִיט חוּצוֹת אֲרִיקֵם:

מד תְּפַלְּטֵנִי מֵרִיבֵי עָם תְּשִׂימֵנִי לְרֹאשׁ גּוֹיִם עַם לֹא־יָדַעְתִּי יַעַבְדוּנִי:

מה לְשֵׁמַע אֹזֶן יִשָּׁמְעוּ לִי בְּנֵי־נֵכָר יְכַחֲשׁוּ־לִי:

מו בְּנֵי־נֵכָר יִבֹּלוּ וְיַחְרְגוּ מִמִּסְגְּרוֹתֵיהֶם:

מז חַי־יְהֹוָה וּבָרוּךְ צוּרִי וְיָרוּם אֱלוֹהֵי יִשְׁעִי:

מח הָאֵל הַנּוֹתֵן נְקָמוֹת לִי וַיַּדְבֵּר עַמִּים תַּחְתָּי:

מט מְפַלְּטִי מֵאֹיְבָי אַף מִן־קָמַי תְּרוֹמְמֵנִי מֵאִישׁ חָמָס תַּצִּילֵנִי:

נ עַל־כֵּן אוֹדְךָ בַגּוֹיִם יְהֹוָה וּלְשִׁמְךָ אֲזַמֵּרָה:

נא מִגְדֹּל [מַגְדִּיל] יְשׁוּעוֹת מַלְכּוֹ וְעֹשֶׂה חֶסֶד לִמְשִׁיחוֹ לְדָוִד וּלְזַרְעוֹ עַד־
עוֹלָם:

30 With Your help I lead a battalion, and with God's assistance I scale a wall.
31 The way of God is perfect; His word is well-refined; He is a protector to all who believe in Him.
32 For who but the Lord is God? Who but our God is a rock?
33 God gives me strength and makes my way straight.
34 He makes my feet light as light as a deer's and puts me upon high places.
35 He trains my arms for war so that my arms can bend a bow of metal.
36 You have also given me Your shield of salvation. Your right hand has strengthened me, and Your humility has made me great.
37 You have made my steps firm beneath me and my feet have not slipped.
38 I pursued my enemies and overtook them, and I did not turn back until they were destroyed.
39 I have destroyed them utterly so they will never rise again; they have fallen beneath my feet.
40 You gave me strength in the battle. You weakened those who fought against me.
41 You also made my enemies run away from me, and I destroyed those who hate me.
42 They cried, even to the Lord, but there was no one to save them. He did not answer them.
43 Then I ground them like the dust before the wind. I threw them out as dust of the streets.
44 You have delivered me from the problems of the people, and You have made me the head of nations. Other peoples serve me also.
45 As soon as they hear of me, they obey me. The sons of the foreigner pretend to be loyal to me.
46 The sons of the foreigner fade away and come trembling out of their hiding places.
47 The Lord lives! Blessed be my Rock, and praised be the God of my help –
48 God, who did great things for me and subdued peoples beneath me.
49 He has delivered me from my enemies. You lift me up above those that rise against me. You save me from violent men.
50 Therefore I will give thanks to You, Lord, among the nations, and I will sing praises to Your name.
51 God provides great salvation to His king and shows mercy to His anointed one, to David and to his descendants for all time.

פרק יט

א לַמְנַצֵּחַ מִזְמוֹר לְדָוִד:

ב הַשָּׁמַיִם מְסַפְּרִים כְּבוֹד־אֵל וּמַעֲשֵׂה יָדָיו מַגִּיד הָרָקִיעַ:

ג יוֹם לְיוֹם יַבִּיעַ אֹמֶר וְלַיְלָה לְּלַיְלָה יְחַוֶּה־דָּעַת:

ד אֵין אֹמֶר וְאֵין דְּבָרִים בְּלִי נִשְׁמָע קוֹלָם:

ה בְּכָל־הָאָרֶץ יָצָא קַוָּם וּבִקְצֵה תֵבֵל מִלֵּיהֶם לַשֶּׁמֶשׁ שָׂם אֹהֶל בָּהֶם:

ו וְהוּא כְּחָתָן יֹצֵא מֵחֻפָּתוֹ יָשִׂישׂ כְּגִבּוֹר לָרוּץ אֹרַח:

ז מִקְצֵה הַשָּׁמַיִם מוֹצָאוֹ וּתְקוּפָתוֹ עַל־קְצוֹתָם וְאֵין נִסְתָּר מֵחַמָּתוֹ:

ח תּוֹרַת יְהֹוָה תְּמִימָה מְשִׁיבַת נָפֶשׁ עֵדוּת יְהֹוָה נֶאֱמָנָה מַחְכִּימַת פֶּתִי:

ט פִּקּוּדֵי יְהֹוָה יְשָׁרִים מְשַׂמְּחֵי־לֵב מִצְוַת יְהֹוָה בָּרָה מְאִירַת עֵינָיִם:

י יִרְאַת יְהֹוָה טְהוֹרָה עוֹמֶדֶת לָעַד מִשְׁפְּטֵי־יְהֹוָה אֱמֶת צָדְקוּ יַחְדָּו:

יא הַנֶּחֱמָדִים מִזָּהָב וּמִפַּז רָב וּמְתוּקִים מִדְּבַשׁ וְנֹפֶת צוּפִים:

יב גַּם־עַבְדְּךָ נִזְהָר בָּהֶם בְּשָׁמְרָם עֵקֶב רָב:

יג שְׁגִיאוֹת מִי־יָבִין מִנִּסְתָּרוֹת נַקֵּנִי:

יד גַּם מִזֵּדִים חֲשֹׂךְ עַבְדֶּךָ אַל־יִמְשְׁלוּ־בִי אָז אֵיתָם וְנִקֵּיתִי מִפֶּשַׁע רָב:

טו יִהְיוּ לְרָצוֹן אִמְרֵי־פִי וְהֶגְיוֹן לִבִּי לְפָנֶיךָ יְהֹוָה צוּרִי וְגֹאֲלִי:

TEHILLIM 19

A song expressing awareness of God.

1 For the chief musician, a psalm of David.

2 The heavens declare the glory of God and heaven shows the work of His hands.

3 Each day tells the day that follows, and every night reveals new knowledge.

4 There is no speech, there are no words, and no voices are heard.

5 The message of God goes out through the entire earth, and the words of Creation extend to the ends of the world. In the heavens He has made a home for the sun,

6 Like a bridegroom emerging from his chamber, as glad as an athlete prepared to run his race.

7 The sun travels from one end of heaven to the other. Nothing is hidden from its heat.

8 The Torah of the Lord is perfect, reviving the soul. The truth of the Lord is certain, making the simple man wise.

9 The law of the Lord is right, giving joy to the heart. The commandments of the Lord are pure, giving light to the eyes.

10 The fear of the Lord is pure and everlasting. The judgments of the Lord are true and righteous.

11 They are more desirable than gold, more than finest gold. They are sweeter than honey from the hive.

12 Your servant understood the warning. By keeping Your Torah, there is great reward.

13 Who can foresee mistakes? Protect me from hidden sins.

14 Prevent Your servant from committing purposeful sins, so that they will have no power over me and I will be pure. Then I will be free from gross sin.

15 May the words of my mouth and the thoughts of my heart be acceptable to You, Lord, my Rock and my Redeemer.

פרק כ

א לַמְנַצֵּחַ מִזְמוֹר לְדָוִד:

ב יַעַנְךָ יְהוָה בְּיוֹם צָרָה יְשַׂגֶּבְךָ שֵׁם אֱלֹהֵי יַעֲקֹב:

ג יִשְׁלַח־עֶזְרְךָ מִקֹּדֶשׁ וּמִצִּיּוֹן יִסְעָדֶךָּ:

ד יִזְכֹּר כָּל־מִנְחֹתֶךָ וְעוֹלָתְךָ יְדַשְּׁנֶה סֶלָה:

ה יִתֶּן־לְךָ כִלְבָבֶךָ וְכָל־עֲצָתְךָ יְמַלֵּא:

ו נְרַנְּנָה בִּישׁוּעָתֶךָ וּבְשֵׁם־אֱלֹהֵינוּ נִדְגֹּל יְמַלֵּא יְהוָה כָּל־מִשְׁאֲלוֹתֶיךָ:

ז עַתָּה יָדַעְתִּי כִּי הוֹשִׁיעַ יְהוָה מְשִׁיחוֹ יַעֲנֵהוּ מִשְּׁמֵי קָדְשׁוֹ בִּגְבֻרוֹת יֵשַׁע יְמִינוֹ:

ח אֵלֶּה בָרֶכֶב וְאֵלֶּה בַסּוּסִים וַאֲנַחְנוּ בְּשֵׁם־יְהוָה אֱלֹהֵינוּ נַזְכִּיר:

ט הֵמָּה כָּרְעוּ וְנָפָלוּ וַאֲנַחְנוּ קַּמְנוּ וַנִּתְעוֹדָד:

י יְהוָה הוֹשִׁיעָה הַמֶּלֶךְ יַעֲנֵנוּ בְיוֹם־קָרְאֵנוּ:

פרק כא

א לַמְנַצֵּחַ מִזְמוֹר לְדָוִד:

ב יְהוָה בְּעָזְּךָ יִשְׂמַח־מֶלֶךְ וּבִישׁוּעָתְךָ מַה־יגיל [יָּגֶל] מְאֹד:

ג תַּאֲוַת לִבּוֹ נָתַתָּה לּוֹ וַאֲרֶשֶׁת שְׂפָתָיו בַּל־מָנַעְתָּ סֶּלָה:

ד כִּי־תְקַדְּמֶנּוּ בִּרְכוֹת טוֹב תָּשִׁית לְרֹאשׁוֹ עֲטֶרֶת פָּז:

ה חַיִּים שָׁאַל מִמְּךָ נָתַתָּה לּוֹ אֹרֶךְ יָמִים עוֹלָם וָעֶד:

ו גָּדוֹל כְּבוֹדוֹ בִּישׁוּעָתֶךָ הוֹד וְהָדָר תְּשַׁוֶּה עָלָיו:

ז כִּי־תְשִׁיתֵהוּ בְרָכוֹת לָעַד תְּחַדֵּהוּ בְשִׂמְחָה אֶת־פָּנֶיךָ:

TEHILLIM 20

A prayer for victory in battle.

1 For the chief musician, a psalm of David.
2 May the Lord answer you on the day of trouble. May the name of the living God of Jacob lift you up high.
3 May he send you help from his Sanctuary, and strength out of Zion.
4 May he remember the memory of all Your meal-offerings and accept the fat of Your burnt-offerings. Selah.
5 May he grant you Your heart's desires and fulfill all your plans.
6 We will shout for joy in Your victory and in the name of our God we will raise our banners. May the Lord fulfill all your wishes.
7 Now I know that the Lord saves His blessed ones. He answers them from His holy heaven with mighty acts of His saving right hand.
8 Some trust in chariots and some in horses, but we will trust in the name of the Lord our God.
9 They sank and fell, but we rose and stood upright.
10 Save us, Lord! May the King answer us on the day that we call.

TEHILLIM 21

A song of thanksgiving after victory in battle

1 For the chief musician, a psalm by David.
2 The king is happy in Your strength, Lord, and deeply he praises Your salvation.
3 You have given him his heart's desire, and have not withheld from him the request of his lips.
4 You presented him with special gifts. You placed a crown of fine gold on his head.
5 He asked You for life, and You gave it to him – long life for ever and ever.
6 Through Your help he has great glory. You have given him honor and majesty.

ח   כִּי־הַמֶּלֶךְ בֹּטֵחַ בַּיהוָה וּבְחֶסֶד עֶלְיוֹן בַּל־יִמּוֹט:

ט   תִּמְצָא יָדְךָ לְכָל־אֹיְבֶיךָ יְמִינְךָ תִּמְצָא שֹׂנְאֶיךָ:

י   תְּשִׁיתֵמוֹ כְּתַנּוּר אֵשׁ לְעֵת פָּנֶיךָ יְהוָה בְּאַפּוֹ יְבַלְּעֵם וְתֹאכְלֵם אֵשׁ:

יא   פִּרְיָמוֹ מֵאֶרֶץ תְּאַבֵּד וְזַרְעָם מִבְּנֵי אָדָם:

יב   כִּי־נָטוּ עָלֶיךָ רָעָה חָשְׁבוּ מְזִמָּה בַּל־יוּכָלוּ:

יג   כִּי תְּשִׁיתֵמוֹ שֶׁכֶם בְּמֵיתָרֶיךָ תְּכוֹנֵן עַל־פְּנֵיהֶם:

יד   רוּמָה יְהוָה בְּעֻזֶּךָ נָשִׁירָה וּנְזַמְּרָה גְּבוּרָתֶךָ:

פרק כב

א   לַמְנַצֵּחַ עַל־אַיֶּלֶת הַשַּׁחַר מִזְמוֹר לְדָוִד:

ב   אֵלִי אֵלִי לָמָה עֲזַבְתָּנִי רָחוֹק מִישׁוּעָתִי דִּבְרֵי שַׁאֲגָתִי:

ג   אֱלֹהַי אֶקְרָא יוֹמָם וְלֹא תַעֲנֶה וְלַיְלָה וְלֹא־דוּמִיָּה לִי:

ד   וְאַתָּה קָדוֹשׁ יוֹשֵׁב תְּהִלּוֹת יִשְׂרָאֵל:

ה   בְּךָ בָּטְחוּ אֲבֹתֵינוּ בָּטְחוּ וַתְּפַלְּטֵמוֹ:

ו   אֵלֶיךָ זָעֲקוּ וְנִמְלָטוּ בְּךָ בָטְחוּ וְלֹא־בוֹשׁוּ:

ז   וְאָנֹכִי תוֹלַעַת וְלֹא־אִישׁ חֶרְפַּת אָדָם וּבְזוּי עָם:

ח   כָּל־רֹאַי יַלְעִגוּ לִי יַפְטִירוּ בְשָׂפָה יָנִיעוּ רֹאשׁ:

ט   גֹּל אֶל־יְהוָה יְפַלְּטֵהוּ יַצִּילֵהוּ כִּי חָפֵץ בּוֹ:

י   כִּי־אַתָּה גֹחִי מִבָּטֶן מַבְטִיחִי עַל־שְׁדֵי אִמִּי:

יא   עָלֶיךָ הָשְׁלַכְתִּי מֵרָחֶם מִבֶּטֶן אִמִּי אֵלִי אָתָּה:

יב   אַל־תִּרְחַק מִמֶּנִּי כִּי־צָרָה קְרוֹבָה כִּי־אֵין עוֹזֵר:

7 You have made him blessed forever. You have made him happy and joyful in Your presence.

8 For the king trusts in the Lord, and will unwaveringly trust in the mercy of the Most High.

9 Your hand is stronger than all Your enemies; Your right hand will overcome all who hate You.

10 You will make them like a fiery oven in the hour of Your anger. The Lord's wrath will destroy them and burn them with fire.

11 You will eliminate their children from the earth and their families from the generations of men, for they intended evil against You.

12 They devised a plot, but they will not succeed.

13 You make them retreat and You prepare Your weapons to strike them.

14 Lord, You are great in strength. We will sing and praise Your power.

TEHILLIM 22

This song about the suffering of the Jewish people asks for Divine help.

1 For the chief musician, on the day's dawning, a psalm by David.

2 My God, my God why have You left me? Your help is far away from my cries of prayer.

3 My God, I call to You during the day but You do not answer me, and at night my suffering does not stop.

4 But You are holy, enthroned as You are upon Israel's praises.

5 Our fathers trusted You. They trusted and You saved them.

6 They cried out to You and were saved. They trusted You completely and were not ashamed.

7 But I am like a worm and not a human being, a disgrace among men and disliked by the people.

8 Everyone who sees me laughs and ridicules me. They curl their lips and shake their heads:

9 "Let him turn to God. Let Him save him. Let Him deliver him, seeing that He loves him."

10 You took me out of the womb and made me trust You from the time I lay upon my mother's breast.

11 I have depended on You since my birth. You were my God even when I was in my mother's womb.

יג סְבָבוּנִי פָּרִים רַבִּים אַבִּירֵי בָשָׁן כִּתְּרוּנִי:

יד פָּצוּ עָלַי פִּיהֶם אַרְיֵה טֹרֵף וְשֹׁאֵג:

טו כַּמַּיִם נִשְׁפַּכְתִּי וְהִתְפָּרְדוּ כָּל־עַצְמוֹתָי הָיָה לִבִּי כַּדּוֹנָג נָמֵס בְּתוֹךְ מֵעָי:

טז יָבֵשׁ כַּחֶרֶשׂ כֹּחִי וּלְשׁוֹנִי מֻדְבָּק מַלְקוֹחָי וְלַעֲפַר־מָוֶת תִּשְׁפְּתֵנִי:

יז כִּי־סְבָבוּנִי כְּלָבִים עֲדַת מְרֵעִים הִקִּיפוּנִי כָּאֲרִי יָדַי וְרַגְלָי:

יח אֲסַפֵּר כָּל־עַצְמוֹתָי הֵמָּה יַבִּיטוּ יִרְאוּ־בִי:

יט יְחַלְּקוּ בְגָדַי לָהֶם וְעַל־לְבוּשִׁי יַפִּילוּ גוֹרָל:

כ וְאַתָּה יְהוָה אַל־תִּרְחָק אֱיָלוּתִי לְעֶזְרָתִי חוּשָׁה:

כא הַצִּילָה מֵחֶרֶב נַפְשִׁי מִיַּד־כֶּלֶב יְחִידָתִי:

כב הוֹשִׁיעֵנִי מִפִּי אַרְיֵה וּמִקַּרְנֵי רֵמִים עֲנִיתָנִי:

כג אֲסַפְּרָה שִׁמְךָ לְאֶחָי בְּתוֹךְ קָהָל אֲהַלְלֶךָּ:

כד יִרְאֵי יְהוָה הַלְלוּהוּ כָּל־זֶרַע יַעֲקֹב כַּבְּדוּהוּ וְגוּרוּ מִמֶּנּוּ כָּל־זֶרַע יִשְׂרָאֵל:

כה כִּי לֹא־בָזָה וְלֹא שִׁקַּץ עֱנוּת עָנִי וְלֹא־הִסְתִּיר פָּנָיו מִמֶּנּוּ וּבְשַׁוְּעוֹ אֵלָיו שָׁמֵעַ:

כו מֵאִתְּךָ תְהִלָּתִי בְּקָהָל רָב נְדָרַי אֲשַׁלֵּם נֶגֶד יְרֵאָיו:

כז יֹאכְלוּ עֲנָוִים וְיִשְׂבָּעוּ יְהַלְלוּ יְהוָה דֹּרְשָׁיו יְחִי לְבַבְכֶם לָעַד:

כח יִזְכְּרוּ וְיָשֻׁבוּ אֶל־יְהוָה כָּל־אַפְסֵי־אָרֶץ וְיִשְׁתַּחֲווּ לְפָנֶיךָ כָּל־מִשְׁפְּחוֹת גּוֹיִם:

כט כִּי לַיהוָה הַמְּלוּכָה וּמֹשֵׁל בַּגּוֹיִם:

ל אָכְלוּ וַיִּשְׁתַּחֲווּ כָּל־דִּשְׁנֵי־אֶרֶץ לְפָנָיו יִכְרְעוּ כָּל־יוֹרְדֵי עָפָר וְנַפְשׁוֹ לֹא חִיָּה:

לא זֶרַע יַעַבְדֶנּוּ יְסֻפַּר לַאדֹנָי לַדּוֹר:

לב יָבֹאוּ וְיַגִּידוּ צִדְקָתוֹ לְעַם נוֹלָד כִּי עָשָׂה:

12 Do not be far from me, for trouble is near and Your help is needed.

13 Many bulls have surrounded me. The strongest bulls of Bashan face me.

14 They open their mouths to seize me like devouring, roaring lions.

15 I am spilled out like water and all my bones are loosened. My heart is faint and my insides weak.

16 My strength is sapped and my tongue sticks to the roof of my mouth. You have put me into the dust of death.

17 Dogs surround me. A group of sinners has surrounded me like a lion, attacking my hands and feet.

18 I can count all my bones, and my enemies look at me and gloat.

19 They divide my clothing among themselves and bid for my clothing.

20 But You, Lord, do not be far from me, for You are my strength. Come quickly to help me.

21 Save my soul from the sword and my life from the power of the dog.

22 Save me from the mouth of the lion. Answer me before the horns of the wild oxen gore me.

23 I will declare Your name to the people and among the people I will praise You.

24 You who revere the Lord, praise Him. All the children of Jacob will praise Him. All the children of Israel will rise in awe of Him.

25 He has not despised nor rejected the suffering of the poor man, nor did He turn His face away from him. When he cried to Him, He listened.

26 My praise in the great assembly comes from You. I will fulfill my vows before those who revere Him.

27 May the humble come and eat and be happy. May they call on the Lord with thanks, and may your hearts beat forever.

28 All the corners of the earth will remember and turn to the Lord. All of the many nations will worship You.

29 For the kingdom is the Lord's and He is the ruler of all nations.

30 All the fat ones of the earth will come and eat and worship. All men made of dust will bow down to Him, even he whose soul is whithered.

31 Their descendants will serve Him; it shall be told to the next generation.

32 Let them come and make known His righteousness to a people that is newly born – that He protects the poor.

פרק כג

א מִזְמוֹר לְדָוִד יְהֹוָה רֹעִי לֹא אֶחְסָר:

ב בִּנְאוֹת דֶּשֶׁא יַרְבִּיצֵנִי עַל־מֵי מְנֻחוֹת יְנַהֲלֵנִי:

ג נַפְשִׁי יְשׁוֹבֵב יַנְחֵנִי בְמַעְגְּלֵי־צֶדֶק לְמַעַן שְׁמוֹ:

ד גַּם כִּי־אֵלֵךְ בְּגֵיא צַלְמָוֶת לֹא־אִירָא רָע כִּי־אַתָּה עִמָּדִי שִׁבְטְךָ וּמִשְׁעַנְתֶּךָ הֵמָּה יְנַחֲמֻנִי:

ה תַּעֲרֹךְ לְפָנַי שֻׁלְחָן נֶגֶד צֹרְרָי דִּשַּׁנְתָּ בַשֶּׁמֶן רֹאשִׁי כּוֹסִי רְוָיָה:

ו אַךְ טוֹב וָחֶסֶד יִרְדְּפוּנִי כָּל־יְמֵי חַיָּי וְשַׁבְתִּי בְּבֵית־יְהֹוָה לְאֹרֶךְ יָמִים:

פרק כד

א לְדָוִד מִזְמוֹר לַיהֹוָה הָאָרֶץ וּמְלוֹאָהּ תֵּבֵל וְיֹשְׁבֵי בָהּ:

ב כִּי־הוּא עַל־יַמִּים יְסָדָהּ וְעַל־נְהָרוֹת יְכוֹנְנֶהָ:

ג מִי־יַעֲלֶה בְהַר יְהֹוָה וּמִי־יָקוּם בִּמְקוֹם קָדְשׁוֹ:

ד נְקִי כַפַּיִם וּבַר לֵבָב אֲשֶׁר לֹא־נָשָׂא לַשָּׁוְא נַפְשִׁי וְלֹא נִשְׁבַּע לְמִרְמָה:

ה יִשָּׂא בְרָכָה מֵאֵת יְהֹוָה וּצְדָקָה מֵאֱלֹהֵי יִשְׁעוֹ:

ו זֶה דּוֹר דרשו [דֹּרְשָׁיו] מְבַקְשֵׁי פָנֶיךָ יַעֲקֹב סֶלָה:

ז שְׂאוּ שְׁעָרִים רָאשֵׁיכֶם וְהִנָּשְׂאוּ פִּתְחֵי עוֹלָם וְיָבוֹא מֶלֶךְ הַכָּבוֹד:

ח מִי זֶה מֶלֶךְ הַכָּבוֹד יְהֹוָה עִזּוּז וְגִבּוֹר יְהֹוָה גִּבּוֹר מִלְחָמָה:

ט שְׂאוּ שְׁעָרִים רָאשֵׁיכֶם וּשְׂאוּ פִּתְחֵי עוֹלָם וְיָבֹא מֶלֶךְ הַכָּבוֹד:

י מִי הוּא זֶה מֶלֶךְ הַכָּבוֹד יְהֹוָה צְבָאוֹת הוּא מֶלֶךְ הַכָּבוֹד סֶלָה:

TEHILLIM 23

*One of the most beautiful songs about human
beings in the Torah, a song of pure faith*

1 A psalm of David. The Lord is my shepherd; I shall not want.
2 He makes me lie down in green pastures. He leads me beside still waters.
3 He restores my soul; he guides me in straight paths for His name's sake.
4 Though I walk through the valley of the shadow of death, I will fear no evil, for You are with me; Your rod and Your staff comfort me.
5 You prepare a table before me in the presence of my enemies; You have anointed my head with oil. My cup overflows.
6 Surely goodness and mercy will follow me all the days of my life, and I will dwell in the house of the Lord forever.

TEHILLIM 24

A song of rejoicing over bringing the Holy Ark to Jerusalem.

1 A psalm of David. The earth and everything in it belong to the Lord, the world and all who dwell in it.
2 He created it upon the seas and established it upon the flood waters.
3 Who will go up to the mountain of the Lord, and who will stand in His holy place?
4 He that has clean hands and a pure heart, who has not taken His name in vain or promised falsely.
5 He will receive a blessing from the Lord and goodness from the God of his salvation.
6 This is the generation that longs for God – the descendants of Jacob long for You. Selah.
7 Lift your heads, you gates, and be raised up, you everlasting doors, that the King of Glory may enter!
8 Who is the King of Glory? The Lord, strong and mighty, the Lord, mighty in battle.
9 Lift your heads, you gates, and be raised up, you everlasting doors, that the King of Glory may enter!
10 Who is the King of Glory? The Lord of Hosts – He is the King of Glory! Selah.

פרק כה

א לְדָוִד אֵלֶיךָ יְהוָה נַפְשִׁי אֶשָּׂא:

ב אֱלֹהַי בְּךָ בָטַחְתִּי אַל־אֵבוֹשָׁה אַל־יַעַלְצוּ אֹיְבַי לִי:

ג גַּם כָּל־קֹוֶיךָ לֹא יֵבֹשׁוּ יֵבֹשׁוּ הַבּוֹגְדִים רֵיקָם:

ד דְּרָכֶיךָ יְהוָה הוֹדִיעֵנִי אֹרְחוֹתֶיךָ לַמְּדֵנִי:

ה הַדְרִיכֵנִי בַאֲמִתֶּךָ וְלַמְּדֵנִי כִּי־אַתָּה אֱלֹהֵי יִשְׁעִי אוֹתְךָ קִוִּיתִי כָּל־הַיּוֹם:

ו זְכֹר־רַחֲמֶיךָ יְהוָה וַחֲסָדֶיךָ כִּי מֵעוֹלָם הֵמָּה:

ז חַטֹּאות נְעוּרַי וּפְשָׁעַי אַל־תִּזְכֹּר כְּחַסְדְּךָ זְכָר־לִי־אַתָּה לְמַעַן טוּבְךָ יְהוָה:

ח טוֹב־וְיָשָׁר יְהוָה עַל־כֵּן יוֹרֶה חַטָּאִים בַּדָּרֶךְ:

ט יַדְרֵךְ עֲנָוִים בַּמִּשְׁפָּט וִילַמֵּד עֲנָוִים דַּרְכּוֹ:

י כָּל־אָרְחוֹת יְהוָה חֶסֶד וֶאֱמֶת לְנֹצְרֵי בְרִיתוֹ וְעֵדֹתָיו:

יא לְמַעַן־שִׁמְךָ יְהוָה וְסָלַחְתָּ לַעֲוֹנִי כִּי רַב־הוּא:

יב מִי זֶה הָאִישׁ יְרֵא יְהוָה יוֹרֶנּוּ בְּדֶרֶךְ יִבְחָר:

יג נַפְשׁוֹ בְּטוֹב תָּלִין וְזַרְעוֹ יִירַשׁ אָרֶץ:

יד סוֹד יְהוָה לִירֵאָיו וּבְרִיתוֹ לְהוֹדִיעָם:

טו עֵינַי תָּמִיד אֶל־יְהוָה כִּי הוּא־יוֹצִיא מֵרֶשֶׁת רַגְלָי:

טז פְּנֵה־אֵלַי וְחָנֵּנִי כִּי־יָחִיד וְעָנִי אָנִי:

יז צָרוֹת לְבָבִי הִרְחִיבוּ מִמְּצוּקוֹתַי הוֹצִיאֵנִי:

יח רְאֵה־עָנְיִי וַעֲמָלִי וְשָׂא לְכָל־חַטֹּאותָי:

יט רְאֵה־אוֹיְבַי כִּי־רָבּוּ וְשִׂנְאַת חָמָס שְׂנֵאוּנִי:

כ שָׁמְרָה נַפְשִׁי וְהַצִּילֵנִי אַל־אֵבוֹשׁ כִּי־חָסִיתִי בָךְ:

כא תֹּם־וָיֹשֶׁר יִצְּרוּנִי כִּי קִוִּיתִיךָ:

כב פְּדֵה אֱלֹהִים אֶת־יִשְׂרָאֵל מִכֹּל צָרוֹתָיו:

TEHILLIM 25

A personal prayer to God for guidance and help

1 A psalm of David. I lift up my soul to You, Lord.

2 I have trusted in You, my God; do not let me be ashamed. Do not let my enemies defeat me.

3 Certainly those who wait for You will never be ashamed. Rather, those who do evil without reason will be punished.

4 Guide me in Your ways, my Lord, and teach me Your paths.

5 Direct me and teach me Your truths, for You are my God and my help. I wait for you all day long.

6 Remember, Lord, Your compassionate acts and Your mercies, for they have endured forever.

7 Do not remember the sins of my youth and my mistakes. Only remember me with Your mercy and with Your goodness, my Lord.

8 The Lord is good and upright, and guides sinners on the path of life.

9 He guides the humble with justice and teaches them His goodness.

10 All the paths of the Lord are mercy and truth, that people may follow His doctrines and His laws.

11 My Lord, for Your name's sake, please forgive my many sins.

12 Which man fears the Lord? The one who fears Him is the one He will teach the right path.

13 His soul will live in abundance, and his children will inherit the land.

14 The secrets of the Lord are revealed to those who fear Him, and they know and value His covenant.

15 My eyes always look to the Lord; he will release my feet from the snare.

16 Turn to me and be kind to me, for I am alone and poor.

17 My heart's troubles are many, and You give me relief from them.

18 Look upon my suffering and pain, and forgive all my sins.

19 See how many my enemies are, and their terrible hatred for me.

20 Protect my soul and save me. Do not let me be ashamed, for I have taken shelter in You.

21 Let my honesty and goodness serve me, because I wait for You.

22 God, please redeem Israel from all its troubles.

פרק כו

א לְדָוִד שָׁפְטֵנִי יְהוָה כִּי־אֲנִי בְּתֻמִּי הָלַכְתִּי וּבַיהוָה בָּטַחְתִּי לֹא אֶמְעָד:

ב בְּחָנֵנִי יְהוָה וְנַסֵּנִי צרופה [צָרְפָה] כִלְיוֹתַי וְלִבִּי:

ג כִּי־חַסְדְּךָ לְנֶגֶד עֵינָי וְהִתְהַלַּכְתִּי בַּאֲמִתֶּךָ:

ד לֹא־יָשַׁבְתִּי עִם־מְתֵי־שָׁוְא וְעִם־נַעֲלָמִים לֹא אָבוֹא:

ה שָׂנֵאתִי קְהַל מְרֵעִים וְעִם־רְשָׁעִים לֹא אֵשֵׁב:

ו אֶרְחַץ בְּנִקָּיוֹן כַּפָּי וַאֲסֹבְבָה אֶת־מִזְבַּחֲךָ יְהוָה:

ז לַשְׁמִעַ בְּקוֹל תּוֹדָה וּלְסַפֵּר כָּל־נִפְלְאוֹתֶיךָ:

ח יְהוָה אָהַבְתִּי מְעוֹן בֵּיתֶךָ וּמְקוֹם מִשְׁכַּן כְּבוֹדֶךָ:

ט אַל־תֶּאֱסֹף עִם־חַטָּאִים נַפְשִׁי וְעִם־אַנְשֵׁי דָמִים חַיָּי:

י אֲשֶׁר־בִּידֵיהֶם זִמָּה וִימִינָם מָלְאָה שֹּׁחַד:

יא וַאֲנִי בְּתֻמִּי אֵלֵךְ פְּדֵנִי וְחָנֵּנִי:

יב רַגְלִי עָמְדָה בְמִישׁוֹר בְּמַקְהֵלִים אֲבָרֵךְ יְהוָה:

פרק כז

א לְדָוִד יְהוָה אוֹרִי וְיִשְׁעִי מִמִּי אִירָא יְהוָה מָעוֹז חַיַּי מִמִּי אֶפְחָד:

ב בִּקְרֹב עָלַי מְרֵעִים לֶאֱכֹל אֶת־בְּשָׂרִי צָרַי וְאֹיְבַי לִי הֵמָּה כָשְׁלוּ וְנָפָלוּ:

ג אִם־תַּחֲנֶה עָלַי מַחֲנֶה לֹא־יִירָא לִבִּי אִם־תָּקוּם עָלַי מִלְחָמָה בְּזֹאת אֲנִי בוֹטֵחַ:

ד אַחַת שָׁאַלְתִּי מֵאֵת־יְהוָה אוֹתָהּ אֲבַקֵּשׁ שִׁבְתִּי בְּבֵית־יְהוָה כָּל־יְמֵי חַיַּי לַחֲזוֹת בְּנֹעַם־יְהוָה וּלְבַקֵּר בְּהֵיכָלוֹ:

TEHILLIM 26

A song that expresses feelings of uncertainty upon being tested

1 By David. Judge me, my Lord, for I have acted with honesty and I have trusted in the Lord completely.

2 Examine me, my Lord, and test me. Test my emotions and my heart.

3 Your mercy is before my eyes and I have walked in Your truth.

4 I have not sat with dishonest men, and I do not keep company with deceivers.

5 I hate the society of evildoers, and I will not be with the wicked.

6 I will wash my hands in purity and approach Your altar.

7 I want to shout with gratitude and tell of all Your wondrous acts.

8 Lord, I love the holiness of Your house and the place where Your glory dwells.

9 Do not place my soul with sinners and my life with murderers,

10 Because in their hands is evil, and their right hand is full of corruption.

11 As for me, I will walk in my honesty. Protect me and be kind to me.

12 My feet stand on level ground and I will bless the Lord among the people.

TEHILLIM 27

A prayer to be permitted to dwell in God's house for all time

1 A psalm of David. The Lord is my light and my help. Whom shall I fear? The Lord is the strength of my life. Of whom shall I be afraid?

2 When sinners came to me to destroy my body, even my enemies and those who hated me, all trembled and fell.

3 If an army were to come against me and I were to be at war, my heart would not fear. Even then I would be confident.

4 One thing I have asked of the Lord, one thing I desire – to live in the house of the Lord all the days of my life, to see the kindness of the Lord and to know the greatness of His house.

פרק כז

ה כִּי יִצְפְּנֵנִי בְּסֻכֹּה בְּיוֹם רָעָה יַסְתִּרֵנִי בְּסֵתֶר אָהֳלוֹ בְּצוּר יְרוֹמְמֵנִי:

ו וְעַתָּה יָרוּם רֹאשִׁי עַל-אֹיְבַי סְבִיבוֹתַי וְאֶזְבְּחָה בְאָהֳלוֹ זִבְחֵי תְרוּעָה אָשִׁירָה וַאֲזַמְּרָה לַיהוָה:

ז שְׁמַע-יְהוָה קוֹלִי אֶקְרָא וְחָנֵּנִי וַעֲנֵנִי:

ח לְךָ אָמַר לִבִּי בַּקְּשׁוּ פָנָי אֶת-פָּנֶיךָ יְהוָה אֲבַקֵּשׁ:

ט אַל-תַּסְתֵּר פָּנֶיךָ מִמֶּנִּי אַל-תַּט בְּאַף עַבְדֶּךָ עֶזְרָתִי הָיִיתָ אַל-תִּטְּשֵׁנִי וְאַל-תַּעַזְבֵנִי אֱלֹהֵי יִשְׁעִי:

י כִּי-אָבִי וְאִמִּי עֲזָבוּנִי וַיהוָה יַאַסְפֵנִי:

יא הוֹרֵנִי יְהוָה דַּרְכֶּךָ וּנְחֵנִי בְּאֹרַח מִישׁוֹר לְמַעַן שׁוֹרְרָי:

יב אַל-תִּתְּנֵנִי בְּנֶפֶשׁ צָרָי כִּי קָמוּ-בִי עֵדֵי-שֶׁקֶר וִיפֵחַ חָמָס:

יג לוּלֵא הֶאֱמַנְתִּי לִרְאוֹת בְּטוּב-יְהוָה בְּאֶרֶץ חַיִּים:

יד קַוֵּה אֶל-יְהוָה חֲזַק וְיַאֲמֵץ לִבֶּךָ וְקַוֵּה אֶל-יְהוָה:

פרק כח

א לְדָוִד אֵלֶיךָ יְהוָה אֶקְרָא צוּרִי אַל-תֶּחֱרַשׁ מִמֶּנִּי פֶּן-תֶּחֱשֶׁה מִמֶּנִּי וְנִמְשַׁלְתִּי עִם-יוֹרְדֵי בוֹר:

ב שְׁמַע קוֹל תַּחֲנוּנַי בְּשַׁוְּעִי אֵלֶיךָ בְּנָשְׂאִי יָדַי אֶל-דְּבִיר קָדְשֶׁךָ:

ג אַל-תִּמְשְׁכֵנִי עִם-רְשָׁעִים וְעִם-פֹּעֲלֵי אָוֶן דֹּבְרֵי שָׁלוֹם עִם-רֵעֵיהֶם וְרָעָה בִּלְבָבָם:

ד תֶּן-לָהֶם כְּפָעֳלָם וּכְרֹעַ מַעַלְלֵיהֶם כְּמַעֲשֵׂה יְדֵיהֶם תֵּן לָהֶם הָשֵׁב גְּמוּלָם לָהֶם:

ה כִּי לֹא יָבִינוּ אֶל-פְּעֻלֹּת יְהוָה וְאֶל-מַעֲשֵׂה יָדָיו יֶהֶרְסֵם וְלֹא יִבְנֵם:

ו בָּרוּךְ יְהוָה כִּי-שָׁמַע קוֹל תַּחֲנוּנָי:

5　He hides me in His house on the day of evil. He hides me in the protection of His house. He lifts me upon a rock.

6　Now my head is raised high above from my enemies that surround me. To the sound of trumpets, I will make offerings in His house. I will sing. I will sing praises to the Lord.

7　Hear, my Lord, when I call. Be gracious and answer me.

8　Regarding you, my heart said: "Seek My face!" I will seek Your face, Lord.

9　Do not hide Your face from me. Do not reject Your servant in anger. You are my help. My saving God, do not leave me or forget me.

10　Even if my own father and mother were to cast me away, the Lord would care for me.

11　Teach me Your way, my Lord, and lead me in a safe path, because people lie in wait for me.

12　Do not give me up to my enemies, for false and violent witnesses have come against me.

13　Had I not believed in and trusted God's goodness in the land of the living!

14　Wait for the Lord. Be strong and let your heart have courage. Wait for the Lord.

TEHILLIM 28

A song combining a request for help and gratitude

1　A psalm by David. To You, my Lord, I call. If You are silent and do not answer me, I will become like those that go down into the grave.

2　Hear my voice when I cry out to You and when I lift my hands to Your holy Temple.

3　Do not put me together with the wicked and with sinners, who speak peacefully with their neighbors while evil is in their hearts.

4　Give them what they deserve, for their ways match the evil of their actions. Give them according to the work of their hands. Give them the punishment that they deserve.

5　They are not interested in God's creations or in the wonders of His hands. He will destroy them without building them back up.

6　Blessed be the Lord for having heard my outcry.

7　The Lord is my strength and my protection. My heart trusts in You. Therefore my heart rejoices greatly, and I will sing songs to You.

ז   יְהֹוָה עֻזִּי וּמָגִנִּי בּוֹ בָטַח לִבִּי וְנֶעֱזָרְתִּי וַיַּעֲלֹז לִבִּי וּמִשִּׁירִי אֲהוֹדֶנּוּ:

ח   יְהֹוָה עֹז־לָמוֹ וּמָעוֹז יְשׁוּעוֹת מְשִׁיחוֹ הוּא:

ט   הוֹשִׁיעָה אֶת־עַמֶּךָ וּבָרֵךְ אֶת־נַחֲלָתֶךָ וּרְעֵם וְנַשְּׂאֵם עַד־הָעוֹלָם:

פרק כט

א   מִזְמוֹר לְדָוִד הָבוּ לַיהֹוָה בְּנֵי אֵלִים הָבוּ לַיהֹוָה כָּבוֹד וָעֹז:

ב   הָבוּ לַיהֹוָה כְּבוֹד שְׁמוֹ הִשְׁתַּחֲווּ לַיהֹוָה בְּהַדְרַת־קֹדֶשׁ:

ג   קוֹל יְהֹוָה עַל־הַמָּיִם אֵל־הַכָּבוֹד הִרְעִים יְהֹוָה עַל־מַיִם רַבִּים:

ד   קוֹל־יְהֹוָה בַּכֹּחַ קוֹל יְהֹוָה בֶּהָדָר:

ה   קוֹל יְהֹוָה שֹׁבֵר אֲרָזִים וַיְשַׁבֵּר יְהֹוָה אֶת־אַרְזֵי הַלְּבָנוֹן:

ו   וַיַּרְקִידֵם כְּמוֹ־עֵגֶל לְבָנוֹן וְשִׂרְיֹן כְּמוֹ בֶן־רְאֵמִים:

ז   קוֹל־יְהֹוָה חֹצֵב לַהֲבוֹת אֵשׁ:

ח   קוֹל יְהֹוָה יָחִיל מִדְבָּר יָחִיל יְהֹוָה מִדְבַּר קָדֵשׁ:

ט   קוֹל יְהֹוָה יְחוֹלֵל אַיָּלוֹת וַיֶּחֱשֹׂף יְעָרוֹת וּבְהֵיכָלוֹ כֻּלּוֹ אֹמֵר כָּבוֹד:

י   יְהֹוָה לַמַּבּוּל יָשָׁב וַיֵּשֶׁב יְהֹוָה מֶלֶךְ לְעוֹלָם:

יא   יְהֹוָה עֹז לְעַמּוֹ יִתֵּן יְהֹוָה יְבָרֵךְ אֶת־עַמּוֹ בַשָּׁלוֹם:

פרק ל

א   מִזְמוֹר שִׁיר חֲנֻכַּת הַבַּיִת לְדָוִד:

ב   אֲרוֹמִמְךָ יְהֹוָה כִּי דִלִּיתָנִי וְלֹא־שִׂמַּחְתָּ אֹיְבַי לִי:

ג   יְהֹוָה אֱלֹהָי שִׁוַּעְתִּי אֵלֶיךָ וַתִּרְפָּאֵנִי:

8 The Lord gives strength to them. He is a great helper to His chosen ones.

9 Save Your people and bless Your inheritance. Care for them and carry them for all time.

TEHILLIM 29

A song describing the power, glory and holiness of God.

1 A psalm of David. Mighty people, acknowledge the Lord's might, glory and strength.

2 Acknowledge the glory that His name deserves. Worship the Lord in beauty and holiness.

3 The thunder of the Lord is upon the waters. The God of greatness is heard upon all the waters.

4 The voice of the Lord is powerful. The voice of the Lord is magnificent.

5 The voice of the Lord breaks the cedar trees; the Lord shatters the very cedar trees of Lebanon.

6 He makes the mountains leap like a calf. The mountains of Lebanon and Sirion shake like a young ox.

7 The voice of the Lord shoots forth flames of fire.

8 The voice of the Lord shakes the wilderness, the Lord shakes the wilderness of Kadesh.

9 The voice of the Lord makes animals give birth and strips the forest's trees of their leaves. In His Temple, everyone declares: "Glory!"

10 The Lord sat on His throne at the time of the flood. The Lord will rule as King forever.

11 The Lord will give strength to His people. The Lord will bless His people with peace.

TEHILLIM 30

A song of gratitude, the dedication of the Second Temple and the festival of Hanukkah

1 A psalm, a song upon the dedication of the Temple by of David.

2 I will praise You, my Lord, for You have saved me, and You did not allow my enemies to gloat over me.

ד   יְהֹוָה הֶעֱלִיתָ מִן־שְׁאוֹל נַפְשִׁי חִיִּיתַנִי מִיּוֹרְדִי־ [מִיׇּרְדִי] בוֹר:

ה   זַמְּרוּ לַיהֹוָה חֲסִידָיו וְהוֹדוּ לְזֵכֶר קׇדְשׁוֹ:

ו   כִּי רֶגַע בְּאַפּוֹ חַיִּים בִּרְצוֹנוֹ בָּעֶרֶב יָלִין בֶּכִי וְלַבֹּקֶר רִנָּה:

ז   וַאֲנִי אָמַרְתִּי בְשַׁלְוִי בַּל־אֶמּוֹט לְעוֹלָם:

ח   יְהֹוָה בִּרְצוֹנְךָ הֶעֱמַדְתָּה לְהַרְרִי עֹז הִסְתַּרְתָּ פָנֶיךָ הָיִיתִי נִבְהָל:

ט   אֵלֶיךָ יְהֹוָה אֶקְרָא וְאֶל־אֲדֹנָי אֶתְחַנָּן:

י   מַה־בֶּצַע בְּדָמִי בְּרִדְתִּי אֶל־שָׁחַת הֲיוֹדְךָ עָפָר הֲיַגִּיד אֲמִתֶּךָ:

יא   שְׁמַע־יְהֹוָה וְחָנֵּנִי יְהֹוָה הֱיֵה עֹזֵר לִי:

יב   הָפַכְתָּ מִסְפְּדִי לְמָחוֹל לִי פִּתַּחְתָּ שַׂקִּי וַתְּאַזְּרֵנִי שִׂמְחָה:

יג   לְמַעַן יְזַמֶּרְךָ כָבוֹד וְלֹא יִדֹּם יְהֹוָה אֱלֹהַי לְעוֹלָם אוֹדֶךָּ:

פרק לא

א   לַמְנַצֵּחַ מִזְמוֹר לְדָוִד:

ב   בְּךָ יְהֹוָה חָסִיתִי אַל־אֵבוֹשָׁה לְעוֹלָם בְּצִדְקָתְךָ פַלְּטֵנִי:

ג   הַטֵּה אֵלַי אׇזְנְךָ מְהֵרָה הַצִּילֵנִי הֱיֵה לִי לְצוּר־מָעוֹז לְבֵית מְצוּדוֹת לְהוֹשִׁיעֵנִי:

ד   כִּי־סַלְעִי וּמְצוּדָתִי אָתָּה וּלְמַעַן שִׁמְךָ תַּנְחֵנִי וּתְנַהֲלֵנִי:

ה   תּוֹצִיאֵנִי מֵרֶשֶׁת זוּ טָמְנוּ לִי כִּי־אַתָּה מָעוּזִּי:

ו   בְּיָדְךָ אַפְקִיד רוּחִי פָּדִיתָה אוֹתִי יְהֹוָה אֵל אֱמֶת:

ז   שָׂנֵאתִי הַשֹּׁמְרִים הַבְלֵי־שָׁוְא וַאֲנִי אֶל־יְהֹוָה בָּטָחְתִּי:

ח   אָגִילָה וְאֶשְׂמְחָה בְּחַסְדֶּךָ אֲשֶׁר רָאִיתָ אֶת־עׇנְיִי יָדַעְתָּ בְּצָרוֹת נַפְשִׁי:

ט   וְלֹא הִסְגַּרְתַּנִי בְּיַד־אוֹיֵב הֶעֱמַדְתָּ בַמֶּרְחָב רַגְלָי:

3 My Lord, my God, I cried to You and You heard me.
4 My Lord, You rescued my soul from the netherworld. You kept me alive and preserved me from death.
5 You who trust the Lord, sing praises to Him and give thanks to His Holy name!
6 His anger lasts only for a moment, but His goodness for a lifetime. Though sadness may come in the evening, joy comes in the morning.
7 Now I know that I will always be attached to You.
8 Lord, for my sake you set up a mountain as a stronghold. You hid Your face and I was afraid.
9 Then I called to You, my Lord, and prayed to You.
10 What value is there in my death, in my going down into the grave? Will the dust praise You? Will it declare Your truth?
11 Hear, my Lord, and be kind to me. Lord, be my helper.
12 You have turned my mourning into dancing. You have removed my sackcloth and clothed me with joy.
13 So that my soul will sing to You and never be silent, My Lord, my God, I will give thanks to You forever.

TEHILLIM 31

A song that prays for strength, courage and patience.

1 For the chief musician, a psalm of David.
2 I have taken shelter in You, my Lord, so do not let me be ashamed. Save me in Your righteousness.
3 Turn Your ear to me and rescue me quickly. Be a rock of strength for me and a fortress to save me.
4 You are my rock and my fortress. Please lead me and guide me for the sake of Your name.
5 Keep me out of the trap that they have set for me, for You are my protector.
6 I have placed myself in Your hand, and You have saved me my Lord, God of truth.
7 I dislike those who follow falsehood. I believe in the Lord.
8 I rejoice in Your loving kindness, for You have seen my suffering. You understood the troubles of my soul.
9 You kept me from the hand of my enemy, and you have directed my feet toward good places.

י חָנֵּנִי יְהוָה כִּי צַר־לִי עָשְׁשָׁה בְכַעַס עֵינִי נַפְשִׁי וּבִטְנִי:

יא כִּי כָלוּ בְיָגוֹן חַיַּי וּשְׁנוֹתַי בַּאֲנָחָה כָּשַׁל בַּעֲוֹנִי כֹחִי וַעֲצָמַי עָשֵׁשׁוּ:

יב מִכָּל־צֹרְרַי הָיִיתִי חֶרְפָּה וְלִשֲׁכֵנַי מְאֹד וּפַחַד לִמְיֻדָּעַי רֹאַי בַּחוּץ נָדְדוּ מִמֶּנִּי:

יג נִשְׁכַּחְתִּי כְּמֵת מִלֵּב הָיִיתִי כִּכְלִי אֹבֵד:

יד כִּי שָׁמַעְתִּי דִּבַּת רַבִּים מָגוֹר מִסָּבִיב בְּהִוָּסְדָם יַחַד עָלַי לָקַחַת נַפְשִׁי זָמָמוּ:

טו וַאֲנִי עָלֶיךָ בָטַחְתִּי יְהוָה אָמַרְתִּי אֱלֹהַי אָתָּה:

טז בְּיָדְךָ עִתֹּתָי הַצִּילֵנִי מִיַּד־אוֹיְבַי וּמֵרֹדְפָי:

יז הָאִירָה פָנֶיךָ עַל־עַבְדֶּךָ הוֹשִׁיעֵנִי בְחַסְדֶּךָ:

יח יְהוָה אַל־אֵבוֹשָׁה כִּי קְרָאתִיךָ יֵבֹשׁוּ רְשָׁעִים יִדְּמוּ לִשְׁאוֹל:

יט תֵּאָלַמְנָה שִׂפְתֵי שָׁקֶר הַדֹּבְרוֹת עַל־צַדִּיק עָתָק בְּגַאֲוָה וָבוּז:

כ מָה רַב טוּבְךָ אֲשֶׁר־צָפַנְתָּ לִּירֵאֶיךָ פָּעַלְתָּ לַחֹסִים בָּךְ נֶגֶד בְּנֵי אָדָם:

כא תַּסְתִּירֵם בְּסֵתֶר פָּנֶיךָ מֵרֻכְסֵי אִישׁ תִּצְפְּנֵם בְּסֻכָּה מֵרִיב לְשֹׁנוֹת:

כב בָּרוּךְ יְהוָה כִּי־הִפְלִיא חַסְדּוֹ לִי בְּעִיר מָצוֹר:

כג וַאֲנִי אָמַרְתִּי בְחָפְזִי נִגְרַזְתִּי מִנֶּגֶד עֵינֶיךָ אָכֵן שָׁמַעְתָּ קוֹל תַּחֲנוּנַי בְּשַׁוְּעִי אֵלֶיךָ:

כד אֶהֱבוּ אֶת־יְהוָה כָּל־חֲסִידָיו אֱמוּנִים נֹצֵר יְהוָה וּמְשַׁלֵּם עַל־יֶתֶר עֹשֵׂה גַאֲוָה:

כה חִזְקוּ וְיַאֲמֵץ לְבַבְכֶם כָּל־הַמְיַחֲלִים לַיהוָה:

פרק לב

א לְדָוִד מַשְׂכִּיל אַשְׁרֵי נְשׂוּי־פֶּשַׁע כְּסוּי חֲטָאָה:

ב אַשְׁרֵי אָדָם לֹא יַחְשֹׁב יְהוָה לוֹ עָוֹן וְאֵין בְּרוּחוֹ רְמִיָּה:

10   Be gracious to me, my Lord, for I am worried. My eyes droop with fatigue, as does my body and my soul.

11   My life is full of sorrow and my years are full of weeping. My strength is failing because of my sins, and my bones have weakened.

12   Because of all my enemies I have become a disgrace to my neighbors and a dread to my friends. When they see me, they run away.

13   I am as forgotten as the dead, like a worthless vessel.

14   I have heard them whispering evil all around me. They have plotted together against me and plan to kill me.

15   I continue to trust You, my Lord, and I declare that You are my God.

16   My life is in Your hands. Save me from the hand of my enemies who attack me.

17   Shine Your face upon Your servant and save me in Your loving kindness.

18   My Lord will not shame me – because I called upon You. Let the evil ones be ashamed and silenced in the netherworld.

19   Silence the lying lips of those who speak with pride, hatred and arrogance against the righteous.

20   How great is the good that you have set aside for those who revere you! That is the reward of those who turn to You, and everyone will witness it.

21   You shelter them in Your presence from the evil conspiracies of men. You protect them in Your presence from wicked tongues.

22   Blessed be the Lord! He has bestowed loving kindness upon me within an embattled city.

23   Under pressure, I said "I am kept away from Your eyes". Yet You heard my pleas when I cried out to You.

24   Love the Lord, all you who follow Him. The Lord protects the faithful. He punishes those who behave arrogantly.

25   All you who wait for the Lord, be strong and fill your hearts with courage.

TEHILLIM 32

*A song about the soul struggling and
subsequently finding happiness*

1   A psalm by David, an instruction. Happy is he whose misdeed is forgiven, whose sin is pardoned.

ג כִּי הֶחֱרַשְׁתִּי בָּלוּ עֲצָמָי בְּשַׁאֲגָתִי כָּל־הַיּוֹם:

ד כִּי יוֹמָם וָלַיְלָה תִּכְבַּד עָלַי יָדֶךָ נֶהְפַּךְ לְשַׁדִּי בְּחַרְבֹנֵי קַיִץ סֶלָה:

ה חַטָּאתִי אוֹדִיעֲךָ וַעֲוֺנִי לֹא־כִסִּיתִי אָמַרְתִּי אוֹדֶה עֲלֵי פְשָׁעַי לַיהוָה וְאַתָּה נָשָׂאתָ עֲוֺן חַטָּאתִי סֶלָה:

ו עַל־זֹאת יִתְפַּלֵּל כָּל־חָסִיד אֵלֶיךָ לְעֵת מְצֹא רַק לְשֵׁטֶף מַיִם רַבִּים אֵלָיו לֹא יַגִּיעוּ:

ז אַתָּה סֵתֶר לִי מִצַּר תִּצְּרֵנִי רָנֵּי פַלֵּט תְּסוֹבְבֵנִי סֶלָה:

ח אַשְׂכִּילְךָ וְאוֹרְךָ בְּדֶרֶךְ־זוּ תֵלֵךְ אִיעֲצָה עָלֶיךָ עֵינִי:

ט אַל־תִּהְיוּ כְּסוּס כְּפֶרֶד אֵין הָבִין בְּמֶתֶג וָרֶסֶן עֶדְיוֹ לִבְלוֹם בַּל קְרֹב אֵלֶיךָ:

י רַבִּים מַכְאוֹבִים לָרָשָׁע וְהַבּוֹטֵחַ בַּיהוָה חֶסֶד יְסוֹבְבֶנּוּ:

יא שִׂמְחוּ בַיהוָה וְגִילוּ צַדִּיקִים וְהַרְנִינוּ כָּל־יִשְׁרֵי־לֵב:

פרק לג

א רַנְּנוּ צַדִּיקִים בַּיהוָה לַיְשָׁרִים נָאוָה תְהִלָּה:

ב הוֹדוּ לַיהוָה בְּכִנּוֹר בְּנֵבֶל עָשׂוֹר זַמְּרוּ־לוֹ:

ג שִׁירוּ לוֹ שִׁיר חָדָשׁ הֵיטִיבוּ נַגֵּן בִּתְרוּעָה:

ד כִּי־יָשָׁר דְּבַר־יְהוָה וְכָל־מַעֲשֵׂהוּ בֶּאֱמוּנָה:

ה אֹהֵב צְדָקָה וּמִשְׁפָּט חֶסֶד יְהוָה מָלְאָה הָאָרֶץ:

ו בִּדְבַר יְהוָה שָׁמַיִם נַעֲשׂוּ וּבְרוּחַ פִּיו כָּל־צְבָאָם:

ז כֹּנֵס כַּנֵּד מֵי הַיָּם נֹתֵן בְּאֹצָרוֹת תְּהוֹמוֹת:

ח יִירְאוּ מֵיהוָה כָּל־הָאָרֶץ מִמֶּנּוּ יָגוּרוּ כָּל־יֹשְׁבֵי תֵבֵל:

2 Happy is the man whom the Lord regards as sinless and in whose soul there is no dishonesty.

3 I remained silent as my bones wasted away, and I groaned all day long.

4 Your strong hand weighed heavily upon me day and night. My body was drained by a dry summer day.

5 I admit my sin. I do not hide my wrongdoing from You. I said:" I will confess my sin to the Lord". Then You forgave me. Selah.

6 Let every God-fearing person pray to You in a time that is favorable. Surely when the flood comes, the waters will not reach him.

7 You are my secure place. You will protect me from the enemy. You will save me with songs of love. Selah.

8 I will teach and guide you in the path that you should go. I will advise for you from my own experience.

9 Do not be like a horse or a mule, for they have no understanding and their mouths are held with bit and bridle, so that they cannot come near you.

10 The wicked have many troubles, but mercy surrounds those who trust in the Lord.

11 You righteous ones, be happy and rejoice in the Lord. All people of integrity, sing out in gladness.

TEHILLIM 33

A song of rejoicing

1 Righteous people, rejoice in the Lord. It is good for the righteous to praise.

2 Give thanks to the Lord with the harp, and sing to Him with ten-stringed instruments.

3 Sing a new song to Him and play it with joy.

4 The word of the Lord is true and all His work is faithful.

5 He loves justice and good, and the earth is full of the Lord's loving kindness.

6 The heavens were made by the word of the Lord and all of creation by the breath of His mouth.

7 He gathered the waters of the sea together and He established the deep wells in their places.

8 Let the whole earth fear the Lord and all people give honor to Him.

ט כִּי הוּא אָמַר וַיֶּהִי הוּא־צִוָּה וַיַּעֲמֹד:

י יְהוָה הֵפִיר עֲצַת גּוֹיִם הֵנִיא מַחְשְׁבוֹת עַמִּים:

יא עֲצַת יְהוָה לְעוֹלָם תַּעֲמֹד מַחְשְׁבוֹת לִבּוֹ לְדֹר וָדֹר:

יב אַשְׁרֵי הַגּוֹי אֲשֶׁר־יְהוָה אֱלֹהָיו הָעָם בָּחַר לְנַחֲלָה לוֹ:

יג מִשָּׁמַיִם הִבִּיט יְהוָה רָאָה אֶת־כָּל־בְּנֵי הָאָדָם:

יד מִמְּכוֹן־שִׁבְתּוֹ הִשְׁגִּיחַ אֶל כָּל־יֹשְׁבֵי הָאָרֶץ:

טו הַיֹּצֵר יַחַד לִבָּם הַמֵּבִין אֶל־כָּל־מַעֲשֵׂיהֶם:

טז אֵין הַמֶּלֶךְ נוֹשָׁע בְּרָב־חָיִל גִּבּוֹר לֹא־יִנָּצֵל בְּרָב־כֹּחַ:

יז שֶׁקֶר הַסּוּס לִתְשׁוּעָה וּבְרֹב חֵילוֹ לֹא יְמַלֵּט:

יח הִנֵּה עֵין יְהוָה אֶל־יְרֵאָיו לַמְיַחֲלִים לְחַסְדּוֹ:

יט לְהַצִּיל מִמָּוֶת נַפְשָׁם וּלְחַיּוֹתָם בָּרָעָב:

כ נַפְשֵׁנוּ חִכְּתָה לַיהוָה עֶזְרֵנוּ וּמָגִנֵּנוּ הוּא:

כא כִּי־בוֹ יִשְׂמַח לִבֵּנוּ כִּי בְשֵׁם קָדְשׁוֹ בָטָחְנוּ:

כב יְהִי־חַסְדְּךָ יְהוָה עָלֵינוּ כַּאֲשֶׁר יִחַלְנוּ לָךְ:

פרק לד

א לְדָוִד בְּשַׁנּוֹתוֹ אֶת־טַעְמוֹ לִפְנֵי אֲבִימֶלֶךְ וַיְגָרֲשֵׁהוּ וַיֵּלַךְ:

ב אֲבָרֲכָה אֶת־יְהוָה בְּכָל־עֵת תָּמִיד תְּהִלָּתוֹ בְּפִי:

ג בַּיהוָה תִּתְהַלֵּל נַפְשִׁי יִשְׁמְעוּ עֲנָוִים וְיִשְׂמָחוּ:

ד גַּדְּלוּ לַיהוָה אִתִּי וּנְרוֹמְמָה שְׁמוֹ יַחְדָּו:

ה דָּרַשְׁתִּי אֶת־יְהוָה וְעָנָנִי וּמִכָּל־מְגוּרוֹתַי הִצִּילָנִי:

ו הִבִּיטוּ אֵלָיו וְנָהָרוּ וּפְנֵיהֶם אַל־יֶחְפָּרוּ:

9 He spoke and it came into being; He commanded and it existed.
10 The Lord renders the counsel of nations empty and the plans of peoples worthless.
11 The counsel of the Lord lasts forever, and the thoughts of His heart remain for all generations.
12 Happy is the nation whose God is the Lord, and the people He has chosen to be His own.
13 The Lord looks out from heaven and sees all the children of men.
14 From His holy place, He looks carefully on all the people of the earth.
15 He created everyone's hearts and looks to see their behavior.
16 A human king is not saved by his army, nor is a powerful man saved by his strength.
17 A horse is useless for safety and is no help.
18 Know that the eye of the Lord is towards those who honor Him and to those that wait for His mercy.
19 He saves their souls from death and keeps them alive in famine.
20 Our souls wait for the Lord because He is our help and our protector.
21 Our hearts rejoice in Him and we trust in His holy name.
22 Bestow Your mercy upon us, God, for we have waited for You.

TEHILLIM 34

A song that describes how to win long life: keep from speaking evil

1 A psalm of David when he pretended to be mad before Avimelech, who drove him away, and he escaped.
2 I will bless the Lord at all times, and His praise will always be in my mouth.
3 My soul will be happy with the Lord, and the humble will hear of this and be glad.
4 Praise the Lord with me and let us exalt His name together.
5 I looked for the Lord and He answered me. He removed all my fears.
6 They looked to Him and their faces shone. They will never fear.

ז זֶה עָנִי קָרָא וַיהֹוָה שָׁמֵעַ וּמִכָּל־צָרוֹתָיו הוֹשִׁיעוֹ׃

ח חֹנֶה מַלְאַךְ־יְהֹוָה סָבִיב לִירֵאָיו וַיְחַלְּצֵם׃

ט טַעֲמוּ וּרְאוּ כִּי־טוֹב יְהֹוָה אַשְׁרֵי הַגֶּבֶר יֶחֱסֶה־בּוֹ׃

י יְראוּ אֶת־יְהֹוָה קְדֹשָׁיו כִּי אֵין מַחְסוֹר לִירֵאָיו׃

יא כְּפִירִים רָשׁוּ וְרָעֵבוּ וְדֹרְשֵׁי יְהֹוָה לֹא־יַחְסְרוּ כָל־טוֹב׃

יב לְכוּ־בָנִים שִׁמְעוּ־לִי יִרְאַת יְהֹוָה אֲלַמֶּדְכֶם׃

יג מִי־הָאִישׁ הֶחָפֵץ חַיִּים אֹהֵב יָמִים לִרְאוֹת טוֹב׃

יד נְצֹר לְשׁוֹנְךָ מֵרָע וּשְׂפָתֶיךָ מִדַּבֵּר מִרְמָה׃

טו סוּר מֵרָע וַעֲשֵׂה־טוֹב בַּקֵּשׁ שָׁלוֹם וְרָדְפֵהוּ׃

טז עֵינֵי יְהֹוָה אֶל־צַדִּיקִים וְאָזְנָיו אֶל־שַׁוְעָתָם׃

יז פְּנֵי יְהֹוָה בְּעֹשֵׂי רָע לְהַכְרִית מֵאֶרֶץ זִכְרָם׃

יח צָעֲקוּ וַיהֹוָה שָׁמֵעַ וּמִכָּל־צָרוֹתָם הִצִּילָם׃

יט קָרוֹב יְהֹוָה לְנִשְׁבְּרֵי־לֵב וְאֶת־דַּכְּאֵי־רוּחַ יוֹשִׁיעַ׃

כ רַבּוֹת רָעוֹת צַדִּיק וּמִכֻּלָּם יַצִּילֶנּוּ יְהֹוָה׃

כא שֹׁמֵר כָּל־עַצְמוֹתָיו אַחַת מֵהֵנָּה לֹא נִשְׁבָּרָה׃

כב תְּמוֹתֵת רָשָׁע רָעָה וְשֹׂנְאֵי צַדִּיק יֶאְשָׁמוּ׃

כג פּוֹדֶה יְהֹוָה נֶפֶשׁ עֲבָדָיו וְלֹא יֶאְשְׁמוּ כָּל־הַחֹסִים בּוֹ׃

פרק לה

א לְדָוִד רִיבָה יְהֹוָה אֶת־יְרִיבַי לְחַם אֶת־לֹחֲמָי׃

ב הַחֲזֵק מָגֵן וְצִנָּה וְקוּמָה בְּעֶזְרָתִי׃

ג וְהָרֵק חֲנִית וּסְגֹר לִקְרַאת רֹדְפָי אֱמֹר לְנַפְשִׁי יְשֻׁעָתֵךְ אָנִי׃

7 Here was a poor man who cried out, and the Lord heard and saved him from all his troubles.

8 The angel of the Lord protects and saves those who fear Him.

9 Consider and witness the goodness of the Lord. Happy is the man who takes refuge in Him.

10 You holy people, revere the Lord, because there is nothing lacking for those that fear Him.

11 Even young lions do not have enough and are hungry, but those who believe in the Lord lack no good thing.

12 Come, children, and listen to me: I will teach you fear of the Lord.

13 Which man desires life, a long span of good days?

14 Keep your tongue from speaking evil and your lips form speaking falsehood.

15 Turn away from evil and do good. Desire peace and go after it.

16 The Lord turns His eyes toward those who are good, and His ears hear their cry.

17 The Lord turns His anger against those who do evil, removing their memory from the earth.

18 They cried and the Lord, Who saves them from all their troubles, heard them.

19 The Lord is near to the broken-hearted and helps those whose hearts suffer.

20 The righteous have many problems, but the Lord save them from all their troubles.

21 He guards all his bones so that not a single one is broken.

22 Evil will destroy the wicked. Those who hate the righteous will be found guilty.

23 The Lord redeems the souls of His servants. Those who desire Him will not be forgotten.

TEHILLIM 35

A song asking for help

1 A psalm by David. My Lord, contend with those who contend against me. Fight against those who fight me.

2 Take up Your shield and sword and come to my aid.

3 Ready your sword and weapons against those who pursue me. Tell my soul: "I am your deliverance."

ד יֵבֹשׁוּ וְיִכָּלְמוּ מְבַקְשֵׁי נַפְשִׁי יִסֹּגוּ אָחוֹר וְיַחְפְּרוּ חֹשְׁבֵי רָעָתִי:

ה יִהְיוּ כְּמֹץ לִפְנֵי־רוּחַ וּמַלְאַךְ יְהוָה דּוֹחֶה:

ו יְהִי־דַרְכָּם חֹשֶׁךְ וַחֲלַקְלַקֹּת וּמַלְאַךְ יְהוָה רֹדְפָם:

ז כִּי־חִנָּם טָמְנוּ־לִי שַׁחַת רִשְׁתָּם חִנָּם חָפְרוּ לְנַפְשִׁי:

ח תְּבוֹאֵהוּ שׁוֹאָה לֹא יֵדָע וְרִשְׁתּוֹ אֲשֶׁר־טָמַן תִּלְכְּדוֹ בְּשׁוֹאָה יִפָּל־בָּהּ:

ט וְנַפְשִׁי תָּגִיל בַּיהוָה תָּשִׂישׂ בִּישׁוּעָתוֹ:

י כָּל עַצְמֹתַי תֹּאמַרְנָה יְהוָה מִי כָמוֹךָ מַצִּיל עָנִי מֵחָזָק מִמֶּנּוּ וְעָנִי וְאֶבְיוֹן מִגֹּזְלוֹ:

יא יְקוּמוּן עֵדֵי חָמָס אֲשֶׁר לֹא־יָדַעְתִּי יִשְׁאָלוּנִי:

יב יְשַׁלְּמוּנִי רָעָה תַּחַת טוֹבָה שְׁכוֹל לְנַפְשִׁי:

יג וַאֲנִי בַּחֲלוֹתָם לְבוּשִׁי שָׂק עִנֵּיתִי בַצּוֹם נַפְשִׁי וּתְפִלָּתִי עַל־חֵיקִי תָשׁוּב:

יד כְּרֵעַ כְּאָח־לִי הִתְהַלָּכְתִּי כַּאֲבֶל־אֵם קֹדֵר שַׁחוֹתִי:

טו וּבְצַלְעִי שָׂמְחוּ וְנֶאֱסָפוּ נֶאֶסְפוּ עָלַי נֵכִים וְלֹא יָדַעְתִּי קָרְעוּ וְלֹא־דָמּוּ:

טז בְּחַנְפֵי לַעֲגֵי מָעוֹג חָרֹק עָלַי שִׁנֵּימוֹ:

יז אֲדֹנָי כַּמָּה תִּרְאֶה הָשִׁיבָה נַפְשִׁי מִשֹּׁאֵיהֶם מִכְּפִירִים יְחִידָתִי:

יח אוֹדְךָ בְּקָהָל רָב בְּעַם עָצוּם אֲהַלְלֶךָּ:

יט אַל־יִשְׂמְחוּ־לִי אֹיְבַי שֶׁקֶר שֹׂנְאַי חִנָּם יִקְרְצוּ־עָיִן:

כ כִּי לֹא שָׁלוֹם יְדַבֵּרוּ וְעַל רִגְעֵי־אֶרֶץ דִּבְרֵי מִרְמוֹת יַחֲשֹׁבוּן:

כא וַיַּרְחִיבוּ עָלַי פִּיהֶם אָמְרוּ הֶאָח הֶאָח רָאֲתָה עֵינֵינוּ:

כב רָאִיתָה יְהוָה אַל־תֶּחֱרַשׁ אֲדֹנָי אַל־תִּרְחַק מִמֶּנִּי:

כג הָעִירָה וְהָקִיצָה לְמִשְׁפָּטִי אֱלֹהַי וַאדֹנָי לְרִיבִי:

כד שָׁפְטֵנִי כְצִדְקְךָ יְהוָה אֱלֹהָי וְאַל־יִשְׂמְחוּ־לִי:

כה אַל־יֹאמְרוּ בְלִבָּם הֶאָח נַפְשֵׁנוּ אַל־יֹאמְרוּ בִּלַּעֲנוּהוּ:

4   May those who wish to take my life be ashamed and confused. May those who wish to hurt me be rejected and defeated.

5   May they be blown away in the wind, may the angel of the Lord thrust them away.

6   May their path be dark and dangerous, with the angel of the Lord pursuing them.

7   For no reason, they have prepared a trap and a snare for my soul to fall into.

8   May sudden punishment come upon them. May the net that they prepared trap them, so that they are punished.

9   My soul will be happy with the Lord and will rejoice in His deliverance.

10   All my bones will say: "Lord, who is like You, Who saves the poor from those who overpower them and the poor and the needy from those who are corrupt?"

11   False witnesses accuse me of things that I know nothing about.

12   They repay me evil for good, and sorrow comes upon my soul.

13   Yet when they were sick, I wore sackcloth and fasted. May my prayer now come to help me.

14   I went about as though he were my friend or my own brother. I bowed down in mourning as if I were mourning my own mother.

15   Now, when I limp, they rejoice and conspire against me, crippled men whom I do not know. They do not cease from tearing me.

16   With mockeries, at banquets and feasts, they grind their teeth at me.

17   Lord, how long will You witness this? Save my life from their destruction, my precious soul from the lions.

18   I will give You thanks in the great assembly, and I will praise you to all the people.

19   Do not let those who hate me without reason gloat over me. Do not let those who hate me without just cause wink their eyes.

20   They do not want peace, and make trouble for those who truly do want peace in the land.

21   They speak loudly against me, shouting, "Aha, aha, we have seen it!"

22   Lord, You witness it all. Do not remain silent. Lord, do not be far from me.

23   Respond and attend to my judgment and to my cause, my God, my Lord.

24   Judge me, my Lord, my God, according to Your goodness, and do not let them gloat over me.

כו יֵבֹשׁוּ וְיַחְפְּרוּ יַחְדָּו שְׂמֵחֵי רָעָתִי יִלְבְּשׁוּ־בֹשֶׁת וּכְלִמָּה הַמַּגְדִּילִים עָלָי:

כז יָרֹנּוּ וְיִשְׂמְחוּ חֲפֵצֵי צִדְקִי וְיֹאמְרוּ תָמִיד יִגְדַּל יְהוָה הֶחָפֵץ שְׁלוֹם עַבְדּוֹ:

כח וּלְשׁוֹנִי תֶּהְגֶּה צִדְקֶךָ כָּל־הַיּוֹם תְּהִלָּתֶךָ:

<h2 style="text-align:center">פרק לו</h2>

א לַמְנַצֵּחַ לְעֶבֶד־יְהוָה לְדָוִד:

ב נְאֻם־פֶּשַׁע לָרָשָׁע בְּקֶרֶב לִבִּי אֵין־פַּחַד אֱלֹהִים לְנֶגֶד עֵינָיו:

ג כִּי־הֶחֱלִיק אֵלָיו בְּעֵינָיו לִמְצֹא עֲוֺנוֹ לִשְׂנֹא:

ד דִּבְרֵי־פִיו אָוֶן וּמִרְמָה חָדַל לְהַשְׂכִּיל לְהֵיטִיב:

ה אָוֶן יַחְשֹׁב עַל־מִשְׁכָּבוֹ יִתְיַצֵּב עַל־דֶּרֶךְ לֹא־טוֹב רָע לֹא יִמְאָס:

ו יְהוָה בְּהַשָּׁמַיִם חַסְדֶּךָ אֱמוּנָתְךָ עַד־שְׁחָקִים:

ז צִדְקָתְךָ כְּהַרְרֵי־אֵל מִשְׁפָּטֶךָ תְּהוֹם רַבָּה אָדָם וּבְהֵמָה תוֹשִׁיעַ יְהוָה:

ח מַה־יָּקָר חַסְדְּךָ אֱלֹהִים וּבְנֵי אָדָם בְּצֵל כְּנָפֶיךָ יֶחֱסָיוּן:

ט יִרְוְיֻן מִדֶּשֶׁן בֵּיתֶךָ וְנַחַל עֲדָנֶיךָ תַשְׁקֵם:

י כִּי־עִמְּךָ מְקוֹר חַיִּים בְּאוֹרְךָ נִרְאֶה־אוֹר:

יא מְשֹׁךְ חַסְדְּךָ לְיֹדְעֶיךָ וְצִדְקָתְךָ לְיִשְׁרֵי־לֵב:

יב אַל־תְּבוֹאֵנִי רֶגֶל גַּאֲוָה וְיַד־רְשָׁעִים אַל־תְּנִדֵנִי:

יג שָׁם נָפְלוּ פֹּעֲלֵי אָוֶן דֹּחוּ וְלֹא־יָכְלוּ קוּם:

25 Do not let them say in their hearts: "Aha, we have what we wanted!" Do not let them say, "We have destroyed him!"

26 Let those who rejoice over my suffering be ashamed. Cover with shame and confusion those who gloat over me.

27 But let those who rejoice to see me victorious sing with joy and gladness. Let them always say: "Praised be the Lord, Who delights in the well-being of His servant."

28 My own tongue will speak of Your goodness and praise You all day long.

TEHILLIM 36

A song describing God's love for us

1 For the chief musician by David, the servant of the Lord.

2 I feel in my heart that the wicked desire sin. There is no fear of God before their eyes.

3 He takes pleasure in his sins, and will continue until he attains his goal of hatred.

4 The words of his mouth are falsehood and dishonesty. They are no longer wise or good.

5 He plans evil at night and leads an evil life. He does not object to evil.

6 Your love and kindness are in the heavens, my Lord. Your faithfulness reaches to the skies.

7 Your goodness is like the mighty mountains. Your judgments are like the deep waters. You support man and beast, my Lord.

8 Your loving kindness is very great, my God. The children of man take refuge in the shadow of Your wings.

9 They take pleasure in Your hospitable house. You give them to drink from the flow of Your goodness.

10 In You is the fountain of life, and through Your light, we see light.

11 Continue Your loving kindness to those who know You, and Your goodness to the faithful in heart.

12 Do not let pride overcome me. Do not let the hand of the wicked drive me away.

13 There the evildoers have fallen. They are thrown down, unable to rise.

פרק לז

א לְדָוִד אַל־תִּתְחַר בַּמְּרֵעִים אַל־תְּקַנֵּא בְּעֹשֵׂי עַוְלָה:

ב כִּי כֶחָצִיר מְהֵרָה יִמָּלוּ וּכְיֶרֶק דֶּשֶׁא יִבּוֹלוּן:

ג בְּטַח בַּיהוָה וַעֲשֵׂה־טוֹב שְׁכָן־אֶרֶץ וּרְעֵה אֱמוּנָה:

ד וְהִתְעַנַּג עַל־יְהוָה וְיִתֶּן־לְךָ מִשְׁאֲלֹת לִבֶּךָ:

ה גּוֹל עַל־יְהוָה דַּרְכֶּךָ וּבְטַח עָלָיו וְהוּא יַעֲשֶׂה:

ו וְהוֹצִיא כָאוֹר צִדְקֶךָ וּמִשְׁפָּטֶךָ כַּצָּהֳרָיִם:

ז דּוֹם לַיהוָה וְהִתְחוֹלֵל לוֹ אַל־תִּתְחַר בְּמַצְלִיחַ דַּרְכּוֹ בְּאִישׁ עֹשֶׂה מְזִמּוֹת:

ח הֶרֶף מֵאַף וַעֲזֹב חֵמָה אַל־תִּתְחַר אַךְ־לְהָרֵעַ:

ט כִּי־מְרֵעִים יִכָּרֵתוּן וְקֹוֵי יְהוָה הֵמָּה יִירְשׁוּ־אָרֶץ:

י וְעוֹד מְעַט וְאֵין רָשָׁע וְהִתְבּוֹנַנְתָּ עַל־מְקוֹמוֹ וְאֵינֶנּוּ:

יא וַעֲנָוִים יִירְשׁוּ־אָרֶץ וְהִתְעַנְּגוּ עַל־רֹב שָׁלוֹם:

יב זֹמֵם רָשָׁע לַצַּדִּיק וְחֹרֵק עָלָיו שִׁנָּיו:

יג אֲדֹנָי יִשְׂחַק־לוֹ כִּי־רָאָה כִּי־יָבֹא יוֹמוֹ:

יד חֶרֶב פָּתְחוּ רְשָׁעִים וְדָרְכוּ קַשְׁתָּם לְהַפִּיל עָנִי וְאֶבְיוֹן לִטְבוֹחַ יִשְׁרֵי־דָרֶךְ:

טו חַרְבָּם תָּבוֹא בְלִבָּם וְקַשְּׁתוֹתָם תִּשָּׁבַרְנָה:

טז טוֹב מְעַט לַצַּדִּיק מֵהֲמוֹן רְשָׁעִים רַבִּים:

יז כִּי זְרוֹעוֹת רְשָׁעִים תִּשָּׁבַרְנָה וְסוֹמֵךְ צַדִּיקִים יְהוָה:

יח יוֹדֵעַ יְהוָה יְמֵי תְמִימִם וְנַחֲלָתָם לְעוֹלָם תִּהְיֶה:

יט לֹא־יֵבֹשׁוּ בְּעֵת רָעָה וּבִימֵי רְעָבוֹן יִשְׂבָּעוּ:

כ כִּי רְשָׁעִים יֹאבֵדוּ וְאֹיְבֵי יְהוָה כִּיקַר כָּרִים כָּלוּ בֶעָשָׁן כָּלוּ:

TEHILLIM 37

A song counseling faith in God.

1 By David. Do not worry because of the wicked, and do not admire those who do evil.

2 They will soon dry up like grass and fade like vegetation.

3 Do good and trust in the Lord. Live in your land and keep faith.

4 Take delight in the Lord, and He will give you your heart's desire.

5 Dedicate yourself to the Lord. Trust Him and all your desires will be fulfilled.

6 He will make your righteousness shine forth like the light, and your judgment like the light of noon.

7 Trust in the Lord and wait patiently for Him. Do not upset yourself because evildoers and sinners are rewarded for their evil ways.

8 Do not become angered or full of hate. Do not worry, because it serves no purpose.

9 The evildoers will be destroyed, but those who wait for the Lord will inherit the land.

10 Soon, the evildoers will no longer exist. You will see that they have vanished.

11 The humble will inherit the land and will enjoy peace.

12 The wicked ones plot against the good and gnashes his teeth at him.

13 The Lord laughs at them, for He knows when his day of judgment will arrive.

14 The wicked have taken out their swords and prepared their bows to cut down the poor and needy and to kill the good.

15 Their swords will enter their own hearts and their bows will be broken.

16 The little that the good have is better than the abundance of the wicked.

17 The arms of evil will be broken, but the Lord supports those who do good.

18 The Lord knows the suffering of the good. Their inheritance will last forever.

19 In evil times they will not be ashamed, and in time of famine they will have food.

20 The wicked will die, and the enemies of the Lord will be like burnt offerings: they will burn in smoke and fade away.

כא לֹוֶה רָשָׁע וְלֹא יְשַׁלֵּם וְצַדִּיק חוֹנֵן וְנוֹתֵן:

כב כִּי מְבֹרָכָיו יִירְשׁוּ אָרֶץ וּמְקֻלָּלָיו יִכָּרֵתוּ:

כג מֵיְהֹוָה מִצְעֲדֵי־גֶבֶר כּוֹנָנוּ וְדַרְכּוֹ יֶחְפָּץ:

כד כִּי־יִפֹּל לֹא־יוּטָל כִּי־יְהֹוָה סוֹמֵךְ יָדוֹ:

כה נַעַר הָיִיתִי גַּם־זָקַנְתִּי וְלֹא־רָאִיתִי צַדִּיק נֶעֱזָב וְזַרְעוֹ מְבַקֶּשׁ־לָחֶם:

כו כָּל־הַיּוֹם חוֹנֵן וּמַלְוֶה וְזַרְעוֹ לִבְרָכָה:

כז סוּר מֵרָע וַעֲשֵׂה־טוֹב וּשְׁכֹן לְעוֹלָם:

כח כִּי יְהֹוָה אֹהֵב מִשְׁפָּט וְלֹא־יַעֲזֹב אֶת־חֲסִידָיו לְעוֹלָם נִשְׁמָרוּ וְזֶרַע רְשָׁעִים נִכְרָת:

כט צַדִּיקִים יִירְשׁוּ־אָרֶץ וְיִשְׁכְּנוּ לָעַד עָלֶיהָ:

ל פִּי־צַדִּיק יֶהְגֶּה חָכְמָה וּלְשׁוֹנוֹ תְּדַבֵּר מִשְׁפָּט:

לא תּוֹרַת אֱלֹהָיו בְּלִבּוֹ לֹא תִמְעַד אֲשֻׁרָיו:

לב צוֹפֶה רָשָׁע לַצַּדִּיק וּמְבַקֵּשׁ לַהֲמִיתוֹ:

לג יְהֹוָה לֹא־יַעַזְבֶנּוּ בְיָדוֹ וְלֹא יַרְשִׁיעֶנּוּ בְּהִשָּׁפְטוֹ:

לד קַוֵּה אֶל־יְהֹוָה וּשְׁמֹר דַּרְכּוֹ וִירוֹמִמְךָ לָרֶשֶׁת אָרֶץ בְּהִכָּרֵת רְשָׁעִים תִּרְאֶה:

לה רָאִיתִי רָשָׁע עָרִיץ וּמִתְעָרֶה כְּאֶזְרָח רַעֲנָן:

לו וַיַּעֲבֹר וְהִנֵּה אֵינֶנּוּ וָאֲבַקְשֵׁהוּ וְלֹא נִמְצָא:

לז שְׁמָר־תָּם וּרְאֵה יָשָׁר כִּי־אַחֲרִית לְאִישׁ שָׁלוֹם:

לח וּפֹשְׁעִים נִשְׁמְדוּ יַחְדָּו אַחֲרִית רְשָׁעִים נִכְרָתָה:

לט וּתְשׁוּעַת צַדִּיקִים מֵיְהֹוָה מָעוּזָּם בְּעֵת צָרָה:

מ וַיַּעְזְרֵם יְהֹוָה וַיְפַלְּטֵם יְפַלְּטֵם מֵרְשָׁעִים וְיוֹשִׁיעֵם כִּי חָסוּ בוֹ:

21 The wicked borrow without repaying, but the good act kindly and give.

22 Those whom God blesses will inherit the land, but those who are cursed will be cut off.

23 The Lord determines whether a man's path pleases Him.

24 If he falls, he will not stay down, for the Lord grips his hand.

25 I was young and now I am old, and I have never seen righteous people forsaken and their children begging for bread.

26 Every day the good person acts kindly and gives, and his children are blessed.

27 Forsake evil and do good, and you will live securely, forever.

28 The Lord loves justice and does not forget His faithful ones. They are supported forever, but the children of the wicked will be cut off.

29 The righteous will inherit the land and live upon it forever.

30 The mouth of the righteous person utters wisdom and his lips speak the truth.

31 The teaching of his God is in his heart, and his footsteps are secure.

32 Evildoers lie in wait for righteous people, wishing to kill them.

33 The Lord will not leave him in the evildoers' hands, or allow him to be judged falsely.

34 Wait for the Lord. Live by His teachings and He will give you strength to inherit the land when the evildoers are destroyed, as you will see.

35 I have seen an evildoer with great power, growing like a strong tree in the soil.

36 But he passed on, and vanished. When I looked for him, he was gone.

37 Notice the man of truth. Look at men of truth, for they are the future of peace.

38 Sinners will be utterly destroyed, and the future of evildoers will vanish.

39 The Lord blesses the righteous. He is security in times of trouble.

40 The Lord helps and saves them. He saves them from evil and protects them because they have taken shelter in Him.

פרק לח

א מִזְמוֹר לְדָוִד לְהַזְכִּיר:

ב יְהוָה אַל־בְּקֶצְפְּךָ תוֹכִיחֵנִי וּבַחֲמָתְךָ תְיַסְּרֵנִי:

ג כִּי־חִצֶּיךָ נִחֲתוּ־בִי וַתִּנְחַת עָלַי יָדֶךָ:

ד אֵין־מְתֹם בִּבְשָׂרִי מִפְּנֵי זַעְמֶךָ אֵין־שָׁלוֹם בַּעֲצָמַי מִפְּנֵי חַטָּאתִי:

ה כִּי־עֲוֹנֹתַי עָבְרוּ רֹאשִׁי כְּמַשָּׂא כָבֵד יִכְבְּדוּ מִמֶּנִּי:

ו הִבְאִישׁוּ נָמַקּוּ חַבּוּרֹתָי מִפְּנֵי אִוַּלְתִּי:

ז נַעֲוֵיתִי שַׁחֹתִי עַד־מְאֹד כָּל־הַיּוֹם קֹדֵר הִלָּכְתִּי:

ח כִּי־כְסָלַי מָלְאוּ נִקְלֶה וְאֵין מְתֹם בִּבְשָׂרִי:

ט נְפוּגֹתִי וְנִדְכֵּיתִי עַד־מְאֹד שָׁאַגְתִּי מִנַּהֲמַת לִבִּי:

י אֲדֹנָי נֶגְדְּךָ כָל־תַּאֲוָתִי וְאַנְחָתִי מִמְּךָ לֹא־נִסְתָּרָה:

יא לִבִּי סְחַרְחַר עֲזָבַנִי כֹחִי וְאוֹר עֵינַי גַּם־הֵם אֵין אִתִּי:

יב אֹהֲבַי וְרֵעַי מִנֶּגֶד נִגְעִי יַעֲמֹדוּ וּקְרוֹבַי מֵרָחֹק עָמָדוּ:

יג וַיְנַקְשׁוּ מְבַקְשֵׁי נַפְשִׁי וְדֹרְשֵׁי רָעָתִי דִּבְּרוּ הַוּוֹת וּמִרְמוֹת כָּל־הַיּוֹם יֶהְגּוּ:

יד וַאֲנִי כְחֵרֵשׁ לֹא אֶשְׁמָע וּכְאִלֵּם לֹא יִפְתַּח־פִּיו:

טו וָאֱהִי כְּאִישׁ אֲשֶׁר לֹא־שֹׁמֵעַ וְאֵין בְּפִיו תּוֹכָחוֹת:

טז כִּי־לְךָ יְהוָה הוֹחָלְתִּי אַתָּה תַעֲנֶה אֲדֹנָי אֱלֹהָי:

יז כִּי־אָמַרְתִּי פֶּן־יִשְׂמְחוּ־לִי בְּמוֹט רַגְלִי עָלַי הִגְדִּילוּ:

יח כִּי־אֲנִי לְצֶלַע נָכוֹן וּמַכְאוֹבִי נֶגְדִּי תָמִיד:

יט כִּי־עֲוֹנִי אַגִּיד אֶדְאַג מֵחַטָּאתִי:

כ וְאֹיְבַי חַיִּים עָצֵמוּ וְרַבּוּ שֹׂנְאַי שָׁקֶר:

כא וּמְשַׁלְּמֵי רָעָה תַּחַת טוֹבָה יִשְׂטְנוּנִי תַּחַת רדופי [רָדְפִי]־טוֹב:

כב אַל־תַּעַזְבֵנִי יְהוָה אֱלֹהַי אַל־תִּרְחַק מִמֶּנִּי:

כג חוּשָׁה לְעֶזְרָתִי אֲדֹנָי תְּשׁוּעָתִי:

TEHILLIM 38

A song asking forgiveness

1 A psalm by David, as a memorial.

2 My Lord, do not chastise me in Your anger. Do not punish me in Your wrath.

3 Your arrows have entered deeply into me and your hand has come down upon me.

4 My flesh is marred because You are upset, and my bones are weak because of my sin.

5 My sins are huge above my head. They are too heavy a burden for me.

6 My wounds are open and infected because of my foolish ways.

7 I am terribly bent and sunk down. All day long I am in mourning.

8 My body is marred and there is no peace in my mind.

9 I am weak and crushed, and I groan because of the pain in my heart.

10 Lord, You know all that I feel. My sighs are not hidden from You.

11 My heart trembles, my strength is gone and the light of my eyes is extinguished.

12 My friends and neighbors stand at a distance from my illness. My family stays away.

13 Those who want to kill me set traps for me. Those who want me to suffer act against me and tell lies all day long.

14 But I am like a deaf man who does not hear. Like one who cannot speak, I do not open my mouth.

15 I have become like a man who hears nothing and cannot speak in his own defense.

16 In You I hope, my Lord. I hope that You will answer me, Lord my God.

17 I said: "Let them not gloat over me. When my foot stumbles, they strengthen themselves against me."

18 I am crippled. My pain is always with me.

19 I have confessed my sins, and I am filled with sorrow over them.

20 But my enemies are in good health, and those who hate me have multiplied.

21 They return evil for good. They are my enemies because I do good.

22 My Lord, do not forget me. My God, do not be far from me.

23 Come quickly to assist me, Lord, my salvation.

פרק לט

א לַמְנַצֵּחַ לִידִיתוּן [לִידוּתוּן] מִזְמוֹר לְדָוִד:

ב אָמַרְתִּי אֶשְׁמְרָה דְרָכַי מֵחֲטוֹא בִלְשׁוֹנִי אֶשְׁמְרָה לְפִי מַחְסוֹם בְּעֹד רָשָׁע לְנֶגְדִּי:

ג נֶאֱלַמְתִּי דוּמִיָּה הֶחֱשֵׁיתִי מִטּוֹב וּכְאֵבִי נֶעְכָּר:

ד חַם־לִבִּי בְּקִרְבִּי בַּהֲגִיגִי תִבְעַר־אֵשׁ דִּבַּרְתִּי בִּלְשׁוֹנִי:

ה הוֹדִיעֵנִי יְהוָה קִצִּי וּמִדַּת יָמַי מַה־הִיא אֵדְעָה מֶה־חָדֵל אָנִי:

ו הִנֵּה טְפָחוֹת נָתַתָּה יָמַי וְחֶלְדִּי כְאַיִן נֶגְדֶּךָ אַךְ־כָּל־הֶבֶל כָּל־אָדָם נִצָּב סֶלָה:

ז אַךְ־בְּצֶלֶם יִתְהַלֶּךְ־אִישׁ אַךְ־הֶבֶל יֶהֱמָיוּן יִצְבֹּר וְלֹא־יֵדַע מִי־אֹסְפָם:

ח וְעַתָּה מַה־קִּוִּיתִי אֲדֹנָי תּוֹחַלְתִּי לְךָ הִיא:

ט מִכָּל־פְּשָׁעַי הַצִּילֵנִי חֶרְפַּת נָבָל אַל־תְּשִׂימֵנִי:

י נֶאֱלַמְתִּי לֹא אֶפְתַּח־פִּי כִּי אַתָּה עָשִׂיתָ:

יא הָסֵר מֵעָלַי נִגְעֶךָ מִתִּגְרַת יָדְךָ אֲנִי כָלִיתִי:

יב בְּתוֹכָחוֹת עַל־עָוֹן יִסַּרְתָּ אִישׁ וַתֶּמֶס כָּעָשׁ חֲמוּדוֹ אַךְ הֶבֶל כָּל־אָדָם סֶלָה:

יג שִׁמְעָה־תְפִלָּתִי יְהוָה וְשַׁוְעָתִי הַאֲזִינָה אֶל־דִּמְעָתִי אַל־תֶּחֱרַשׁ כִּי גֵר אָנֹכִי עִמָּךְ תּוֹשָׁב כְּכָל־אֲבוֹתָי:

יד הָשַׁע מִמֶּנִּי וְאַבְלִיגָה בְּטֶרֶם אֵלֵךְ וְאֵינֶנִּי:

TEHILLIM 39

A song asking the Lord to hear his cry

1 For the chief musician, for Jeduthun. A psalm by David.

2 I said "I will control myself, and I will not sin with my tongue. I will restrain my mouth while the wicked are near me".

3 I remained silent and kept quiet, hoping for good things. I kept my pain inside me.

4 My heart burned within me while I held back the fire. Then I spoke with my tongue.

5 "Lord, let me know my end and how many are the length of my days. Let me know how short my life will be.

6 Now You have given me only a few days. My years are nothing to You. Even men at their best are not immortal." Selah.

7 Man is nothing but a semblance of himself, and he worries over nothing. He accumulates riches but does not know who will receive them.

8 Now, Lord, what do I wait for? My hope is in You.

9 Save me from all my sins, and do not let me be ashamed in front of the wicked.

10 I am silent and do not open my mouth because You have done this.

11 Remove your judgment from me. I have been punished by your hand.

12 You punish man for his sin with anger. You make his beauty vanish as if consumed by moths. Surely every man is vain. Selah.

13 Lord, hear my prayer and listen to my cry. Do not remain quiet when You see my tears, for I am a stranger with You, a traveler, as all my ancestors were.

14 Look away from me so that I will have comfort before I depart and exist no more.

פרק מ

א לַמְנַצֵּחַ לְדָוִד מִזְמוֹר:

ב קַוֺּה קִוִּיתִי יְהוָה וַיֵּט אֵלַי וַיִּשְׁמַע שַׁוְעָתִי:

ג וַיַּעֲלֵנִי מִבּוֹר שָׁאוֹן מִטִּיט הַיָּוֵן וַיָּקֶם עַל־סֶלַע רַגְלַי כּוֹנֵן אֲשֻׁרָי:

ד וַיִּתֵּן בְּפִי שִׁיר חָדָשׁ תְּהִלָּה לֵאלֹהֵינוּ יִרְאוּ רַבִּים וְיִירָאוּ וְיִבְטְחוּ בַּיהוָה:

ה אַשְׁרֵי־הַגֶּבֶר אֲשֶׁר־שָׂם יְהוָה מִבְטַחוֹ וְלֹא־פָנָה אֶל־רְהָבִים וְשָׂטֵי כָזָב:

ו רַבּוֹת עָשִׂיתָ אַתָּה יְהוָה אֱלֹהַי נִפְלְאֹתֶיךָ וּמַחְשְׁבֹתֶיךָ אֵלֵינוּ אֵין עֲרֹךְ אֵלֶיךָ אַגִּידָה וַאֲדַבֵּרָה עָצְמוּ מִסַּפֵּר:

ז זֶבַח וּמִנְחָה לֹא־חָפַצְתָּ אָזְנַיִם כָּרִיתָ לִּי עוֹלָה וַחֲטָאָה לֹא שָׁאָלְתָּ:

ח אָז אָמַרְתִּי הִנֵּה־בָאתִי בִּמְגִלַּת־סֵפֶר כָּתוּב עָלָי:

ט לַעֲשׂוֹת רְצוֹנְךָ אֱלֹהַי חָפָצְתִּי וְתוֹרָתְךָ בְּתוֹךְ מֵעָי:

י בִּשַּׂרְתִּי צֶדֶק בְּקָהָל רָב הִנֵּה שְׂפָתַי לֹא אֶכְלָא יְהוָה אַתָּה יָדָעְתָּ:

יא צִדְקָתְךָ לֹא־כִסִּיתִי בְּתוֹךְ לִבִּי אֱמוּנָתְךָ וּתְשׁוּעָתְךָ אָמָרְתִּי לֹא־כִחַדְתִּי חַסְדְּךָ וַאֲמִתְּךָ לְקָהָל רָב:

יב אַתָּה יְהוָה לֹא־תִכְלָא רַחֲמֶיךָ מִמֶּנִּי חַסְדְּךָ וַאֲמִתְּךָ תָּמִיד יִצְּרוּנִי:

יג כִּי אָפְפוּ עָלַי רָעוֹת עַד־אֵין מִסְפָּר הִשִּׂיגוּנִי עֲוֺנֹתַי וְלֹא־יָכֹלְתִּי לִרְאוֹת עָצְמוּ מִשַּׂעֲרוֹת רֹאשִׁי וְלִבִּי עֲזָבָנִי:

יד רְצֵה־יְהוָה לְהַצִּילֵנִי יְהוָה לְעֶזְרָתִי חוּשָׁה:

טו יֵבֹשׁוּ וְיַחְפְּרוּ יַחַד מְבַקְשֵׁי נַפְשִׁי לִסְפּוֹתָהּ יִסֹּגוּ אָחוֹר וְיִכָּלְמוּ חֲפֵצֵי רָעָתִי:

טז יָשֹׁמּוּ עַל־עֵקֶב בָּשְׁתָּם הָאֹמְרִים לִי הֶאָח הֶאָח:

יז יָשִׂישׂוּ וְיִשְׂמְחוּ בְּךָ כָּל־מְבַקְשֶׁיךָ יֹאמְרוּ תָמִיד יִגְדַּל יְהוָה אֹהֲבֵי תְּשׁוּעָתֶךָ:

יח וַאֲנִי עָנִי וְאֶבְיוֹן אֲדֹנָי יַחֲשָׁב לִי עֶזְרָתִי וּמְפַלְטִי אַתָּה אֱלֹהַי אַל־תְּאַחַר:

TEHILLIM 40

A song of thanks and a prayer for help

1 For the chief musician, a psalm by David.

2 I waited patiently for the Lord, and He turned to me to hear my cry.

3 He took me out of the pit of turmoil and out of the mire. He placed my feet on a rock and supported my path.

4 He placed a new song into my mouth – the praise of our God. Many will witness and fear, and trust in the Lord.

5 Happy is the man who trusts in the Lord and has not turned to the arrogant, or to those who commit treachery.

6 My Lord, my God, You have done many great things. Your thoughts are with us. There is no one to compare to You. If I were to list Your wonders and speak of them, I would not be able to tell everything.

7 You take no pleasure in sacrifices or meal-offerings. You have made me hear You do not need burnt offerings or sin-offerings.

8 Then I said:" I come with a scroll written about me.

9 I am to do Your will. Your law is deep inside me."

10 I have preached righteousness to all of the people. I did not close my lips – this You know, my Lord.

11 I did not hide Your goodness in my heart. I told of Your faithfulness and Your salvation. I did not hide Your mercy and truth from the assembly.

12 Lord, do not keep Your mercy from me. Let Your mercy and truth always preserve me.

13 Many troubles come upon me. My sins overtake me. I cannot look up. They number more than the hairs of my head, and my heart fails.

14 My Lord, be pleased to save me, and hurry to help me.

15 Let those who seek my life be ashamed and embarrassed. May those who rejoice in my suffering be turned backward and thrown into confusion.

16 Let those who say "Aha! aha!" to me be appalled by their shame.

17 But may all who desire You rejoice and be happy with You. May all who love Your salvation always say: "May the Lord be magnified!"

18 I am poor and needy, but You, Lord, think well of me. You are my help and my savior. My Lord, do not delay.

פרק מא

א לַמְנַצֵּחַ מִזְמוֹר לְדָוִד:

ב אַשְׁרֵי מַשְׂכִּיל אֶל־דָּל בְּיוֹם רָעָה יְמַלְּטֵהוּ יְהוָה:

ג יְהוָה יִשְׁמְרֵהוּ וִיחַיֵּהוּ יאשר [וְאֻשַּׁר] בָּאָרֶץ וְאַל־תִּתְּנֵהוּ בְּנֶפֶשׁ אֹיְבָיו:

ד יְהוָה יִסְעָדֶנּוּ עַל־עֶרֶשׂ דְּוָי כָּל־מִשְׁכָּבוֹ הָפַכְתָּ בְחָלְיוֹ:

ה אֲנִי־אָמַרְתִּי יְהוָה חָנֵּנִי רְפָאָה נַפְשִׁי כִּי־חָטָאתִי לָךְ:

ו אוֹיְבַי יֹאמְרוּ רַע לִי מָתַי יָמוּת וְאָבַד שְׁמוֹ:

ז וְאִם־בָּא לִרְאוֹת שָׁוְא יְדַבֵּר לִבּוֹ יִקְבָּץ־אָוֶן לוֹ יֵצֵא לַחוּץ יְדַבֵּר:

ח יַחַד עָלַי יִתְלַחֲשׁוּ כָּל־שֹׂנְאָי עָלַי יַחְשְׁבוּ רָעָה לִי:

ט דְּבַר־בְּלִיַּעַל יָצוּק בּוֹ וַאֲשֶׁר שָׁכַב לֹא־יוֹסִיף לָקוּם:

י גַּם־אִישׁ־שְׁלוֹמִי אֲשֶׁר־בָּטַחְתִּי בוֹ אוֹכֵל לַחְמִי הִגְדִּיל עָלַי עָקֵב:

יא וְאַתָּה יְהוָה חָנֵּנִי וַהֲקִימֵנִי וַאֲשַׁלְּמָה לָהֶם:

יב בְּזֹאת יָדַעְתִּי כִּי־חָפַצְתָּ בִּי כִּי לֹא־יָרִיעַ אֹיְבִי עָלָי:

יג וַאֲנִי בְּתֻמִּי תָּמַכְתָּ בִּי וַתַּצִּיבֵנִי לְפָנֶיךָ לְעוֹלָם:

יד בָּרוּךְ יְהוָה אֱלֹהֵי יִשְׂרָאֵל מֵהָעוֹלָם וְעַד הָעוֹלָם אָמֵן וְאָמֵן:

פרק מב

א לַמְנַצֵּחַ מַשְׂכִּיל לִבְנֵי־קֹרַח:

ב כְּאַיָּל תַּעֲרֹג עַל־אֲפִיקֵי־מָיִם כֵּן נַפְשִׁי תַעֲרֹג אֵלֶיךָ אֱלֹהִים:

TEHILLIM 41

A prayer for healing from illness

1 For the chief musician, a psalm by David.

2 Happy is he that feels for the poor; the Lord will save him the time of evil.

3 The Lord will protect him and keep him healthy, and everyone will know that he is happy in the land. You will not put him into the waiting hands of his enemies.

4 The Lord supports him in time of illness. May You heal him from his sickness.

5 To my Lord I said: "Please be gracious to me. Heal my soul, for I have sinned against You."

6 My enemies say evil things about me: "When will he die and his name be erased?"

7 If they come to visit me, they dishonestly wish for my recovery, while they become more hateful toward me. When they leave me, they speak evil of me.

8 Together they whisper against me and wish suffering upon me:

9 "An evil thing is affecting him, and now that he is ill, he will not recover."

10 Even my very good friend, whom I trusted and who ate my bread, has turned against me.

11 But You, my Lord – be good to me and support me so that I may repay them.

12 Then I will know that You are with me and that my enemies will not be victorious over me.

13 You support me because of my honesty, and set me before You always.

14 Blessed is the Lord, the God of Israel, forever and ever. Amen and Amen.

TEHILLIM 42

A song expressing the desire to pray once more in God's Temple

1 For the leader, an instruction by the sons of Korach.

2 As the hart pants for brooks of water, so my soul desires You, my God.

ג צָמְאָה נַפְשִׁי לֵאלֹהִים לְאֵל חָי מָתַי אָבוֹא וְאֵרָאֶה פְּנֵי אֱלֹהִים:

ד הָיְתָה־לִּי דִמְעָתִי לֶחֶם יוֹמָם וָלָיְלָה בֶּאֱמֹר אֵלַי כָּל־הַיּוֹם אַיֵּה אֱלֹהֶיךָ:

ה אֵלֶּה אֶזְכְּרָה וְאֶשְׁפְּכָה עָלַי נַפְשִׁי כִּי אֶעֱבֹר בַּסָּךְ אֶדַּדֵּם עַד־בֵּית אֱלֹהִים בְּקוֹל־רִנָּה וְתוֹדָה הָמוֹן חוֹגֵג:

ו מַה־תִּשְׁתּוֹחֲחִי נַפְשִׁי וַתֶּהֱמִי עָלָי הוֹחִילִי לֵאלֹהִים כִּי־עוֹד אוֹדֶנּוּ יְשׁוּעוֹת פָּנָיו:

ז אֱלֹהַי עָלַי נַפְשִׁי תִשְׁתּוֹחָח עַל־כֵּן אֶזְכָּרְךָ מֵאֶרֶץ יַרְדֵּן וְחֶרְמוֹנִים מֵהַר מִצְעָר:

ח תְּהוֹם אֶל־תְּהוֹם קוֹרֵא לְקוֹל צִנּוֹרֶיךָ כָּל־מִשְׁבָּרֶיךָ וְגַלֶּיךָ עָלַי עָבָרוּ:

ט יוֹמָם יְצַוֶּה יְהוָה חַסְדּוֹ וּבַלַּיְלָה שִׁירה [שִׁירוֹ] עִמִּי תְּפִלָּה לְאֵל חַיָּי:

י אוֹמְרָה לְאֵל סַלְעִי לָמָה שְׁכַחְתָּנִי לָמָּה־קֹדֵר אֵלֵךְ בְּלַחַץ אוֹיֵב:

יא בְּרֶצַח בְּעַצְמוֹתַי חֵרְפוּנִי צוֹרְרָי בְּאָמְרָם אֵלַי כָּל־הַיּוֹם אַיֵּה אֱלֹהֶיךָ:

יב מַה־תִּשְׁתּוֹחֲחִי נַפְשִׁי וּמַה־תֶּהֱמִי עָלָי הוֹחִילִי לֵאלֹהִים כִּי־עוֹד אוֹדֶנּוּ יְשׁוּעֹת פָּנַי וֵאלֹהָי:

פרק מג

א שָׁפְטֵנִי אֱלֹהִים וְרִיבָה רִיבִי מִגּוֹי לֹא־חָסִיד מֵאִישׁ־מִרְמָה וְעַוְלָה תְפַלְּטֵנִי:

ב כִּי־אַתָּה אֱלֹהֵי מָעוּזִּי לָמָה זְנַחְתָּנִי לָמָּה־קֹדֵר אֶתְהַלֵּךְ בְּלַחַץ אוֹיֵב:

ג שְׁלַח־אוֹרְךָ וַאֲמִתְּךָ הֵמָּה יַנְחוּנִי יְבִיאוּנִי אֶל־הַר־קָדְשְׁךָ וְאֶל־ מִשְׁכְּנוֹתֶיךָ:

ד וְאָבוֹאָה אֶל־מִזְבַּח אֱלֹהִים אֶל־אֵל שִׂמְחַת גִּילִי וְאוֹדְךָ בְכִנּוֹר אֱלֹהִים אֱלֹהָי:

ה מַה־תִּשְׁתּוֹחֲחִי נַפְשִׁי וּמַה־תֶּהֱמִי עָלָי הוֹחִילִי לֵאלֹהִים כִּי־עוֹד אוֹדֶנּוּ יְשׁוּעֹת פָּנַי וֵאלֹהָי:

3 My soul desires my God. He is my God, Who can fulfill my desire. When will I come to pray in His holy Temple?

4 My tears have been my food for days and nights, while they say to me, "Where is your God?"

5 When I remember how I used to walk with the people and lead them to the house of God with joy and song, keeping Your holy days, my soul cries out within me.

6 Why are you upset, my soul, and why do you weep? Keep hoping in the Lord, for I will continue to praise Him for the help of His greatness.

7 My God, my soul is upset. I remember You from the land of the Jordan, the hills of Hermon and the hill of Mizah.

8 Your voice commanded the events and troubles. All Your waters and floods are drowning me.

9 During the day, the Lord commands His loving kindness, and in the night His song will be with me. I pray to the God of my life.

10 I will say to God, my Rock: "Why have You forgotten me? Why do I suffer from my enemy's attack?"

11 Like one whose bones have been crushed, my enemies laugh at me. All day long, they say to me, "Where is your God?"

12 My soul, why are you upset? Why do you weep within me? Hope in God, because I still worship Him, my Helper.

TEHILLIM 43

A continuation of the wish to pray at God's holy Temple

1 You are my Judge, my God. Take up my cause against the wrongdoers and save me from the evil and untruthful man.

2 You are the God of my strength. Why have You left me? Why am I alone, under attack by the enemy?

3 Send out Your light and Your truth and let them guide me. Let them bring me to Your holy mountain and to Your holy Temple.

4 Then I will go to the altar of God, of God who is my great happiness, and praise You upon the harp, Lord, my God.

5 Why are you upset, my soul, and why do you weep within me? Hope in God, because I continue to praise Him, my salvation and my God.

פרק מד

א לַמְנַצֵּחַ לִבְנֵי־קֹרַח מַשְׂכִּיל:

ב אֱלֹהִים בְּאָזְנֵינוּ שָׁמַעְנוּ אֲבוֹתֵינוּ סִפְּרוּ־לָנוּ פֹּעַל־פָּעַלְתָּ בִימֵיהֶם בִּימֵי קֶדֶם:

ג אַתָּה יָדְךָ גּוֹיִם הוֹרַשְׁתָּ וַתִּטָּעֵם תָּרַע לְאֻמִּים וַתְּשַׁלְּחֵם:

ד כִּי לֹא בְחַרְבָּם יָרְשׁוּ־אָרֶץ וּזְרוֹעָם לֹא־הוֹשִׁיעָה לָּמוֹ כִּי־יְמִינְךָ וּזְרוֹעֲךָ וְאוֹר פָּנֶיךָ כִּי רְצִיתָם:

ה אַתָּה־הוּא מַלְכִּי אֱלֹהִים צַוֵּה יְשׁוּעוֹת יַעֲקֹב:

ו בְּךָ צָרֵינוּ נְנַגֵּחַ בְּשִׁמְךָ נָבוּס קָמֵינוּ:

ז כִּי לֹא בְקַשְׁתִּי אֶבְטָח וְחַרְבִּי לֹא תוֹשִׁיעֵנִי:

ח כִּי הוֹשַׁעְתָּנוּ מִצָּרֵינוּ וּמְשַׂנְאֵינוּ הֱבִישׁוֹתָ:

ט בֵּאלֹהִים הִלַּלְנוּ כָל־הַיּוֹם וְשִׁמְךָ לְעוֹלָם נוֹדֶה סֶלָה:

י אַף־זָנַחְתָּ וַתַּכְלִימֵנוּ וְלֹא־תֵצֵא בְּצִבְאוֹתֵינוּ:

יא תְּשִׁיבֵנוּ אָחוֹר מִנִּי־צָר וּמְשַׂנְאֵינוּ שָׁסוּ לָמוֹ:

יב תִּתְּנֵנוּ כְּצֹאן מַאֲכָל וּבַגּוֹיִם זֵרִיתָנוּ:

יג תִּמְכֹּר עַמְּךָ בְלֹא־הוֹן וְלֹא־רִבִּיתָ בִּמְחִירֵיהֶם:

יד תְּשִׂימֵנוּ חֶרְפָּה לִשְׁכֵנֵינוּ לַעַג וָקֶלֶס לִסְבִיבוֹתֵינוּ:

טו תְּשִׂימֵנוּ מָשָׁל בַּגּוֹיִם מְנוֹד־רֹאשׁ בַּלְאֻמִּים:

טז כָּל־הַיּוֹם כְּלִמָּתִי נֶגְדִּי וּבֹשֶׁת פָּנַי כִּסָּתְנִי:

יז מִקּוֹל מְחָרֵף וּמְגַדֵּף מִפְּנֵי אוֹיֵב וּמִתְנַקֵּם:

יח כָּל־זֹאת בָּאַתְנוּ וְלֹא שְׁכַחֲנוּךָ וְלֹא־שִׁקַּרְנוּ בִּבְרִיתֶךָ:

יט לֹא־נָסוֹג אָחוֹר לִבֵּנוּ וַתֵּט אֲשֻׁרֵינוּ מִנִּי אָרְחֶךָ:

כ כִּי דִכִּיתָנוּ בִּמְקוֹם תַּנִּים וַתְּכַס עָלֵינוּ בְצַלְמָוֶת:

TEHILLIM 44

A song asking for God's help in battle

1 For the chief musician, by the sons of Korach, an instruction.

2 My God, our fathers have told us, and we ourselves have heard the things that you did in their days, at that time.

3 You drove out the nations with Your hand and then You established our ancestors. You defeated the nations and dispersed them at a distance.

4 They did not win possession of the land by their own might, and their own strength did not save them. Instead, it was Your right hand, Your arm and Your light, because You were good to them.

5 You are my King, my God – command the salvation of Jacob!

6 Thanks to You, we defeat our enemies. Thanks to Your name, we defeat the enemies who rise up against us.

7 I do not trust in my weapons. My sword cannot save me.

8 However, You have saved us from our enemies and have put to shame those who hate us.

9 All day long we praised God, and we will give thanks to Your name forever. Selah.

10 Even though You left us, and we are troubled. You do not go out with our army.

11 You cause us to turn back from our enemy, and those who hate us rejoice.

12 You made us like sheep to be eaten and have scattered us among the nations.

13 You sold Your people cheaply, and have not set their value high.

14 You make us a laughingstock to our neighbors, an object of pity and derision to those around us.

15 You make us an example to the nations, and make peoples shake their heads at us.

16 All day I am in confusion, and covered with shame

17 Because of the voice of the one who taunts and blasphemes, from the enemy and the vengeful.

18 All this has come upon us even though we have not forgotten You, nor have we been false to Your Torah.

19 Our hearts have not turned away, nor have we gone off Your path.

20 Even though You pushed us into a place of wild jackals and covered us with the shadow of death.

כא אִם־שָׁכַחְנוּ שֵׁם אֱלֹהֵינוּ וַנִּפְרֹשׂ כַּפֵּינוּ לְאֵל זָר:

כב הֲלֹא אֱלֹהִים יַחֲקָר־זֹאת כִּי־הוּא יֹדֵעַ תַּעֲלֻמוֹת לֵב:

כג כִּי־עָלֶיךָ הֹרַגְנוּ כָל־הַיּוֹם נֶחְשַׁבְנוּ כְּצֹאן טִבְחָה:

כד עוּרָה לָמָּה תִישַׁן אֲדֹנָי הָקִיצָה אַל־תִּזְנַח לָנֶצַח:

כה לָמָּה פָנֶיךָ תַסְתִּיר תִּשְׁכַּח עָנְיֵנוּ וְלַחֲצֵנוּ:

כו כִּי שָׁחָה לֶעָפָר נַפְשֵׁנוּ דָּבְקָה לָאָרֶץ בִּטְנֵנוּ:

כז קוּמָה עֶזְרָתָה לָּנוּ וּפְדֵנוּ לְמַעַן חַסְדֶּךָ:

פרק מה

א לַמְנַצֵּחַ עַל־שֹׁשַׁנִּים לִבְנֵי־קֹרַח מַשְׂכִּיל שִׁיר יְדִידֹת:

ב רָחַשׁ לִבִּי דָּבָר טוֹב אֹמֵר אָנִי מַעֲשַׂי לְמֶלֶךְ לְשׁוֹנִי עֵט סוֹפֵר מָהִיר:

ג יָפְיָפִיתָ מִבְּנֵי אָדָם הוּצַק חֵן בְּשִׂפְתוֹתֶיךָ עַל־כֵּן בֵּרַכְךָ אֱלֹהִים לְעוֹלָם:

ד חֲגוֹר חַרְבְּךָ עַל־יָרֵךְ גִּבּוֹר הוֹדְךָ וַהֲדָרֶךָ:

ה וַהֲדָרְךָ צְלַח רְכַב עַל־דְּבַר־אֱמֶת וְעַנְוָה־צֶדֶק וְתוֹרְךָ נוֹרָאוֹת יְמִינֶךָ:

ו חִצֶּיךָ שְׁנוּנִים עַמִּים תַּחְתֶּיךָ יִפְּלוּ בְּלֵב אוֹיְבֵי הַמֶּלֶךְ:

ז כִּסְאֲךָ אֱלֹהִים עוֹלָם וָעֶד שֵׁבֶט מִישֹׁר שֵׁבֶט מַלְכוּתֶךָ:

ח אָהַבְתָּ צֶּדֶק וַתִּשְׂנָא רֶשַׁע עַל־כֵּן מְשָׁחֲךָ אֱלֹהִים אֱלֹהֶיךָ שֶׁמֶן שָׂשׂוֹן מֵחֲבֵרֶיךָ:

ט מֹר וַאֲהָלוֹת קְצִיעוֹת כָּל־בִּגְדֹתֶיךָ מִן־הֵיכְלֵי שֵׁן מִנִּי שִׂמְּחוּךָ:

י בְּנוֹת מְלָכִים בְּיִקְּרוֹתֶיךָ נִצְּבָה שֵׁגַל לִימִינְךָ בְּכֶתֶם אוֹפִיר:

יא שִׁמְעִי־בַת וּרְאִי וְהַטִּי אָזְנֵךְ וְשִׁכְחִי עַמֵּךְ וּבֵית אָבִיךְ:

יב וְיִתְאָו הַמֶּלֶךְ יָפְיֵךְ כִּי־הוּא אֲדֹנַיִךְ וְהִשְׁתַּחֲוִי־לוֹ:

21 If we had forgotten the name of God or spread our hands to a false god,

22 Would You, our God, not have checked to see if it were so? You know the secrets of man's heart.

23 Yet for Your sake we are killed each day and we are like sheep for slaughter.

24 Awake! Why do You sleep, my Lord? Please reconsider and do not leave us forever.

25 Why do You hide Your face and forget our troubles and our suffering?

26 Our souls have fallen to the dust and our bodies lie upon the earth.

27 Come to help us and save us in Your mercy.

TEHILLIM 45

A song about the relationship of God and His people Israel

1 For the chief musician, upon Shoshannim, by the sons of Korach, an instructor, a love song.

2 My heart overflows with good. My song is about a King. My tongue is like the pen of a composer.

3 You are more beautiful than the children of men, and your lips speak pleasant words. God has blessed you forever.

4 Buckle your sword upon your thigh, mighty one; it is your glory and your majesty.

5 In your glory, ride on to victory – in the name of truth, humility and righteousness – and let your right hand accomplish mighty things.

6 Your arrows are sharp and the people surrender to you; they fall into the heart of the king's enemies.

7 Your God-given throne is forever. The torch of truth symbolizes your kingdom.

8 Therefore God, your God, has made you king, crowned with the oil of rejoicing above the others.

9 Myrrh, aloes and cassia are your garments. Stringed instruments playing from ivory palaces give us joy.

10 Kings' daughters are among your favorites, and at your right hand is the jewelry of Ophir.

11 Listen and hear, bride, and forget your people and your former home.

12 The king admires your beauty, and he is your lord – give him honor.

13 Daughter of Tyre, the wealthiest of the people will ask your favor with a gift.

יג   וּבַת־צֹר בְּמִנְחָה פָּנַיִךְ יְחַלּוּ עֲשִׁירֵי עָם:

יד   כָּל־כְּבוּדָּה בַת־מֶלֶךְ פְּנִימָה מִמִּשְׁבְּצוֹת זָהָב לְבוּשָׁהּ:

טו   לִרְקָמוֹת תּוּבַל לַמֶּלֶךְ בְּתוּלוֹת אַחֲרֶיהָ רֵעוֹתֶיהָ מוּבָאוֹת לָךְ:

טז   תּוּבַלְנָה בִּשְׂמָחֹת וָגִיל תְּבֹאֶינָה בְּהֵיכַל מֶלֶךְ:

יז   תַּחַת אֲבֹתֶיךָ יִהְיוּ בָנֶיךָ תְּשִׁיתֵמוֹ לְשָׂרִים בְּכָל־הָאָרֶץ:

יח   אַזְכִּירָה שִׁמְךָ בְּכָל־דֹּר וָדֹר עַל־כֵּן עַמִּים יְהוֹדֻךָ לְעֹלָם וָעֶד:

פרק מו

א   לַמְנַצֵּחַ לִבְנֵי־קֹרַח עַל־עֲלָמוֹת שִׁיר:

ב   אֱלֹהִים לָנוּ מַחֲסֶה וָעֹז עֶזְרָה בְצָרוֹת נִמְצָא מְאֹד:

ג   עַל־כֵּן לֹא־נִירָא בְּהָמִיר אָרֶץ וּבְמוֹט הָרִים בְּלֵב יַמִּים:

ד   יֶהֱמוּ יֶחְמְרוּ מֵימָיו יִרְעֲשׁוּ הָרִים בְּגַאֲוָתוֹ סֶלָה:

ה   נָהָר פְּלָגָיו יְשַׂמְּחוּ עִיר־אֱלֹהִים קְדֹשׁ מִשְׁכְּנֵי עֶלְיוֹן:

ו   אֱלֹהִים בְּקִרְבָּהּ בַּל־תִּמּוֹט יַעְזְרֶהָ אֱלֹהִים לִפְנוֹת בֹּקֶר:

ז   הָמוּ גוֹיִם מָטוּ מַמְלָכוֹת נָתַן בְּקוֹלוֹ תָּמוּג אָרֶץ:

ח   יְהֹוָה צְבָאוֹת עִמָּנוּ מִשְׂגָּב־לָנוּ אֱלֹהֵי יַעֲקֹב סֶלָה:

ט   לְכוּ־חֲזוּ מִפְעֲלוֹת יְהֹוָה אֲשֶׁר־שָׂם שַׁמּוֹת בָּאָרֶץ:

י   מַשְׁבִּית מִלְחָמוֹת עַד־קְצֵה הָאָרֶץ קֶשֶׁת יְשַׁבֵּר וְקִצֵּץ חֲנִית עֲגָלוֹת יִשְׂרֹף בָּאֵשׁ:

יא   הַרְפּוּ וּדְעוּ כִּי־אָנֹכִי אֱלֹהִים אָרוּם בַּגּוֹיִם אָרוּם בָּאָרֶץ:

יב   יְהֹוָה צְבָאוֹת עִמָּנוּ מִשְׂגָּב־לָנוּ אֱלֹהֵי יַעֲקֹב סֶלָה:

14 The king's daughter is beautiful in the palace; her clothing is specially worked in gold.

15 She will be brought to the king on beautiful carpets, and maidens will accompany her.

16 They will be led with gladness and rejoicing; they will enter the king's palace.

17 Your sons will take the place of your father, and you will make them princes in the land.

18 I will make Your name to be remembered for all generations and the nations will praise You forever.

TEHILLIM 46

A song describing God's protection of the Jewish nation

1 For the chief musician, by the sons of Korach, using *alamoth*. A song.

2 God is our protection and our strength, always helping in the time of trouble.

3 We do not fear no matter what happens – even if the mountains move into the heart of the sea,

4 Even if the waters roar and overflow, even if the mountains shake before his glory. Selah.

5 God has made a river that brings peace to the City of God, Zion, the holiest home of God, the Most High.

6 God is in Zion, and it will not be moved. God will help Zion when dawn comes.

7 Nations were in shock and kingdoms tattered. At God's voice, the earth trembled.

8 The Lord of Hosts is with us; the God of Jacob is our Tower of protection. Selah.

9 Come see the creations of the Lord; He has made desolation upon the earth.

10 He stops wars to the throughout the world. He breaks the bow and cuts the spear, and sets chariots on fire.

11 "Be still and know that I am God. I will be praised by all nations. I will be praised on earth."

12 The Lord of Hosts is with us; the God of Jacob is our Tower of protection. Selah.

פרק מז

א לַמְנַצֵּחַ לִבְנֵי־קֹרַח מִזְמוֹר:

ב כָּל־הָעַמִּים תִּקְעוּ־כָף הָרִיעוּ לֵאלֹהִים בְּקוֹל רִנָּה:

ג כִּי־יְהוָה עֶלְיוֹן נוֹרָא מֶלֶךְ גָּדוֹל עַל־כָּל־הָאָרֶץ:

ד יַדְבֵּר עַמִּים תַּחְתֵּינוּ וּלְאֻמִּים תַּחַת רַגְלֵינוּ:

ה יִבְחַר־לָנוּ אֶת־נַחֲלָתֵנוּ אֶת גְּאוֹן יַעֲקֹב אֲשֶׁר־אָהֵב סֶלָה:

ו עָלָה אֱלֹהִים בִּתְרוּעָה יְהוָה בְּקוֹל שׁוֹפָר:

ז זַמְּרוּ אֱלֹהִים זַמֵּרוּ זַמְּרוּ לְמַלְכֵּנוּ זַמֵּרוּ:

ח כִּי מֶלֶךְ כָּל־הָאָרֶץ אֱלֹהִים זַמְּרוּ מַשְׂכִּיל:

ט מָלַךְ אֱלֹהִים עַל־גּוֹיִם אֱלֹהִים יָשַׁב עַל־כִּסֵּא קָדְשׁוֹ:

י נְדִיבֵי עַמִּים נֶאֱסָפוּ עַם אֱלֹהֵי אַבְרָהָם כִּי לֵאלֹהִים מָגִנֵּי־אֶרֶץ מְאֹד נַעֲלָה:

פרק מח

א שִׁיר מִזְמוֹר לִבְנֵי־קֹרַח:

ב גָּדוֹל יְהוָה וּמְהֻלָּל מְאֹד בְּעִיר אֱלֹהֵינוּ הַר־קָדְשׁוֹ:

ג יְפֵה נוֹף מְשׂוֹשׂ כָּל־הָאָרֶץ הַר־צִיּוֹן יַרְכְּתֵי צָפוֹן קִרְיַת מֶלֶךְ רָב:

ד אֱלֹהִים בְּאַרְמְנוֹתֶיהָ נוֹדַע לְמִשְׂגָּב:

ה כִּי־הִנֵּה הַמְּלָכִים נוֹעֲדוּ עָבְרוּ יַחְדָּו:

ו הֵמָּה רָאוּ כֵּן תָּמָהוּ נִבְהֲלוּ נֶחְפָּזוּ:

ז רְעָדָה אֲחָזָתַם שָׁם חִיל כַּיּוֹלֵדָה:

TEHILLIM 47

A song honoring God, the King

1 For the chief musician, a psalm by the sons of Korach.
2 Clap your hands, all you nations. With a victorious voice, shout to God.
3 The Lord, the Most High, is powerful, and He is the great King of all the earth.
4 He defeats peoples under us, and nations under our feet.
5 He gives us this land, our inheritance, the pride of Jacob whom He loved. Selah.
6 God, the Lord, is exalted with shouting and the blowing of the horn.
7 Sing praises to our God, sing praises. Sing praises to our King, sing praises.
8 God is the King of all the earth. Sing a song of understanding.
9 God rules over all the nations and sits upon His holy throne.
10 The princes of the people are assembled, together with the people of the God of Abraham. The shields of the earth belong to God, Who is greatly to be praised.

TEHILLIM 48

A song of thanksgiving and a prayer that
God will always protect Jerusalem

1 A song. A psalm by the sons of Korach.
2 The Lord is great, and we truly praise Him in the city of our God, the holy mountain, Zion.
3 It is beautifully located and is the joy of the whole world, including Mt. Zion in the northernmost parts, the city of our great King.
4 This is the palace of God. He has made His power known.
5 The kings joined together and marched out to attack.
6 Immediately they saw and were amazed. They were frightened and fled.
7 They were shocked and in pain, like a woman in labor.
8 You destroy the ships of Tarshish with powerful eastern winds.

ח בְּרוּחַ קָדִים תְּשַׁבֵּר אֳנִיּוֹת תַּרְשִׁישׁ:

ט כַּאֲשֶׁר שָׁמַעְנוּ כֵּן רָאִינוּ בְּעִיר יְהוָה צְבָאוֹת בְּעִיר אֱלֹהֵינוּ אֱלֹהִים יְכוֹנְנֶהָ עַד־עוֹלָם סֶלָה:

י דִּמִּינוּ אֱלֹהִים חַסְדֶּךָ בְּקֶרֶב הֵיכָלֶךָ:

יא כְּשִׁמְךָ אֱלֹהִים כֵּן תְּהִלָּתְךָ עַל־קַצְוֵי־אֶרֶץ צֶדֶק מָלְאָה יְמִינֶךָ:

יב יִשְׂמַח הַר־צִיּוֹן תָּגֵלְנָה בְּנוֹת יְהוּדָה לְמַעַן מִשְׁפָּטֶיךָ:

יג סֹבּוּ צִיּוֹן וְהַקִּיפוּהָ סִפְרוּ מִגְדָּלֶיהָ:

יד שִׁיתוּ לִבְּכֶם לְחֵילָה פַּסְּגוּ אַרְמְנוֹתֶיהָ לְמַעַן תְּסַפְּרוּ לְדוֹר אַחֲרוֹן:

טו כִּי זֶה אֱלֹהִים אֱלֹהֵינוּ עוֹלָם וָעֶד הוּא יְנַהֲגֵנוּ עַל־מוּת:

פרק מט

א לַמְנַצֵּחַ לִבְנֵי־קֹרַח מִזְמוֹר:

ב שִׁמְעוּ־זֹאת כָּל־הָעַמִּים הַאֲזִינוּ כָּל־יֹשְׁבֵי חָלֶד:

ג גַּם־בְּנֵי אָדָם גַּם־בְּנֵי־אִישׁ יַחַד עָשִׁיר וְאֶבְיוֹן:

ד פִּי יְדַבֵּר חָכְמוֹת וְהָגוּת לִבִּי תְבוּנוֹת:

ה אַטֶּה לְמָשָׁל אָזְנִי אֶפְתַּח בְּכִנּוֹר חִידָתִי:

ו לָמָּה אִירָא בִּימֵי רָע עֲוֹן עֲקֵבַי יְסוּבֵּנִי:

ז הַבֹּטְחִים עַל־חֵילָם וּבְרֹב עָשְׁרָם יִתְהַלָּלוּ:

ח אָח לֹא־פָדֹה יִפְדֶּה אִישׁ לֹא־יִתֵּן לֵאלֹהִים כָּפְרוֹ:

ט וְיֵקַר פִּדְיוֹן נַפְשָׁם וְחָדַל לְעוֹלָם:

י וִיחִי־עוֹד לָנֶצַח לֹא יִרְאֶה הַשָּׁחַת:

יא כִּי יִרְאֶה חֲכָמִים יָמוּתוּ יַחַד כְּסִיל וָבַעַר יֹאבֵדוּ וְעָזְבוּ לַאֲחֵרִים חֵילָם:

9 These facts we have heard and have seen in the city of the Lord of Hosts, in the city of our God. God has established the city forever. Selah.

10 In Your holy Temple we have thought of Your loving kindness, our God.

11 Your honor and Your name, our God, extend to the ends of the earth, and Your right hand is full of righteousness.

12 Mount Zion will be happy and the daughters of Judah will rejoice over Your wisdom.

13 Walk around Zion and encircle it. Count all of its high towers.

14 Notice all her defenses and enter her palaces, so that you may tell future generations about them.

15 He is God, our God forever and ever. He will lead us for all time.

TEHILLIM 49

*A song describing how truth and goodness are
more important than worldly wealth*

1 For the chief musician, a psalm by the sons of Korach.

2 Listen, all you people, and all you men of the decaying world, hear this:

3 Men of low degree and high degree, rich and poor together.

4 My mouth will speak with wisdom and the thoughts of my heart with understanding.

5 I will receive the word of God in my ear. I will play this important message on the harp.

6 Will I fear evil in the future because of the sins of those who surround me?

7 Of those who trust in their wealth and take pride in their riches?

8 Not one of them will redeem his brother, or ransom him from God.

9 It is not possible to stay alive and avoid death.

10 Nor use one's riches to live forever and never see the grave.

11 He sees that even wise men pass away, and fools and evil people must leave their wealth to others.

12 They think that their families and their estates will last forever, and they name their lands after themselves.

פרק נ

יב   קִרְבָּם בָּתֵּימוֹ לְעוֹלָם מִשְׁכְּנֹתָם לְדֹר וָדֹר קָרְאוּ בִשְׁמוֹתָם עֲלֵי אֲדָמוֹת:

יג   וְאָדָם בִּיקָר בַּל־יָלִין נִמְשַׁל כַּבְּהֵמוֹת נִדְמוּ:

יד   זֶה דַרְכָּם כֵּסֶל לָמוֹ וְאַחֲרֵיהֶם בְּפִיהֶם יִרְצוּ סֶלָה:

טו   כַּצֹּאן לִשְׁאוֹל שַׁתּוּ מָוֶת יִרְעֵם וַיִּרְדּוּ בָם יְשָׁרִים לַבֹּקֶר וְצִירָם [וְצוּרָם] לְבַלּוֹת שְׁאוֹל מִזְּבֻל לוֹ:

טז   אַךְ־אֱלֹהִים יִפְדֶּה נַפְשִׁי מִיַּד־שְׁאוֹל כִּי יִקָּחֵנִי סֶלָה:

יז   אַל־תִּירָא כִּי־יַעֲשִׁר אִישׁ כִּי־יִרְבֶּה כְּבוֹד בֵּיתוֹ:

יח   כִּי לֹא בְמוֹתוֹ יִקַּח הַכֹּל לֹא־יֵרֵד אַחֲרָיו כְּבוֹדוֹ:

יט   כִּי־נַפְשׁוֹ בְּחַיָּיו יְבָרֵךְ וְיוֹדֻךָ כִּי־תֵיטִיב לָךְ:

כ   תָּבוֹא עַד־דּוֹר אֲבוֹתָיו עַד־נֵצַח לֹא יִרְאוּ־אוֹר:

כא   אָדָם בִּיקָר וְלֹא יָבִין נִמְשַׁל כַּבְּהֵמוֹת נִדְמוּ:

פרק נ

א   מִזְמוֹר לְאָסָף אֵל אֱלֹהִים יְהוָה דִּבֶּר וַיִּקְרָא־אָרֶץ מִמִּזְרַח־שֶׁמֶשׁ עַד־מְבֹאוֹ:

ב   מִצִּיּוֹן מִכְלַל־יֹפִי אֱלֹהִים הוֹפִיעַ:

ג   יָבֹא אֱלֹהֵינוּ וְאַל־יֶחֱרַשׁ אֵשׁ־לְפָנָיו תֹּאכֵל וּסְבִיבָיו נִשְׂעֲרָה מְאֹד:

ד   יִקְרָא אֶל־הַשָּׁמַיִם מֵעָל וְאֶל־הָאָרֶץ לָדִין עַמּוֹ:

ה   אִסְפוּ־לִי חֲסִידָי כֹּרְתֵי בְרִיתִי עֲלֵי־זָבַח:

ו   וַיַּגִּידוּ שָׁמַיִם צִדְקוֹ כִּי־אֱלֹהִים שֹׁפֵט הוּא סֶלָה:

ז   שִׁמְעָה עַמִּי וַאֲדַבֵּרָה יִשְׂרָאֵל וְאָעִידָה בָּךְ אֱלֹהִים אֱלֹהֶיךָ אָנֹכִי:

13 But man's honor does not last forever. He is like the beasts that perish.

14 These are the thoughts of fools and their children agree with what they say. Selah.

15 Like sheep they go to the netherworld, and death is their shepherd. Worthy people will rule over them in the morning, and their bodies will decay in the grave. There is no place for them.

16 But God will save my soul from the netherworld. He will protect me. Selah.

17 Do not be afraid when someone becomes rich and the wealth of his family is increased.

18 When they die they will not take their wealth with them, and it will not go down after them.

19 Even if he blessed himself while he lived, saying, "Men will honor you because you do well."

20 He will pass away like his fathers in previous generations, and they will never see the light.

21 A man who seeks prestige does not understand; he is like the beasts that perish.

TEHILLIM 50

A song describing Israel's trial for having violated the Torah before God, the Judge

1 A psalm by Asaph. God, God, the Lord, has spoken, calling the earth from sunrise to sunset.

2 The perfection of holiness, the Torah, shines out of Zion.

3 God's light shines brightly. Our God comes and is not silent. Fire bursts out before Him and all around there is a violent storm.

4 He calls to the heavens and to the earth to witness that he is judging His nation, Israel.

5 "Gather my pious ones before Me, those who made a covenant with me by sacrifice."

6 The heavens announce that God is the Judge. Selah.

7 Listen and I will speak to you, my people. My nation Israel, I will testify against you. I am God, Your God.

ח   לֹא עַל־זְבָחֶיךָ אוֹכִיחֶךָ וְעוֹלֹתֶיךָ לְנֶגְדִּי תָמִיד:

ט   לֹא־אֶקַּח מִבֵּיתְךָ פָר מִמִּכְלְאֹתֶיךָ עַתּוּדִים:

י   כִּי־לִי כָל־חַיְתוֹ־יָעַר בְּהֵמוֹת בְּהַרְרֵי־אָלֶף:

יא   יָדַעְתִּי כָּל־עוֹף הָרִים וְזִיז שָׂדַי עִמָּדִי:

יב   אִם־אֶרְעַב לֹא־אֹמַר לָךְ כִּי־לִי תֵבֵל וּמְלֹאָהּ:

יג   הַאוֹכַל בְּשַׂר אַבִּירִים וְדַם עַתּוּדִים אֶשְׁתֶּה:

יד   זְבַח לֵאלֹהִים תּוֹדָה וְשַׁלֵּם לְעֶלְיוֹן נְדָרֶיךָ:

טו   וּקְרָאֵנִי בְּיוֹם צָרָה אֲחַלֶּצְךָ וּתְכַבְּדֵנִי:

טז   וְלָרָשָׁע אָמַר אֱלֹהִים מַה־לְּךָ לְסַפֵּר חֻקָּי וַתִּשָּׂא בְרִיתִי עֲלֵי־פִיךָ:

יז   וְאַתָּה שָׂנֵאתָ מוּסָר וַתַּשְׁלֵךְ דְּבָרַי אַחֲרֶיךָ:

יח   אִם־רָאִיתָ גַנָּב וַתִּרֶץ עִמּוֹ וְעִם מְנָאֲפִים חֶלְקֶךָ:

יט   פִּיךָ שָׁלַחְתָּ בְרָעָה וּלְשׁוֹנְךָ תַּצְמִיד מִרְמָה:

כ   תֵּשֵׁב בְּאָחִיךָ תְדַבֵּר בְּבֶן־אִמְּךָ תִּתֶּן־דֹּפִי:

כא   אֵלֶּה עָשִׂיתָ וְהֶחֱרַשְׁתִּי דִּמִּיתָ הֱיוֹת־אֶהְיֶה כָמוֹךָ אוֹכִיחֲךָ וְאֶעֶרְכָה לְעֵינֶיךָ:

כב   בִּינוּ־נָא זֹאת שֹׁכְחֵי אֱלוֹהַּ פֶּן־אֶטְרֹף וְאֵין מַצִּיל:

כג   זֹבֵחַ תּוֹדָה יְכַבְּדָנְנִי וְשָׂם דֶּרֶךְ אַרְאֶנּוּ בְּיֵשַׁע אֱלֹהִים:

פרק נא

א   לַמְנַצֵּחַ מִזְמוֹר לְדָוִד:

ב   בְּבוֹא־אֵלָיו נָתָן הַנָּבִיא כַּאֲשֶׁר־בָּא אֶל־בַּת־שָׁבַע:

8 I will not reprimand you for the sacrifices and for the burnt-offerings that are always before Me.

9 I will take no bulls from your houses or he-goats from your fields because I do not need them.

10 All the cattle and every animal of the forest and on all the mountains belong to Me.

11 I know all the birds of the thousands of mountains, and the beasts of the forest are Mine.

12 If I were hungry I would not tell you, because the whole world and everything in it belong to Me.

13 Do I eat the meat of the bulls or drink the blood of goats?

14 Rather, you should offer God sacrifices of thanksgiving and pay your vows to the Most High.

15 "Pray to Me in your time of need and I will save you, and you will honor me."

16 But I say to evildoers, "Why should you mention My laws or keep My covenant on your lips?

17 It is known that you hate instruction and you cast My words away.

18 When you saw a thief, you ran to be with him, and you keep company with adulterers.

19 You use your mouth for evil and your tongue for falsehood.

20 You sit and speak evil about your brother and slander your own mother's son.

21 Should I keep silent when you have done all these evil things? Perhaps you thought that I was the same as you, but I will accuse you and prove your evil before your eyes.

22 Now, those of you who have forgotten God, understand this lest I destroy and there are none left to save.

23 Those who offer the thanksgiving sacrifice honor Me, and to those who walk in the right path, I will show Divine salvation.

TEHILLIM 51

A song of repentance, asking God's forgiveness for all His children.

1 For the chief musician, a psalm by David,

2 When the prophet Nathan went to David after he had come to Batsheva.

ג   חָנֵּנִי אֱלֹהִים כְּחַסְדֶּךָ כְּרֹב רַחֲמֶיךָ מְחֵה פְשָׁעָי:

ד   הרבה [הֶרֶב] כַּבְּסֵנִי מֵעֲוֹנִי וּמֵחַטָּאתִי טַהֲרֵנִי:

ה   כִּי־פְשָׁעַי אֲנִי אֵדָע וְחַטָּאתִי נֶגְדִּי תָמִיד:

ו   לְךָ לְבַדְּךָ חָטָאתִי וְהָרַע בְּעֵינֶיךָ עָשִׂיתִי לְמַעַן־תִּצְדַּק בְּדָבְרֶךָ תִּזְכֶּה בְשָׁפְטֶךָ:

ז   הֵן־בְּעָווֹן חוֹלָלְתִּי וּבְחֵטְא יֶחֱמַתְנִי אִמִּי:

ח   הֵן־אֱמֶת חָפַצְתָּ בַטֻּחוֹת וּבְסָתֻם חָכְמָה תוֹדִיעֵנִי:

ט   תְּחַטְּאֵנִי בְאֵזוֹב וְאֶטְהָר תְּכַבְּסֵנִי וּמִשֶּׁלֶג אַלְבִּין:

י   תַּשְׁמִיעֵנִי שָׂשׂוֹן וְשִׂמְחָה תָּגֵלְנָה עֲצָמוֹת דִּכִּיתָ:

יא   הַסְתֵּר פָּנֶיךָ מֵחֲטָאָי וְכָל־עֲוֹנֹתַי מְחֵה:

יב   לֵב טָהוֹר בְּרָא־לִי אֱלֹהִים וְרוּחַ נָכוֹן חַדֵּשׁ בְּקִרְבִּי:

יג   אַל־תַּשְׁלִיכֵנִי מִלְּפָנֶיךָ וְרוּחַ קָדְשְׁךָ אַל־תִּקַּח מִמֶּנִּי:

יד   הָשִׁיבָה לִּי שְׂשׂוֹן יִשְׁעֶךָ וְרוּחַ נְדִיבָה תִסְמְכֵנִי:

טו   אֲלַמְּדָה פֹשְׁעִים דְּרָכֶיךָ וְחַטָּאִים אֵלֶיךָ יָשׁוּבוּ:

טז   הַצִּילֵנִי מִדָּמִים אֱלֹהִים אֱלֹהֵי תְּשׁוּעָתִי תְּרַנֵּן לְשׁוֹנִי צִדְקָתֶךָ:

יז   אֲדֹנָי שְׂפָתַי תִּפְתָּח וּפִי יַגִּיד תְּהִלָּתֶךָ:

יח   כִּי לֹא־תַחְפֹּץ זֶבַח וְאֶתֵּנָה עוֹלָה לֹא תִרְצֶה:

יט   זִבְחֵי אֱלֹהִים רוּחַ נִשְׁבָּרָה לֵב־נִשְׁבָּר וְנִדְכֶּה אֱלֹהִים לֹא תִבְזֶה:

כ   הֵיטִיבָה בִרְצוֹנְךָ אֶת־צִיּוֹן תִּבְנֶה חוֹמוֹת יְרוּשָׁלָ͏ִם:

כא   אָז תַּחְפֹּץ זִבְחֵי־צֶדֶק עוֹלָה וְכָלִיל אָז יַעֲלוּ עַל־מִזְבַּחֲךָ פָרִים:

3 My God, be merciful to me according to Your goodness, and with Your great compassion, erase my sins.

4 Forgive my mistakes and remove my sin completely.

5 I know my sins. They are always before me.

6 I have sinned only against You and done that which is evil in Your eyes because You speak truth and You are truthful in judgment.

7 I was born an imperfect human being. In sin did my mother conceive me.

8 You want a truthful heart. Make me understand wisdom in my heart.

9 Purify me with hyssop and I will be pure. Wash me and I will be whiter than snow.

10 Help me to hear joy and happiness, so that these bones that You have crushed may rejoice.

11 Turn Your face from my sins and remove all my evil deeds.

12 Create a pure heart in me, my God, and give me a strong spirit.

13 Do not cast me away or take Your holy spirit away from me.

14 Return to me the joy of Your salvation and let a willing spirit support me.

15 Then I will teach sinners Your ways and they will return to You.

16 Save me from sin, my God, God of my salvation and my heart will sing of Your goodness.

17 My Lord, open my lips so that my mouth may utter Your praise.

18 I would offer sacrifices to You but You do not desire it; You take no pleasure in burnt-offerings.

19 You, my God, accept the sacrifice of a broken spirit. You do not reject a repentant heart.

20 Do kindness in Your love for Zion, and build the walls of Jerusalem.

21 Then You will happily accept burnt-offerings and whole-offerings, sacrifices of the righteous. They will offer the bullocks on Your altar.

פרק נב

א לַמְנַצֵּחַ מַשְׂכִּיל לְדָוִד:

ב בְּבוֹא דּוֹאֵג הָאֲדֹמִי וַיַּגֵּד לְשָׁאוּל וַיֹּאמֶר לוֹ בָּא דָוִד אֶל־בֵּית אֲחִימֶלֶךְ:

ג מַה־תִּתְהַלֵּל בְּרָעָה הַגִּבּוֹר חֶסֶד אֵל כָּל־הַיּוֹם:

ד הַוּוֹת תַּחְשֹׁב לְשׁוֹנֶךָ כְּתַעַר מְלֻטָּשׁ עֹשֵׂה רְמִיָּה:

ה אָהַבְתָּ רָּע מִטּוֹב שֶׁקֶר מִדַּבֵּר צֶדֶק סֶלָה:

ו אָהַבְתָּ כָל־דִּבְרֵי־בָלַע לְשׁוֹן מִרְמָה:

ז גַּם־אֵל יִתָּצְךָ לָנֶצַח יַחְתְּךָ וְיִסָּחֲךָ מֵאֹהֶל וְשֵׁרֶשְׁךָ מֵאֶרֶץ חַיִּים סֶלָה:

ח וְיִרְאוּ צַדִּיקִים וְיִירָאוּ וְעָלָיו יִשְׂחָקוּ:

ט הִנֵּה הַגֶּבֶר לֹא יָשִׂים אֱלֹהִים מָעוּזּוֹ וַיִּבְטַח בְּרֹב עָשְׁרוֹ יָעֹז בְּהַוָּתוֹ:

י וַאֲנִי כְּזַיִת רַעֲנָן בְּבֵית אֱלֹהִים בָּטַחְתִּי בְחֶסֶד אֱלֹהִים עוֹלָם וָעֶד:

יא אוֹדְךָ לְעוֹלָם כִּי עָשִׂיתָ וַאֲקַוֶּה שִׁמְךָ כִי־טוֹב נֶגֶד חֲסִידֶיךָ:

פרק נג

א לַמְנַצֵּחַ עַל־מָחֲלַת מַשְׂכִּיל לְדָוִד:

ב אָמַר נָבָל בְּלִבּוֹ אֵין אֱלֹהִים הִשְׁחִיתוּ וְהִתְעִיבוּ עָוֶל אֵין עֹשֵׂה־טוֹב:

ג אֱלֹהִים מִשָּׁמַיִם הִשְׁקִיף עַל־בְּנֵי אָדָם לִרְאוֹת הֲיֵשׁ מַשְׂכִּיל דֹּרֵשׁ אֶת־אֱלֹהִים:

ד כֻּלּוֹ סָג יַחְדָּו נֶאֱלָחוּ אֵין עֹשֵׂה־טוֹב אֵין גַּם אֶחָד:

ה הֲלֹא יָדְעוּ פֹּעֲלֵי אָוֶן אֹכְלֵי עַמִּי אָכְלוּ לֶחֶם אֱלֹהִים לֹא קָרָאוּ:

TEHILLIM 52

A song about a public official who did evil and caused evil to others

1 For the chief musician, an instructor of David,
2 When Doeg, the Edomite, came and told Shaul: "David has arrived at the house of Achimelech."
3 Mighty man, why do you boast of evil? God's mercy lasts forever.
4 Your plotting tongue plans destruction like a knife. You act dishonestly.
5 You love evil more than good and you tell lies rather than truth. Selah.
6 You love all the insulting words of a plotting tongue.
7 Therefore God will destroy you forever. He will seize you and take you from your tent. He will remove you from the land of the living. Selah.
8 The righteous will see this and fear, and will laugh at him.
9 This will happen to the man who does not believe in God, but rather trusted in his great wealth and made himself strong in his wickedness.
10 However, I am like a strong, green olive tree in the house of God; I trust in the goodness of God forever.
11 I will give You thanks forever because of what You have done. I will await the continuation of Your goodness, for Your name is great in the midst of Your saintly people.

TEHILLIM 53

A song about the evil of non-believers

1 For the chief musician, on the *mahalath*, an instructor by David.
2 The fool says in his heart: "There is no God." They act corruptly and commit terrible sins. There is none who does good.
3 God looks out from heaven upon the children of men to see whether there is any man of understanding who seeks God.
4 They have all become unclean and are all impure. There is none who does good, not even one.
5 Should not these sinners know about this, who destroy my people like they eat bread, and do not call upon God?

ו שָׁם פָּחֲדוּ־פַחַד לֹא־הָיָה פָחַד כִּי־אֱלֹהִים פִּזַּר עַצְמוֹת חֹנָךְ הֱבִשֹׁתָה כִּי־אֱלֹהִים מְאָסָם:

ז מִי־יִתֵּן מִצִּיּוֹן יְשֻׁעוֹת יִשְׂרָאֵל בְּשׁוּב אֱלֹהִים שְׁבוּת עַמּוֹ יָגֵל יַעֲקֹב יִשְׂמַח יִשְׂרָאֵל:

פרק נד

א לַמְנַצֵּחַ בִּנְגִינֹת מַשְׂכִּיל לְדָוִד:

ב בְּבוֹא הַזִּיפִים וַיֹּאמְרוּ לְשָׁאוּל הֲלֹא־דָוִד מִסְתַּתֵּר עִמָּנוּ:

ג אֱלֹהִים בְּשִׁמְךָ הוֹשִׁיעֵנִי וּבִגְבוּרָתְךָ תְדִינֵנִי:

ד אֱלֹהִים שְׁמַע תְּפִלָּתִי הַאֲזִינָה לְאִמְרֵי־פִי:

ה כִּי זָרִים קָמוּ עָלַי וְעָרִיצִים בִּקְשׁוּ נַפְשִׁי לֹא שָׂמוּ אֱלֹהִים לְנֶגְדָּם סֶלָה:

ו הִנֵּה אֱלֹהִים עֹזֵר לִי אֲדֹנָי בְּסֹמְכֵי נַפְשִׁי:

ז יָשׁוּב [יָשִׁיב] הָרַע לְשֹׁרְרָי בַּאֲמִתְּךָ הַצְמִיתֵם:

ח בִּנְדָבָה אֶזְבְּחָה־לָּךְ אוֹדֶה שִּׁמְךָ יְהוָה כִּי־טוֹב:

ט כִּי מִכָּל־צָרָה הִצִּילָנִי וּבְאֹיְבַי רָאֲתָה עֵינִי:

פרק נה

א לַמְנַצֵּחַ בִּנְגִינֹת מַשְׂכִּיל לְדָוִד:

ב הַאֲזִינָה אֱלֹהִים תְּפִלָּתִי וְאַל־תִּתְעַלַּם מִתְּחִנָּתִי:

ג הַקְשִׁיבָה לִּי וַעֲנֵנִי אָרִיד בְּשִׂיחִי וְאָהִימָה:

ד מִקּוֹל אוֹיֵב מִפְּנֵי עָקַת רָשָׁע כִּי־יָמִיטוּ עָלַי אָוֶן וּבְאַף יִשְׂטְמוּנִי:

6 There is no reason to fear, yet they are fearful, even though God has defeated the attacking enemy army and scattered their bones. You have put the non-believers to shame because G-d rejected them.

7 If only Israel's salvation would come from Zion! When God brings back the captives among His people, let Jacob rejoice and let Israel be glad.

TEHILLIM 54

A song asking for help

1 For the chief musician, with string music. An instruction by David.

2 When the Ziphites came to Shaul and said, "David is hiding among us."

3 My God, save me with Your name, and judge me with Your might.

4 My God, hear my prayer and listen to the words of my mouth.

5 Strangers have attacked me and violent men seek my life. They do not accept God. Selah.

6 Indeed God is my helper. The Lord supports my my soul.

7 He will turn their evil deeds back upon them. Destroy them with Your truth.

8 I will sacrifice a free will offering to You. I will offer thanks to Your name, my Lord, because it is good.

9 You have saved me from all my troubles, and my eyes have seen my enemies downfall.

TEHILLIM 55

A prayer for help against sudden, unexpected attack

1 For the chief musician with string music, an instructor of David.

2 Listen to my prayer, my God, and do not hide Yourself from my pleas.

3 Come to me and answer me. My soul is upset and cries out

4 Because of the lies of the enemy and the pressure of the evildoers. They cause trouble for me and harm me in their anger.

5 My heart suffers within me and the terrors of death are upon me.

ה   לִבִּי יָחִיל בְּקִרְבִּי וְאֵימוֹת מָוֶת נָפְלוּ עָלָי:

ו   יִרְאָה וָרַעַד יָבֹא בִי וַתְּכַסֵּנִי פַּלָּצוּת:

ז   וָאֹמַר מִי־יִתֶּן־לִי אֵבֶר כַּיּוֹנָה אָעוּפָה וְאֶשְׁכֹּנָה:

ח   הִנֵּה אַרְחִיק נְדֹד אָלִין בַּמִּדְבָּר סֶלָה:

ט   אָחִישָׁה מִפְלָט לִי מֵרוּחַ סֹעָה מִסָּעַר:

י   בַּלַּע אֲדֹנָי פַּלַּג לְשׁוֹנָם כִּי־רָאִיתִי חָמָס וְרִיב בָּעִיר:

יא   יוֹמָם וָלַיְלָה יְסוֹבְבֻהָ עַל־חוֹמֹתֶיהָ וְאָוֶן וְעָמָל בְּקִרְבָּהּ:

יב   הַוּוֹת בְּקִרְבָּהּ וְלֹא־יָמִישׁ מֵרְחֹבָהּ תֹּךְ וּמִרְמָה:

יג   כִּי לֹא־אוֹיֵב יְחָרְפֵנִי וְאֶשָּׂא לֹא־מְשַׂנְאִי עָלַי הִגְדִּיל וְאֶסָּתֵר מִמֶּנּוּ:

יד   וְאַתָּה אֱנוֹשׁ כְּעֶרְכִּי אַלּוּפִי וּמְיֻדָּעִי:

טו   אֲשֶׁר יַחְדָּו נַמְתִּיק סוֹד בְּבֵית אֱלֹהִים נְהַלֵּךְ בְּרָגֶשׁ:

טז   ישימות [יַשִּׁיא מָוֶת] עָלֵימוֹ יֵרְדוּ שְׁאוֹל חַיִּים כִּי־רָעוֹת בִּמְגוּרָם בְּקִרְבָּם:

יז   אֲנִי אֶל־אֱלֹהִים אֶקְרָא וַיהֹוָה יוֹשִׁיעֵנִי:

יח   עֶרֶב וָבֹקֶר וְצָהֳרַיִם אָשִׂיחָה וְאֶהֱמֶה וַיִּשְׁמַע קוֹלִי:

יט   פָּדָה בְשָׁלוֹם נַפְשִׁי מִקֲּרָב־לִי כִּי־בְרַבִּים הָיוּ עִמָּדִי:

כ   יִשְׁמַע אֵל וְיַעֲנֵם וְיֹשֵׁב קֶדֶם סֶלָה אֲשֶׁר אֵין חֲלִיפוֹת לָמוֹ וְלֹא יָרְאוּ אֱלֹהִים:

כא   שָׁלַח יָדָיו בִּשְׁלֹמָיו חִלֵּל בְּרִיתוֹ:

כב   חָלְקוּ מַחְמָאֹת פִּיו וּקֲרָב־לִבּוֹ רַכּוּ דְבָרָיו מִשֶּׁמֶן וְהֵמָּה פְתִחוֹת:

כג   הַשְׁלֵךְ עַל־יְהֹוָה יְהָבְךָ וְהוּא יְכַלְכְּלֶךָ לֹא־יִתֵּן לְעוֹלָם מוֹט לַצַּדִּיק:

כד   וְאַתָּה אֱלֹהִים תּוֹרִדֵם לִבְאֵר שַׁחַת אַנְשֵׁי דָמִים וּמִרְמָה לֹא־יֶחֱצוּ יְמֵיהֶם וַאֲנִי אֶבְטַח־בָּךְ:

6 Fear and trembling over powers me, and horror overcomes me.

7 I say, "If only I had the wings of a dove, I would fly away and be at rest."

8 Indeed I would go far away and live in the wilderness. Selah.

9 I would hurry to take refuge from the storm wind and the tempest.

10 My Lord, destroy and confuse their speech. I have seen violence and fighting in the city.

11 Day and night they walk about the city walls. Sins and evil are all within it.

12 Wickedness is within it. The public places are full of hatred and deceit.

13 It is not first one enemy that attacks me, for this I could have overcome. It was not a great army that came to fight me for then I would have hidden myself.

14 No – it was you, a man like me, my companion and my good friend.

15 We shared our secrets, and together we worshipped in the house of God with the people.

16 May God bring death upon them. May they go down alive into the netherworld because they live to be evil.

17 But I will call on God, and the Lord will save me.

18 I will call and cry out to Him in the evening, the morning and at midday. God will hear my voice.

19 He has redeemed my soul in peace and those who are against me now, were once with me.

20 God will hear and punish them, those that are the leaders. Selah. They do not worry and do not fear God.

21 My attacker went against me even though I was at peace with him. He broke his covenant.

22 His words were spoken like smooth butter but in his heart he intended to fight. Although his words were softer than oil, they were sharper than swords.

23 Entrust the Lord with your burden and He will support you. He will never cause the righteous to be moved.

24 You, my God, will take them down into the pit of the netherworld. Blood thirsty and deceitful men will not live even half their lives. But for myself, I will trust in You.

פרק נו

א לַמְנַצֵּחַ עַל־יוֹנַת אֵלֶם רְחֹקִים לְדָוִד מִכְתָּם בֶּאֱחֹז אֹתוֹ פְלִשְׁתִּים בְּגַת:

ב חָנֵּנִי אֱלֹהִים כִּי־שְׁאָפַנִי אֱנוֹשׁ כָּל־הַיּוֹם לֹחֵם יִלְחָצֵנִי:

ג שָׁאֲפוּ שׁוֹרְרַי כָּל־הַיּוֹם כִּי־רַבִּים לֹחֲמִים לִי מָרוֹם:

ד יוֹם אִירָא אֲנִי אֵלֶיךָ אֶבְטָח:

ה בֵּאלֹהִים אֲהַלֵּל דְּבָרוֹ בֵּאלֹהִים בָּטַחְתִּי לֹא אִירָא מַה־יַּעֲשֶׂה בָשָׂר לִי:

ו כָּל־הַיּוֹם דְּבָרַי יְעַצֵּבוּ עָלַי כָּל־מַחְשְׁבֹתָם לָרָע:

ז יָגוּרוּ יצפינו [יִצְפּוֹנוּ] הֵמָּה עֲקֵבַי יִשְׁמֹרוּ כַּאֲשֶׁר קִוּוּ נַפְשִׁי:

ח עַל־אָוֶן פַּלֶּט־לָמוֹ בְּאַף עַמִּים הוֹרֵד אֱלֹהִים:

ט נֹדִי סָפַרְתָּה אָתָּה שִׂימָה דִמְעָתִי בְנֹאדֶךָ הֲלֹא בְּסִפְרָתֶךָ:

י אָז יָשׁוּבוּ אוֹיְבַי אָחוֹר בְּיוֹם אֶקְרָא זֶה־יָדַעְתִּי כִּי־אֱלֹהִים לִי:

יא בֵּאלֹהִים אֲהַלֵּל דָּבָר בַּיהוָה אֲהַלֵּל דָּבָר:

יב בֵּאלֹהִים בָּטַחְתִּי לֹא אִירָא מַה־יַּעֲשֶׂה אָדָם לִי:

יג עָלַי אֱלֹהִים נְדָרֶיךָ אֲשַׁלֵּם תּוֹדֹת לָךְ:

יד כִּי הִצַּלְתָּ נַפְשִׁי מִמָּוֶת הֲלֹא רַגְלַי מִדֶּחִי לְהִתְהַלֵּךְ לִפְנֵי אֱלֹהִים בְּאוֹר הַחַיִּים:

פרק נז

א לַמְנַצֵּחַ אַל־תַּשְׁחֵת לְדָוִד מִכְתָּם בְּבָרְחוֹ מִפְּנֵי־שָׁאוּל בַּמְּעָרָה:

ב חָנֵּנִי אֱלֹהִים חָנֵּנִי כִּי בְךָ חָסָיָה נַפְשִׁי וּבְצֵל־כְּנָפֶיךָ אֶחְסֶה עַד יַעֲבֹר הַוּוֹת:

TEHILLIM 56

A song about living life with God

1 For the chief musician, upon the silenced dove who was far away, a memorial by David, when the Philstines held him in Gath.
2 My God, be gracious to me or I will be swallowed up by man. His constant fighting weakens me.
3 They prepare to attack me all day long in order to destroy me. There are many who fight me, from above.
4 When I am afraid, I put my trust in You.
5 I have confidence in the word of God. My trust is in God and I am not afraid. What harm can man do to me?
6 All day long they cause me to speak sadly. They have only evil plans against me.
7 They gather and hide themselves. They track my steps and lie in ambush for my life.
8 Will you let them escape with their sins? My God, throw them down!
9 You know how many times I have fled. You have preserved my tears in your flask. Is not all of this recorded in Your book?
10 On the day that I call You, my enemies will be defeated, for I know that God is with me.
11 I will praise the Lord for His word; I will praise God's loving kindness for His word.
12 I trust in the Lord and am not afraid. What can man do to me?
13 I will fulfill my vows, my God, and I will bring thanksgiving offerings to You.
14 For You have saved my spirit from death and my feet from stumbling, that I may walk before my God in the light of the living.

TEHILLIM 57

A song of confidence in Divine help

1 For the chief musician, do not destroy a memorial by David, when he fled from Saul, in the cave.
2 My God, be gracious to me, be kind to me, be kind to me, for my soul has taken refuge in You. I have taken shelter in the shadow of Your wings until all the threats have passed.

ג אֶקְרָא לֵאלֹהִים עֶלְיוֹן לָאֵל גֹּמֵר עָלָי:

ד יִשְׁלַח מִשָּׁמַיִם וְיוֹשִׁיעֵנִי חֵרֵף שֹׁאֲפִי סֶלָה יִשְׁלַח אֱלֹהִים חַסְדּוֹ וַאֲמִתּוֹ:

ה נַפְשִׁי בְּתוֹךְ לְבָאִם אֶשְׁכְּבָה לֹהֲטִים בְּנֵי־אָדָם שִׁנֵּיהֶם חֲנִית וְחִצִּים וּלְשׁוֹנָם חֶרֶב חַדָּה:

ו רוּמָה עַל־הַשָּׁמַיִם אֱלֹהִים עַל כָּל־הָאָרֶץ כְּבוֹדֶךָ:

ז רֶשֶׁת הֵכִינוּ לִפְעָמַי כָּפַף נַפְשִׁי כָּרוּ לְפָנַי שִׁיחָה נָפְלוּ בְתוֹכָהּ סֶלָה:

ח נָכוֹן לִבִּי אֱלֹהִים נָכוֹן לִבִּי אָשִׁירָה וַאֲזַמֵּרָה:

ט עוּרָה כְבוֹדִי עוּרָה הַנֵּבֶל וְכִנּוֹר אָעִירָה שָּׁחַר:

י אוֹדְךָ בָעַמִּים אֲדֹנָי אֲזַמֶּרְךָ בַּל־אֻמִּים:

יא כִּי־גָדֹל עַד־שָׁמַיִם חַסְדֶּךָ וְעַד־שְׁחָקִים אֲמִתֶּךָ:

יב רוּמָה עַל־שָׁמַיִם אֱלֹהִים עַל כָּל־הָאָרֶץ כְּבוֹדֶךָ:

פרק נח

א לַמְנַצֵּחַ אַל־תַּשְׁחֵת לְדָוִד מִכְתָּם:

ב הַאֻמְנָם אֵלֶם צֶדֶק תְּדַבֵּרוּן מֵישָׁרִים תִּשְׁפְּטוּ בְּנֵי אָדָם:

ג אַף־בְּלֵב עוֹלֹת תִּפְעָלוּן בָּאָרֶץ חֲמַס יְדֵיכֶם תְּפַלֵּסוּן:

ד זֹרוּ רְשָׁעִים מֵרָחֶם תָּעוּ מִבֶּטֶן דֹּבְרֵי כָזָב:

ה חֲמַת־לָמוֹ כִּדְמוּת חֲמַת־נָחָשׁ כְּמוֹ־פֶתֶן חֵרֵשׁ יַאְטֵם אָזְנוֹ:

ו אֲשֶׁר לֹא־יִשְׁמַע לְקוֹל מְלַחֲשִׁים חוֹבֵר חֲבָרִים מְחֻכָּם:

ז אֱלֹהִים הֲרָס־שִׁנֵּימוֹ בְּפִימוֹ מַלְתְּעוֹת כְּפִירִים נְתֹץ יְהוָה:

ח יִמָּאֲסוּ כְמוֹ־מַיִם יִתְהַלְּכוּ־לָמוֹ יִדְרֹךְ חִצָּו [חִצָּיו] כְּמוֹ יִתְמֹלָלוּ:

3 I will cry to God, the Most High, to God, Who cares for me.

4 He will send from heaven and save me from the humiliation of those who try to destroy me. Selah. God will send His mercy and truth.

5 My soul lies among lions, among whose hatred rage against me, the sons of man whose teeth are weapons and sears and arrows whose tongues are sharp swords.

6 In the heavens You are praised, my God. Your glory is upon the entire earth.

7 They have prepared a net to trap me. My soul is bowed down. They have prepared a pit for me, but they have fallen into it themselves. Selah.

8 My God, my heart is confident. My heart is confident and I will sing praises.

9 Awaken, my soul! Awaken, my lyre and harp, and I will awake the dawn.

10 I will give thanks to You, my Lord among the peoples, and I will sing praises to You among the nations.

11 Your kindness reaches to the heavens, and your truth reaches to the skies.

12 My God, May You be exalted above the earth and Your glory above the heavens.

TEHILLIM 58

This song cries out against corrupt judges

1 For the chief musician, do not destroy a memorial by David.

2 Why don't you judges speak in the name of truth? Do you judge the sons of man equally?

3 You do evil in your hearts and do violence to justice in the land.

4 Evildoers reject good from the womb. Liars go astray from their birth.

5 Their poison is like the venom of a snake, like the deaf viper that closes its ear,

6 So as not to listen to the voice of enchanters or to the cleverest maker of spells.

7 God, break their teeth in their mouths. Break the teeth of the young lions, Lord.

ט כְּמוֹ שַׁבְּלוּל תֶּמֶס יַהֲלֹךְ נֵפֶל אֵשֶׁת בַּל־חָזוּ שָׁמֶשׁ:

י בְּטֶרֶם יָבִינוּ סִירֹתֵיכֶם אָטָד כְּמוֹ־חַי כְּמוֹ־חָרוֹן יִשְׂעָרֶנּוּ:

יא יִשְׂמַח צַדִּיק כִּי־חָזָה נָקָם פְּעָמָיו יִרְחַץ בְּדַם הָרָשָׁע:

יב וְיֹאמַר אָדָם אַךְ־פְּרִי לַצַּדִּיק אַךְ יֵשׁ־אֱלֹהִים שֹׁפְטִים בָּאָרֶץ:

פרק נט

א לַמְנַצֵּחַ אַל־תַּשְׁחֵת לְדָוִד מִכְתָּם בִּשְׁלֹחַ שָׁאוּל וַיִּשְׁמְרוּ אֶת־הַבַּיִת לַהֲמִיתוֹ:

ב הַצִּילֵנִי מֵאֹיְבַי אֱלֹהָי מִמִּתְקוֹמְמַי תְּשַׂגְּבֵנִי:

ג הַצִּילֵנִי מִפֹּעֲלֵי אָוֶן וּמֵאַנְשֵׁי דָמִים הוֹשִׁיעֵנִי:

ד כִּי הִנֵּה אָרְבוּ לְנַפְשִׁי יָגוּרוּ עָלַי עַזִּים לֹא־פִשְׁעִי וְלֹא־חַטָּאתִי יְהוָה:

ה בְּלִי־עָוֺן יְרוּצוּן וְיִכּוֹנָנוּ עוּרָה לִקְרָאתִי וּרְאֵה:

ו וְאַתָּה יְהוָה־אֱלֹהִים צְבָאוֹת אֱלֹהֵי יִשְׂרָאֵל הָקִיצָה לִפְקֹד כָּל־הַגּוֹיִם אַל־תָּחֹן כָּל־בֹּגְדֵי אָוֶן סֶלָה:

ז יָשׁוּבוּ לָעֶרֶב יֶהֱמוּ כַכָּלֶב וִיסוֹבְבוּ עִיר:

ח הִנֵּה יַבִּיעוּן בְּפִיהֶם חֲרָבוֹת בְּשִׂפְתוֹתֵיהֶם כִּי־מִי שֹׁמֵעַ:

ט וְאַתָּה יְהוָה תִּשְׂחַק־לָמוֹ תִּלְעַג לְכָל־גּוֹיִם:

י עֻזּוֹ אֵלֶיךָ אֶשְׁמֹרָה כִּי אֱלֹהִים מִשְׂגַּבִּי:

יא אֱלֹהֵי חסדו [חַסְדִּי] יְקַדְּמֵנִי אֱלֹהִים יַרְאֵנִי בְשֹׁרְרָי:

יב אַל־תַּהַרְגֵם פֶּן־יִשְׁכְּחוּ עַמִּי הֲנִיעֵמוֹ בְחֵילְךָ וְהוֹרִידֵמוֹ מָגִנֵּנוּ אֲדֹנָי:

יג חַטַּאת־פִּימוֹ דְּבַר־שְׂפָתֵימוֹ וְיִלָּכְדוּ בִגְאוֹנָם וּמֵאָלָה וּמִכַּחַשׁ יְסַפֵּרוּ:

8 Let them melt away like flowing water, and break the weapons that they shoot.

9 Let them be like a snail that melts away and like the stillborn of a mole that will never see the sun.

10 Before their cooking pots are heated, God will blow it away with a storm.

11 The righteous will rejoice when they see vengeance, and will wash their feet in the blood of the wicked.

12 Men will say: "Yes, there is a reward for the righteous; surely God judges on earth."

TEHILLIM 59

A song asking for protection

1 For the chief musician, do not destroy a memorial by David, when Saul sent men to watch the house, waiting to kill him.

2 My God, deliver me from my enemies. Protect me from those who attack me.

3 Save me from those who do evil. Save me from the murderers.

4 They are waiting to take my life. The sinners gather about me – not because I have sinned or done evil.

5 They prepare themselves even though I am not guilty. Awake and help me, and see.

6 My Lord, God of Israel, come and punish all the nations, and grant no mercy to traitors. Selah.

7 They come back in the evening, around the city, and bark like dogs.

8 They lie with their mouths and their lips are like swords. They say: "God will not hear."

9 However, my Lord, You will laugh at them, and mock all these nations.

10 I will wait for Your great strength because God is my protector.

11 My merciful God will go ahead of me, and let me see my enemies.

12 Do not kill them, because people will quickly forget the reason. Let them drift about, and then bring down with Your power, Lord, my protector.

13 For the sinful words of their mouths and lips asked: Who will hear? – They cursed and they lied – let them be taken in their pride.

יד כַּלֵּה בְחֵמָה כַּלֵּה וְאֵינֵמוֹ וְיֵדְעוּ כִּי־אֱלֹהִים מֹשֵׁל בְּיַעֲקֹב לְאַפְסֵי הָאָרֶץ סֶלָה:

טו וְיָשֻׁבוּ לָעֶרֶב יֶהֱמוּ כַכָּלֶב וִיסוֹבְבוּ עִיר:

טז הֵמָּה יְנוּעוּן [יְנִיעוּן] לֶאֱכֹל אִם־לֹא יִשְׂבְּעוּ וַיָּלִינוּ:

יז וַאֲנִי אָשִׁיר עֻזֶּךָ וַאֲרַנֵּן לַבֹּקֶר חַסְדֶּךָ כִּי־הָיִיתָ מִשְׂגָּב לִי וּמָנוֹס בְּיוֹם צַר־לִי:

יח עֻזִּי אֵלֶיךָ אֲזַמֵּרָה כִּי־אֱלֹהִים מִשְׂגַּבִּי אֱלֹהֵי חַסְדִּי:

פרק ס

א לַמְנַצֵּחַ עַל־שׁוּשַׁן עֵדוּת מִכְתָּם לְדָוִד לְלַמֵּד:

ב בְּהַצּוֹתוֹ אֶת אֲרַם נַהֲרַיִם וְאֶת־אֲרַם צוֹבָה וַיָּשָׁב יוֹאָב וַיַּךְ אֶת־אֱדוֹם בְּגֵיא־מֶלַח שְׁנֵים עָשָׂר אָלֶף:

ג אֱלֹהִים זְנַחְתָּנוּ פְרַצְתָּנוּ אָנַפְתָּ תְּשׁוֹבֵב לָנוּ:

ד הִרְעַשְׁתָּה אֶרֶץ פְּצַמְתָּהּ רְפָה שְׁבָרֶיהָ כִי־מָטָה:

ה הִרְאִיתָה עַמְּךָ קָשָׁה הִשְׁקִיתָנוּ יַיִן תַּרְעֵלָה:

ו נָתַתָּה לִּירֵאֶיךָ נֵּס לְהִתְנוֹסֵס מִפְּנֵי קֹשֶׁט סֶלָה:

ז לְמַעַן יֵחָלְצוּן יְדִידֶיךָ הוֹשִׁיעָה יְמִינְךָ וענוו [וַעֲנֵנִי]:

ח אֱלֹהִים דִּבֶּר בְּקָדְשׁוֹ אֶעְלֹזָה אֲחַלְּקָה שְׁכֶם וְעֵמֶק סֻכּוֹת אֲמַדֵּד:

ט לִי גִלְעָד וְלִי מְנַשֶּׁה וְאֶפְרַיִם מָעוֹז רֹאשִׁי יְהוּדָה מְחֹקְקִי:

י מוֹאָב סִיר רַחְצִי עַל־אֱדוֹם אַשְׁלִיךְ נַעֲלִי עָלַי פְּלֶשֶׁת הִתְרֹעָעִי:

יא מִי יֹבִלֵנִי עִיר מָצוֹר מִי נָחַנִי עַד־אֱדוֹם:

יב הֲלֹא־אַתָּה אֱלֹהִים זְנַחְתָּנוּ וְלֹא־תֵצֵא אֱלֹהִים בְּצִבְאוֹתֵינוּ:

יג הָבָה־לָּנוּ עֶזְרָת מִצָּר וְשָׁוְא תְּשׁוּעַת אָדָם:

יד בֵּאלֹהִים נַעֲשֶׂה־חָיִל וְהוּא יָבוּס צָרֵינוּ:

14 Destroy them completely. Destroy them so that none remain. Let them know that God rules in Jacob to the ends of the earth. Selah.

15 They return in the evening barking like dogs, around the city.

16 They wander around to eat and stay all night long until they satisfied.

17 However, I will sing of Your might. I will sing loudly of Your loving kindness in the morning, for You have been my protector and my shelter in my day of trouble.

18 To You, my Strength, I will sing songs, for God is my protector and the God of my loving kindness.

TEHILLIM 60

The song describes a military defeat that God turned into victory

1 For the chief musician, in honor of the Sanhedrin, an instructor by David to teach,

2 When he fought against Aram-naharaim and Aram-zobah, and Joab returned and killed twelve thousand men of Edom in the Valley of Salt.

3 My God, You have left us and defeated us. You have become angry. Please take us back.

4 You have made the land to shake and split. Heal its broken places, for it totters.

5 You have forced Your people to witness terrible things. You have made them drink wine of confusion.

6 To those who fear You, You have given a flag that gives hope and represents truth. Selah.

7 So that those whom You love may be delivered, save them with Your right hand and answer me.

8 The holy God said that He will rejoice in the defeat of Shechem and divide the Valley of Succoth.

9 Gilead is mine and Manasseh is mine. Ephraim is my main fortress. Judah is the giver of my laws.

10 Moab is my wash basin. Upon Edom I put my foot. Philistia cries out because of me.

11 Who will bring us into the fortified city? Who will lead the army to Edom?

פרק סא

א לַמְנַצֵּחַ עַל־נְגִינַת לְדָוִד׃

ב שִׁמְעָה אֱלֹהִים רִנָּתִי הַקְשִׁיבָה תְּפִלָּתִי׃

ג מִקְצֵה הָאָרֶץ אֵלֶיךָ אֶקְרָא בַּעֲטֹף לִבִּי בְּצוּר־יָרוּם מִמֶּנִּי תַנְחֵנִי׃

ד כִּי־הָיִיתָ מַחְסֶה לִי מִגְדַּל־עֹז מִפְּנֵי אוֹיֵב׃

ה אָגוּרָה בְאָהָלְךָ עוֹלָמִים אֶחֱסֶה בְסֵתֶר כְּנָפֶיךָ סֶּלָה׃

ו כִּי־אַתָּה אֱלֹהִים שָׁמַעְתָּ לִנְדָרָי נָתַתָּ יְרֻשַּׁת יִרְאֵי שְׁמֶךָ׃

ז יָמִים עַל־יְמֵי־מֶלֶךְ תּוֹסִיף שְׁנוֹתָיו כְּמוֹ־דֹר וָדֹר׃

ח יֵשֵׁב עוֹלָם לִפְנֵי אֱלֹהִים חֶסֶד וֶאֱמֶת מַן יִנְצְרֻהוּ׃

ט כֵּן אֲזַמְּרָה שִׁמְךָ לָעַד לְשַׁלְּמִי נְדָרַי יוֹם יוֹם׃

פרק סב

א לַמְנַצֵּחַ עַל־יְדוּתוּן מִזְמוֹר לְדָוִד׃

ב אַךְ אֶל־אֱלֹהִים דּוּמִיָּה נַפְשִׁי מִמֶּנּוּ יְשׁוּעָתִי׃

ג אַךְ־הוּא צוּרִי וִישׁוּעָתִי מִשְׂגַּבִּי לֹא־אֶמּוֹט רַבָּה׃

ד עַד־אָנָה תְּהוֹתְתוּ עַל־אִישׁ תְּרָצְּחוּ כֻלְּכֶם כְּקִיר נָטוּי גָּדֵר הַדְּחוּיָה׃

ה אַךְ מִשְּׂאֵתוֹ יָעֲצוּ לְהַדִּיחַ יִרְצוּ כָזָב בְּפִיו יְבָרֵכוּ וּבְקִרְבָּם יְקַלְלוּ־סֶלָה׃

12 My God, have You left us? Do You do not lead our army?
13 Give us Your help against the enemy, for the help of man is worthless.
14 With God we will be victorious, for God will defeat the enemy.

TEHILLIM 61

A song asking that the king be given long life

1 For the chief musician with string music, by David.
2 My God, hear my cry and listen to my prayer.
3 With my fainting heart from the ends of the earth I will call to You. With Your help, take me to a safe, high place.
4 You have been a shelter to me and a pillar of strength before the enemy.
5 I will live in Your protecting tent and take shelter under Your wings. Selah.
6 You have heard my vows, my God. You have given the Land of Israel to those that fear Your name.
7 Please add to the king's life. May his years continue through many generations.
8 May he sit on the throne before God forever and command mercy and truth to guard him always.
9 I will sing thanks to Your name forever, and pay my vows every day.

TEHILLIM 62

A song that describes God as the only hope

1 For the chief musician, for Jeduthun. A psalm by David.
2 My soul waits quietly only for God, and from Him comes my help.
3 He alone is my rock, help and strength, and this I believe.
4 How long will all the evildoers attack, wanting to kill me, as though my wall of truth were a falling fence?
5 They love to lie and plan to remove him as king. They utter blessings with their mouths but truly, they curse. Selah.
6 My soul, waits quietly only for God, for from Him comes my hope.
7 Only He is my strength and my deliverance. I believe in God.

ו אַךְ לֵאלֹהִים דּוּמִּי נַפְשִׁי כִּי־מִמֶּנּוּ תִּקְוָתִי:

ז אַךְ־הוּא צוּרִי וִישׁוּעָתִי מִשְׂגַּבִּי לֹא אֶמּוֹט:

ח עַל־אֱלֹהִים יִשְׁעִי וּכְבוֹדִי צוּר־עֻזִּי מַחְסִי בֵּאלֹהִים:

ט בִּטְחוּ בוֹ בְכָל־עֵת עָם שִׁפְכוּ לְפָנָיו לְבַבְכֶם אֱלֹהִים מַחֲסֶה־לָּנוּ סֶלָה:

י אַךְ הֶבֶל בְּנֵי־אָדָם כָּזָב בְּנֵי אִישׁ בְּמֹאזְנַיִם לַעֲלוֹת הֵמָּה מֵהֶבֶל יָחַד:

יא אַל־תִּבְטְחוּ בְעֹשֶׁק וּבְגָזֵל אַל־תֶּהְבָּלוּ חַיִל כִּי־יָנוּב אַל־תָּשִׁיתוּ לֵב:

יב אַחַת דִּבֶּר אֱלֹהִים שְׁתַּיִם־זוּ שָׁמָעְתִּי כִּי עֹז לֵאלֹהִים:

יג וּלְךָ־אֲדֹנָי חָסֶד כִּי־אַתָּה תְשַׁלֵּם לְאִישׁ כְּמַעֲשֵׂהוּ:

פרק סג

א מִזְמוֹר לְדָוִד בִּהְיוֹתוֹ בְּמִדְבַּר יְהוּדָה:

ב אֱלֹהִים אֵלִי אַתָּה אֲשַׁחֲרֶךָּ צָמְאָה לְךָ נַפְשִׁי כָּמַהּ לְךָ בְשָׂרִי בְּאֶרֶץ־צִיָּה וְעָיֵף בְּלִי־מָיִם:

ג כֵּן בַּקֹּדֶשׁ חֲזִיתִיךָ לִרְאוֹת עֻזְּךָ וּכְבוֹדֶךָ:

ד כִּי־טוֹב חַסְדְּךָ מֵחַיִּים שְׂפָתַי יְשַׁבְּחוּנְךָ:

ה כֵּן אֲבָרֶכְךָ בְחַיָּי בְּשִׁמְךָ אֶשָּׂא כַפָּי:

ו כְּמוֹ חֵלֶב וָדֶשֶׁן תִּשְׂבַּע נַפְשִׁי וְשִׂפְתֵי רְנָנוֹת יְהַלֶּל־פִּי:

ז אִם־זְכַרְתִּיךָ עַל־יְצוּעָי בְּאַשְׁמֻרוֹת אֶהְגֶּה־בָּךְ:

ח כִּי־הָיִיתָ עֶזְרָתָה לִּי וּבְצֵל כְּנָפֶיךָ אֲרַנֵּן:

ט דָּבְקָה נַפְשִׁי אַחֲרֶיךָ בִּי תָּמְכָה יְמִינֶךָ:

י וְהֵמָּה לְשׁוֹאָה יְבַקְשׁוּ נַפְשִׁי יָבֹאוּ בְּתַחְתִּיּוֹת הָאָרֶץ:

יא יַגִּירֻהוּ עַל־יְדֵי־חָרֶב מְנָת שֻׁעָלִים יִהְיוּ:

יב וְהַמֶּלֶךְ יִשְׂמַח בֵּאלֹהִים יִתְהַלֵּל כָּל־הַנִּשְׁבָּע בּוֹ כִּי יִסָּכֵר פִּי דוֹבְרֵי־שָׁקֶר:

8 My honor and my kingdom depend on God. The rock of my strength and refuge is in God.

9 People, always trust in Him. Open your hearts to Him, for God is our refuge. Selah.

10 Wealthy men are liars and ordinary men are weak. If they are put on a scale, they are weightless.

11 Do not trust in evil ways and do not trust in theft. Do not depend on riches.

12 God has spoken once, and again I heard this: Might belongs to God.

13 My Lord, mercy belongs to You. You reward every man according to his actions.

TEHILLIM 63

The song of a soul that seeks God

1 A psalm by David when he was in the wilderness of Judah.

2 My God, You are my God. I truly long for You. My soul desires You and my body searches for You as in a desolate place where there is no water.

3 I looked for You in the Sanctuary in order to behold Your power and glory.

4 Your goodness and kindness are better than life. My lips will thank You.

5 I will bless You as long as I live. In Your name, I will lift my hands to thank you.

6 My soul is satisfied as though it consumed marrow and fat. My mouth thanks You with rejoicing lips.

7 I remember You at night and think about You during the night-watches.

8 You have been my help, and I rejoice in the shadow of Your wings.

9 My soul is connected to You, and Your right hand holds me firmly.

10 Those who want to destroy my soul will go to the netherworld.

11 They will be killed by a powerful sword, to become food for foxes.

12 But the king will rejoice in God, and everyone who believes in God will be glad because those who speak falsehood will be no more.

פרק סד

א לַמְנַצֵּחַ מִזְמוֹר לְדָוִד:

ב שְׁמַע אֱלֹהִים קוֹלִי בְשִׂיחִי מִפַּחַד אוֹיֵב תִּצֹּר חַיָּי:

ג תַּסְתִּירֵנִי מִסּוֹד מְרֵעִים מֵרִגְשַׁת פֹּעֲלֵי אָוֶן:

ד אֲשֶׁר שָׁנְנוּ כַחֶרֶב לְשׁוֹנָם דָּרְכוּ חִצָּם דָּבָר מָר:

ה לִירוֹת בַּמִּסְתָּרִים תָּם פִּתְאֹם יֹרֻהוּ וְלֹא יִירָאוּ:

ו יְחַזְּקוּ־לָמוֹ דָּבָר רָע יְסַפְּרוּ לִטְמוֹן מוֹקְשִׁים אָמְרוּ מִי יִרְאֶה־לָּמוֹ:

ז יַחְפְּשׂוּ עוֹלֹת תַּמְנוּ חֵפֶשׂ מְחֻפָּשׂ וְקֶרֶב אִישׁ וְלֵב עָמֹק:

ח וַיֹּרֵם אֱלֹהִים חֵץ פִּתְאוֹם הָיוּ מַכּוֹתָם:

ט וַיַּכְשִׁילֻהוּ עָלֵימוֹ לְשׁוֹנָם יִתְנֹדֲדוּ כָּל־רֹאֵה בָם:

י וַיִּירְאוּ כָּל־אָדָם וַיַּגִּידוּ פֹּעַל אֱלֹהִים וּמַעֲשֵׂהוּ הִשְׂכִּילוּ:

יא יִשְׂמַח צַדִּיק בַּיהוָה וְחָסָה בוֹ וְיִתְהַלְלוּ כָּל־יִשְׁרֵי־לֵב:

פרק סה

א לַמְנַצֵּחַ מִזְמוֹר לְדָוִד שִׁיר:

ב לְךָ דֻמִיָּה תְהִלָּה אֱלֹהִים בְּצִיּוֹן וּלְךָ יְשֻׁלַּם־נֶדֶר:

ג שֹׁמֵעַ תְּפִלָּה עָדֶיךָ כָּל־בָּשָׂר יָבֹאוּ:

ד דִּבְרֵי עֲוֹנֹת גָּבְרוּ מֶנִּי פְּשָׁעֵינוּ אַתָּה תְכַפְּרֵם:

ה אַשְׁרֵי תִּבְחַר וּתְקָרֵב יִשְׁכֹּן חֲצֵרֶיךָ נִשְׂבְּעָה בְּטוּב בֵּיתֶךָ קְדֹשׁ הֵיכָלֶךָ:

ו נוֹרָאוֹת בְּצֶדֶק תַּעֲנֵנוּ אֱלֹהֵי יִשְׁעֵנוּ מִבְטָח כָּל־קַצְוֵי־אֶרֶץ וְיָם רְחֹקִים:

TEHILLIM 64

A song of a good heart's happiness with God

1 For the chief musician, a psalm by David.

2 My God, hear my troubled voice. Save my life from the terror of the enemy.

3 Protect me from the council of sinners and from the actions of the evildoers.

4 They have prepared their tongues like swords and their weapons are bitter words.

5 They shoot at the innocent in secret places, suddenly and without fear.

6 They encourage each other to do evil and they speak softly of setting traps. They say, "who will see us?"

7 They have carefully planned and prepared their evil acts deep within their hearts.

8 But God suddenly shoots an arrow at them, wounding them.

9 Their own lying tongue betrays them. Everyone shakes their heads to see them.

10 Then all men revered and spoke of the acts of God, and understood His works.

11 The righteous will be happy in the Lord and take refuge in Him, and all people of integrity will rejoice.

TEHILLIM 65

A song of thanks to God for an abundant harvest

1 For the chief musician, a psalm, a song by David.

2 Silent gratitude is yours, my God in Zion, and to You vows are fulfilled.

3 To You who accept prayer, all people will come.

4 My countless sins are too heavy for me, but You will pardon them.

5 Happy is the man whom You choose and bring close to you to live in Your house. May we be satisfied with the goodness of Your House, the holy place of your Sanctuary.

6 Answer us with good and wonderful things. My saving God, You are trusted by those who live at the ends of the earth and in the distant seas.

ז   מֵכִין הָרִים בְּכֹחוֹ נֶאְזָר בִּגְבוּרָה:

ח   מַשְׁבִּיחַ שְׁאוֹן יַמִּים שְׁאוֹן גַּלֵּיהֶם וַהֲמוֹן לְאֻמִּים:

ט   וַיִּירְאוּ יֹשְׁבֵי קְצָוֹת מֵאוֹתֹתֶיךָ מוֹצָאֵי־בֹקֶר וָעֶרֶב תַּרְנִין:

י   פָּקַדְתָּ הָאָרֶץ וַתְּשֹׁקְקֶהָ רַבַּת תַּעְשְׁרֶנָּה פֶּלֶג אֱלֹהִים מָלֵא מָיִם תָּכִין דְּגָנָם כִּי־כֵן תְּכִינֶהָ:

יא   תְּלָמֶיהָ רַוֵּה נַחֵת גְּדוּדֶהָ בִּרְבִיבִים תְּמֹגְגֶנָּה צִמְחָהּ תְּבָרֵךְ:

יב   עִטַּרְתָּ שְׁנַת טוֹבָתֶךָ וּמַעְגָּלֶיךָ יִרְעֲפוּן דָּשֶׁן:

יג   יִרְעֲפוּ נְאוֹת מִדְבָּר וְגִיל גְּבָעוֹת תַּחְגֹּרְנָה:

יד   לָבְשׁוּ כָרִים הַצֹּאן וַעֲמָקִים יַעַטְפוּ־בָר יִתְרוֹעֲעוּ אַף־יָשִׁירוּ:

פרק סו

א   לַמְנַצֵּחַ שִׁיר מִזְמוֹר הָרִיעוּ לֵאלֹהִים כָּל־הָאָרֶץ:

ב   זַמְּרוּ כְבוֹד־שְׁמוֹ שִׂימוּ כָבוֹד תְּהִלָּתוֹ:

ג   אִמְרוּ לֵאלֹהִים מַה־נּוֹרָא מַעֲשֶׂיךָ בְּרֹב עֻזְּךָ יְכַחֲשׁוּ־לְךָ אֹיְבֶיךָ:

ד   כָּל־הָאָרֶץ יִשְׁתַּחֲווּ לְךָ וִיזַמְּרוּ־לָךְ יְזַמְּרוּ שִׁמְךָ סֶלָה:

ה   לְכוּ וּרְאוּ מִפְעֲלוֹת אֱלֹהִים נוֹרָא עֲלִילָה עַל־בְּנֵי אָדָם:

ו   הָפַךְ יָם לְיַבָּשָׁה בַּנָּהָר יַעַבְרוּ בְרָגֶל שָׁם נִשְׂמְחָה־בּוֹ:

ז   מֹשֵׁל בִּגְבוּרָתוֹ עוֹלָם עֵינָיו בַּגּוֹיִם תִּצְפֶּינָה הַסּוֹרְרִים אַל־[יָרִימוּ] [יָרוּמוּ] לָמוֹ סֶלָה:

ח   בָּרְכוּ עַמִּים אֱלֹהֵינוּ וְהַשְׁמִיעוּ קוֹל תְּהִלָּתוֹ:

ט   הַשָּׂם נַפְשֵׁנוּ בַּחַיִּים וְלֹא־נָתַן לַמּוֹט רַגְלֵנוּ:

י   כִּי־בְחַנְתָּנוּ אֱלֹהִים צְרַפְתָּנוּ כִּצְרָף־כָּסֶף:

7 With Your strength, You establish the mountains. You are mighty and powerful.

8 You control the mighty seas and their roaring waves, and calm the troubles of people.

9 Those who live far away see Your acts with amazement. You cause the coming of the mornings and the evenings to be joyous.

10 You remember the earth and give it water to make it bear fruit. God's river of rain is full. You prepare the earth to give them food.

11 You give abundant water to the valleys and prepare the earth. You make it soft with showers. You bless the earth's growth.

12 You crown the year with goodness and Your paths cause abundance to flow.

13 The pastures of the wilderness receive Your rain, and the hills are full of joy.

14 The meadows are clothed with flocks and the valleys are covered with corn. They shout for joy and sing.

TEHILLIM 66

*A song of thanksgiving to God for having
saved the nation from attackers*

1 For the chief musician, a song, a psalm. Shout to God, all the earth!

2 Sing thanks to the greatness of His name and make His praise beautiful.

3 Say to God: How very great is Your creation! Your great power forces Your enemies to pay homage to you.

4 The whole earth will worship You and will sing thanks to You. They will sing praises to Your name. Selah.

5 Come and see the works of God. He does awe-inspiring deeds for the children of men.

6 He turned the sea into dry land, and they went through the river with dry feet. There we praised Him!

7 He rules with power, forever. His eyes watch over the nations. Let rebellious people not glory in themselves. Selah.

8 Nations, bless our God, and shout His praises.

9 He gave us life and keeps our feet from stumbling.

10 God, You have tested us, and You purified us as silver is purified.

11 You have isolated us and made our bodies bear burdens.

יא הֲבֵאתָנוּ בַמְּצוּדָה שַׂמְתָּ מוּעָקָה בְמָתְנֵינוּ:

יב הִרְכַּבְתָּ אֱנוֹשׁ לְרֹאשֵׁנוּ בָּאנוּ־בָאֵשׁ וּבַמַּיִם וַתּוֹצִיאֵנוּ לָרְוָיָה:

יג אָבוֹא בֵיתְךָ בְעוֹלוֹת אֲשַׁלֵּם לְךָ נְדָרָי:

יד אֲשֶׁר־פָּצוּ שְׂפָתָי וְדִבֶּר־פִּי בַּצַּר־לִי:

טו עֹלוֹת מֵחִים אַעֲלֶה־לָּךְ עִם־קְטֹרֶת אֵילִים אֶעֱשֶׂה בָקָר עִם־עַתּוּדִים סֶלָה:

טז לְכוּ שִׁמְעוּ וַאֲסַפְּרָה כָּל־יִרְאֵי אֱלֹהִים אֲשֶׁר עָשָׂה לְנַפְשִׁי:

יז אֵלָיו פִּי־קָרָאתִי וְרוֹמַם תַּחַת לְשׁוֹנִי:

יח אָוֶן אִם־רָאִיתִי בְלִבִּי לֹא יִשְׁמַע אֲדֹנָי:

יט אָכֵן שָׁמַע אֱלֹהִים הִקְשִׁיב בְּקוֹל תְּפִלָּתִי:

כ בָּרוּךְ אֱלֹהִים אֲשֶׁר לֹא־הֵסִיר תְּפִלָּתִי וְחַסְדּוֹ מֵאִתִּי:

פרק סז

א לַמְנַצֵּחַ בִּנְגִינֹת מִזְמוֹר שִׁיר:

ב אֱלֹהִים יְחָנֵּנוּ וִיבָרְכֵנוּ יָאֵר פָּנָיו אִתָּנוּ סֶלָה:

ג לָדַעַת בָּאָרֶץ דַּרְכֶּךָ בְּכָל־גּוֹיִם יְשׁוּעָתֶךָ:

ד יוֹדוּךָ עַמִּים אֱלֹהִים יוֹדוּךָ עַמִּים כֻּלָּם:

ה יִשְׂמְחוּ וִירַנְּנוּ לְאֻמִּים כִּי־תִשְׁפֹּט עַמִּים מִישׁוֹר וּלְאֻמִּים בָּאָרֶץ תַּנְחֵם סֶלָה:

ו יוֹדוּךָ עַמִּים אֱלֹהִים יוֹדוּךָ עַמִּים כֻּלָּם:

ז אֶרֶץ נָתְנָה יְבוּלָהּ יְבָרְכֵנוּ אֱלֹהִים אֱלֹהֵינוּ:

ח יְבָרְכֵנוּ אֱלֹהִים וְיִירְאוּ אֹתוֹ כָּל־אַפְסֵי־אָרֶץ:

12 You brought the enemy to be victorious over us. We went through fire and water, but then You took us out into abundance.

13 I will come to Your house with burnt-offerings. I will keep my vows

14 That my lips uttered and that my mouth spoke when I was suffering.

15 I will offer burnt-offerings to You with the sweet smoke of rams. I will offer bulls with goats. Selah.

16 Come and hear, all who love God! I will tell of the good that He has done for me.

17 I cried to Him with my mouth and worshipped Him with my tongue.

18 If I had thought of sin in my heart, the Lord would not have listened.

19 However, the Lord has surely heard, and He has listened to the voice of my prayer.

20 Blessed be God, Who has not turned away from my prayer or from His loving kindness toward me.

TEHILLIM 67

A song calling for all people to sing to God

1 For the chief musician with string music, a psalm, a song.

2 May God be good to us and bless us. May He make His face to shine upon us. Selah.

3 So that Your way be known on earth, and Your ability to save man, among the nations.

4 Nations will give thanks to You, my God, Everyone will give thanks to You.

5 May the nations be glad and sing joyfully, for You will judge the people with fairness and guide the nations upon the earth. Selah.

6 Nations will give thanks to You, my God. Everyone will give thanks to You.

7 The earth has produced its harvest; God, our own God, bless us.

8 May God bless us. May those from one end of the earth to the other, revere Him.

פרק סח

א לַמְנַצֵּחַ לְדָוִד מִזְמוֹר שִׁיר:

ב יָקוּם אֱלֹהִים יָפוּצוּ אוֹיְבָיו וְיָנוּסוּ מְשַׂנְאָיו מִפָּנָיו:

ג כְּהִנְדֹּף עָשָׁן תִּנְדֹּף כְּהִמֵּס דּוֹנַג מִפְּנֵי־אֵשׁ יֹאבְדוּ רְשָׁעִים מִפְּנֵי אֱלֹהִים:

ד וְצַדִּיקִים יִשְׂמְחוּ יַעַלְצוּ לִפְנֵי אֱלֹהִים וְיָשִׂישׂוּ בְשִׂמְחָה:

ה שִׁירוּ לֵאלֹהִים זַמְּרוּ שְׁמוֹ סֹלּוּ לָרֹכֵב בָּעֲרָבוֹת בְּיָהּ שְׁמוֹ וְעִלְזוּ לְפָנָיו:

ו אֲבִי יְתוֹמִים וְדַיַּן אַלְמָנוֹת אֱלֹהִים בִּמְעוֹן קָדְשׁוֹ:

ז אֱלֹהִים מוֹשִׁיב יְחִידִים בַּיְתָה מוֹצִיא אֲסִירִים בַּכּוֹשָׁרוֹת אַךְ־סוֹרְרִים שָׁכְנוּ צְחִיחָה:

ח אֱלֹהִים בְּצֵאתְךָ לִפְנֵי עַמֶּךָ בְּצַעְדְּךָ בִישִׁימוֹן סֶלָה:

ט אֶרֶץ רָעָשָׁה אַף־שָׁמַיִם נָטְפוּ מִפְּנֵי אֱלֹהִים זֶה סִינַי מִפְּנֵי אֱלֹהִים אֱלֹהֵי יִשְׂרָאֵל:

י גֶּשֶׁם נְדָבוֹת תָּנִיף אֱלֹהִים נַחֲלָתְךָ וְנִלְאָה אַתָּה כוֹנַנְתָּהּ:

יא חַיָּתְךָ יָשְׁבוּ־בָהּ תָּכִין בְּטוֹבָתְךָ לֶעָנִי אֱלֹהִים:

יב אֲדֹנָי יִתֶּן־אֹמֶר הַמְבַשְּׂרוֹת צָבָא רָב:

יג מַלְכֵי צְבָאוֹת יִדֹּדוּן יִדֹּדוּן וּנְוַת בַּיִת תְּחַלֵּק שָׁלָל:

יד אִם־תִּשְׁכְּבוּן בֵּין שְׁפַתָּיִם כַּנְפֵי יוֹנָה נֶחְפָּה בַכֶּסֶף וְאֶבְרוֹתֶיהָ בִּירַקְרַק חָרוּץ:

טו בְּפָרֵשׂ שַׁדַּי מְלָכִים בָּהּ תַּשְׁלֵג בְּצַלְמוֹן:

טז הַר־אֱלֹהִים הַר־בָּשָׁן הַר גַּבְנֻנִּים הַר־בָּשָׁן:

יז לָמָּה תְּרַצְּדוּן הָרִים גַּבְנֻנִּים הָהָר חָמַד אֱלֹהִים לְשִׁבְתּוֹ אַף־יְהוָה יִשְׁכֹּן לָנֶצַח:

יח רֶכֶב אֱלֹהִים רִבֹּתַיִם אַלְפֵי שִׁנְאָן אֲדֹנָי בָם סִינַי בַּקֹּדֶשׁ:

TEHILLIM 68

A song of Israel's faith and hope in God's greatness

1 For the chief musician. A psalm by David, a song.

2 May God come and scatter His enemies. May those who hate Him run away.

3 Chase them away like smoke in the wind and like wax melted in fire: Thus will evildoers disappear from before God.

4 But may the righteous be glad and rejoice with God. May they be happy with goodness.

5 Sing to God. Sing thanks to His name. Praise God Who rides over in the heavens. His name is the Lord. Rejoice in Him.

6 He is the father to orphans and the judge of widows. God is holy in his holy Sanctuary.

7 God gives the lonely houses to live in. He frees the slaves forever. But the wicked live in a barren land.

8 My God, when You went out together with Your people, You stayed in the wilderness with them. Selah.

9 The earth shook and the heavens dropped down before the presence of God. Sinai also shook at the presence of God, the God of Israel.

10 You brought down generous rain, and when the Land of Israel was dry, You sent rain to water it.

11 Your flock settled there. My God, in Your goodness You helped the poor.

12 The Lord gave his promise. Those who bore the tidings were a numerous.

13 "The kings of the armies flee quickly away. She who lives with God, divides the plunder."

14 When you lie down with within your boundaries, you will relax protected by the wings of the the Torah and their Mitzvoth.

15 It will snow on the peaks of Zalmon when the Almighty scatters kings and their armies.

16 Mount Bashan is a mountain of God. Mount Bashan is a mountain of peaks.

17 Mountain of peaks, why do you question Him who chose Mount Zion for His home? Surely the Lord will live there forever.

18 The chariots of God arrive by the thousands with the Lord as He did at Sinai in holiness.

יט עָלִיתָ לַמָּרוֹם שָׁבִיתָ שֶּׁבִי לָקַחְתָּ מַתָּנוֹת בָּאָדָם וְאַף סוֹרְרִים לִשְׁכֹּן יָהּ אֱלֹהִים:

כ בָּרוּךְ אֲדֹנָי יוֹם יוֹם יַעֲמָס־לָנוּ הָאֵל יְשׁוּעָתֵנוּ סֶלָה:

כא הָאֵל לָנוּ אֵל לְמוֹשָׁעוֹת וְלֵיהוִה אֲדֹנָי לַמָּוֶת תּוֹצָאוֹת:

כב אַךְ־אֱלֹהִים יִמְחַץ רֹאשׁ אֹיְבָיו קָדְקֹד שֵׂעָר מִתְהַלֵּךְ בַּאֲשָׁמָיו:

כג אָמַר אֲדֹנָי מִבָּשָׁן אָשִׁיב אָשִׁיב מִמְּצֻלוֹת יָם:

כד לְמַעַן תִּמְחַץ רַגְלְךָ בְּדָם לְשׁוֹן כְּלָבֶיךָ מֵאֹיְבִים מִנֵּהוּ:

כה רָאוּ הֲלִיכוֹתֶיךָ אֱלֹהִים הֲלִיכוֹת אֵלִי מַלְכִּי בַקֹּדֶשׁ:

כו קִדְּמוּ שָׁרִים אַחַר נֹגְנִים בְּתוֹךְ עֲלָמוֹת תּוֹפֵפוֹת:

כז בְּמַקְהֵלוֹת בָּרְכוּ אֱלֹהִים יְהוָה מִמְּקוֹר יִשְׂרָאֵל:

כח שָׁם בִּנְיָמִן צָעִיר רֹדֵם שָׂרֵי יְהוּדָה רִגְמָתָם שָׂרֵי זְבֻלוּן שָׂרֵי נַפְתָּלִי:

כט צִוָּה אֱלֹהֶיךָ עֻזֶּךָ עוּזָּה אֱלֹהִים זוּ פָּעַלְתָּ לָּנוּ:

ל מֵהֵיכָלֶךָ עַל־יְרוּשָׁלָ͏ִם לְךָ יוֹבִילוּ מְלָכִים שָׁי:

לא גְּעַר חַיַּת קָנֶה עֲדַת אַבִּירִים בְּעֶגְלֵי עַמִּים מִתְרַפֵּס בְּרַצֵּי־כָסֶף בִּזַּר עַמִּים קְרָבוֹת יֶחְפָּצוּ:

לב יֶאֱתָיוּ חַשְׁמַנִּים מִנִּי מִצְרָיִם כּוּשׁ תָּרִיץ יָדָיו לֵאלֹהִים:

לג מַמְלְכוֹת הָאָרֶץ שִׁירוּ לֵאלֹהִים זַמְּרוּ אֲדֹנָי סֶלָה:

לד לָרֹכֵב בִּשְׁמֵי שְׁמֵי־קֶדֶם הֵן יִתֵּן בְּקוֹלוֹ קוֹל עֹז:

לה תְּנוּ עֹז לֵאלֹהִים עַל־יִשְׂרָאֵל גַּאֲוָתוֹ וְעֻזּוֹ בַּשְּׁחָקִים:

לו נוֹרָא אֱלֹהִים מִמִּקְדָּשֶׁיךָ אֵל יִשְׂרָאֵל הוּא נֹתֵן עֹז וְתַעֲצֻמוֹת לָעָם בָּרוּךְ אֱלֹהִים:

19 You went up to Your throne. The enemy was captured. You are praised by human beings. Now even the rebellious lives with You.

20 Blessed be the Lord every day, for He gives us a burden to bear even He helps us. Selah.

21 He is the God who saves us, and to God, the Lord, belong the ways of death.

22 God will strike the heads of His enemies, the hairy head of those untroubled by their guilt.

23 The Lord said, "I will bring you back from the nations of Bashan and from the deep sea."

24 Israel's feet will wade through blood, and your dogs will take portions from your enemies.

25 They see You, my God, my King, going there in Holiness.

26 The singers are followed by the minstrels in the midst of women playing on the drums.

27 Let us bless God in full assembly. Bless the Lord, the Master of Israel from the beginning.

28 There Benjamin, the youngest of the tribes, rules the enemy; the princes of Judah, stone them as do, the princes of Zevulun and the princes of Naphtali.

29 Through Your strength, our God, You helped us to win. Our God is strong. You have fought for us.

30 You rule from Your Sanctuary in Jerusalem, and the kings will give You honor there.

31 Chastise the wild beast of the reeds, the herd of bulls, among the calves of the nations, who bow down for pieces of silver. He has scattered the nations that desired war.

32 The nobles will come out of Egypt, and Ethiopia will hurry to stretch out its hands to You.

33 Sing to God, nations of the earth! Sing praises to the Lord. Selah.

34 Sing to Him as He moves in the heaven of heavens, from the time of creation speaking with His mighty voice.

35 Beware of the might of God. His beauty is over Israel and His strength is in the heavens.

36 Powerful is God in His holy places. The God of Israel gives strength and power to His people. Blessed be God.

פרק סט

א לַמְנַצֵּחַ עַל־שׁוֹשַׁנִּים לְדָוִד:

ב הוֹשִׁיעֵנִי אֱלֹהִים כִּי בָאוּ מַיִם עַד־נָפֶשׁ:

ג טָבַעְתִּי בִּיוֵן מְצוּלָה וְאֵין מָעֳמָד בָּאתִי בְמַעֲמַקֵּי־מַיִם וְשִׁבֹּלֶת שְׁטָפָתְנִי:

ד יָגַעְתִּי בְקָרְאִי נִחַר גְּרוֹנִי כָּלוּ עֵינַי מְיַחֵל לֵאלֹהָי:

ה רַבּוּ מִשַּׂעֲרוֹת רֹאשִׁי שֹׂנְאַי חִנָּם עָצְמוּ מַצְמִיתַי אֹיְבַי שֶׁקֶר אֲשֶׁר לֹא־גָזַלְתִּי אָז אָשִׁיב:

ו אֱלֹהִים אַתָּה יָדַעְתָּ לְאִוַּלְתִּי וְאַשְׁמוֹתַי מִמְּךָ לֹא־נִכְחָדוּ:

ז אַל־יֵבֹשׁוּ בִי קֹוֶיךָ אֲדֹנָי יְהוִה צְבָאוֹת אַל־יִכָּלְמוּ בִי מְבַקְשֶׁיךָ אֱלֹהֵי יִשְׂרָאֵל:

ח כִּי־עָלֶיךָ נָשָׂאתִי חֶרְפָּה כִּסְּתָה כְלִמָּה פָנָי:

ט מוּזָר הָיִיתִי לְאֶחָי וְנָכְרִי לִבְנֵי אִמִּי:

י כִּי־קִנְאַת בֵּיתְךָ אֲכָלָתְנִי וְחֶרְפּוֹת חוֹרְפֶיךָ נָפְלוּ עָלָי:

יא וָאֶבְכֶּה בַצּוֹם נַפְשִׁי וַתְּהִי לַחֲרָפוֹת לִי:

יב וָאֶתְּנָה לְבוּשִׁי שָׂק וָאֱהִי לָהֶם לְמָשָׁל:

יג יָשִׂיחוּ בִי יֹשְׁבֵי שָׁעַר וּנְגִינוֹת שׁוֹתֵי שֵׁכָר:

יד וַאֲנִי תְפִלָּתִי־לְךָ יְהוָה עֵת רָצוֹן אֱלֹהִים בְּרָב־חַסְדֶּךָ עֲנֵנִי בֶּאֱמֶת יִשְׁעֶךָ:

טו הַצִּילֵנִי מִטִּיט וְאַל־אֶטְבָּעָה אִנָּצְלָה מִשֹּׂנְאַי וּמִמַּעֲמַקֵּי־מָיִם:

טז אַל־תִּשְׁטְפֵנִי שִׁבֹּלֶת מַיִם וְאַל־תִּבְלָעֵנִי מְצוּלָה וְאַל־תֶּאְטַר עָלַי בְּאֵר פִּיהָ:

יז עֲנֵנִי יְהוָה כִּי־טוֹב חַסְדֶּךָ כְּרֹב רַחֲמֶיךָ פְּנֵה אֵלָי:

יח וְאַל־תַּסְתֵּר פָּנֶיךָ מֵעַבְדֶּךָ כִּי־צַר־לִי מַהֵר עֲנֵנִי:

TEHILLIM 69

A cry to God for salvation

1 For the chief musician, on the rose of Israel, by David.

2 Save me, my God, because the flooding water has reached my soul.

3 I have sunk into deep trouble and I am not safe. I have come into deep waters and the whirlpool has swept me away.

4 I am tired from weeping and my throat is dry. My eyes will not stay open as I wait for my God.

5 Those who hate me without reason are more numerous than the hair on my head. They are many who are my enemies who accuse me of falsehood. How can I give back something that I did not steal?

6 God, You know how foolish I have been. My sins are not hidden from You.

7 Let those who wait for You not suffer shame because of me, Lord God of Hosts. Do not let me become a source of disgrace to those who seek You, God of Israel.

8 For Your sake, I have suffered insult; my face has been covered by disgrace.

9 I have become a stranger to my brothers and an alien to my mother's children

10 Because zeal for Your house has devoured me, and the insults of those who would insult You has fallen upon me.

11 My soul has wept with fasting, and it was humiliating to me.

12 I made sackcloth my clothing, and I became an example to them.

13 Those who sit at the gate talk about me, and I have become a song for drunkards.

14 Still, let my prayer come to You, Lord, at an acceptable time, God, in Your great mercy; answer me with the truth of Your salvation.

15 Save me from the quicksand, and do not let me sink. Let me be rescued from my enemies, and from the deep waters.

16 Don't let the flood waters overwhelm me. Don't not let me go down into the deep, and don't let the grave shut its mouth over me.

17 Answer me, Lord, for Your loving kindness is good; as one of Your many compassionate acts, turn toward me.

18 Do not hide Your face from Your servant, for I am in trouble; quickly answer me.

19 Come near and save my life, and ransom me because of my enemies.

יט קָרְבָה אֶל־נַפְשִׁי גְאָלָהּ לְמַעַן אֹיְבַי פְּדֵנִי׃

כ אַתָּה יָדַעְתָּ חֶרְפָּתִי וּבָשְׁתִּי וּכְלִמָּתִי נֶגְדְּךָ כָּל־צוֹרְרָי׃

כא חֶרְפָּה שָׁבְרָה לִבִּי וָאָנוּשָׁה וָאֲקַוֶּה לָנוּד וָאַיִן וְלַמְנַחֲמִים וְלֹא מָצָאתִי׃

כב וַיִּתְּנוּ בְּבָרוּתִי רֹאשׁ וְלִצְמָאִי יַשְׁקוּנִי חֹמֶץ׃

כג יְהִי שֻׁלְחָנָם לִפְנֵיהֶם לְפָח וְלִשְׁלוֹמִים לְמוֹקֵשׁ׃

כד תֶּחְשַׁכְנָה עֵינֵיהֶם מֵרְאוֹת וּמָתְנֵיהֶם תָּמִיד הַמְעַד׃

כה שְׁפָךְ־עֲלֵיהֶם זַעְמֶךָ וַחֲרוֹן אַפְּךָ יַשִּׂיגֵם׃

כו תְּהִי־טִירָתָם נְשַׁמָּה בְּאָהֳלֵיהֶם אַל־יְהִי יֹשֵׁב׃

כז כִּי־אַתָּה אֲשֶׁר־הִכִּיתָ רָדָפוּ וְאֶל־מַכְאוֹב חֲלָלֶיךָ יְסַפֵּרוּ׃

כח תְּנָה־עָוֺן עַל־עֲוֺנָם וְאַל־יָבֹאוּ בְּצִדְקָתֶךָ׃

כט יִמָּחוּ מִסֵּפֶר חַיִּים וְעִם צַדִּיקִים אַל־יִכָּתֵבוּ׃

ל וַאֲנִי עָנִי וְכוֹאֵב יְשׁוּעָתְךָ אֱלֹהִים תְּשַׂגְּבֵנִי׃

לא אֲהַלְלָה שֵׁם־אֱלֹהִים בְּשִׁיר וַאֲגַדְּלֶנּוּ בְתוֹדָה׃

לב וְתִיטַב לַיהוָה מִשּׁוֹר פָּר מַקְרִן מַפְרִיס׃

לג רָאוּ עֲנָוִים יִשְׂמָחוּ דֹּרְשֵׁי אֱלֹהִים וִיחִי לְבַבְכֶם׃

לד כִּי־שֹׁמֵעַ אֶל־אֶבְיוֹנִים יְהוָה וְאֶת־אֲסִירָיו לֹא בָזָה׃

לה יְהַלְלוּהוּ שָׁמַיִם וָאָרֶץ יַמִּים וְכָל־רֹמֵשׂ בָּם׃

לו כִּי אֱלֹהִים יוֹשִׁיעַ צִיּוֹן וְיִבְנֶה עָרֵי יְהוּדָה וְיָשְׁבוּ שָׁם וִירֵשׁוּהָ׃

לז וְזֶרַע עֲבָדָיו יִנְחָלוּהָ וְאֹהֲבֵי שְׁמוֹ יִשְׁכְּנוּ־בָהּ׃

20 You are aware of my suffering, my shame and my confusion. My enemies are known to You.

21 Humiliation has broken my heart and I am very sick. I looked for someone to show me compassion and comfort me, but there was none to be found.

22 They poisoned my food and gave me vinegar to quench my thirst.

23 May their own table cause trouble for them and let their peace be a trap for them.

24 May their eyes be darkened so they do not see and their hips always tremble.

25 Bring Your punishment on them and cause Your hot anger to come to them.

26 May their dwellings be destroyed so that no one can live in their tents.

27 They persecute the Israelites you have attacked and recount the suffering of those you have wounded.

28 Add sin to their sin so they can never enjoy Your righteousness.

29 May they be removed from the book of life and not be mentioned with the righteous.

30 But I am suffering and in pain. My God, put me up on high with Your salvation.

31 I will sing to the name of God with a song and praise Him with gratitude.

32 It will please the Lord better than the sacrifice of a bull with horns and hoofs.

33 The humble will see this and rejoice, and their hearts, which seek God, will revive.

34 The Lord listens to the needy and does not forget His prisoners.

35 May heaven and earth praise Him, and also the seas and everything that moves within it.

36 God will save Zion and build the cities of Judah, and will live there and possess it, once more.

37 The children of His servants will inherit it, and those who love His name will dwell in Zion.

פרק ע

א לַמְנַצֵּחַ לְדָוִד לְהַזְכִּיר:

ב אֱלֹהִים לְהַצִּילֵנִי יְהֹוָה לְעֶזְרָתִי חוּשָׁה:

ג יֵבשׁוּ וְיַחְפְּרוּ מְבַקְשֵׁי נַפְשִׁי יִסֹּגוּ אָחוֹר וְיִכָּלְמוּ חֲפֵצֵי רָעָתִי:

ד יָשׁוּבוּ עַל־עֵקֶב בָּשְׁתָּם הָאֹמְרִים הֶאָח הֶאָח:

ה יָשִׂישׂוּ וְיִשְׂמְחוּ בְּךָ כָּל־מְבַקְשֶׁיךָ וְיֹאמְרוּ תָמִיד יִגְדַּל אֱלֹהִים אֹהֲבֵי יְשׁוּעָתֶךָ:

ו וַאֲנִי עָנִי וְאֶבְיוֹן אֱלֹהִים חוּשָׁה־לִּי עֶזְרִי וּמְפַלְטִי אַתָּה יְהֹוָה אַל־תְּאַחַר:

פרק עא

א בְּךָ־יְהֹוָה חָסִיתִי אַל־אֵבוֹשָׁה לְעוֹלָם:

ב בְּצִדְקָתְךָ תַּצִּילֵנִי וּתְפַלְּטֵנִי הַטֵּה־אֵלַי אָזְנְךָ וְהוֹשִׁיעֵנִי:

ג הֱיֵה לִי לְצוּר מָעוֹן לָבוֹא תָּמִיד צִוִּיתָ לְהוֹשִׁיעֵנִי כִּי־סַלְעִי וּמְצוּדָתִי אָתָּה:

ד אֱלֹהַי פַּלְּטֵנִי מִיַּד רָשָׁע מִכַּף מְעַוֵּל וְחוֹמֵץ:

ה כִּי־אַתָּה תִקְוָתִי אֲדֹנָי יְהֹוָה מִבְטַחִי מִנְּעוּרָי:

ו עָלֶיךָ נִסְמַכְתִּי מִבֶּטֶן מִמְּעֵי אִמִּי אַתָּה גוֹזִי בְּךָ תְהִלָּתִי תָמִיד:

ז כְּמוֹפֵת הָיִיתִי לְרַבִּים וְאַתָּה מַחֲסִי־עֹז:

ח יִמָּלֵא פִי תְּהִלָּתֶךָ כָּל־הַיּוֹם תִּפְאַרְתֶּךָ:

ט אַל־תַּשְׁלִיכֵנִי לְעֵת זִקְנָה כִּכְלוֹת כֹּחִי אַל־תַּעַזְבֵנִי:

י כִּי־אָמְרוּ אוֹיְבַי לִי וְשֹׁמְרֵי נַפְשִׁי נוֹעֲצוּ יַחְדָּו:

TEHILLIM 70

A song asking God not to delay His help

1 For the chief musician, by David, to serve as a memorial.
2 My God, save me. My Lord, hurry to help me.
3 May those who seek my life be ashamed and embarrassed. May those who are pleased when I suffer fall back and be disgraced.
4 May their shame cause them to turn back – those who laugh and say "Aha, aha!"
5 But let everyone who seeks You be happy and rejoice with You. Everyone who appreciates Your help will always say, "May God be greatly praised."
6 As for me, I am poor and needy. My God, please hurry to me. You are my help and my rescuer. My God, do not delay.

TEHILLIM 71

A song of confidence in God

1 I have taken shelter in You, my Lord. Let me never be put to shame.
2 Help me with Your kindness and save me. Listen to me and save me.
3 Be a rock of protection to me so that I may always turn to You. You are prepared to save me because You are my Rock and my safety.
4 My God, rescue me from the hand of evildoers and from the hand of evil and cruel people.
5 For You, my Lord God, are my hope and my trust from my youth.
6 I have relied on You from my birth. You took me from my mother's womb. I am always grateful to You.
7 Many people were amazed by me, but You were always my strong shelter.
8 My mouth utters praises and songs to You all day long.
9 Do not cast me off in my old age. Do not leave me when my strength runs out.
10 My enemies speak about me. They conspire against my life.
11 They say, "God has forgotten him. Pursue him and capture him because no one will save him."
12 My God, be close to me and hurry to help me.

יא לֵאמֹר אֱלֹהִים עֲזָבוֹ רִדְפוּ וְתִפְשׂוּהוּ כִּי אֵין מַצִּיל:

יב אֱלֹהִים אַל־תִּרְחַק מִמֶּנִּי אֱלֹהַי לְעֶזְרָתִי חִישָׁה [חוּשָׁה]:

יג יֵבֹשׁוּ יִכְלוּ שֹׂטְנֵי נַפְשִׁי יַעֲטוּ חֶרְפָּה וּכְלִמָּה מְבַקְשֵׁי רָעָתִי:

יד וַאֲנִי תָּמִיד אֲיַחֵל וְהוֹסַפְתִּי עַל־כָּל־תְּהִלָּתֶךָ:

טו פִּי יְסַפֵּר צִדְקָתֶךָ כָּל־הַיּוֹם תְּשׁוּעָתֶךָ כִּי לֹא יָדַעְתִּי סְפֹרוֹת:

טז אָבוֹא בִּגְבֻרוֹת אֲדֹנָי יְהוִה אַזְכִּיר צִדְקָתְךָ לְבַדֶּךָ:

יז אֱלֹהִים לִמַּדְתַּנִי מִנְּעוּרָי וְעַד־הֵנָּה אַגִּיד נִפְלְאוֹתֶיךָ:

יח וְגַם עַד־זִקְנָה וְשֵׂיבָה אֱלֹהִים אַל־תַּעַזְבֵנִי עַד־אַגִּיד זְרוֹעֲךָ לְדוֹר לְכָל־
יָבוֹא גְּבוּרָתֶךָ:

יט וְצִדְקָתְךָ אֱלֹהִים עַד־מָרוֹם אֲשֶׁר־עָשִׂיתָ גְדֹלוֹת אֱלֹהִים מִי כָמוֹךָ:

כ אֲשֶׁר הראיתנו [הִרְאִיתַנִי] צָרוֹת רַבּוֹת וְרָעוֹת תָּשׁוּב תחיינו [תְּחַיֵּינִי]
וּמִתְּהֹמוֹת הָאָרֶץ תָּשׁוּב תַּעֲלֵנִי:

כא תֶּרֶב גְּדֻלָּתִי וְתִסֹּב תְּנַחֲמֵנִי:

כב גַּם־אֲנִי אוֹדְךָ בִכְלִי־נֶבֶל אֲמִתְּךָ אֱלֹהָי אֲזַמְּרָה לְךָ בְכִנּוֹר קְדוֹשׁ יִשְׂרָאֵל:

כג תְּרַנֵּנָּה שְׂפָתַי כִּי אֲזַמְּרָה־לָּךְ וְנַפְשִׁי אֲשֶׁר פָּדִיתָ:

כד גַּם־לְשׁוֹנִי כָּל־הַיּוֹם תֶּהְגֶּה צִדְקָתֶךָ כִּי־בֹשׁוּ כִי־חָפְרוּ מְבַקְשֵׁי רָעָתִי:

פרק עב

א לִשְׁלֹמֹה אֱלֹהִים מִשְׁפָּטֶיךָ לְמֶלֶךְ תֵּן וְצִדְקָתְךָ לְבֶן־מֶלֶךְ:

ב יָדִין עַמְּךָ בְצֶדֶק וַעֲנִיֶּיךָ בְמִשְׁפָּט:

ג יִשְׂאוּ הָרִים שָׁלוֹם לָעָם וּגְבָעוֹת בִּצְדָקָה:

ד יִשְׁפֹּט עֲנִיֵּי־עָם יוֹשִׁיעַ לִבְנֵי אֶבְיוֹן וִידַכֵּא עוֹשֵׁק:

13 May those who seek my life be ashamed and punished. May those who seek to harm me be covered with humiliation and disgrace.

14 I will always hope, and will thank You more and more.

15 I will tell of Your righteousness and Your salvation every day, for they are infinite.

16 I will tell of Your greatness, the righteousness that is Yours alone.

17 My God, You have taught me from my youth and I continue to speak of Your great acts.

18 My God, do not leave me in old age and weakness until I have told the next generation of Your greatness and power to everyone.

19 My God, Your goodness reaches to the high heavens. You have performed the greatest things. My God, who is like You?

20 You have sent me many terrible troubles, but You will quickly save me and bring me up from the depths of the earth.

21 You will increase my greatness, and come and comfort me.

22 I will give thanks to You with music of the lyre, for your faithfulness. I will sing praises with the harp – to You, the Holy One of Israel.

23 My lips will rejoice when I sing thanks to You, together with my soul, which You have saved.

24 Let those who seek to harm me be ashamed and embarrassed – and I will tell of Your greatness all day long.

TEHILLIM 72

This song presents the ideal for the nation's happiness and safety

1 [A psalm] for Solomon. God, give the king Your judgments, and give Your righteousness to the king's son

2 So that he will judge Your people with righteousness and Your poor with justice.

3 May peace come to the people from the mountains and the hills, through righteousness.

ה יִירָאוּךָ עִם־שָׁמֶשׁ וְלִפְנֵי יָרֵחַ דּוֹר דּוֹרִים:

ו יֵרֵד כְּמָטָר עַל־גֵּז כִּרְבִיבִים זַרְזִיף אָרֶץ:

ז יִפְרַח־בְּיָמָיו צַדִּיק וְרֹב שָׁלוֹם עַד־בְּלִי יָרֵחַ:

ח וְיֵרְדְּ מִיָּם עַד־יָם וּמִנָּהָר עַד־אַפְסֵי־אָרֶץ:

ט לְפָנָיו יִכְרְעוּ צִיִּים וְאֹיְבָיו עָפָר יְלַחֵכוּ:

י מַלְכֵי תַרְשִׁישׁ וְאִיִּים מִנְחָה יָשִׁיבוּ מַלְכֵי שְׁבָא וּסְבָא אֶשְׁכָּר יַקְרִיבוּ:

יא וְיִשְׁתַּחֲווּ־לוֹ כָל־מְלָכִים כָּל־גּוֹיִם יַעַבְדוּהוּ:

יב כִּי־יַצִּיל אֶבְיוֹן מְשַׁוֵּעַ וְעָנִי וְאֵין־עֹזֵר לוֹ:

יג יָחֹס עַל־דַּל וְאֶבְיוֹן וְנַפְשׁוֹת אֶבְיוֹנִים יוֹשִׁיעַ:

יד מִתּוֹךְ וּמֵחָמָס יִגְאַל נַפְשָׁם וְיֵיקַר דָּמָם בְּעֵינָיו:

טו וִיחִי וְיִתֶּן־לוֹ מִזְּהַב שְׁבָא וְיִתְפַּלֵּל בַּעֲדוֹ תָמִיד כָּל־הַיּוֹם יְבָרֲכֶנְהוּ:

טז יְהִי פִסַּת־בַּר בָּאָרֶץ בְּרֹאשׁ הָרִים יִרְעַשׁ כַּלְּבָנוֹן פִּרְיוֹ וְיָצִיצוּ מֵעִיר כְּעֵשֶׂב הָאָרֶץ:

יז יְהִי שְׁמוֹ לְעוֹלָם לִפְנֵי שֶׁמֶשׁ ינין [יִנּוֹן] שְׁמוֹ וְיִתְבָּרְכוּ בוֹ כָּל־גּוֹיִם יְאַשְּׁרוּהוּ:

יח בָּרוּךְ יְהוָה אֱלֹהִים אֱלֹהֵי יִשְׂרָאֵל עֹשֵׂה נִפְלָאוֹת לְבַדּוֹ:

יט וּבָרוּךְ שֵׁם כְּבוֹדוֹ לְעוֹלָם וְיִמָּלֵא כְבוֹדוֹ אֶת־כָּל־הָאָרֶץ אָמֵן וְאָמֵן:

כ כָּלּוּ תְפִלּוֹת דָּוִד בֶּן־יִשָׁי:

4 May he judge the poor among the people and save the needy children, and crush the oppressor.

5 While there is yet a sun they will fear him, and as long as the moon exists all generations will know him.

6 May his words come down like rain upon the cut grass and like showers that water the earth.

7 May the righteous benefit during his reign and may there be only peace until the moon is no more.

8 May he rule from sea to sea and from the river to the ends of the earth.

9 May those who live in the wilderness bow down to him, and may his enemies be defeated.

10 The kings of Tarshish and of all the islands will send tribute, and the kings of Sheba and Seba will offer him gifts.

11 All the kings will bow down before him, and all the nations will serve him.

12 He will save the poor when they cry out. He will save the needy and of those who have no one to help them.

13 He will have compassion upon the poor and the needy, and he will save their lives.

14 He will save their souls from oppression and violence, and hold their blood precious in his sight.

15 Then they will live, and he will give them gold from Sheba, so that they will pray for him always and bless him all day long.

16 May the rich grains of the land extend to the top of the mountains. May the corn blow in the wind like the cedars of Mount Lebanon, and may they thrive outside the city like the grass in the fields.

17 May the king's name be known for ever and continue for as long as the sun. May people be blessed through him, and may all nations praise him.

18 Blessed be the Lord God, the God of Israel, Who alone does wondrous things.

19 Blessed be His glorious name forever, and may the whole earth be filed with His glory. Amen and amen.

20 The prayers of David, son of Yishai are complete.[1]

---

1 The prayers of King David have not ended. They exist forever and we cherish them with love.

פרק עג

א מִזְמוֹר לְאָסָף אַךְ טוֹב לְיִשְׂרָאֵל אֱלֹהִים לְבָרֵי לֵבָב:

ב וַאֲנִי כִּמְעַט נטוי [נָטָיוּ] רַגְלָי כְּאַיִן שפכה [שֻׁפְּכוּ] אֲשֻׁרָי:

ג כִּי־קִנֵּאתִי בַּהוֹלְלִים שְׁלוֹם רְשָׁעִים אֶרְאֶה:

ד כִּי אֵין חַרְצֻבּוֹת לְמוֹתָם וּבָרִיא אוּלָם:

ה בַּעֲמַל אֱנוֹשׁ אֵינֵמוֹ וְעִם־אָדָם לֹא יְנֻגָּעוּ:

ו לָכֵן עֲנָקַתְמוֹ גַאֲוָה יַעֲטָף־שִׁית חָמָס לָמוֹ:

ז יָצָא מֵחֵלֶב עֵינֵמוֹ עָבְרוּ מַשְׂכִּיּוֹת לֵבָב:

ח יָמִיקוּ וִידַבְּרוּ בְרָע עֹשֶׁק מִמָּרוֹם יְדַבֵּרוּ:

ט שַׁתּוּ בַשָּׁמַיִם פִּיהֶם וּלְשׁוֹנָם תִּהֲלַךְ בָּאָרֶץ:

י לָכֵן ישיב [יָשׁוּב] עַמּוֹ הֲלֹם וּמֵי מָלֵא יִמָּצוּ לָמוֹ:

יא וְאָמְרוּ אֵיכָה יָדַע־אֵל וְיֵשׁ דֵּעָה בְעֶלְיוֹן:

יב הִנֵּה־אֵלֶּה רְשָׁעִים וְשַׁלְוֵי עוֹלָם הִשְׂגּוּ־חָיִל:

יג אַךְ־רִיק זִכִּיתִי לְבָבִי וָאֶרְחַץ בְּנִקָּיוֹן כַּפָּי:

יד וָאֱהִי נָגוּעַ כָּל־הַיּוֹם וְתוֹכַחְתִּי לַבְּקָרִים:

טו אִם־אָמַרְתִּי אֲסַפְּרָה כְמוֹ הִנֵּה דוֹר בָּנֶיךָ בָגָדְתִּי:

טז וָאֲחַשְּׁבָה לָדַעַת זֹאת עָמָל היא [הוּא] בְעֵינָי:

יז עַד־אָבוֹא אֶל־מִקְדְּשֵׁי־אֵל אָבִינָה לְאַחֲרִיתָם:

יח אַךְ בַּחֲלָקוֹת תָּשִׁית לָמוֹ הִפַּלְתָּם לְמַשּׁוּאוֹת:

יט אֵיךְ הָיוּ לְשַׁמָּה כְרָגַע סָפוּ תַמּוּ מִן־בַּלָּהוֹת:

כ כַּחֲלוֹם מֵהָקִיץ אֲדֹנָי בָּעִיר צַלְמָם תִּבְזֶה:

כא כִּי־יִתְחַמֵּץ לְבָבִי וְכִלְיוֹתַי אֶשְׁתּוֹנָן:

TEHILLIM 73

While evildoers may appear to prosper, this song provides faith that righteous people are always rewarded

1 A psalm by Asaph. God is certainly good to Israel and to the pure of heart.

2 But I was very weak. My feet were almost turned away, and my footsteps almost swept aside

3 Because I saw how evildoers prospered, and I was envious.

4 They did not suffer at death, and their bodies were sound.

5 They have no troubles making a living and are not punished like other people.

6 They show their pride and their violence openly and publicly.

7 Their eyes show confidence bulging from fat bodies while their hearts meditate on terrible evil.

8 They laugh and speak evilly. They speak out of the feeling that they are above everyone.

9 Their mouths speak against heaven and their tongues have no fear of mankind.

10 The people of God are influenced by them, and their understanding of Torah is drained out of them.

11 They began to ask "Does God know? Is God aware of what's happening?"

12 This the way of evildoers. Though they do not worry, they still become richer.

13 "For nothing have I kept my heart pure and my hands innocent of wrongdoing.

14 My sorrows come upon me all day and I suffer anew each morning".

15 Had I thought to express my feelings, this would have caused me to be unfaithful to the generation of Your children.

16 When I wondered about my feelings, I became upset.

17 Then I went to the Sanctuaries of God and understood what is in store for those who do evil.

18 You put them in unsafe places and send them to destruction.

19 Suddenly they are desolate and utterly destroyed by punishment.

20 Like a dream after we awaken, so you despise their appearance in Jerusalem.

21 When my heart is upset and my passions control me.

22 I behave terribly, stupidly, like a beast toward You.

כב וַאֲנִי־בַעַר וְלֹא אֵדָע בְּהֵמוֹת הָיִיתִי עִמָּךְ:

כג וַאֲנִי תָמִיד עִמָּךְ אָחַזְתָּ בְּיַד־יְמִינִי:

כד בַּעֲצָתְךָ תַנְחֵנִי וְאַחַר כָּבוֹד תִּקָּחֵנִי:

כה מִי־לִי בַשָּׁמָיִם וְעִמְּךָ לֹא־חָפַצְתִּי בָאָרֶץ:

כו כָּלָה שְׁאֵרִי וּלְבָבִי צוּר־לְבָבִי וְחֶלְקִי אֱלֹהִים לְעוֹלָם:

כז כִּי־הִנֵּה רְחֵקֶיךָ יֹאבֵדוּ הִצְמַתָּה כָּל־זוֹנֶה מִמֶּךָּ:

כח וַאֲנִי קִרֲבַת אֱלֹהִים לִי־טוֹב שַׁתִּי בַּאדֹנָי יְהֹוִה מַחְסִי לְסַפֵּר כָּל־מַלְאֲכוֹתֶיךָ:

פרק עד

א מַשְׂכִּיל לְאָסָף לָמָה אֱלֹהִים זָנַחְתָּ לָנֶצַח יֶעְשַׁן אַפְּךָ בְּצֹאן מַרְעִיתֶךָ:

ב זְכֹר עֲדָתְךָ קָנִיתָ קֶּדֶם גָּאַלְתָּ שֵׁבֶט נַחֲלָתֶךָ הַר־צִיּוֹן זֶה שָׁכַנְתָּ בּוֹ:

ג הָרִימָה פְעָמֶיךָ לְמַשֻּׁאוֹת נֶצַח כָּל־הֵרַע אוֹיֵב בַּקֹּדֶשׁ:

ד שָׁאֲגוּ צֹרְרֶיךָ בְּקֶרֶב מוֹעֲדֶךָ שָׂמוּ אוֹתֹתָם אֹתוֹת:

ה יִוָּדַע כְּמֵבִיא לְמָעְלָה בִּסֲבָךְ־עֵץ קַרְדֻּמּוֹת:

ו ועת [וְעַתָּה] פִּתּוּחֶיהָ יָּחַד בְּכַשִּׁיל וְכֵילַפֹּת יַהֲלֹמוּן:

ז שִׁלְחוּ בָאֵשׁ מִקְדָּשֶׁךָ לָאָרֶץ חִלְּלוּ מִשְׁכַּן־שְׁמֶךָ:

ח אָמְרוּ בְלִבָּם נִינָם יָחַד שָׂרְפוּ כָל־מוֹעֲדֵי־אֵל בָּאָרֶץ:

ט אֹתוֹתֵינוּ לֹא רָאִינוּ אֵין־עוֹד נָבִיא וְלֹא־אִתָּנוּ יֹדֵעַ עַד־מָה:

י עַד־מָתַי אֱלֹהִים יְחָרֶף צָר יְנָאֵץ אוֹיֵב שִׁמְךָ לָנֶצַח:

יא לָמָּה תָשִׁיב יָדְךָ וִימִינֶךָ מִקֶּרֶב חוקך [חֵיקְךָ] כַלֵּה:

יב וֵאלֹהִים מַלְכִּי מִקֶּדֶם פֹּעֵל יְשׁוּעוֹת בְּקֶרֶב הָאָרֶץ:

23 Yet I am always with You. You hold my right hand.

24 You guide me to Your truth, and You receive me with honor.

25 Whom do I have in heaven but You? I desire only You on earth.

26 Though my body and my heart fail, God is the support of my heart and always saves me.

27 They who are far from You will cease to exist. You destroy those who turn from You.

28 But I am close to God, and that is good. I have made the Lord God my shelter, and I will speak of your acts.

TEHILLIM 74

A song about the destruction of the Sanctuary

1 An instruction by Asaph. Why, my God, have You left us forever? Why does Your anger fume against the flock of Your pasture?

2 Remember Your people whom You chose and rescued, and made Your nation. Remember Mount Zion, where You dwell.

3 Lift up your anger because of the destruction that has been committed and all the other shameful things that the enemy has done to the Sanctuary.

4 Your enemies shouted in Your Sanctuary and raised their banners there.

5 Their attack was against God. They destroyed the Sanctuary with axes, as though they were cutting down trees.

6 They destroyed and ruined all the Sanctuary furniture with hatchets and hammers.

7 They set Your Sanctuary on fire and they razed the House of Your Name to the ground.

8 They said "Let us destroy all their houses of worship together." They burned all the meeting places of God in the land.

9 We do not see our signs of redemption. There is no prophet who knows how long this will last.

10 How long will the enemy continue to destroy? Will the enemy curse Your name forever?

יג אַתָּה פוֹרַרְתָּ בְעָזְּךָ יָם שִׁבַּרְתָּ רָאשֵׁי תַנִּינִים עַל־הַמָּיִם:

יד אַתָּה רִצַּצְתָּ רָאשֵׁי לִוְיָתָן תִּתְּנֶנּוּ מַאֲכָל לְעָם לְצִיִּים:

טו אַתָּה בָקַעְתָּ מַעְיָן וָנָחַל אַתָּה הוֹבַשְׁתָּ נַהֲרוֹת אֵיתָן:

טז לְךָ יוֹם אַף־לְךָ לָיְלָה אַתָּה הֲכִינוֹתָ מָאוֹר וָשָׁמֶשׁ:

יז אַתָּה הִצַּבְתָּ כָּל־גְּבוּלוֹת אָרֶץ קַיִץ וָחֹרֶף אַתָּה יְצַרְתָּם:

יח זְכָר־זֹאת אוֹיֵב חֵרֵף יְהוָה וְעַם־נָבָל נִאֲצוּ שְׁמֶךָ:

יט אַל־תִּתֵּן לְחַיַּת נֶפֶשׁ תּוֹרֶךָ חַיַּת עֲנִיֶּיךָ אַל־תִּשְׁכַּח לָנֶצַח:

כ הַבֵּט־לַבְּרִית כִּי־מָלְאוּ מַחֲשַׁכֵּי־אָרֶץ נְאוֹת חָמָס:

כא אַל־יָשֹׁב דַּךְ נִכְלָם עָנִי וְאֶבְיוֹן יְהַלְלוּ שְׁמֶךָ:

כב קוּמָה אֱלֹהִים רִיבָה רִיבֶךָ זְכֹר חֶרְפָּתְךָ מִנִּי־נָבָל כָּל־הַיּוֹם:

כג אַל־תִּשְׁכַּח קוֹל צֹרְרֶיךָ שְׁאוֹן קָמֶיךָ עֹלֶה תָמִיד:

פרק עה

א לַמְנַצֵּחַ אַל־תַּשְׁחֵת מִזְמוֹר לְאָסָף שִׁיר:

ב הוֹדִינוּ לְךָ אֱלֹהִים הוֹדִינוּ וְקָרוֹב שְׁמֶךָ סִפְּרוּ נִפְלְאוֹתֶיךָ:

ג כִּי־אֶקַּח מוֹעֵד אֲנִי מֵישָׁרִים אֶשְׁפֹּט:

ד נְמֹגִים־אֶרֶץ וְכָל־יֹשְׁבֶיהָ אָנֹכִי תִכַּנְתִּי עַמּוּדֶיהָ סֶּלָה:

ה אָמַרְתִּי לַהוֹלְלִים אַל־תָּהֹלּוּ וְלָרְשָׁעִים אַל־תָּרִימוּ קָרֶן:

ו אַל־תָּרִימוּ לַמָּרוֹם קַרְנְכֶם תְּדַבְּרוּ בְצַוָּאר עָתָק:

11 Why do You not use Your right hand? Draw it from your bosom and destroy them.

12 God has always been my King, helping the people of the earth.

13 You split the sea with Your strength. You broke the heads of the sea monsters in the waters.

14 You crushed the head of Leviathan. You gave him as food to the people living in the wilderness.

15 You split the rocks to give water to the people. You dried up mighty rivers.

16 Day and night alike belong to You; You made the moon and the sun.

17 You made all the boundaries of the world. You made summer and winter.

18 Now remember how the enemy sinned against the Lord, how wicked people cursed Your name.

19 Don't give Your turtledove to the wild beast. Don't forget the lives of Your poor forever.

20 Remember Your agreement with Your people Israel. The land is full of unsafe places filled with violence.

21 Do not make those who suffer wander in confusion. Let the poor and needy praise Your name.

22 My God, arise and act for Your own sake. Remember the terrible deeds of these wicked people all day long.

23 Do not forget the voice of Your enemies or the loud commotion against You that rises up all the time.

TEHILLIM 75

A song of the people's thanksgiving

1 For the chief musician, do not destroy a memorial, a psalm by Asaph, a song.

2 We give thanks to You, my God. We give thanks to Your name, which is close to us. We recount of Your great acts.

3 God says: "I will choose the time in which I Myself will judge justly.

4 When the earth and all the people fell apart, I Myself saved the foundations of the earth." Selah.

5 God tells the ungrateful: Do not act selfishly, and to evildoers He says: Do not act like wild beasts.

6 Do not act wickedly. Do not utter insults with confidence.

ז   כִּי לֹא מִמּוֹצָא וּמִמַּעֲרָב וְלֹא מִמִּדְבַּר הָרִים:

ח   כִּי־אֱלֹהִים שֹׁפֵט זֶה יַשְׁפִּיל וְזֶה יָרִים:

ט   כִּי כוֹס בְּיַד־יְהוָה וְיַיִן חָמַר מָלֵא מֶסֶךְ וַיַּגֵּר מִזֶּה אַךְ־שְׁמָרֶיהָ יִמְצוּ יִשְׁתּוּ כֹּל רִשְׁעֵי־אָרֶץ:

י   וַאֲנִי אַגִּיד לְעֹלָם אֲזַמְּרָה לֵאלֹהֵי יַעֲקֹב:

יא   וְכָל־קַרְנֵי רְשָׁעִים אֲגַדֵּעַ תְּרוֹמַמְנָה קַרְנוֹת צַדִּיק:

פרק עז

א   לַמְנַצֵּחַ בִּנְגִינֹת מִזְמוֹר לְאָסָף שִׁיר:

ב   נוֹדָע בִּיהוּדָה אֱלֹהִים בְּיִשְׂרָאֵל גָּדוֹל שְׁמוֹ:

ג   וַיְהִי בְשָׁלֵם סֻכּוֹ וּמְעוֹנָתוֹ בְצִיּוֹן:

ד   שָׁמָּה שִׁבַּר רִשְׁפֵי־קָשֶׁת מָגֵן וְחֶרֶב וּמִלְחָמָה סֶלָה:

ה   נָאוֹר אַתָּה אַדִּיר מֵהַרְרֵי־טָרֶף:

ו   אֶשְׁתּוֹלְלוּ אַבִּירֵי לֵב נָמוּ שְׁנָתָם וְלֹא־מָצְאוּ כָל־אַנְשֵׁי־חַיִל יְדֵיהֶם:

ז   מִגַּעֲרָתְךָ אֱלֹהֵי יַעֲקֹב נִרְדָּם וְרֶכֶב וָסוּס:

ח   אַתָּה נוֹרָא אַתָּה וּמִי־יַעֲמֹד לְפָנֶיךָ מֵאָז אַפֶּךָ:

ט   מִשָּׁמַיִם הִשְׁמַעְתָּ דִּין אֶרֶץ יָרְאָה וְשָׁקָטָה:

י   בְּקוּם־לַמִּשְׁפָּט אֱלֹהִים לְהוֹשִׁיעַ כָּל־עַנְוֵי־אֶרֶץ סֶלָה:

יא   כִּי־חֲמַת אָדָם תּוֹדֶךָּ שְׁאֵרִית חֵמֹת תַּחְגֹּר:

יב   נִדֲרוּ וְשַׁלְּמוּ לַיהוָה אֱלֹהֵיכֶם כָּל־סְבִיבָיו יוֹבִילוּ שַׁי לַמּוֹרָא:

יג   יִבְצֹר רוּחַ נְגִידִים נוֹרָא לְמַלְכֵי־אָרֶץ:

7 No support for evil will come neither from east or west, nor from the wilderness.

8 God is the judge. He raises one high and brings another down.

9 The Lord has a cup of strong wine in His hand, and He pours it out. All evildoers, all the wicked people of the earth will drink only the dregs at the bottom of this wine.

10 But I will always speak and sing thanks to the God of Jacob.

11 I will cut off the pride of the wicked, but the fortunes of the righteous will be raised.

TEHILLIM 76

A song about God's victories

1 For the chief musician, with string music: a psalm by Asaph, a song.

2 God is known in Judah, and His name is great in Israel.

3 His Tabernacle was in Shalem, and He dwelled in Zion.

4 He destroyed the enemy's arrows, shield, sword and the battle. Selah.

5 You are awesome, mightier than the mountains filled with prey.

6 The strong-hearted soldiers have lost their senses and sleep the sleep of the dead. All the fighting men are helpless.

7 My God of Jacob, with Your rebuke You have brought the sleep of death upon the horses and their riders.

8 You, God, inspire awe. When You are angry, who can stand in Your sight?

9 You pronounced sentence from heaven, and the earth was still out of fear.

10 When God arises to judge it is to save all the humble, good people of the earth. Selah.

11 Even the raging of the wicked will bring praise to You, God. If necessary, You are prepared to fight any further evil.

12 Now fulfill the vows that you made to God. Let all those who are around Him bring gifts to the Awesome One.

13 He destroys the evil thoughts of the princes; the kings of the earth hold him in awe.

פרק עז

א לַמְנַצֵּחַ עַל־יְדִיתוּן [יְדוּתוּן] לְאָסָף מִזְמוֹר:

ב קוֹלִי אֶל־אֱלֹהִים וְאֶצְעָקָה קוֹלִי אֶל־אֱלֹהִים וְהַאֲזִין אֵלָי:

ג בְּיוֹם צָרָתִי אֲדֹנָי דָּרָשְׁתִּי יָדִי לַיְלָה נִגְּרָה וְלֹא תָפוּג מֵאֲנָה הִנָּחֵם נַפְשִׁי:

ד אֶזְכְּרָה אֱלֹהִים וְאֶהֱמָיָה אָשִׂיחָה וְתִתְעַטֵּף רוּחִי סֶלָה:

ה אָחַזְתָּ שְׁמֻרוֹת עֵינָי נִפְעַמְתִּי וְלֹא אֲדַבֵּר:

ו חִשַּׁבְתִּי יָמִים מִקֶּדֶם שְׁנוֹת עוֹלָמִים:

ז אֶזְכְּרָה נְגִינָתִי בַּלָּיְלָה עִם־לְבָבִי אָשִׂיחָה וַיְחַפֵּשׂ רוּחִי:

ח הַלְעוֹלָמִים יִזְנַח אֲדֹנָי וְלֹא־יֹסִיף לִרְצוֹת עוֹד:

ט הֶאָפֵס לָנֶצַח חַסְדּוֹ גָּמַר אֹמֶר לְדֹר וָדֹר:

י הֲשָׁכַח חַנּוֹת אֵל אִם־קָפַץ בְּאַף רַחֲמָיו סֶלָה:

יא וָאֹמַר חַלּוֹתִי הִיא שְׁנוֹת יְמִין עֶלְיוֹן:

יב אזכיר [אֶזְכּוֹר] מַעַלְלֵי־יָהּ כִּי־אֶזְכְּרָה מִקֶּדֶם פִּלְאֶךָ:

יג וְהָגִיתִי בְכָל־פָּעֳלֶךָ וּבַעֲלִילוֹתֶיךָ אָשִׂיחָה:

יד אֱלֹהִים בַּקֹּדֶשׁ דַּרְכֶּךָ מִי־אֵל גָּדוֹל כֵּאלֹהִים:

טו אַתָּה הָאֵל עֹשֵׂה פֶלֶא הוֹדַעְתָּ בָעַמִּים עֻזֶּךָ:

טז גָּאַלְתָּ בִּזְרוֹעַ עַמֶּךָ בְּנֵי־יַעֲקֹב וְיוֹסֵף סֶלָה:

יז רָאוּךָ מַּיִם אֱלֹהִים רָאוּךָ מַּיִם יָחִילוּ אַף יִרְגְּזוּ תְהֹמוֹת:

יח זֹרְמוּ מַיִם עָבוֹת קוֹל נָתְנוּ שְׁחָקִים אַף־חֲצָצֶיךָ יִתְהַלָּכוּ:

יט קוֹל רַעַמְךָ בַּגַּלְגַּל הֵאִירוּ בְרָקִים תֵּבֵל רָגְזָה וַתִּרְעַשׁ הָאָרֶץ:

כ בַּיָּם דַּרְכֶּךָ ושבילך [וּשְׁבִילְךָ] בְּמַיִם רַבִּים וְעִקְּבוֹתֶיךָ לֹא נֹדָעוּ:

כא נָחִיתָ כַצֹּאן עַמֶּךָ בְּיַד־מֹשֶׁה וְאַהֲרֹן:

TEHILLIM 77

A song of the people's suffering

1 For the chief musician, for Jeduthun, a song by Asaph.

2 I will lift up my voice to God and cry. I will lift up my voice to God that He may listen to me.

3 I search for the Lord in the day of my trouble. With my hand raised to You, I searched for You all night long. My soul would not be comforted.

4 I think of how good God has been to me and I get nervous. My soul faints from worry. Selah.

5 You prevented my eyelids from resting. I was in pain and could not speak.

6 I think about the days and years gone by.

7 At night I remember the songs that I used to sing. I meditate, and my soul searches for answers.

8 Has the Lord left me forever? Will He not be good to me anymore?

9 Is there no more loving kindness? Has His promise vanished forever?

10 Has God decided to withhold His goodness? Has His anger prevented Him from being compassionate? Selah.

11 So I say: "It is to frighten me. That is the reason for this change.

12 From now on, I will mention Your great deeds. I will remember your miracles of former days.

13 I will think about all Your great acts and all the great things that You have done".

14 My God, Yours is the way of holiness. Who is like You, mighty God?

15 You are God, Who works wonders, and Your power is known to everyone.

16 With Your power You saved the people, the sons of Jacob and Joseph. Selah.

17 The water of the seas saw You, my God. The waters saw You and trembled; even the depths shook.

18 The clouds poured forth rain and the skies thundered, and Your arrows sped outward.

19 The sound of Your thunder rolled, and lightning lit up the world. The earth trembled and shook.

20 You came through the sea and along the waves. Your footsteps were invisible.

21 You led Your people like children by the hand of Moshe and Aaron.

פרק עח

א מַשְׂכִּיל לְאָסָף הַאֲזִינָה עַמִּי תּוֹרָתִי הַטּוּ אָזְנְכֶם לְאִמְרֵי־פִי:

ב אֶפְתְּחָה בְמָשָׁל פִּי אַבִּיעָה חִידוֹת מִנִּי־קֶדֶם:

ג אֲשֶׁר שָׁמַעְנוּ וַנֵּדָעֵם וַאֲבוֹתֵינוּ סִפְּרוּ־לָנוּ:

ד לֹא נְכַחֵד מִבְּנֵיהֶם לְדוֹר אַחֲרוֹן מְסַפְּרִים תְּהִלּוֹת יְהוָה וֶעֱזוּזוֹ וְנִפְלְאוֹתָיו אֲשֶׁר עָשָׂה:

ה וַיָּקֶם עֵדוּת בְּיַעֲקֹב וְתוֹרָה שָׂם בְּיִשְׂרָאֵל אֲשֶׁר צִוָּה אֶת־אֲבוֹתֵינוּ לְהוֹדִיעָם לִבְנֵיהֶם:

ו לְמַעַן יֵדְעוּ דּוֹר אַחֲרוֹן בָּנִים יִוָּלֵדוּ יָקֻמוּ וִיסַפְּרוּ לִבְנֵיהֶם:

ז וְיָשִׂימוּ בֵאלֹהִים כִּסְלָם וְלֹא יִשְׁכְּחוּ מַעַלְלֵי־אֵל וּמִצְוֹתָיו יִנְצֹרוּ:

ח וְלֹא יִהְיוּ כַּאֲבוֹתָם דּוֹר סוֹרֵר וּמֹרֶה דּוֹר לֹא־הֵכִין לִבּוֹ וְלֹא־נֶאֶמְנָה אֶת־אֵל רוּחוֹ:

ט בְּנֵי־אֶפְרַיִם נוֹשְׁקֵי רוֹמֵי־קָשֶׁת הָפְכוּ בְּיוֹם קְרָב:

י לֹא שָׁמְרוּ בְּרִית אֱלֹהִים וּבְתוֹרָתוֹ מֵאֲנוּ לָלֶכֶת:

יא וַיִּשְׁכְּחוּ עֲלִילוֹתָיו וְנִפְלְאוֹתָיו אֲשֶׁר הֶרְאָם:

יב נֶגֶד אֲבוֹתָם עָשָׂה פֶלֶא בְּאֶרֶץ מִצְרַיִם שְׂדֵה־צֹעַן:

יג בָּקַע יָם וַיַּעֲבִירֵם וַיַּצֶּב־מַיִם כְּמוֹ־נֵד:

יד וַיַּנְחֵם בֶּעָנָן יוֹמָם וְכָל־הַלַּיְלָה בְּאוֹר אֵשׁ:

טו יְבַקַּע צֻרִים בַּמִּדְבָּר וַיַּשְׁקְ כִּתְהֹמוֹת רַבָּה:

טז וַיּוֹצִא נוֹזְלִים מִסָּלַע וַיּוֹרֶד כַּנְּהָרוֹת מָיִם:

יז וַיּוֹסִיפוּ עוֹד לַחֲטֹא־לוֹ לַמְרוֹת עֶלְיוֹן בַּצִּיָּה:

יח וַיְנַסּוּ־אֵל בִּלְבָבָם לִשְׁאָל־אֹכֶל לְנַפְשָׁם:

יט וַיְדַבְּרוּ בֵּאלֹהִים אָמְרוּ הֲיוּכַל אֵל לַעֲרֹךְ שֻׁלְחָן בַּמִּדְבָּר:

TEHILLIM 78

A song instructing people to be faithful to God

1 An instruction by Asaph. My people, be careful to keep the Torah. Hear with your ears the words of my mouth.

2 I will begin with a story. I will speak of solving life's riddles, concerning days past,

3 Things that we heard and knew and that our forebears told us.

4 We will tell the generation of our children to come and thank the Lord for His mighty help and for the great things that he has done for us.

5 He made a tradition for the children of Jacob and gave the Torah to Israel, commanding our forebears that they teach the Torah to their children,

6 So that the children yet to be born and all future generations will know the Torah. They will come and teach all their children

7 To put their trust in God, not to forget all God's deeds and to keep His commandments.

8 So that their children will not be like their forebears, a stubborn and rebellious generation, a generation whose heart did not accept God and were not loyal to God, in spirit.

9 The tribe of Ephraim, who shot the bow, retreated in time of battle.

10 They did not keep their agreement with God, to follow His law.

11 They forgot all that He had done and all the great things that He had revealed to them.

12 He worked miracles in the sight of their ancestors in the land of Egypt, in the field of Zoan.

13 He split the sea and allowed them to pass through. He made the waters to stand like a wall.

14 He led them with a cloud during the day and with a light of fire during the night.

15 He split the rocks in the desert and provided them with abundant water to drink, as if from a deep sea.

16 He brought flowing streams out of the rock and caused water to flow like rivers.

17 But they sinned against Him and opposed Him in the desert.

18 They doubted God in their hearts and asked for food to satisfy their desires.

כ הֵן הִכָּה־צוּר וַיָּזוּבוּ מַיִם וּנְחָלִים יִשְׁטֹפוּ הֲגַם־לֶחֶם יוּכַל־תֵּת אִם־יָכִין שְׁאֵר לְעַמּוֹ:

כא לָכֵן שָׁמַע יְהוָה וַיִּתְעַבָּר וְאֵשׁ נִשְּׂקָה בְיַעֲקֹב וְגַם־אַף עָלָה בְיִשְׂרָאֵל:

כב כִּי לֹא הֶאֱמִינוּ בֵּאלֹהִים וְלֹא בָטְחוּ בִּישׁוּעָתוֹ:

כג וַיְצַו שְׁחָקִים מִמָּעַל וְדַלְתֵי שָׁמַיִם פָּתָח:

כד וַיַּמְטֵר עֲלֵיהֶם מָן לֶאֱכֹל וּדְגַן שָׁמַיִם נָתַן לָמוֹ:

כה לֶחֶם אַבִּירִים אָכַל אִישׁ צֵידָה שָׁלַח לָהֶם לָשֹׂבַע:

כו יַסַּע קָדִים בַּשָּׁמָיִם וַיְנַהֵג בְּעֻזּוֹ תֵימָן:

כז וַיַּמְטֵר עֲלֵיהֶם כֶּעָפָר שְׁאֵר וּכְחוֹל יַמִּים עוֹף כָּנָף:

כח וַיַּפֵּל בְּקֶרֶב מַחֲנֵהוּ סָבִיב לְמִשְׁכְּנֹתָיו:

כט וַיֹּאכְלוּ וַיִּשְׂבְּעוּ מְאֹד וְתַאֲוָתָם יָבִא לָהֶם:

ל לֹא־זָרוּ מִתַּאֲוָתָם עוֹד אָכְלָם בְּפִיהֶם:

לא וְאַף אֱלֹהִים עָלָה בָהֶם וַיַּהֲרֹג בְּמִשְׁמַנֵּיהֶם וּבַחוּרֵי יִשְׂרָאֵל הִכְרִיעַ:

לב בְּכָל־זֹאת חָטְאוּ־עוֹד וְלֹא הֶאֱמִינוּ בְּנִפְלְאוֹתָיו:

לג וַיְכַל־בַּהֶבֶל יְמֵיהֶם וּשְׁנוֹתָם בַּבֶּהָלָה:

לד אִם־הֲרָגָם וּדְרָשׁוּהוּ וְשָׁבוּ וְשִׁחֲרוּ־אֵל:

לה וַיִּזְכְּרוּ כִּי־אֱלֹהִים צוּרָם וְאֵל עֶלְיוֹן גֹּאֲלָם:

לו וַיְפַתּוּהוּ בְּפִיהֶם וּבִלְשׁוֹנָם יְכַזְּבוּ־לוֹ:

לז וְלִבָּם לֹא־נָכוֹן עִמּוֹ וְלֹא נֶאֶמְנוּ בִּבְרִיתוֹ:

לח וְהוּא רַחוּם יְכַפֵּר עָוֹן וְלֹא־יַשְׁחִית וְהִרְבָּה לְהָשִׁיב אַפּוֹ וְלֹא־יָעִיר כָּל־חֲמָתוֹ:

לט וַיִּזְכֹּר כִּי־בָשָׂר הֵמָּה רוּחַ הוֹלֵךְ וְלֹא יָשׁוּב:

מ כַּמָּה יַמְרוּהוּ בַמִּדְבָּר יַעֲצִיבוּהוּ בִּישִׁימוֹן:

19 They spoke against God, saying:" Can God prepare a table in the desert?

20 True, He struck the rock and waters poured out and the streams flooded. But can He also provide bread and meat for His people?"

21 The Lord heard them, and His anger burned like a fire against the children of Jacob, His anger also against Israel

22 Because they did not believe in God and did not trust His salvation.

23 He commanded the skies above, and opened the doors of heaven.

24 He made the manna to fall on them for food, giving them the grain of heaven.

25 They ate the food of angels, food that satisfied them greatly.

26 He commanded the east wind to blow from heaven and with His power brought the south wind.

27 He caused meat to rain upon them like dust, and fowl like the sand of the sea.

28 He let it fall in their camp and near their tents

29 They ate and were satisfied. He gave them what they had desired.

30 They had not yet satisfied their craving, and the food was still in their mouths

31 When the anger of God came upon them and killed the obese among them, the young men of Israel.

32 Even after all this they continued to sin and did not believe in His mighty deeds.

33 So He ended their days unfulfilled, their lives in terror.

34 When He killed them, those remaining would return to seek and ask about Him.

35 Then they remembered that God was their Rock and their savior.

36 However, they only paid Him lip-service and lied to Him with their tongues.

37 Their hearts were not true to Him, and they were not faithful to the covenant.

38 But He did not destroy them because of His compassion, and He forgave their sins. Many times He suppresses His anger and does not impose punishment.

39 He remembers that they are but human beings, like a wind that passes away, never to return.

40 How many times did they rebel against Him and anger Him in the desert?

41 They continued to test God and set bounds for Him.

מא וַיָּשׁוּבוּ וַיְנַסּוּ אֵל וּקְדוֹשׁ יִשְׂרָאֵל הִתְווּ:

מב לֹא־זָכְרוּ אֶת־יָדוֹ יוֹם אֲשֶׁר־פָּדָם מִנִּי־צָר:

מג אֲשֶׁר־שָׂם בְּמִצְרַיִם אֹתוֹתָיו וּמוֹפְתָיו בִּשְׂדֵה־צֹעַן:

מד וַיַּהֲפֹךְ לְדָם יְאֹרֵיהֶם וְנֹזְלֵיהֶם בַּל־יִשְׁתָּיוּן:

מה יְשַׁלַּח בָּהֶם עָרֹב וַיֹּאכְלֵם וּצְפַרְדֵּעַ וַתַּשְׁחִיתֵם:

מו וַיִּתֵּן לֶחָסִיל יְבוּלָם וִיגִיעָם לָאַרְבֶּה:

מז יַהֲרֹג בַּבָּרָד גַּפְנָם וְשִׁקְמוֹתָם בַּחֲנָמַל:

מח וַיַּסְגֵּר לַבָּרָד בְּעִירָם וּמִקְנֵיהֶם לָרְשָׁפִים:

מט יְשַׁלַּח־בָּם חֲרוֹן אַפּוֹ עֶבְרָה וָזַעַם וְצָרָה מִשְׁלַחַת מַלְאֲכֵי רָעִים:

נ יְפַלֵּס נָתִיב לְאַפּוֹ לֹא־חָשַׂךְ מִמָּוֶת נַפְשָׁם וְחַיָּתָם לַדֶּבֶר הִסְגִּיר:

נא וַיַּךְ כָּל־בְּכוֹר בְּמִצְרָיִם רֵאשִׁית אוֹנִים בְּאָהֳלֵי־חָם:

נב וַיַּסַּע כַּצֹּאן עַמּוֹ וַיְנַהֲגֵם כַּעֵדֶר בַּמִּדְבָּר:

נג וַיַּנְחֵם לָבֶטַח וְלֹא פָחָדוּ וְאֶת־אוֹיְבֵיהֶם כִּסָּה הַיָּם:

נד וַיְבִיאֵם אֶל־גְּבוּל קָדְשׁוֹ הַר־זֶה קָנְתָה יְמִינוֹ:

נה וַיְגָרֶשׁ מִפְּנֵיהֶם גּוֹיִם וַיַּפִּילֵם בְּחֶבֶל נַחֲלָה וַיַּשְׁכֵּן בְּאָהֳלֵיהֶם שִׁבְטֵי יִשְׂרָאֵל:

נו וַיְנַסּוּ וַיַּמְרוּ אֶת־אֱלֹהִים עֶלְיוֹן וְעֵדוֹתָיו לֹא שָׁמָרוּ:

נז וַיִּסֹּגוּ וַיִּבְגְּדוּ כַּאֲבוֹתָם נֶהְפְּכוּ כְּקֶשֶׁת רְמִיָּה:

נח וַיַּכְעִיסוּהוּ בְּבָמוֹתָם וּבִפְסִילֵיהֶם יַקְנִיאוּהוּ:

נט שָׁמַע אֱלֹהִים וַיִּתְעַבָּר וַיִּמְאַס מְאֹד בְּיִשְׂרָאֵל:

ס וַיִּטֹּשׁ מִשְׁכַּן שִׁלוֹ אֹהֶל שִׁכֵּן בָּאָדָם:

סא וַיִּתֵּן לַשְּׁבִי עֻזּוֹ וְתִפְאַרְתּוֹ בְיַד־צָר:

סב וַיַּסְגֵּר לַחֶרֶב עַמּוֹ וּבְנַחֲלָתוֹ הִתְעַבָּר:

42 They did not remember His power or the day on which He freed them from the enemy,

43 How He performed His miracles in Egypt and His wonders in the field of Zoan.

44 He turned their rivers and streams into blood so that they could not drink water.

45 He sent wild beasts to devour them and frogs to destroy them.

46 He destroyed their work and produce with the plague of locusts.

47 He destroyed their vines and their fruit trees with hail.

48 He destroyed their cattle and their flocks with hail and lightning.

49 He released His anger, wrath, fury and distress on them, His messengers of punishment.

50 He sent a stream of anger and did not prevent their deaths, just as he had destroyed their cattle with pestilence.

51 He killed all the first-born of Egypt, the first fruit of their strength, the descendants of Cham.

52 He made His people depart to freedom and guided them in the desert like a shepherd leading his sheep.

53 He led them in safety, and they were not afraid when the sea drowned their Egyptian enemies.

54 He led them to His holy land, to this mountain that His right hand possessed.

55 He drove all the nations from the land and gave it to His people as a perpetual legacy, and made the tribes of Israel live in their tents.

56 But they tested and rebelled against the mighty God and did not follow His laws.

57 They changed and acted disloyally, behaving dishonestly like their ancestors.

58 They angered Him with their high places and provoked His jealousy with their idols.

59 God heard and was angry, and rejected Israel.

60 He forgot the Ark of Shiloh in the tent where He dwelled among His people.

61 He allowed his strength to be captured, and gave His glory into the enemy's hands.

62 He gave His people to the sword and was angry with His inheritance.

63 Fire consumed the young men, and the young maidens never married.

סג בַּחוּרָיו אָכְלָה־אֵשׁ וּבְתוּלֹתָיו לֹא הוּלָּלוּ:

סד כֹּהֲנָיו בַּחֶרֶב נָפָלוּ וְאַלְמְנֹתָיו לֹא תִבְכֶּינָה:

סה וַיִּקַץ כְּיָשֵׁן אֲדֹנָי כְּגִבּוֹר מִתְרוֹנֵן מִיָּיִן:

סו וַיַּךְ־צָרָיו אָחוֹר חֶרְפַּת עוֹלָם נָתַן לָמוֹ:

סז וַיִּמְאַס בְּאֹהֶל יוֹסֵף וּבְשֵׁבֶט אֶפְרַיִם לֹא בָחָר:

סח וַיִּבְחַר אֶת־שֵׁבֶט יְהוּדָה אֶת־הַר צִיּוֹן אֲשֶׁר אָהֵב:

סט וַיִּבֶן כְּמוֹ־רָמִים מִקְדָּשׁוֹ כְּאֶרֶץ יְסָדָהּ לְעוֹלָם:

ע וַיִּבְחַר בְּדָוִד עַבְדּוֹ וַיִּקָּחֵהוּ מִמִּכְלְאֹת צֹאן:

עא מֵאַחַר עָלוֹת הֱבִיאוֹ לִרְעוֹת בְּיַעֲקֹב עַמּוֹ וּבְיִשְׂרָאֵל נַחֲלָתוֹ:

עב וַיִּרְעֵם כְּתֹם לְבָבוֹ וּבִתְבוּנוֹת כַּפָּיו יַנְחֵם:

פרק עט

א מִזְמוֹר לְאָסָף אֱלֹהִים בָּאוּ גוֹיִם בְּנַחֲלָתֶךָ טִמְּאוּ אֶת־הֵיכַל קָדְשֶׁךָ שָׂמוּ אֶת־יְרוּשָׁלַ͏ִם לְעִיִּים:

ב נָתְנוּ אֶת־נִבְלַת עֲבָדֶיךָ מַאֲכָל לְעוֹף הַשָּׁמָיִם בְּשַׂר חֲסִידֶיךָ לְחַיְתוֹ־אָרֶץ:

ג שָׁפְכוּ דָמָם כַּמַּיִם סְבִיבוֹת יְרוּשָׁלָ͏ִם וְאֵין קוֹבֵר:

ד הָיִינוּ חֶרְפָּה לִשְׁכֵנֵינוּ לַעַג וָקֶלֶס לִסְבִיבוֹתֵינוּ:

ה עַד־מָה יְהוָה תֶּאֱנַף לָנֶצַח תִּבְעַר כְּמוֹ־אֵשׁ קִנְאָתֶךָ:

ו שְׁפֹךְ חֲמָתְךָ אֶל־הַגּוֹיִם אֲשֶׁר לֹא־יְדָעוּךָ וְעַל מַמְלָכוֹת אֲשֶׁר בְּשִׁמְךָ לֹא קָרָאוּ:

ז כִּי־אָכַל אֶת־יַעֲקֹב וְאֶת־נָוֵהוּ הֵשַׁמּוּ:

ח אַל־תִּזְכָּר־לָנוּ עֲוֺנֹת רִאשֹׁנִים מַהֵר יְקַדְּמוּנוּ רַחֲמֶיךָ כִּי דַלּוֹנוּ מְאֹד:

64 The priests were killed by the sword, and their widows did not mourn for them.

65 Then the Lord awoke from sleep, like a mighty man who awakens from the effects of wine.

66 He destroyed His enemies as before. He destroyed them in total defeat.

67 He despised the tent of Joseph and did not choose the tribe of Ephraim.

68 He chose the tribe of Judah and Mount Zion, which He loves.

69 He built His Sanctuary like a high mountain, like the earth which He established for all time.

70 He chose David, His servant, taking him from the sheep.

71 He took David from caring for nursing sheep, making him the shepherd over Jacob and His chosen people, Israel.

72 He cared for them with integrity and led them with the skill of his hands.

TEHILLIM 79

A song lamenting the destruction of Jerusalem and the Temple

1 A psalm by Asaph. My God, the enemy has invaded Your Land. They have desecrated Your holy Sanctuary, and they have turned Jerusalem into ruins.

2 They have left the bodies of Your devoted people as food for the birds and the beasts of the earth.

3 They have spilled their blood like water all around Jerusalem, with none to bury them.

4 We have become an object of mockery to the other nations and an embarrassment to other peoples.

5 How long will You remain angry with us, my Lord? How long will Your jealousy burn like fire?

6 Pour out Your anger upon the nations that do not accept You and upon the nations that do not call upon Your name,

7 For they have destroyed Jacob and ruined his home.

8 Do not punish us for the sins of our forefathers. Let Your compassion come quickly to us, for we are in great need.

ט עֶזְרֵנוּ אֱלֹהֵי יִשְׁעֵנוּ עַל־דְּבַר כְּבוֹד־שְׁמֶךָ וְהַצִּילֵנוּ וְכַפֵּר עַל־חַטֹּאתֵינוּ לְמַעַן שְׁמֶךָ:

י לָמָּה יֹאמְרוּ הַגּוֹיִם אַיֵּה אֱלֹהֵיהֶם יִוָּדַע בגיים [בַּגּוֹיִם] לְעֵינֵינוּ נִקְמַת דַּם־עֲבָדֶיךָ הַשָּׁפוּךְ:

יא תָּבוֹא לְפָנֶיךָ אֶנְקַת אָסִיר כְּגֹדֶל זְרוֹעֲךָ הוֹתֵר בְּנֵי תְמוּתָה:

יב וְהָשֵׁב לִשְׁכֵנֵינוּ שִׁבְעָתַיִם אֶל־חֵיקָם חֶרְפָּתָם אֲשֶׁר חֵרְפוּךָ אֲדֹנָי:

יג וַאֲנַחְנוּ עַמְּךָ וְצֹאן מַרְעִיתֶךָ נוֹדֶה לְּךָ לְעוֹלָם לְדֹר וָדֹר נְסַפֵּר תְּהִלָּתֶךָ:

פרק פ

א לַמְנַצֵּחַ אֶל־שֹׁשַׁנִּים עֵדוּת לְאָסָף מִזְמוֹר:

ב רֹעֵה יִשְׂרָאֵל הַאֲזִינָה נֹהֵג כַּצֹּאן יוֹסֵף יֹשֵׁב הַכְּרוּבִים הוֹפִיעָה:

ג לִפְנֵי אֶפְרַיִם וּבִנְיָמִן וּמְנַשֶּׁה עוֹרְרָה אֶת־גְּבוּרָתֶךָ וּלְכָה לִישֻׁעָתָה לָּנוּ:

ד אֱלֹהִים הֲשִׁיבֵנוּ וְהָאֵר פָּנֶיךָ וְנִוָּשֵׁעָה:

ה יְהוָה אֱלֹהִים צְבָאוֹת עַד־מָתַי עָשַׁנְתָּ בִּתְפִלַּת עַמֶּךָ:

ו הֶאֱכַלְתָּם לֶחֶם דִּמְעָה וַתַּשְׁקֵמוֹ בִּדְמָעוֹת שָׁלִישׁ:

ז תְּשִׂימֵנוּ מָדוֹן לִשְׁכֵנֵינוּ וְאֹיְבֵינוּ יִלְעֲגוּ־לָמוֹ:

ח אֱלֹהִים צְבָאוֹת הֲשִׁיבֵנוּ וְהָאֵר פָּנֶיךָ וְנִוָּשֵׁעָה:

ט גֶּפֶן מִמִּצְרַיִם תַּסִּיעַ תְּגָרֵשׁ גּוֹיִם וַתִּטָּעֶהָ:

י פִּנִּיתָ לְפָנֶיהָ וַתַּשְׁרֵשׁ שָׁרָשֶׁיהָ וַתְּמַלֵּא־אָרֶץ:

יא כָּסּוּ הָרִים צִלָּהּ וַעֲנָפֶיהָ אַרְזֵי־אֵל:

יב תְּשַׁלַּח קְצִירֶהָ עַד־יָם וְאֶל־נָהָר יוֹנְקוֹתֶיהָ:

יג לָמָּה פָּרַצְתָּ גְדֵרֶיהָ וְאָרוּהָ כָּל־עֹבְרֵי דָרֶךְ:

9 Help us, God of our salvation, for the honor of Your name. Save us and forgive our sins for Your name's sake.

10 Why should the nations say, "Where is their God?" Let us witness the vengeance done to the nations for the spilled blood of Your servants.

11 May the prisoner's groans come before You. With Your great power, free those who are about to be killed.

12 Avenge seven times over, to their very hearts, the insults of the nations against you, my Lord.

13 Then we, Your people, the flock of Your pasture, will give thanks to You forever, and we will tell of Your goodness to all generations.

TEHILLIM 80

*A song praying for the exiled ten tribes
and asking for national reunion*

1 For the chief musician, to the rose of Israel, a testimony, a psalm by Asaph.

2 Shepherd of Israel, You Who lead Joseph like a flock, please listen to us. You who are enthroned upon the cherubim, send us Your light.

3 Arouse Your might for Ephraim, Benjamin and Manasseh, and save us.

4 My God, bring us back and let Your goodness come to us, and we will be saved.

5 My Lord God of Hosts, how long will You reject the prayers of Your people?

6 You have fed them the bread of tears and made them drink many tears.

7 You have made us a target for our neighbors, and our enemies rejoice over our troubles.

8 Our Lord of Hosts, bring us back and send us Your goodness, and we will be saved.

9 You brought up a vine from Egypt, drove out the nations, and then planted it.

10 You cleared a place for them, it took root deeply and filled the land.

11 Its shadow covered the mountains like the spreading branches of the giant cedar trees.

12 It sent out its branches to the sea and its shoots as far as the river.

יד יְכַרְסְמֶנָּה חֲזִיר מִיָּעַר וְזִיז שָׂדַי יִרְעֶנָּה:

טו אֱלֹהִים צְבָאוֹת שׁוּב־נָא הַבֵּט מִשָּׁמַיִם וּרְאֵה וּפְקֹד גֶּפֶן זֹאת:

טז וְכַנָּה אֲשֶׁר־נָטְעָה יְמִינֶךָ וְעַל־בֵּן אִמַּצְתָּה לָּךְ:

יז שְׂרֻפָה בָאֵשׁ כְּסוּחָה מִגַּעֲרַת פָּנֶיךָ יֹאבֵדוּ:

יח תְּהִי־יָדְךָ עַל־אִישׁ יְמִינֶךָ עַל־בֶּן־אָדָם אִמַּצְתָּ לָּךְ:

יט וְלֹא־נָסוֹג מִמֶּךָּ תְּחַיֵּנוּ וּבְשִׁמְךָ נִקְרָא:

כ יְהוָה אֱלֹהִים צְבָאוֹת הֲשִׁיבֵנוּ הָאֵר פָּנֶיךָ וְנִוָּשֵׁעָה:

פרק פא

א לַמְנַצֵּחַ עַל־הַגִּתִּית לְאָסָף:

ב הַרְנִינוּ לֵאלֹהִים עוּזֵּנוּ הָרִיעוּ לֵאלֹהֵי יַעֲקֹב:

ג שְׂאוּ־זִמְרָה וּתְנוּ־תֹף כִּנּוֹר נָעִים עִם־נָבֶל:

ד תִּקְעוּ בַחֹדֶשׁ שׁוֹפָר בַּכֵּסֶה לְיוֹם חַגֵּנוּ:

ה כִּי חֹק לְיִשְׂרָאֵל הוּא מִשְׁפָּט לֵאלֹהֵי יַעֲקֹב:

ו עֵדוּת בִּיהוֹסֵף שָׂמוֹ בְּצֵאתוֹ עַל־אֶרֶץ מִצְרָיִם שְׂפַת לֹא־יָדַעְתִּי אֶשְׁמָע:

ז הֲסִירוֹתִי מִסֵּבֶל שִׁכְמוֹ כַּפָּיו מִדּוּד תַּעֲבֹרְנָה:

ח בַּצָּרָה קָרָאתָ וָאֲחַלְּצֶךָּ אֶעֶנְךָ בְּסֵתֶר רַעַם אֶבְחָנְךָ עַל־מֵי מְרִיבָה סֶלָה:

ט שְׁמַע עַמִּי וְאָעִידָה בָּךְ יִשְׂרָאֵל אִם־תִּשְׁמַע־לִי:

י לֹא־יִהְיֶה בְךָ אֵל זָר וְלֹא תִשְׁתַּחֲוֶה לְאֵל נֵכָר:

יא אָנֹכִי יְהוָה אֱלֹהֶיךָ הַמַּעַלְךָ מֵאֶרֶץ מִצְרָיִם הַרְחֶב־פִּיךָ וַאֲמַלְאֵהוּ:

13 Why have You removed its protective fences so that anyone can pluck its fruit?

14 The wild boar from the forest gnaws on it, and the animals of the field graze on it.

15 God of Hosts, we beg You to return. Look out from heaven and take thought for this vine,

16 And of the foundation which Your right hand planted and the son, Israel that You took to Yourself.

17 It has been burned with fire, cut down, and perishes at Your rebuke.

18 May Your saving hand be upon Your chosen one, upon the man whom you strengthened for Yourself.

19 So that we will not turn away from You, revive us, and we will call upon Your name.

20 Lord of Hosts, bring us back. Turn Your bright face toward us, and we will be saved.

TEHILLIM 81

*A song of holiday thanksgiving to God
for providing for His nation*

1 For the chief musician, upon the *gittith*. A psalm by Asaph.

2 Sing loudly to God, our strength. Shout for joy to the God of Jacob.

3 Play a melody on timbrel, lyre and harp.

4 Blow the shofar on the new moon and on the unseen moon of Rosh Hashanah.

5 This is a law for Israel, a judgment day of the God of Jacob.

6 He made this a remembrance for Joseph when He went out against Egypt. Israel heard God speaking but did not yet know Him fully.

7 I removed the burden from his shoulders; his hands were freed from hard labor.

8 You cried out in trouble and I saved you; I answered you thunderously from heaven; I tested you at Meribah. Selah.

9 Listen carefully, my people, and I will teach you. My people Israel, if only you would listen to me!

10 There shall be no alien god among you, and you shall not worship a foreign deity.

11 I am the Lord Your God Who brought you up out of the land of Egypt. Open your mouth wide and I will fill it.

יב וְלֹא־שָׁמַע עַמִּי לְקוֹלִי וְיִשְׂרָאֵל לֹא־אָבָה לִי:

יג וָאֲשַׁלְּחֵהוּ בִּשְׁרִירוּת לִבָּם יֵלְכוּ בְּמוֹעֲצוֹתֵיהֶם:

יד לוּ עַמִּי שֹׁמֵעַ לִי יִשְׂרָאֵל בִּדְרָכַי יְהַלֵּכוּ:

טו כִּמְעַט אוֹיְבֵיהֶם אַכְנִיעַ וְעַל־צָרֵיהֶם אָשִׁיב יָדִי:

טז מְשַׂנְאֵי יְהוָה יְכַחֲשׁוּ־לוֹ וִיהִי עִתָּם לְעוֹלָם:

יז וַיַּאֲכִילֵהוּ מֵחֵלֶב חִטָּה וּמִצּוּר דְּבַשׁ אַשְׂבִּיעֶךָ:

פרק פב

א מִזְמוֹר לְאָסָף אֱלֹהִים נִצָּב בַּעֲדַת־אֵל בְּקֶרֶב אֱלֹהִים יִשְׁפֹּט:

ב עַד־מָתַי תִּשְׁפְּטוּ־עָוֶל וּפְנֵי רְשָׁעִים תִּשְׂאוּ־סֶלָה:

ג שִׁפְטוּ־דַל וְיָתוֹם עָנִי וָרָשׁ הַצְדִּיקוּ:

ד פַּלְּטוּ־דַל וְאֶבְיוֹן מִיַּד רְשָׁעִים הַצִּילוּ:

ה לֹא יָדְעוּ וְלֹא יָבִינוּ בַּחֲשֵׁכָה יִתְהַלָּכוּ יִמּוֹטוּ כָּל־מוֹסְדֵי אָרֶץ:

ו אֲנִי אָמַרְתִּי אֱלֹהִים אַתֶּם וּבְנֵי עֶלְיוֹן כֻּלְּכֶם:

ז אָכֵן כְּאָדָם תְּמוּתוּן וּכְאַחַד הַשָּׂרִים תִּפֹּלוּ:

ח קוּמָה אֱלֹהִים שָׁפְטָה הָאָרֶץ כִּי־אַתָּה תִנְחַל בְּכָל־הַגּוֹיִם:

12 But my people did not listen to my voice; Israel turned away from me.

13 I allowed them to follow their stubborn hearts, and they followed their own ways.

14 If only my people would listen to Me and observe My ways!

15 I would quickly defeat their enemies and turn my hand against those who oppose them.

16 Those who hate the Lord will be removed from before them, and their punishment will last forever.

17 Israel will be given the cream of the wheat, and I will satisfy them with honey from the rock.

TEHILLIM 82

A song that deals with the conduct of human judges

1 A psalm by Asaph. God comes to the midst of the people of God; in the midst of the judges He will judge.

2 God says to the judges: "How long will you judge dishonestly and show favoritism to the wicked? Selah.

3 Judge the poor and the fatherless with truth. Give justice to the suffering and the needy.

4 Save the poor and the needy and rescue them from the hands of the wicked.

5 But the judges do not know and they do not understand. They go in darkness, causing the earth's foundations to quake.

6 I said: "You are God like people, and you are sons of the Supreme One.

7 However, you will die like ordinary men, and you will fall like one of the princes."

8 Arise God, come to judge the earth, for You are the ruler of all nations.

פרק פג

א שִׁיר מִזְמוֹר לְאָסָף:

ב אֱלֹהִים אַל־דֳּמִי־לָךְ אַל־תֶּחֱרַשׁ וְאַל־תִּשְׁקֹט אֵל:

ג כִּי־הִנֵּה אוֹיְבֶיךָ יֶהֱמָיוּן וּמְשַׂנְאֶיךָ נָשְׂאוּ רֹאשׁ:

ד עַל־עַמְּךָ יַעֲרִימוּ סוֹד וְיִתְיָעֲצוּ עַל־צְפוּנֶיךָ:

ה אָמְרוּ לְכוּ וְנַכְחִידֵם מִגּוֹי וְלֹא־יִזָּכֵר שֵׁם־יִשְׂרָאֵל עוֹד:

ו כִּי נוֹעֲצוּ לֵב יַחְדָּו עָלֶיךָ בְּרִית יִכְרֹתוּ:

ז אָהֳלֵי אֱדוֹם וְיִשְׁמְעֵאלִים מוֹאָב וְהַגְרִים:

ח גְּבָל וְעַמּוֹן וַעֲמָלֵק פְּלֶשֶׁת עִם־יֹשְׁבֵי צוֹר:

ט גַּם־אַשּׁוּר נִלְוָה עִמָּם הָיוּ זְרוֹעַ לִבְנֵי־לוֹט סֶלָה:

י עֲשֵׂה־לָהֶם כְּמִדְיָן כְּסִיסְרָא כְיָבִין בְּנַחַל קִישׁוֹן:

יא נִשְׁמְדוּ בְעֵין־דֹּאר הָיוּ דֹּמֶן לָאֲדָמָה:

יב שִׁיתֵמוֹ נְדִיבֵמוֹ כְּעֹרֵב וְכִזְאֵב וּכְזֶבַח וּכְצַלְמֻנָּע כָּל־נְסִיכֵמוֹ:

יג אֲשֶׁר אָמְרוּ נִירֲשָׁה לָּנוּ אֵת נְאוֹת אֱלֹהִים:

יד אֱלֹהַי שִׁיתֵמוֹ כַגַּלְגַּל כְּקַשׁ לִפְנֵי־רוּחַ:

טו כְּאֵשׁ תִּבְעַר־יָעַר וּכְלֶהָבָה תְּלַהֵט הָרִים:

טז כֵּן תִּרְדְּפֵם בְּסַעֲרֶךָ וּבְסוּפָתְךָ תְבַהֲלֵם:

יז מַלֵּא פְנֵיהֶם קָלוֹן וִיבַקְשׁוּ שִׁמְךָ יְהוָה:

יח יֵבֹשׁוּ וְיִבָּהֲלוּ עֲדֵי־עַד וְיַחְפְּרוּ וְיֹאבֵדוּ:

יט וְיֵדְעוּ כִּי־אַתָּה שִׁמְךָ יְהוָה לְבַדֶּךָ עֶלְיוֹן עַל־כָּל־הָאָרֶץ:

TEHILLIM 83

*A song calling for God's help against the
combined attack of the nations*

1 A song, a psalm by Asaph.

2 Our God, do not remain silent. Do not be quiet, and do not remain calm, God.

3 Your enemies are in commotion, and those who hate You have lifted up their heads.

4 They have conspired against Your people and threaten Your chosen ones.

5 They say: "Come, let us destroy them as a nation so that the name of Israel will be remembered no more."

6 The nations have joined together with one heart. They scheme against You.

7 The nations of Edom; the Ishmaelites, Moab, the Hagrites,

8 Gebal, Ammon and Amalek; Philistia with the people of Tyre.

9 Assyria has also allied with them, and they have aided the descendants of Lot. Selah.

10 Do to them as You did to Midian, as You did to Sisera, to Jabin at the brook of Kishon;

11 They were destroyed at En-dor and became the dirt of the earth.

12 Do to their rulers as You did to Oreb, Zeeb, Zebah, to Zalmunna and to all their princes.

13 For they had said: "Let us take possession of all God's dwellings."

14 My God, make them like whirling dust and chaff in the wind,

15 Like a fire that burns the forest and a flame that sets fire to the mountains.

16 Pursue them with Your anger and terrify them with Your storm.

17 Bring shame upon them so that they may seek Your name.

18 May they be ashamed and frightened forever. Let them be disgraced and die,

19 That they may know that You alone, Whose name is the Lord, are the most powerful upon all the earth.

פרק פד

א לַמְנַצֵּחַ עַל־הַגִּתִּית לִבְנֵי־קֹרַח מִזְמוֹר:

ב מַה־יְּדִידוֹת מִשְׁכְּנוֹתֶיךָ יְהוָה צְבָאוֹת:

ג נִכְסְפָה וְגַם־כָּלְתָה נַפְשִׁי לְחַצְרוֹת יְהוָה לִבִּי וּבְשָׂרִי יְרַנְּנוּ אֶל־אֵל חָי:

ד גַּם־צִפּוֹר מָצְאָה בַיִת וּדְרוֹר קֵן לָהּ אֲשֶׁר־שָׁתָה אֶפְרֹחֶיהָ אֶת־ מִזְבְּחוֹתֶיךָ יְהוָה צְבָאוֹת מַלְכִּי וֵאלֹהָי:

ה אַשְׁרֵי יוֹשְׁבֵי בֵיתֶךָ עוֹד יְהַלְלוּךָ סֶּלָה:

ו אַשְׁרֵי אָדָם עוֹז לוֹ־בָךְ מְסִלּוֹת בִּלְבָבָם:

ז עֹבְרֵי בְּעֵמֶק הַבָּכָא מַעְיָן יְשִׁיתוּהוּ גַּם־בְּרָכוֹת יַעְטֶה מוֹרֶה:

ח יֵלְכוּ מֵחַיִל אֶל־חָיִל יֵרָאֶה אֶל־אֱלֹהִים בְּצִיּוֹן:

ט יְהוָה אֱלֹהִים צְבָאוֹת שִׁמְעָה תְפִלָּתִי הַאֲזִינָה אֱלֹהֵי יַעֲקֹב סֶלָה:

י מָגִנֵּנוּ רְאֵה אֱלֹהִים וְהַבֵּט פְּנֵי מְשִׁיחֶךָ:

יא כִּי טוֹב־יוֹם בַּחֲצֵרֶיךָ מֵאָלֶף בָּחַרְתִּי הִסְתּוֹפֵף בְּבֵית אֱלֹהַי מִדּוּר בְּאָהֳלֵי־רֶשַׁע:

יב כִּי שֶׁמֶשׁ וּמָגֵן יְהוָה אֱלֹהִים חֵן וְכָבוֹד יִתֵּן יְהוָה לֹא־יִמְנַע טוֹב לַהֹלְכִים בְּתָמִים:

יג יְהוָה צְבָאוֹת אַשְׁרֵי אָדָם בֹּטֵחַ בָּךְ:

פרק פה

א לַמְנַצֵּחַ לִבְנֵי־קֹרַח מִזְמוֹר:

ב רָצִיתָ יְהוָה אַרְצֶךָ שַׁבְתָּ שְׁבִית [שְׁבוּת] יַעֲקֹב:

ג נָשָׂאתָ עֲוֺן עַמֶּךָ כִּסִּיתָ כָל־חַטָּאתָם סֶלָה:

TEHILLIM 84

A song of closeness and love for God

1 For the chief musician, on the *gittith*, a psalm by the sons of Korah.
2 Your dwelling places are very lovely, Lord of Hosts.
3 My soul desires and yearns to be in the places of the Lord. My heart and my body sing joyfully to the living God.
4 Like the sparrow and the swallow that have made nests for their young in Your dwelling places, I also wish to rest in Your home, Lord of Hosts, my King, my God.
5 Happy are those who live in Your house; they praise you always. Selah.
6 Happy is the man who serves You and whose heart leads to Your house.
7 As they pass through the Valley of Weeping, they make it into a spring, which the early rains cover with blessings.
8 They go from strength from strength, and everyone comes before God in Zion.
9 Lord of Hosts, hear my prayer; listen, God of Jacob. Selah.
10 Please, God our Protector, look and see the face of Your anointed.
11 One day in Your house is better than a thousand anywhere else. I prefer to stand at the doorstep of Your house, my God, than to live in the houses of the wicked.
12 The Lord God is my sun and my shield. The Lord gives grace and honor. He does not withhold any good thing from those who act truthfully.
13 Lord of Hosts, happy is the man who trusts in You.

TEHILLIM 85

A song that the people returning from Babylon sang to God, asking for His help

1 For the chief musician, a psalm by the sons of Korah.
2 Lord, You have been good to Your land, and You have brought the people of Jacob back from captivity in Babylon.
3 You have forgiven and pardoned all their sins. Selah.

ד אָסַפְתָּ כָל־עֶבְרָתֶךָ הֱשִׁיבוֹתָ מֵחֲרוֹן אַפֶּךָ:

ה שׁוּבֵנוּ אֱלֹהֵי יִשְׁעֵנוּ וְהָפֵר כַּעַסְךָ עִמָּנוּ:

ו הַלְעוֹלָם תֶּאֱנַף־בָּנוּ תִּמְשֹׁךְ אַפְּךָ לְדֹר וָדֹר:

ז הֲלֹא־אַתָּה תָּשׁוּב תְּחַיֵּנוּ וְעַמְּךָ יִשְׂמְחוּ־בָךְ:

ח הַרְאֵנוּ יְהוָה חַסְדֶּךָ וְיֶשְׁעֲךָ תִּתֶּן־לָנוּ:

ט אֶשְׁמְעָה מַה־יְדַבֵּר הָאֵל יְהוָה כִּי יְדַבֵּר שָׁלוֹם אֶל־עַמּוֹ וְאֶל־חֲסִידָיו וְאַל־יָשׁוּבוּ לְכִסְלָה:

י אַךְ קָרוֹב לִירֵאָיו יִשְׁעוֹ לִשְׁכֹּן כָּבוֹד בְּאַרְצֵנוּ:

יא חֶסֶד־וֶאֱמֶת נִפְגָּשׁוּ צֶדֶק וְשָׁלוֹם נָשָׁקוּ:

יב אֱמֶת מֵאֶרֶץ תִּצְמָח וְצֶדֶק מִשָּׁמַיִם נִשְׁקָף:

יג גַּם־יְהוָה יִתֵּן הַטּוֹב וְאַרְצֵנוּ תִּתֵּן יְבוּלָהּ:

יד צֶדֶק לְפָנָיו יְהַלֵּךְ וְיָשֵׂם לְדֶרֶךְ פְּעָמָיו:

פרק פו

א תְּפִלָּה לְדָוִד הַטֵּה יְהוָה אָזְנְךָ עֲנֵנִי כִּי־עָנִי וְאֶבְיוֹן אָנִי:

ב שָׁמְרָה נַפְשִׁי כִּי־חָסִיד אָנִי הוֹשַׁע עַבְדְּךָ אַתָּה אֱלֹהַי הַבּוֹטֵחַ אֵלֶיךָ:

ג חָנֵּנִי אֲדֹנָי כִּי־אֵלֶיךָ אֶקְרָא כָּל־הַיּוֹם:

ד שַׂמֵּחַ נֶפֶשׁ עַבְדֶּךָ כִּי אֵלֶיךָ אֲדֹנָי נַפְשִׁי אֶשָּׂא:

ה כִּי־אַתָּה אֲדֹנָי טוֹב וְסַלָּח וְרַב־חֶסֶד לְכָל־קֹרְאֶיךָ:

ו הַאֲזִינָה יְהוָה תְּפִלָּתִי וְהַקְשִׁיבָה בְּקוֹל תַּחֲנוּנוֹתָי:

ז בְּיוֹם צָרָתִי אֶקְרָאֶךָּ כִּי תַעֲנֵנִי:

ח אֵין־כָּמוֹךָ בָאֱלֹהִים אֲדֹנָי וְאֵין כְּמַעֲשֶׂיךָ:

4 In the past, You have taken away Your anger and turned back from Your fierce wrath.

5 My God, take us back again, and remove Your anger from us.

6 Will You be angry with us forever? Will You draw your anger out for all generations?

7 Will You not revive us once more so that Your people may rejoice in You?

8 My Lord, show us Your mercy and save us.

9 I will hear what the Lord has to say. He will speak of peace to His people and His holy ones – only let them not turn again to foolishness.

10 Certainly His salvation is close to those who revere Him, that honor may dwell in our land.

11 Loving kindness and truth have met; and righteousness and peace have kissed.

12 Truth grows from the earth and righteousness looks down from heaven.

13 The Lord provides what is good, and our land will grow her produce.

14 Righteousness will go before Him, and provide a path to His footsteps.

TEHILLIM 86

A song of the soul crying out for help in time of trouble

1 A prayer by David. My Lord, please listen to me and answer me. I am poor and needy.

2 Care for my soul, for I am Your servant who trusts in You.

3 My Lord, be merciful to me for I pray to You all day long.

4 My Lord, make the soul of Your servant joyful, because I lift up my soul to You.

5 Lord, you are good and eager to forgive. You are abundantly kind to all who call upon You.

6 My Lord, listen to my prayer and answer the voice of my pleading.

7 In the time of my trouble I call to You, and You answer me.

8 There is none like You, my Lord, and there are no creations like Yours.

9 All the nations that You made will come and bow down to You, my Lord, and praise Your name.

ט כָּל־גּוֹיִם אֲשֶׁר עָשִׂיתָ יָבוֹאוּ וְיִשְׁתַּחֲווּ לְפָנֶיךָ אֲדֹנָי וִיכַבְּדוּ לִשְׁמֶךָ:

י כִּי־גָדוֹל אַתָּה וְעֹשֵׂה נִפְלָאוֹת אַתָּה אֱלֹהִים לְבַדֶּךָ:

יא הוֹרֵנִי יְהוָה דַּרְכֶּךָ אֲהַלֵּךְ בַּאֲמִתֶּךָ יַחֵד לְבָבִי לְיִרְאָה שְׁמֶךָ:

יב אוֹדְךָ אֲדֹנָי אֱלֹהַי בְּכָל־לְבָבִי וַאֲכַבְּדָה שִׁמְךָ לְעוֹלָם:

יג כִּי־חַסְדְּךָ גָּדוֹל עָלָי וְהִצַּלְתָּ נַפְשִׁי מִשְּׁאוֹל תַּחְתִּיָּה:

יד אֱלֹהִים זֵדִים קָמוּ עָלַי וַעֲדַת עָרִיצִים בִּקְשׁוּ נַפְשִׁי וְלֹא שָׂמוּךָ לְנֶגְדָּם:

טו וְאַתָּה אֲדֹנָי אֵל־רַחוּם וְחַנּוּן אֶרֶךְ אַפַּיִם וְרַב־חֶסֶד וֶאֱמֶת:

טז פְּנֵה אֵלַי וְחָנֵּנִי תְּנָה־עֻזְּךָ לְעַבְדֶּךָ וְהוֹשִׁיעָה לְבֶן־אֲמָתֶךָ:

יז עֲשֵׂה־עִמִּי אוֹת לְטוֹבָה וְיִרְאוּ שֹׂנְאַי וְיֵבֹשׁוּ כִּי־אַתָּה יְהוָה עֲזַרְתַּנִי
וְנִחַמְתָּנִי:

פרק פז

א לִבְנֵי־קֹרַח מִזְמוֹר שִׁיר יְסוּדָתוֹ בְּהַרְרֵי־קֹדֶשׁ:

ב אֹהֵב יְהוָה שַׁעֲרֵי צִיּוֹן מִכֹּל מִשְׁכְּנוֹת יַעֲקֹב:

ג נִכְבָּדוֹת מְדֻבָּר בָּךְ עִיר הָאֱלֹהִים סֶלָה:

ד אַזְכִּיר רַהַב וּבָבֶל לְיֹדְעָי הִנֵּה פְלֶשֶׁת וְצוֹר עִם־כּוּשׁ זֶה יֻלַּד־שָׁם:

ה וּלֲצִיּוֹן יֵאָמַר אִישׁ וְאִישׁ יֻלַּד־בָּהּ וְהוּא יְכוֹנְנֶהָ עֶלְיוֹן:

ו יְהוָה יִסְפֹּר בִּכְתוֹב עַמִּים זֶה יֻלַּד־שָׁם סֶלָה:

ז וְשָׁרִים כְּחֹלְלִים כָּל־מַעְיָנַי בָּךְ:

10 You are great and You perform miracles. You alone are God.

11 My Lord, teach me Your ways so that I may walk in Your way of truth. Help my heart to revere Your name.

12 With my whole heart I give thanks to You, my Lord, my God. I will praise Your name forever.

13 Your kindness to me is great, and You have saved my soul from the lowest netherworld.

14 My God, haughty people are attacking me, and a group of violent men seeks my life. They do not fear You.

15 But You, my Lord, my God, are full of mercy and grace, slow to anger and abundant in kindness and truth.

16 Turn to me and be gracious to me. Give strength to Your servant, and save the son of Your handmaid.

17 Show me a sign of Your good so that my enemies may see it and be ashamed, because You, my Lord, have helped me and comforted me.

TEHILLIM 87

A song about our eternal God, Whose dwelling place is in Zion

1 A psalm by the sons of Korah, a song. His foundation is on the sacred mountains.

2 The Lord loves the gates of Zion more than all the other dwellings of Jacob.

3 Great things are said of you, City of God. Selah.

4 I will mention Egypt and Babylon to those who know Me; and they say, "Here are Philistia, Tyre and Ethiopia – This great person was born there."

5 But of Zion, people will say: "This great man and that great man were born there, and the Supreme One Himself establishes her."

6 The Lord will make a list of the nations: "This one was born there." Selah.

7 They will sing and dance – for all my thoughts are of you.

פרק פח

א שִׁיר מִזְמוֹר לִבְנֵי קֹרַח לַמְנַצֵּחַ עַל־מָחֲלַת לְעַנּוֹת מַשְׂכִּיל לְהֵימָן הָאֶזְרָחִי:

ב יְהֹוָה אֱלֹהֵי יְשׁוּעָתִי יוֹם צָעַקְתִּי בַלַּיְלָה נֶגְדֶּךָ:

ג תָּבוֹא לְפָנֶיךָ תְּפִלָּתִי הַטֵּה־אָזְנְךָ לְרִנָּתִי:

ד כִּי־שָׂבְעָה בְרָעוֹת נַפְשִׁי וְחַיַּי לִשְׁאוֹל הִגִּיעוּ:

ה נֶחְשַׁבְתִּי עִם־יוֹרְדֵי בוֹר הָיִיתִי כְּגֶבֶר אֵין־אֱיָל:

ו בַּמֵּתִים חָפְשִׁי כְּמוֹ חֲלָלִים שֹׁכְבֵי קֶבֶר אֲשֶׁר לֹא זְכַרְתָּם עוֹד וְהֵמָּה מִיָּדְךָ נִגְזָרוּ:

ז שַׁתַּנִי בְּבוֹר תַּחְתִּיּוֹת בְּמַחֲשַׁכִּים בִּמְצֹלוֹת:

ח עָלַי סָמְכָה חֲמָתֶךָ וְכָל־מִשְׁבָּרֶיךָ עִנִּיתָ סֶּלָה:

ט הִרְחַקְתָּ מְיֻדָּעַי מִמֶּנִּי שַׁתַּנִי תוֹעֵבוֹת לָמוֹ כָּלֻא וְלֹא אֵצֵא:

י עֵינִי דָאֲבָה מִנִּי עֹנִי קְרָאתִיךָ יְהֹוָה בְּכָל־יוֹם שִׁטַּחְתִּי אֵלֶיךָ כַפָּי:

יא הֲלַמֵּתִים תַּעֲשֶׂה־פֶּלֶא אִם־רְפָאִים יָקוּמוּ יוֹדוּךָ סֶּלָה:

יב הַיְסֻפַּר בַּקֶּבֶר חַסְדֶּךָ אֱמוּנָתְךָ בָּאֲבַדּוֹן:

יג הֲיִוָּדַע בַּחֹשֶׁךְ פִּלְאֶךָ וְצִדְקָתְךָ בְּאֶרֶץ נְשִׁיָּה:

יד וַאֲנִי אֵלֶיךָ יְהֹוָה שִׁוַּעְתִּי וּבַבֹּקֶר תְּפִלָּתִי תְקַדְּמֶךָּ:

טו לָמָה יְהֹוָה תִּזְנַח נַפְשִׁי תַּסְתִּיר פָּנֶיךָ מִמֶּנִּי:

טז עָנִי אֲנִי וְגֹוֵעַ מִנֹּעַר נָשָׂאתִי אֵמֶיךָ אָפוּנָה:

יז עָלַי עָבְרוּ חֲרוֹנֶיךָ בִּעוּתֶיךָ צִמְּתוּתֻנִי:

יח סַבּוּנִי כַמַּיִם כָּל־הַיּוֹם הִקִּיפוּ עָלַי יָחַד:

יט הִרְחַקְתָּ מִמֶּנִּי אֹהֵב וָרֵעַ מְיֻדָּעַי מַחְשָׁךְ:

TEHILLIM 88

A song recalling a difficult life

1 A song, a psalm by the sons of Korah, for the chief musician on the *mahalath le-annoth*, an *instruction* of Heman the Ezrahite.

2 My Lord, God of my salvation, I cry out to You by day and by night.

3 May my prayer come before You. May You hear my cry.

4 My soul is full of sorrow and my life approaches the grave.

5 I am considered as dead because I am a man with no strength.

6 I am like the dead who are free, who lie in the grave separated from You. Like those whom You no longer remember nor punish.

7 You have put me in the lowest pit, in the deepest and darkest places. Selah.

8 Your anger is hard for me to bear, and You press hard upon me.

9 You have taken my close friends away from me and have made me hateful to them. I am isolated and I cannot go out.

10 My eyes are weakened with suffering. Every day I call to You, my Lord, and I spread out my hands to You.

11 Will You perform miracles for the dead? Will the dead rise and give thanks to You? Selah.

12 Will Your loving kindness be told in the grave? Will Your faithfulness be recalled in destruction?

13 Will Your miracles be known in the dark and Your righteousness in the land of oblivion?

14 But I cry out to You, my Lord, and each morning my prayer comes before You.

15 Lord, why do you reject me? Why do You hide Your presence from me?

16 I have been suffering and dying from the time of my youth. I have borne Your punishments and I am weak.

17 Your terrible anger has covered me, and Your terrors have cut me off.

18 Suffering surrounds me like a sea of water, and it covers me all at once.

19 You have taken my friends and companions away from me, and given me darkness for an acquaintance.

פרק פט

א מַשְׂכִּיל לְאֵיתָן הָאֶזְרָחִי:

ב חַסְדֵי יְהוָה עוֹלָם אָשִׁירָה לְדֹר וָדֹר אוֹדִיעַ אֱמוּנָתְךָ בְּפִי:

ג כִּי־אָמַרְתִּי עוֹלָם חֶסֶד יִבָּנֶה שָׁמַיִם תָּכִן אֱמוּנָתְךָ בָהֶם:

ד כָּרַתִּי בְרִית לִבְחִירִי נִשְׁבַּעְתִּי לְדָוִד עַבְדִּי:

ה עַד־עוֹלָם אָכִין זַרְעֶךָ וּבָנִיתִי לְדֹר־וָדוֹר כִּסְאֲךָ סֶלָה:

ו וְיוֹדוּ שָׁמַיִם פִּלְאֲךָ יְהוָה אַף־אֱמוּנָתְךָ בִּקְהַל קְדֹשִׁים:

ז כִּי מִי בַשַּׁחַק יַעֲרֹךְ לַיהוָה יִדְמֶה לַיהוָה בִּבְנֵי אֵלִים:

ח אֵל נַעֲרָץ בְּסוֹד־קְדֹשִׁים רַבָּה וְנוֹרָא עַל־כָּל־סְבִיבָיו:

ט יְהוָה אֱלֹהֵי צְבָאוֹת מִי־כָמוֹךָ חֲסִין יָהּ וֶאֱמוּנָתְךָ סְבִיבוֹתֶיךָ:

י אַתָּה מוֹשֵׁל בְּגֵאוּת הַיָּם בְּשׂוֹא גַלָּיו אַתָּה תְשַׁבְּחֵם:

יא אַתָּה דִכִּאתָ כֶחָלָל רָהַב בִּזְרוֹעַ עֻזְּךָ פִּזַּרְתָּ אוֹיְבֶיךָ:

יב לְךָ שָׁמַיִם אַף־לְךָ אָרֶץ תֵּבֵל וּמְלֹאָהּ אַתָּה יְסַדְתָּם:

יג צָפוֹן וְיָמִין אַתָּה בְרָאתָם תָּבוֹר וְחֶרְמוֹן בְּשִׁמְךָ יְרַנֵּנוּ:

יד לְךָ זְרוֹעַ עִם־גְּבוּרָה תָּעֹז יָדְךָ תָּרוּם יְמִינֶךָ:

טו צֶדֶק וּמִשְׁפָּט מְכוֹן כִּסְאֶךָ חֶסֶד וֶאֱמֶת יְקַדְּמוּ פָנֶיךָ:

טז אַשְׁרֵי הָעָם יוֹדְעֵי תְרוּעָה יְהוָה בְּאוֹר־פָּנֶיךָ יְהַלֵּכוּן:

יז בְּשִׁמְךָ יְגִילוּן כָּל־הַיּוֹם וּבְצִדְקָתְךָ יָרוּמוּ:

יח כִּי־תִפְאֶרֶת עֻזָּמוֹ אָתָּה וּבִרְצֹנְךָ תָּרִים [תָּרוּם] קַרְנֵנוּ:

יט כִּי לַיהוָה מָגִנֵּנוּ וְלִקְדוֹשׁ יִשְׂרָאֵל מַלְכֵּנוּ:

כ אָז דִּבַּרְתָּ־בְחָזוֹן לַחֲסִידֶיךָ וַתֹּאמֶר שִׁוִּיתִי עֵזֶר עַל־גִּבּוֹר הֲרִימוֹתִי בָחוּר מֵעָם:

TEHILLIM 89

A song about the glory and the downfall of the Kingdom of David

1 An instruction by Ethan the Ezrahite.

2 I will sing about the loving kindness of the Lord forever. I will tell every generation of Your faithfulness.

3 I say: loving kindness is built forever, and Your faithfulness is established in heaven.

4 I have made a covenant with My chosen one; I have promised My servant David:

5 I will establish your children and build your kingdom for all generations. Selah.

6 The heavens will praise Your wonders, my Lord, and Your faithfulness to all the holy ones.

7 Who in the heavens compares to the Lord? Can any mighty one be compared to the Lord?

8 God is feared by the angels and by all around Him.

9 Lord of Hosts, Who is as powerful as You, my Lord? Your faithfulness surrounds You.

10 You control the powerful waves of the sea, and when the waves rise up, You calm them.

11 You destroyed Egypt like a corpse, and You scattered Your enemies with Your powerful arm.

12 Heaven and earth are Yours. You created the world and everything in it.

13 You created the whole world from the north to the south. The mountains of Tabor and Hermon rejoice at Your name.

14 Yours is the mighty arm; Your hand is strong, and Your right hand is exalted.

15 Righteousness and justice, loving kindness and truth are the pillars of Your world, and go before You.

16 Happy are the people that know the sound of the shofar; they walk in the light of Your countenance, my Lord.

17 They rejoice in Your name all day long and are raised up by Your righteousness.

18 You are the glory of their strength, and in Your honor our pride is raised high.

19 The Lord is our protector, and the holy God of Israel is our King.

כא מָצָאתִי דָּוִד עַבְדִּי בְּשֶׁמֶן קָדְשִׁי מְשַׁחְתִּיו:

כב אֲשֶׁר יָדִי תִּכּוֹן עִמּוֹ אַף־זְרוֹעִי תְאַמְּצֶנּוּ:

כג לֹא־יַשִּׁא אוֹיֵב בּוֹ וּבֶן־עַוְלָה לֹא יְעַנֶּנּוּ:

כד וְכַתּוֹתִי מִפָּנָיו צָרָיו וּמְשַׂנְאָיו אֶגּוֹף:

כה וֶאֱמוּנָתִי וְחַסְדִּי עִמּוֹ וּבִשְׁמִי תָּרוּם קַרְנוֹ:

כו וְשַׂמְתִּי בַיָּם יָדוֹ וּבַנְּהָרוֹת יְמִינוֹ:

כז הוּא יִקְרָאֵנִי אָבִי אָתָּה אֵלִי וְצוּר יְשׁוּעָתִי:

כח אַף־אָנִי בְּכוֹר אֶתְּנֵהוּ עֶלְיוֹן לְמַלְכֵי־אָרֶץ:

כט לְעוֹלָם אשמור [אֶשְׁמָר]־לוֹ חַסְדִּי וּבְרִיתִי נֶאֱמֶנֶת לוֹ:

ל וְשַׂמְתִּי לָעַד זַרְעוֹ וְכִסְאוֹ כִּימֵי שָׁמָיִם:

לא אִם־יַעַזְבוּ בָנָיו תּוֹרָתִי וּבְמִשְׁפָּטַי לֹא יֵלֵכוּן:

לב אִם־חֻקֹּתַי יְחַלֵּלוּ וּמִצְוֹתַי לֹא יִשְׁמֹרוּ:

לג וּפָקַדְתִּי בְשֵׁבֶט פִּשְׁעָם וּבִנְגָעִים עֲוֹנָם:

לד וְחַסְדִּי לֹא־אָפִיר מֵעִמּוֹ וְלֹא אֲשַׁקֵּר בֶּאֱמוּנָתִי:

לה לֹא־אֲחַלֵּל בְּרִיתִי וּמוֹצָא שְׂפָתַי לֹא אֲשַׁנֶּה:

לו אַחַת נִשְׁבַּעְתִּי בְקָדְשִׁי אִם־לְדָוִד אֲכַזֵּב:

לז זַרְעוֹ לְעוֹלָם יִהְיֶה וְכִסְאוֹ כַשֶּׁמֶשׁ נֶגְדִּי:

לח כְּיָרֵחַ יִכּוֹן עוֹלָם וְעֵד בַּשַּׁחַק נֶאֱמָן סֶלָה:

לט וְאַתָּה זָנַחְתָּ וַתִּמְאָס הִתְעַבַּרְתָּ עִם־מְשִׁיחֶךָ:

מ נֵאַרְתָּה בְּרִית עַבְדֶּךָ חִלַּלְתָּ לָאָרֶץ נִזְרוֹ:

מא פָּרַצְתָּ כָל־גְּדֵרֹתָיו שַׂמְתָּ מִבְצָרָיו מְחִתָּה:

מב שַׁסֻּהוּ כָּל־עֹבְרֵי דָרֶךְ הָיָה חֶרְפָּה לִשְׁכֵנָיו:

מג הֲרִימוֹתָ יְמִין צָרָיו הִשְׂמַחְתָּ כָּל־אוֹיְבָיו:

20 In a vision You spoke to Your holy ones and said: "I have aided the powerful man and I have chosen him from among My people.

21 I have chosen David, My servant, and with My holy oil I have anointed him.

22 Through David My power will be firm, and I will strengthen him.

23 The enemy will not overcome him, and wicked people will not harm him.

24 I will destroy his enemies completely and kill those who hate him.

25 My love and loving kindness will be with him and through My name, his kingdom will be uplifted.

26 I will set his hand upon the sea, and his right hand upon the rivers.

27 He will say to me, "You are my Father, my Rock and my Savior."

28 I will make him My firstborn, the highest of all the kings of the earth.

29 I will be kind to him and keep my covenant with him forever.

30 I will keep his children forever and his kingdom will remain to the end of days.

31 If his children forget My teaching, if they do not observe My ordinances,

32 If they profane My law and do not keep My commandments,

33 Then I will punish their sins with my rod and their wrong doing with My plagues.

34 But I will not take away My kindness from David or prove false to My faithfulness.

35 I will not violate my covenant, nor will I change what My lips have uttered.

36 Surely I will not be false to David, since I have sworn by My holiness.

37 His children will endure forever and his kingdom will continue before me as does the sun.

38 His kingdom will be as permanent as the moon and as a faithful witness in the sky. Selah.

39 But You, God, turned away and left us; You became angry with Your anointed one.

40 You rejected the covenant with Your servant, and You cast his crown to the earth.

41 You have removed all his fences and destroyed his fortresses.

42 Everyone who passes by loots him, and he has become an object of disgrace to his neighbors.

43 You strengthened the power of his enemies and made them rejoice.

פרק פט

מד אַף־תָּשִׁיב צוּר חַרְבּוֹ וְלֹא הֲקֵימֹתוֹ בַּמִּלְחָמָה:

מה הִשְׁבַּתָּ מִטְּהָרוֹ וְכִסְאוֹ לָאָרֶץ מִגַּרְתָּה:

מו הִקְצַרְתָּ יְמֵי עֲלוּמָיו הֶעֱטִיתָ עָלָיו בּוּשָׁה סֶלָה:

מז עַד־מָה יְהוָה תִּסָּתֵר לָנֶצַח תִּבְעַר כְּמוֹ־אֵשׁ חֲמָתֶךָ:

מח זְכָר־אֲנִי מֶה־חָלֶד עַל־מַה־שָּׁוְא בָּרָאתָ כָל־בְּנֵי־אָדָם:

מט מִי גֶבֶר יִחְיֶה וְלֹא יִרְאֶה־מָּוֶת יְמַלֵּט נַפְשׁוֹ מִיַּד־שְׁאוֹל סֶלָה:

נ אַיֵּה חֲסָדֶיךָ הָרִאשֹׁנִים אֲדֹנָי נִשְׁבַּעְתָּ לְדָוִד בֶּאֱמוּנָתֶךָ:

נא זְכֹר אֲדֹנָי חֶרְפַּת עֲבָדֶיךָ שְׂאֵתִי בְחֵיקִי כָּל־רַבִּים עַמִּים:

נב אֲשֶׁר חֵרְפוּ אוֹיְבֶיךָ יְהוָה אֲשֶׁר חֵרְפוּ עִקְּבוֹת מְשִׁיחֶךָ:

נג בָּרוּךְ יְהוָה לְעוֹלָם אָמֵן וְאָמֵן:

פרק צ

א תְּפִלָּה לְמֹשֶׁה אִישׁ־הָאֱלֹהִים אֲדֹנָי מָעוֹן אַתָּה הָיִיתָ לָּנוּ בְּדֹר וָדֹר:

ב בְּטֶרֶם הָרִים יֻלָּדוּ וַתְּחוֹלֵל אֶרֶץ וְתֵבֵל וּמֵעוֹלָם עַד־עוֹלָם אַתָּה אֵל:

ג תָּשֵׁב אֱנוֹשׁ עַד־דַּכָּא וַתֹּאמֶר שׁוּבוּ בְנֵי־אָדָם:

ד כִּי אֶלֶף שָׁנִים בְּעֵינֶיךָ כְּיוֹם אֶתְמוֹל כִּי יַעֲבֹר וְאַשְׁמוּרָה בַלָּיְלָה:

ה זְרַמְתָּם שֵׁנָה יִהְיוּ בַּבֹּקֶר כֶּחָצִיר יַחֲלֹף:

ו בַּבֹּקֶר יָצִיץ וְחָלָף לָעֶרֶב יְמוֹלֵל וְיָבֵשׁ:

ז כִּי־כָלִינוּ בְאַפֶּךָ וּבַחֲמָתְךָ נִבְהָלְנוּ:

ח שת [שַׁתָּה] עֲוֹנֹתֵינוּ לְנֶגְדֶּךָ עֲלֻמֵנוּ לִמְאוֹר פָּנֶיךָ:

ט כִּי כָל־יָמֵינוּ פָּנוּ בְעֶבְרָתֶךָ כִּלִּינוּ שָׁנֵינוּ כְמוֹ־הֶגֶה:

44 You turned back the edge of the sword and took away his strength in battle.

45 You have taken away his light and thrown his throne down to the ground.

46 The king's youth has been cut short and he is brought down in shame. Selah.

47 How long, my Lord, will You hide Yourself – forever? How long will Your anger burn?

48 Remember that my time is short, so for what vain purpose have You created man?

49 Is there any living man who will never die and be saved from the power of the grave? Selah.

50 Where are Your previous kindnesses, my Lord, which You swore to David with faithfulness?

51 Lord, remember the insults to Your servants, how I have bear the future nations in my bosom.

52 Your enemies taunt, Lord, they taunt the footsteps of Your anointed one.

53 Blessed be the Lord forever: Amen and amen.

TEHILLIM 90

A song by Moshe recounting how, while human beings pass away, God is eternal

1 A prayer by Moshe, the man of God. Lord, You are our house of safety for all generations. Before You created the mountains,

2 Before You created the earth and the universe, You, God, are the everlasting Creator with no beginning or end.

3 You humble mankind, saying, "Return, children of men."

4 To You a thousand years is like yesterday, like a brief night watch.

5 Their lives flow away like a flood of water and it is as though they sleep. In the morning they are like fresh grass.

6 In the morning it thrives and grows, and in the evening it is cut down and withers.

7 So too, are consumed in Your anger, and by Your wrath, we are terrified.

8 You know our sins. Even our secret sins lie before the brightness of Your face.

י יְמֵי שְׁנוֹתֵינוּ בָהֶם שִׁבְעִים שָׁנָה וְאִם בִּגְבוּרֹת שְׁמוֹנִים שָׁנָה וְרָהְבָּם
עָמָל וָאָוֶן כִּי־גָז חִישׁ וַנָּעֻפָה:

יא מִי־יוֹדֵעַ עֹז אַפֶּךָ וּכְיִרְאָתְךָ עֶבְרָתֶךָ:

יב לִמְנוֹת יָמֵינוּ כֵּן הוֹדַע וְנָבִא לְבַב חָכְמָה:

יג שׁוּבָה יְהֹוָה עַד־מָתָי וְהִנָּחֵם עַל־עֲבָדֶיךָ:

יד שַׂבְּעֵנוּ בַבֹּקֶר חַסְדֶּךָ וּנְרַנְּנָה וְנִשְׂמְחָה בְּכָל־יָמֵינוּ:

טו שַׂמְּחֵנוּ כִּימוֹת עִנִּיתָנוּ שְׁנוֹת רָאִינוּ רָעָה:

טז יֵרָאֶה אֶל־עֲבָדֶיךָ פָּעֳלֶךָ וַהֲדָרְךָ עַל־בְּנֵיהֶם:

יז וִיהִי נֹעַם אֲדֹנָי אֱלֹהֵינוּ עָלֵינוּ וּמַעֲשֵׂה יָדֵינוּ כּוֹנְנָה עָלֵינוּ וּמַעֲשֵׂה יָדֵינוּ
כּוֹנְנֵהוּ:

א יֹשֵׁב בְּסֵתֶר עֶלְיוֹן בְּצֵל שַׁדַּי יִתְלוֹנָן:

ב אֹמַר לַיהֹוָה מַחְסִי וּמְצוּדָתִי אֱלֹהַי אֶבְטַח־בּוֹ:

ג כִּי הוּא יַצִּילְךָ מִפַּח יָקוּשׁ מִדֶּבֶר הַוּוֹת:

ד בְּאֶבְרָתוֹ יָסֶךְ לָךְ וְתַחַת כְּנָפָיו תֶּחְסֶה צִנָּה וְסֹחֵרָה אֲמִתּוֹ:

ה לֹא־תִירָא מִפַּחַד לָיְלָה מֵחֵץ יָעוּף יוֹמָם:

ו מִדֶּבֶר בָּאֹפֶל יַהֲלֹךְ מִקֶּטֶב יָשׁוּד צָהֳרָיִם:

ז יִפֹּל מִצִּדְּךָ אֶלֶף וּרְבָבָה מִימִינֶךָ אֵלֶיךָ לֹא יִגָּשׁ:

ח רַק בְּעֵינֶיךָ תַבִּיט וְשִׁלֻּמַת רְשָׁעִים תִּרְאֶה:

ט כִּי־אַתָּה יְהֹוָה מַחְסִי עֶלְיוֹן שַׂמְתָּ מְעוֹנֶךָ:

9 Your anger causes our lives to pass away. Our lives come to an end like a story that is untold.

10 The days of our lives are seventy in all, or with strength, perhaps eighty, yet their pride is nothing but hard labor and vanity, for it goes quickly, and we fly away.

11 Who knows the power of Your anger? And Your wrath is in accord to the reverence that is due to You.

12 Teach us to number our days so that our hearts will become wise.

13 Return, my Lord! How long? Have mercy upon Your servants.

14 Satisfy us with Your kindness in the morning, so that we may be joyful and glad all our lives.

15 Give us joy according to the length of time that You have afflicted us, according to the years in which we saw evil.

16 Let Your acts appear to Your servants, and Your splendor upon their children.

17 May the graciousness of our Lord be upon us. Grant lasting success to the work of our hands. Grant the work of our hands lasting success.

TEHILLIM 91

A song of God in answer to the prayers of human beings

1 You who live in the concealment of the Most High, who shelter in the shadow of the Almighty:

2 I say of the Lord, who is my shelter and my protector, my God in whom I trust.

3 That He will save you from the trap, and from terrible plague.

4 He will cover you with His wings, and you will be protected; His truth is a broad, round shield.

5 You will fear no terror at night, nor arrows that fly by day,

6 Nor the plague that comes by night, nor the destruction that rages at noon.

7 A thousand people may fall beside you, ten thousand at your right hand, but it will not come near you.

8 Only your eyes will see and witness the punishment of the wicked.

9 For you have made the Lord, the Most High, who is my shelter, your dwelling place.

י‏ לֹא־תְאֻנֶּה אֵלֶיךָ רָעָה וְנֶגַע לֹא־יִקְרַב בְּאָהֳלֶךָ:

יא‏ כִּי מַלְאָכָיו יְצַוֶּה־לָּךְ לִשְׁמָרְךָ בְּכָל־דְּרָכֶיךָ:

יב‏ עַל־כַּפַּיִם יִשָּׂאוּנְךָ פֶּן־תִּגֹּף בָּאֶבֶן רַגְלֶךָ:

יג‏ עַל־שַׁחַל וָפֶתֶן תִּדְרֹךְ תִּרְמֹס כְּפִיר וְתַנִּין:

יד‏ כִּי בִי חָשַׁק וַאֲפַלְּטֵהוּ אֲשַׂגְּבֵהוּ כִּי־יָדַע שְׁמִי:

טו‏ יִקְרָאֵנִי וְאֶעֱנֵהוּ עִמּוֹ אָנֹכִי בְצָרָה אֲחַלְּצֵהוּ וַאֲכַבְּדֵהוּ:

טז‏ אֹרֶךְ יָמִים אַשְׂבִּיעֵהוּ וְאַרְאֵהוּ בִּישׁוּעָתִי:

פרק צב

א‏ מִזְמוֹר שִׁיר לְיוֹם הַשַּׁבָּת:

ב‏ טוֹב לְהֹדוֹת לַיהוָה וּלְזַמֵּר לְשִׁמְךָ עֶלְיוֹן:

ג‏ לְהַגִּיד בַּבֹּקֶר חַסְדֶּךָ וֶאֱמוּנָתְךָ בַּלֵּילוֹת:

ד‏ עֲלֵי־עָשׂוֹר וַעֲלֵי־נָבֶל עֲלֵי הִגָּיוֹן בְּכִנּוֹר:

ה‏ כִּי שִׂמַּחְתַּנִי יְהוָה בְּפָעֳלֶךָ בְּמַעֲשֵׂי יָדֶיךָ אֲרַנֵּן:

ו‏ מַה־גָּדְלוּ מַעֲשֶׂיךָ יְהוָה מְאֹד עָמְקוּ מַחְשְׁבֹתֶיךָ:

ז‏ אִישׁ בַּעַר לֹא יֵדָע וּכְסִיל לֹא־יָבִין אֶת־זֹאת:

ח‏ בִּפְרֹחַ רְשָׁעִים כְּמוֹ עֵשֶׂב וַיָּצִיצוּ כָּל־פֹּעֲלֵי אָוֶן לְהִשָּׁמְדָם עֲדֵי־עַד:

ט‏ וְאַתָּה מָרוֹם לְעֹלָם יְהוָה:

י‏ כִּי הִנֵּה אֹיְבֶיךָ יְהוָה כִּי־הִנֵּה אֹיְבֶיךָ יֹאבֵדוּ יִתְפָּרְדוּ כָּל־פֹּעֲלֵי אָוֶן:

יא‏ וַתָּרֶם כִּרְאֵים קַרְנִי בַּלֹּתִי בְּשֶׁמֶן רַעֲנָן:

יב‏ וַתַּבֵּט עֵינִי בְּשׁוּרָי בַּקָּמִים עָלַי מְרֵעִים תִּשְׁמַעְנָה אָזְנָי:

10 Nothing evil will happen to you, nor will any plague come near your tent.

11 God will command His angels to guard you everywhere you go.

12 They will support you with their hands, so that you will never injure your toe against a stone.

13 You will walk upon the lion and the venomous snake; you will trample the young lion and the serpent under your feet.

14 "He desires Me, so I will save him. I will raise him high because He knows My name."

15 When he calls to Me, I will answer him. I will be with him in time of trouble; I will save him and show him honor.

16 I will satisfy him with long life, and allow him to witness My salvation."

TEHILLIM 92

Adam sings about the beauty of Shabbat and about God's love for the world that He created

1 A psalm, a song for the Sabbath day.

2 It is good to thank the Lord and to sing praises to Your name, God,

3 To speak of Your loving kindness in the morning and Your faithfulness at nighttime,

4 With the ten-stringed instrument and with the lyre, with a solemn sound upon the harp.

5 You have made me rejoice in Your works, God; the work of Your hands makes me glad.

6 How great are Your works, Lord! Your thoughts are profound indeed.

7 An ignorant man does not know this, and a foolish person does not understand it:

8 When wicked people thrive like grass and all the evildoers prosper, it is so they will be destroyed for all time.

9 But You, my Lord, are raised on high forever.

10 See, Your enemies, Lord – Behold, Your enemies will perish; all the evildoers will be scattered.

11 But You have raised my fortunes like the wild ox; I am anointed with fresh oil.

יג צַדִּיק כַּתָּמָר יִפְרָח כְּאֶרֶז בַּלְּבָנוֹן יִשְׂגֶּה:

יד שְׁתוּלִים בְּבֵית יְהוָה בְּחַצְרוֹת אֱלֹהֵינוּ יַפְרִיחוּ:

טו עוֹד יְנוּבוּן בְּשֵׂיבָה דְּשֵׁנִים וְרַעֲנַנִּים יִהְיוּ:

טז לְהַגִּיד כִּי־יָשָׁר יְהוָה צוּרִי וְלֹא־עלתה [עַוְלָתָה] בּוֹ:

פרק צג

א יְהוָה מָלָךְ גֵּאוּת לָבֵשׁ לָבֵשׁ יְהוָה עֹז הִתְאַזָּר אַף־תִּכּוֹן תֵּבֵל בַּל־תִּמּוֹט:

ב נָכוֹן כִּסְאֲךָ מֵאָז מֵעוֹלָם אָתָּה:

ג נָשְׂאוּ נְהָרוֹת יְהוָה נָשְׂאוּ נְהָרוֹת קוֹלָם יִשְׂאוּ נְהָרוֹת דָּכְיָם:

ד מִקֹּלוֹת מַיִם רַבִּים אַדִּירִים מִשְׁבְּרֵי־יָם אַדִּיר בַּמָּרוֹם יְהוָה:

ה עֵדֹתֶיךָ נֶאֶמְנוּ מְאֹד לְבֵיתְךָ נָאֲוָה־קֹדֶשׁ יְהוָה לְאֹרֶךְ יָמִים:

פרק צד

א אֵל־נְקָמוֹת יְהוָה אֵל נְקָמוֹת הוֹפִיעַ:

ב הִנָּשֵׂא שֹׁפֵט הָאָרֶץ הָשֵׁב גְּמוּל עַל־גֵּאִים:

ג עַד־מָתַי רְשָׁעִים יְהוָה עַד־מָתַי רְשָׁעִים יַעֲלֹזוּ:

ד יַבִּיעוּ יְדַבְּרוּ עָתָק יִתְאַמְּרוּ כָּל־פֹּעֲלֵי אָוֶן:

ה עַמְּךָ יְהוָה יְדַכְּאוּ וְנַחֲלָתְךָ יְעַנּוּ:

12 I have looked upon the destruction of my enemies who lie in wait for me; my ears have heard of the judgment of the wicked people who rise up against me.

13 The righteous will blossom like the palm tree; they shall grow like the cedars of Lebanon.

14 Planted in the House of our Lord, they shall thrive in the courts of our God.

15 Even in old age they shall be fruitful; they shall be full of sap and freshness,

16 Declaring that God is upright, that my Rock does no wrong.

TEHILLIM 93

A song about God the King

1 The Lord reigns, clothed in majesty. The Lord has clothed Himself, has girded Himself with strength. The world is firmly established and cannot be moved.

2 Your Throne has always existed and You are eternal.

3 The floods have raised, Lord, the floods have raised their voices; the floods roar.

4 Above the voices of many waters, the roaring waves of the ocean, the Lord is mighty on high.

5 Your laws are very faithful and holiness is the foundation of Your house, My Lord, for all time.

TEHILLIM 94

A song asking for Divine justice

1 God of vengeance, Lord, God of vengeance, appear!

2 Arise, Judge of the earth, and punish the haughty as they deserve.

3 How long will the wicked, Lord, how long will the wicked rejoice?

4 They spread out and speak in arrogance; all the evildoers put on airs.

5 They crush Your people, God, and torment Your heritage.

6 They kill the widow and the stranger and murder the orphan.

7 They say: The Lord will never see, nor will the God of Jacob be concerned.

8 Think, you ignorant ones! You fools, when will you understand?

ו   אַלְמָנָה וְגֵר יַהֲרֹגוּ וִיתוֹמִים יְרַצֵּחוּ:

ז   וַיֹּאמְרוּ לֹא יִרְאֶה־יָּהּ וְלֹא־יָבִין אֱלֹהֵי יַעֲקֹב:

ח   בִּינוּ בֹּעֲרִים בָּעָם וּכְסִילִים מָתַי תַּשְׂכִּילוּ:

ט   הֲנֹטַע אֹזֶן הֲלֹא יִשְׁמָע אִם־יֹצֵר עַיִן הֲלֹא יַבִּיט:

י   הֲיֹסֵר גּוֹיִם הֲלֹא יוֹכִיחַ הַמְלַמֵּד אָדָם דָּעַת:

יא   יְהוָה יֹדֵעַ מַחְשְׁבוֹת אָדָם כִּי הֵמָּה הָבֶל:

יב   אַשְׁרֵי הַגֶּבֶר אֲשֶׁר־תְּיַסְּרֶנּוּ יָּהּ וּמִתּוֹרָתְךָ תְלַמְּדֶנּוּ:

יג   לְהַשְׁקִיט לוֹ מִימֵי רָע עַד יִכָּרֶה לָרָשָׁע שָׁחַת:

יד   כִּי לֹא־יִטֹּשׁ יְהוָה עַמּוֹ וְנַחֲלָתוֹ לֹא יַעֲזֹב:

טו   כִּי־עַד־צֶדֶק יָשׁוּב מִשְׁפָּט וְאַחֲרָיו כָּל־יִשְׁרֵי־לֵב:

טז   מִי־יָקוּם לִי עִם־מְרֵעִים מִי־יִתְיַצֵּב לִי עִם־פֹּעֲלֵי אָוֶן:

יז   לוּלֵי יְהוָה עֶזְרָתָה לִּי כִּמְעַט שָׁכְנָה דוּמָה נַפְשִׁי:

יח   אִם־אָמַרְתִּי מָטָה רַגְלִי חַסְדְּךָ יְהוָה יִסְעָדֵנִי:

יט   בְּרֹב שַׂרְעַפַּי בְּקִרְבִּי תַּנְחוּמֶיךָ יְשַׁעַשְׁעוּ נַפְשִׁי:

כ   הַיְחָבְרְךָ כִּסֵּא הַוּוֹת יֹצֵר עָמָל עֲלֵי־חֹק:

כא   יָגוֹדּוּ עַל־נֶפֶשׁ צַדִּיק וְדָם נָקִי יַרְשִׁיעוּ:

כב   וַיְהִי יְהוָה לִי לְמִשְׂגָּב וֵאלֹהַי לְצוּר מַחְסִי:

כג   וַיָּשֶׁב עֲלֵיהֶם אֶת־אוֹנָם וּבְרָעָתָם יַצְמִיתֵם יַצְמִיתֵם יְהוָה אֱלֹהֵינוּ:

פרק צה

א   לְכוּ נְרַנְּנָה לַיהוָה נָרִיעָה לְצוּר יִשְׁעֵנוּ:

ב   נְקַדְּמָה פָנָיו בְּתוֹדָה בִּזְמִרוֹת נָרִיעַ לוֹ:

9 Will the One who created the ear not hear? Will the One who formed the eye not see?

10 He who teaches nations – will He not rebuke? – the One Who gives man knowledge?

11 God knows the thoughts of human beings – that they are vanity.

12 My Lord, fortunate is the man whom You reproach, and whom you Your Torah.

13 You will shelter him in quiet from evil times, until the pit is dug for the wicked.

14 The Lord will not reject His people and will not forget His inheritance, Israel.

15 Nations shall return to justice, and all those of integrity shall go after it.

16 Who will come forward for me against the sinners? Who will fight against evildoers for me?

17 If it had not been for the Lord helping me, my life would have been silenced.

18 If I said "My foot stumbles," Your loving kindness supported me.

19 I had worries but Your comfort soothed me.

20 Will the wicked make a partnership with You to make the law evil?

21 They join together against the good people and condemn the innocent.

22 But the Lord has been my protector, God you are the rock of my refuge.

23 God brings the evil of the wicked upon them, and will cut them off with their own evil; the Lord our God will destroy them.

TEHILLIM 95

A song of thanks and praise, and the day of rest

1 Come and let us sing to the Lord; let us shout joyfully to the Rock of our salvation.

2 Let us come before Him with thanks and shout joyful psalms to Him.

ג כִּי אֵל גָּדוֹל יְהוָה וּמֶלֶךְ גָּדוֹל עַל־כָּל־אֱלֹהִים:

ד אֲשֶׁר בְּיָדוֹ מֶחְקְרֵי־אָרֶץ וְתוֹעֲפוֹת הָרִים לוֹ:

ה אֲשֶׁר־לוֹ הַיָּם וְהוּא עָשָׂהוּ וְיַבֶּשֶׁת יָדָיו יָצָרוּ:

ו בֹּאוּ נִשְׁתַּחֲוֶה וְנִכְרָעָה נִבְרְכָה לִפְנֵי־יְהוָה עֹשֵׂנוּ:

ז כִּי הוּא אֱלֹהֵינוּ וַאֲנַחְנוּ עַם מַרְעִיתוֹ וְצֹאן יָדוֹ הַיּוֹם אִם־בְּקֹלוֹ תִשְׁמָעוּ:

ח אַל־תַּקְשׁוּ לְבַבְכֶם כִּמְרִיבָה כְּיוֹם מַסָּה בַּמִּדְבָּר:

ט אֲשֶׁר נִסּוּנִי אֲבוֹתֵיכֶם בְּחָנוּנִי גַּם־רָאוּ פָעֳלִי:

י אַרְבָּעִים שָׁנָה אָקוּט בְּדוֹר וָאֹמַר עַם תֹּעֵי לֵבָב הֵם וְהֵם לֹא־יָדְעוּ דְרָכָי:

יא אֲשֶׁר־נִשְׁבַּעְתִּי בְאַפִּי אִם־יְבֹאוּן אֶל־מְנוּחָתִי:

פרק צו

א שִׁירוּ לַיהוָה שִׁיר חָדָשׁ שִׁירוּ לַיהוָה כָּל־הָאָרֶץ:

ב שִׁירוּ לַיהוָה בָּרְכוּ שְׁמוֹ בַּשְּׂרוּ מִיּוֹם־לְיוֹם יְשׁוּעָתוֹ:

ג סַפְּרוּ בַגּוֹיִם כְּבוֹדוֹ בְּכָל־הָעַמִּים נִפְלְאוֹתָיו:

ד כִּי גָדוֹל יְהוָה וּמְהֻלָּל מְאֹד נוֹרָא הוּא עַל־כָּל־אֱלֹהִים:

ה כִּי כָּל־אֱלֹהֵי הָעַמִּים אֱלִילִים וַיהוָה שָׁמַיִם עָשָׂה:

ו הוֹד־וְהָדָר לְפָנָיו עֹז וְתִפְאֶרֶת בְּמִקְדָּשׁוֹ:

ז הָבוּ לַיהוָה מִשְׁפְּחוֹת עַמִּים הָבוּ לַיהוָה כָּבוֹד וָעֹז:

ח הָבוּ לַיהוָה כְּבוֹד שְׁמוֹ שְׂאוּ־מִנְחָה וּבֹאוּ לְחַצְרוֹתָיו:

ט הִשְׁתַּחֲווּ לַיהוָה בְּהַדְרַת־קֹדֶשׁ חִילוּ מִפָּנָיו כָּל־הָאָרֶץ:

3 The Lord is a great God and a great King above all gods.
4 He controls the depths of earth and the height of the mountains.
5 He made the sea and it belongs to Him. He created the dry land.
6 Let us kneel and bend the knee. Let us bow down to our Creator.
7 He is our God and we are the people of His pasture, the flock of His hand. Today, if you would but listen to His voice!
8 "Do not harden your hearts as you did at Meribah, as on the day of Massah in the wilderness,
9 Where your ancestors tested Me even though they had witnessed My miracles.
10 I was troubled by that generation for forty years. I said:" These people act wrongly in their hearts and do not know My ways".
11 Therefore in My anger I swore that they would not enter into Israel My resting place."

TEHILLIM 96

All the nations will sing to God

1 Sing a new song to the Lord. Let the entire earth sing to the Lord.
2 Sing to the Lord and bless His name. Proclaim His salvation each and every day.
3 Speak of His glory among the nations and of His wonderful deeds among the people.
4 The Lord is great and He should be greatly praised. He should be feared above all gods.
5 All the gods of the nations are nothing, but the Lord made the heavens.
6 Majesty and splendor go before Him. Strength and beauty are in His Sanctuary.
7 Ascribe to the Lord, families of nations, ascribe to the Lord glory and might.
8 Give to the lord the honor he is due. Bring an offering and come into His courts.
9 Bow down to the Lord in the glory of the Sanctuary. Tremble before him, all the world!

י אִמְרוּ בַגּוֹיִם יְהֹוָה מָלָךְ אַף־תִּכּוֹן תֵּבֵל בַּל־תִּמּוֹט יָדִין עַמִּים
בְּמֵישָׁרִים:

יא יִשְׂמְחוּ הַשָּׁמַיִם וְתָגֵל הָאָרֶץ יִרְעַם הַיָּם וּמְלֹאוֹ:

יב יַעֲלֹז שָׂדַי וְכָל־אֲשֶׁר־בּוֹ אָז יְרַנְּנוּ כָּל־עֲצֵי־יָעַר:

יג לִפְנֵי יְהֹוָה כִּי בָא כִּי בָא לִשְׁפֹּט הָאָרֶץ יִשְׁפֹּט־תֵּבֵל בְּצֶדֶק וְעַמִּים
בֶּאֱמוּנָתוֹ:

פרק צז

א יְהֹוָה מָלָךְ תָּגֵל הָאָרֶץ יִשְׂמְחוּ אִיִּים רַבִּים:

ב עָנָן וַעֲרָפֶל סְבִיבָיו צֶדֶק וּמִשְׁפָּט מְכוֹן כִּסְאוֹ:

ג אֵשׁ לְפָנָיו תֵּלֵךְ וּתְלַהֵט סָבִיב צָרָיו:

ד הֵאִירוּ בְרָקָיו תֵּבֵל רָאֲתָה וַתָּחֵל הָאָרֶץ:

ה הָרִים כַּדּוֹנַג נָמַסּוּ מִלִּפְנֵי יְהֹוָה מִלִּפְנֵי אֲדוֹן כָּל־הָאָרֶץ:

ו הִגִּידוּ הַשָּׁמַיִם צִדְקוֹ וְרָאוּ כָל־הָעַמִּים כְּבוֹדוֹ:

ז יֵבֹשׁוּ כָּל־עֹבְדֵי פֶסֶל הַמִּתְהַלְלִים בָּאֱלִילִים הִשְׁתַּחֲווּ־לוֹ כָּל־אֱלֹהִים:

ח שָׁמְעָה וַתִּשְׂמַח צִיּוֹן וַתָּגֵלְנָה בְּנוֹת יְהוּדָה לְמַעַן מִשְׁפָּטֶיךָ יְהֹוָה:

ט כִּי־אַתָּה יְהֹוָה עֶלְיוֹן עַל־כָּל־הָאָרֶץ מְאֹד נַעֲלֵיתָ עַל־כָּל־אֱלֹהִים:

י אֹהֲבֵי יְהֹוָה שִׂנְאוּ רָע שֹׁמֵר נַפְשׁוֹת חֲסִידָיו מִיַּד רְשָׁעִים יַצִּילֵם:

יא אוֹר זָרֻעַ לַצַּדִּיק וּלְיִשְׁרֵי־לֵב שִׂמְחָה:

יב שִׂמְחוּ צַדִּיקִים בַּיהֹוָה וְהוֹדוּ לְזֵכֶר קָדְשׁוֹ:

10 Declare to all the nations: "The Lord reigns!" He created the world so that it cannot be moved. He will judge the nations fairly.

11 Let the heavens be glad and the earth rejoice. Let the sea roar with all that is in it.

12 Let the field rejoice, with all it contains. Then the trees of the forest will sing for joy

13 Before the Lord, for He has come, He has come to judge the earth. He will judge the world with righteousness and the nations with His faithfulness.

TEHILLIM 97

A song about God, the King of all the earth

1 When the Lord rules the earth, the earth will be glad. The many islands will be happy.

2 Clouds and darkness surround Him. His throne is established upon righteousness and justice.

3 A fire goes before Him, surrounding and destroying all His enemies.

4 His lightning lights the entire world. The earth sees and shakes.

5 The mountains melt away like wax in the Lord's presence, before the Lord of the whole earth.

6 The heavens will declare His righteousness and all the nations will witness His glory.

7 Let all who serve graven idols and boast of their false gods be ashamed. Bow down to Him, all you gods.

8 Zion hears and is glad. The daughters of Judah rejoice because of Your judgments, Lord.

9 You, Lord, are most high above the earth. You are lifted high above all gods.

10 You who love the Lord, hate evil. He preserves the souls of His servants and has saved them from the wicked.

11 Light is sown for the righteous, and gladness for those with integrity.

12 Rejoice in the Lord, righteous people, and give thanks to His holy name.

פרק צח

א מִזְמוֹר שִׁירוּ לַיהוָה שִׁיר חָדָשׁ כִּי־נִפְלָאוֹת עָשָׂה הוֹשִׁיעָה־לּוֹ יְמִינוֹ וּזְרוֹעַ קָדְשׁוֹ:

ב הוֹדִיעַ יְהוָה יְשׁוּעָתוֹ לְעֵינֵי הַגּוֹיִם גִּלָּה צִדְקָתוֹ:

ג זָכַר חַסְדּוֹ וֶאֱמוּנָתוֹ לְבֵית יִשְׂרָאֵל רָאוּ כָל־אַפְסֵי־אָרֶץ אֵת יְשׁוּעַת אֱלֹהֵינוּ:

ד הָרִיעוּ לַיהוָה כָּל־הָאָרֶץ פִּצְחוּ וְרַנְּנוּ וְזַמֵּרוּ:

ה זַמְּרוּ לַיהוָה בְּכִנּוֹר בְּכִנּוֹר וְקוֹל זִמְרָה:

ו בַּחֲצֹצְרוֹת וְקוֹל שׁוֹפָר הָרִיעוּ לִפְנֵי הַמֶּלֶךְ יְהוָה:

ז יִרְעַם הַיָּם וּמְלֹאוֹ תֵּבֵל וְיֹשְׁבֵי בָהּ:

ח נְהָרוֹת יִמְחֲאוּ־כָף יַחַד הָרִים יְרַנֵּנוּ:

ט לִפְנֵי־יְהוָה כִּי בָא לִשְׁפֹּט הָאָרֶץ יִשְׁפֹּט־תֵּבֵל בְּצֶדֶק וְעַמִּים בְּמֵישָׁרִים:

פרק צט

א יְהוָה מָלָךְ יִרְגְּזוּ עַמִּים יֹשֵׁב כְּרוּבִים תָּנוּט הָאָרֶץ:

ב יְהוָה בְּצִיּוֹן גָּדוֹל וְרָם הוּא עַל־כָּל־הָעַמִּים:

ג יוֹדוּ שִׁמְךָ גָּדוֹל וְנוֹרָא קָדוֹשׁ הוּא:

ד וְעֹז מֶלֶךְ מִשְׁפָּט אָהֵב אַתָּה כּוֹנַנְתָּ מֵישָׁרִים מִשְׁפָּט וּצְדָקָה בְּיַעֲקֹב אַתָּה עָשִׂיתָ:

ה רוֹמְמוּ יְהוָה אֱלֹהֵינוּ וְהִשְׁתַּחֲווּ לַהֲדֹם רַגְלָיו קָדוֹשׁ הוּא:

ו מֹשֶׁה וְאַהֲרֹן בְּכֹהֲנָיו וּשְׁמוּאֵל בְּקֹרְאֵי שְׁמוֹ קֹרִאים אֶל־יְהוָה וְהוּא יַעֲנֵם:

TEHILLIM 98

A song of rejoicing for the nation of Israel

1 A psalm. Sing a new song to the Lord because He has done wonders. His strong right arm and His holiness have brought victories for Israel.

2 The Lord has proved and revealed His salvation and His righteousness for the nations to see.

3 He remembered His kindness and faithfulness toward the house of Israel; all the ends of the earth have witnessed God's salvation.

4 Shout to the Lord, all the earth! Break into joyous song and sing!

5 Sing praises to the Lord with the harp, with the harp and voices of harmony.

6 With trumpets and the shofar, shout before the King, the Lord!

7 Let the sea and everything in it roar, the world and all who inhabit it.

8 Let the floods clap their hands. Let the mountains sing joyously together

9 Before the Lord, for He has come to judge the earth. He will judge the world with righteousness and the people with truth.

TEHILLIM 99

A song of thanksgiving to God

1 The Lord rules – let the nations tremble. He is enthroned upon the cherubim. Let the earth quake.

2 The Lord is great in Zion, and He is high above all nations.

3 Let all worship Your great and powerful name; holy is He!

4 The mighty King loves justice. You have established truth; You have carried out justice and righteousness within Jacob.

5 Worship the Lord our God, and bow down at His Santuary; holy is He!

6 Moshe and Aharon among His priests and Shmuel among those who call upon His name – they called upon the Lord and He answered them.

7 He spoke to them from a pillar of cloud. They kept His observances, and He gave them laws.

ז בְּעַמּוּד עָנָן יְדַבֵּר אֲלֵיהֶם שָׁמְרוּ עֵדֹתָיו וְחֹק נָתַן־לָמוֹ:

ח יְהוָה אֱלֹהֵינוּ אַתָּה עֲנִיתָם אֵל נֹשֵׂא הָיִיתָ לָהֶם וְנֹקֵם עַל־עֲלִילוֹתָם:

ט רוֹמְמוּ יְהוָה אֱלֹהֵינוּ וְהִשְׁתַּחֲווּ לְהַר קָדְשׁוֹ כִּי־קָדוֹשׁ יְהוָה אֱלֹהֵינוּ:

פרק ק

א מִזְמוֹר לְתוֹדָה הָרִיעוּ לַיהוָה כָּל־הָאָרֶץ:

ב עִבְדוּ אֶת־יְהוָה בְּשִׂמְחָה בֹּאוּ לְפָנָיו בִּרְנָנָה:

ג דְּעוּ כִּי־יְהוָה הוּא אֱלֹהִים הוּא עָשָׂנוּ וְלֹא [וְלוֹ] אֲנַחְנוּ עַמּוֹ וְצֹאן מַרְעִיתוֹ:

ד בֹּאוּ שְׁעָרָיו בְּתוֹדָה חֲצֵרֹתָיו בִּתְהִלָּה הוֹדוּ לוֹ בָּרְכוּ שְׁמוֹ:

ה כִּי־טוֹב יְהוָה לְעוֹלָם חַסְדּוֹ וְעַד־דֹּר וָדֹר אֱמוּנָתוֹ:

פרק קא

א לְדָוִד מִזְמוֹר חֶסֶד־וּמִשְׁפָּט אָשִׁירָה לְךָ יְהוָה אֲזַמֵּרָה:

ב אַשְׂכִּילָה בְּדֶרֶךְ תָּמִים מָתַי תָּבוֹא אֵלָי אֶתְהַלֵּךְ בְּתָם־לְבָבִי בְּקֶרֶב בֵּיתִי:

ג לֹא־אָשִׁית לְנֶגֶד עֵינַי דְּבַר־בְּלִיָּעַל עֲשֹׂה־סֵטִים שָׂנֵאתִי לֹא יִדְבַּק בִּי:

ד לֵבָב עִקֵּשׁ יָסוּר מִמֶּנִּי רָע לֹא אֵדָע:

ה מְלוֹשְׁנִי [מְלָשְׁנִי] בַסֵּתֶר רֵעֵהוּ אוֹתוֹ אַצְמִית גְּבַהּ־עֵינַיִם וּרְחַב לֵבָב אֹתוֹ
לֹא אוּכָל:

ו עֵינַי בְּנֶאֶמְנֵי־אֶרֶץ לָשֶׁבֶת עִמָּדִי הֹלֵךְ בְּדֶרֶךְ תָּמִים הוּא יְשָׁרְתֵנִי:

ז לֹא־יֵשֵׁב בְּקֶרֶב בֵּיתִי עֹשֵׂה רְמִיָּה דֹּבֵר שְׁקָרִים לֹא־יִכּוֹן לְנֶגֶד עֵינָי:

ח לַבְּקָרִים אַצְמִית כָּל־רִשְׁעֵי־אָרֶץ לְהַכְרִית מֵעִיר־יְהוָה כָּל־פֹּעֲלֵי אָוֶן:

8 Lord our God, You answered them. You were a forgiving God to them even as you meted out punishment for their sins.

9 Worship the Lord our God, and bow down at His holy mountain, for the Lord our God is holy.

TEHILLIM 100

An invitation to worship God

1 A psalm of thanksgiving. Shout for joy to the Lord, all the earth!

2 Serve the Lord with gladness and come before Him with fervent singing.

3 Know that the Lord is God. He created us and we, His people, are the flock of His pasture.

4 Come to His gates with thanksgiving and into His courts with praise. Give thanks to Him and bless His name.

5 The Lord is good and His loving kindness lasts forever. His faithfulness lasts for all generations.

TEHILLIM 101

A song about preparing Jerusalem to receive God's Holy Ark

1 A psalm of David. I will sing of mercy and justice to You, my Lord. To You, Lord, I will sing praises.

2 I will choose the path of truth. God, when will you come to me? I will walk in my home with a pure heart.

3 I will keep no wicked thing before my eyes. I hate dishonesty; it will not cleave to me.

4 A stubborn heart will stay away from me. I will know no evil.

5 I will destroy anyone who lies about his neighbors even in secret. I will not tolerate anyone who has arrogant eyes and a prideful heart.

6 My eyes look to the faithful people of the land. They will live with me. Those who walk in the path of truth shall serve me.

7 Those who commit deceit will not live in my house; those who speak falsely will not be acceptable to me.

8 Morning after morning I will destroy all the wicked of the land, to cut off all evildoers from the city of the Lord. Selah.

פרק קב

א תְּפִלָּה לְעָנִי כִי־יַעֲטֹף וְלִפְנֵי יְהֹוָה יִשְׁפֹּךְ שִׂיחוֹ:

ב יְהֹוָה שִׁמְעָה תְפִלָּתִי וְשַׁוְעָתִי אֵלֶיךָ תָבוֹא:

ג אַל־תַּסְתֵּר פָּנֶיךָ מִמֶּנִּי בְּיוֹם צַר לִי הַטֵּה־אֵלַי אָזְנֶךָ בְּיוֹם אֶקְרָא מַהֵר עֲנֵנִי:

ד כִּי־כָלוּ בְעָשָׁן יָמָי וְעַצְמוֹתַי כְּמוֹקֵד נִחָרוּ:

ה הוּכָּה־כָעֵשֶׂב וַיִּבַשׁ לִבִּי כִּי־שָׁכַחְתִּי מֵאֲכֹל לַחְמִי:

ו מִקּוֹל אַנְחָתִי דָּבְקָה עַצְמִי לִבְשָׂרִי:

ז דָּמִיתִי לִקְאַת מִדְבָּר הָיִיתִי כְּכוֹס חֳרָבוֹת:

ח שָׁקַדְתִּי וָאֶהְיֶה כְּצִפּוֹר בּוֹדֵד עַל־גָּג:

ט כָּל־הַיּוֹם חֵרְפוּנִי אוֹיְבָי מְהוֹלָלַי בִּי נִשְׁבָּעוּ:

י כִּי אֵפֶר כַּלֶּחֶם אָכָלְתִּי וְשִׁקֻּוַי בִּבְכִי מָסָכְתִּי:

יא מִפְּנֵי־זַעַמְךָ וְקִצְפֶּךָ כִּי נְשָׂאתַנִי וַתַּשְׁלִיכֵנִי:

יב יָמַי כְּצֵל נָטוּי וַאֲנִי כָּעֵשֶׂב אִיבָשׁ:

יג וְאַתָּה יְהֹוָה לְעוֹלָם תֵּשֵׁב וְזִכְרְךָ לְדֹר וָדֹר:

יד אַתָּה תָקוּם תְּרַחֵם צִיּוֹן כִּי־עֵת לְחֶנְנָהּ כִּי בָא מוֹעֵד:

טו כִּי־רָצוּ עֲבָדֶיךָ אֶת־אֲבָנֶיהָ וְאֶת־עֲפָרָהּ יְחֹנֵנוּ:

טז וְיִירְאוּ גוֹיִם אֶת־שֵׁם יְהֹוָה וְכָל־מַלְכֵי הָאָרֶץ אֶת־כְּבוֹדֶךָ:

יז כִּי־בָנָה יְהֹוָה צִיּוֹן נִרְאָה בִּכְבוֹדוֹ:

יח פָּנָה אֶל־תְּפִלַּת הָעַרְעָר וְלֹא־בָזָה אֶת־תְּפִלָּתָם:

יט תִּכָּתֶב זֹאת לְדוֹר אַחֲרוֹן וְעַם נִבְרָא יְהַלֶּל־יָהּ:

כ כִּי־הִשְׁקִיף מִמְּרוֹם קָדְשׁוֹ יְהֹוָה מִשָּׁמַיִם אֶל־אֶרֶץ הִבִּיט:

TEHILLIM 102

A song of faith and hope for the future

1 A prayer of a poor man who is suffering, who feels faint and desires to pour out his heart to the Lord.

2 My Lord, hear my prayer. Let my cry come to You.

3 Do not hide from me in my time of trouble. Listen to me, and answer me quickly when I call to You.

4 My days have vanished in smoke, and my bones are burned as if they were on a pyre.

5 My heart is struck and dried out like grass, for I have forgotten to eat my food.

6 My bones stick to my flesh because of my sighing.

7 I am like a pelican of the wilderness, like an owl that lives in ruins.

8 I sit by myself and watch like a lone bird on a rooftop.

9 My enemies insult me all day long, and those who hate me use my name as a curse.

10 I have eaten ashes instead of bread, and mixed tears into my drink

11 Because of Your fury and anger, for You took me up and then cast me away.

12 My days are like a shadow that lengthens, and I am like withered grass.

13 You, Lord, are enthroned forever, and Your name will be remembered for all generations.

14 You will arise and have compassion upon Zion, for the time has come for You to favor her.

15 Your servants desire its very stones and love its dust.

16 Then all the nations will revere the name of the Lord, and all the kings of the earth will revere Your glory;

17 When the Lord rebuilds Zion and appears there in glory;

18 When he accepts the prayer of the shattered ones, and has not scorned their prayer.

19 This will be written down for future generations, and a nation that will yet be created shall praise the Lord.

20 He looked down to the earth from His high and sacred place; the Lord looked down from Heaven to earth,

21 To hear the groan of the prisoner and to save those who have been sentenced to death,

כא לִשְׁמֹעַ אֶנְקַת אָסִיר לְפַתֵּחַ בְּנֵי תְמוּתָה:

כב לְסַפֵּר בְּצִיּוֹן שֵׁם יְהוָה וּתְהִלָּתוֹ בִּירוּשָׁלָם:

כג בְּהִקָּבֵץ עַמִּים יַחְדָּו וּמַמְלָכוֹת לַעֲבֹד אֶת־יְהוָה:

כד עִנָּה בַדֶּרֶךְ כחו [כֹּחִי] קִצַּר יָמָי:

כה אֹמַר אֵלִי אַל־תַּעֲלֵנִי בַּחֲצִי יָמָי בְּדוֹר דּוֹרִים שְׁנוֹתֶיךָ:

כו לְפָנִים הָאָרֶץ יָסַדְתָּ וּמַעֲשֵׂה יָדֶיךָ שָׁמָיִם:

כז הֵמָּה יֹאבֵדוּ וְאַתָּה תַעֲמֹד וְכֻלָּם כַּבֶּגֶד יִבְלוּ כַּלְּבוּשׁ תַּחֲלִיפֵם וְיַחֲלֹפוּ:

כח וְאַתָּה־הוּא וּשְׁנוֹתֶיךָ לֹא יִתָּמּוּ:

כט בְּנֵי־עֲבָדֶיךָ יִשְׁכּוֹנוּ וְזַרְעָם לְפָנֶיךָ יִכּוֹן:

פרק קג

א לְדָוִד בָּרֲכִי נַפְשִׁי אֶת־יְהוָה וְכָל־קְרָבַי אֶת־שֵׁם קָדְשׁוֹ:

ב בָּרֲכִי נַפְשִׁי אֶת־יְהוָה וְאַל־תִּשְׁכְּחִי כָּל־גְּמוּלָיו:

ג הַסֹּלֵחַ לְכָל־עֲוֹנֵכִי הָרֹפֵא לְכָל־תַּחֲלֻאָיְכִי:

ד הַגּוֹאֵל מִשַּׁחַת חַיָּיְכִי הַמְעַטְּרֵכִי חֶסֶד וְרַחֲמִים:

ה הַמַּשְׂבִּיעַ בַּטּוֹב עֶדְיֵךְ תִּתְחַדֵּשׁ כַּנֶּשֶׁר נְעוּרָיְכִי:

ו עֹשֵׂה צְדָקוֹת יְהוָה וּמִשְׁפָּטִים לְכָל־עֲשׁוּקִים:

ז יוֹדִיעַ דְּרָכָיו לְמֹשֶׁה לִבְנֵי יִשְׂרָאֵל עֲלִילוֹתָיו:

ח רַחוּם וְחַנּוּן יְהוָה אֶרֶךְ אַפַּיִם וְרַב־חָסֶד:

ט לֹא־לָנֶצַח יָרִיב וְלֹא לְעוֹלָם יִטּוֹר:

י לֹא כַחֲטָאֵינוּ עָשָׂה לָנוּ וְלֹא כַעֲוֹנֹתֵינוּ גָּמַל עָלֵינוּ:

יא כִּי כִגְבֹהַּ שָׁמַיִם עַל־הָאָרֶץ גָּבַר חַסְדּוֹ עַל־יְרֵאָיו:

22 So that people may tell of the Lord's name in Zion, and His fame in Jerusalem;

23 When the nations and the kingdoms are assembled to serve the Lord.

24 If he weakened my strength along the way; and shortened my life,

25 I say: my God, do not take me away in the midst of my life; You Whose years last throughout all generations.

26 In the beginning You laid the earth's foundations, and the heavens are the work of Your hands.

27 They will perish, but You will endure. They will all wear out like clothing. You will change them like a garment, and they will pass away.

28 But You remain the same, and Your years have no end".

29 The children of Your servants will live in safety, and their descendants shall be established before You.

TEHILLIM 103

A song of joy and happiness

1 A [psalm] of David. My soul, bless the Lord. Let everything that is within me bless His holy Name.

2 Bless the Lord, my soul, and do not forget all His kindnesses toward you:

3 He forgives all your sins and heals all your diseases,

4 Saves your life from the grave and surrounds you with loving kindness and mercy.

5 He satisfies you with good in your old age, so that your youth is renewed like the feathers of an eagle.

6 The Lord does righteously and acts justly towards all who are oppressed.

7 He showed His ways to Moshe and His acts to the children of Israel.

8 The Lord is full of compassion and gracious; slow to anger and full of kindness.

9 He will not always chastise; He will not keep hold of His anger forever.

10 He has not repaid us according to our sins, nor paid us back according to our wrongdoing.

יב כִּרְחֹק מִזְרָח מִמַּעֲרָב הִרְחִיק מִמֶּנּוּ אֶת־פְּשָׁעֵינוּ:

יג כְּרַחֵם אָב עַל־בָּנִים רִחַם יְהוָה עַל־יְרֵאָיו:

יד כִּי הוּא יָדַע יִצְרֵנוּ זָכוּר כִּי־עָפָר אֲנָחְנוּ:

טו אֱנוֹשׁ כֶּחָצִיר יָמָיו כְּצִיץ הַשָּׂדֶה כֵּן יָצִיץ:

טז כִּי רוּחַ עָבְרָה־בּוֹ וְאֵינֶנּוּ וְלֹא־יַכִּירֶנּוּ עוֹד מְקוֹמוֹ:

יז וְחֶסֶד יְהוָה מֵעוֹלָם וְעַד־עוֹלָם עַל־יְרֵאָיו וְצִדְקָתוֹ לִבְנֵי בָנִים:

יח לְשֹׁמְרֵי בְרִיתוֹ וּלְזֹכְרֵי פִקֻּדָיו לַעֲשׂוֹתָם:

יט יְהוָה בַּשָּׁמַיִם הֵכִין כִּסְאוֹ וּמַלְכוּתוֹ בַּכֹּל מָשָׁלָה:

כ בָּרֲכוּ יְהוָה מַלְאָכָיו גִּבֹּרֵי כֹחַ עֹשֵׂי דְבָרוֹ לִשְׁמֹעַ בְּקוֹל דְּבָרוֹ:

כא בָּרֲכוּ יְהוָה כָּל־צְבָאָיו מְשָׁרְתָיו עֹשֵׂי רְצוֹנוֹ:

כב בָּרֲכוּ יְהוָה כָּל־מַעֲשָׂיו בְּכָל־מְקֹמוֹת מֶמְשַׁלְתּוֹ בָּרֲכִי נַפְשִׁי אֶת־יְהוָה:

פרק קד

א בָּרֲכִי נַפְשִׁי אֶת־יְהוָה יְהוָה אֱלֹהַי גָּדַלְתָּ מְּאֹד הוֹד וְהָדָר לָבָשְׁתָּ:

ב עֹטֶה אוֹר כַּשַּׂלְמָה נוֹטֶה שָׁמַיִם כַּיְרִיעָה:

ג הַמְקָרֶה בַמַּיִם עֲלִיּוֹתָיו הַשָּׂם־עָבִים רְכוּבוֹ הַמְהַלֵּךְ עַל־כַּנְפֵי־רוּחַ:

ד עֹשֶׂה מַלְאָכָיו רוּחוֹת מְשָׁרְתָיו אֵשׁ לֹהֵט:

ה יָסַד אֶרֶץ עַל־מְכוֹנֶיהָ בַּל־תִּמּוֹט עוֹלָם וָעֶד:

ו תְּהוֹם כַּלְּבוּשׁ כִּסִּיתוֹ עַל־הָרִים יַעַמְדוּ־מָיִם:

ז מִן־גַּעֲרָתְךָ יְנוּסוּן מִן־קוֹל רַעַמְךָ יֵחָפֵזוּן:

ח יַעֲלוּ הָרִים יֵרְדוּ בְקָעוֹת אֶל־מְקוֹם זֶה יָסַדְתָּ לָהֶם:

11 As high as heaven is above the earth, so great is His kindness toward those who revere Him.

12 As far as east is from west, so far has God removed our sins from us.

13 As a father has compassion upon his children, so God has compassion on those who revere Him.

14 He knows that we are only human. He remembers that we are nothing but dust.

15 The days of man are like grass. He blossoms like a flower of the field.

16 The wind passes over him and he is gone. His own place no longer remembers him.

17 But the Lord's kindness lasts forever, for all time, for those who revere Him, and His righteousness to children's children,

18 To those who keep the covenant and remember and perform His commandments.

19 The Lord has set up His throne in the heaven; His kingship is over all.

20 Bless the Lord, his angels, you who are mighty, who perform His bidding, heeding His word.

21 Bless the Lord, His hosts, His servants, who do His will.

22 Bless the Lord, all his works, in all the places that He governs: bless the Lord, my soul!

TEHILLIM 104

A song about the beautiful universe that God created

1 Bless the Lord, my soul! My Lord God, You are very great. You are clothed in glory and majesty.

2 You wrap Yourself in a clothing of light as in clothing and stretch out the heavens like a curtain.

3 You lay the beams of your upper rooms in the waters. You make the clouds Your chariot and walk upon the wings of wind.

4 You make the wind Your messenger and flaming fire Your servant.

5 You established the earth upon its foundations so that it will never be moved.

6 You covered it with the deep as with a garment. The waters stood above the mountains.

7 At your rebuke, the waters fled. They hurried away from the voice of Your thunder.

ט   גְּבוּל־שַׂמְתָּ בַּל־יַעֲבֹרוּן בַּל־יְשׁוּבוּן לְכַסּוֹת הָאָרֶץ׃

י   הַמְשַׁלֵּחַ מַעְיָנִים בַּנְּחָלִים בֵּין הָרִים יְהַלֵּכוּן׃

יא   יַשְׁקוּ כָּל־חַיְתוֹ שָׂדָי יִשְׁבְּרוּ פְרָאִים צְמָאָם׃

יב   עֲלֵיהֶם עוֹף־הַשָּׁמַיִם יִשְׁכּוֹן מִבֵּין עֳפָאִים יִתְּנוּ־קוֹל׃

יג   מַשְׁקֶה הָרִים מֵעֲלִיּוֹתָיו מִפְּרִי מַעֲשֶׂיךָ תִּשְׂבַּע הָאָרֶץ׃

יד   מַצְמִיחַ חָצִיר לַבְּהֵמָה וְעֵשֶׂב לַעֲבֹדַת הָאָדָם לְהוֹצִיא לֶחֶם מִן־הָאָרֶץ׃

טו   וְיַיִן יְשַׂמַּח לְבַב־אֱנוֹשׁ לְהַצְהִיל פָּנִים מִשָּׁמֶן וְלֶחֶם לְבַב־אֱנוֹשׁ יִסְעָד׃

טז   יִשְׂבְּעוּ עֲצֵי יְהוָה אַרְזֵי לְבָנוֹן אֲשֶׁר נָטָע׃

יז   אֲשֶׁר־שָׁם צִפֳּרִים יְקַנֵּנוּ חֲסִידָה בְּרוֹשִׁים בֵּיתָהּ׃

יח   הָרִים הַגְּבֹהִים לַיְּעֵלִים סְלָעִים מַחְסֶה לַשְׁפַנִּים׃

יט   עָשָׂה יָרֵחַ לְמוֹעֲדִים שֶׁמֶשׁ יָדַע מְבוֹאוֹ׃

כ   תָּשֶׁת חֹשֶׁךְ וִיהִי לָיְלָה בּוֹ־תִרְמֹשׂ כָּל־חַיְתוֹ־יָעַר׃

כא   הַכְּפִירִים שֹׁאֲגִים לַטָּרֶף וּלְבַקֵּשׁ מֵאֵל אָכְלָם׃

כב   תִּזְרַח הַשֶּׁמֶשׁ יֵאָסֵפוּן וְאֶל־מְעוֹנֹתָם יִרְבָּצוּן׃

כג   יֵצֵא אָדָם לְפָעֳלוֹ וְלַעֲבֹדָתוֹ עֲדֵי־עָרֶב׃

כד   מָה־רַבּוּ מַעֲשֶׂיךָ יְהוָה כֻּלָּם בְּחָכְמָה עָשִׂיתָ מָלְאָה הָאָרֶץ קִנְיָנֶךָ׃

כה   זֶה הַיָּם גָּדוֹל וּרְחַב יָדָיִם שָׁם־רֶמֶשׂ וְאֵין מִסְפָּר חַיּוֹת קְטַנּוֹת עִם־
גְּדֹלוֹת׃

כו   שָׁם אֳנִיּוֹת יְהַלֵּכוּן לִוְיָתָן זֶה־יָצַרְתָּ לְשַׂחֶק־בּוֹ׃

כז   כֻּלָּם אֵלֶיךָ יְשַׂבֵּרוּן לָתֵת אָכְלָם בְּעִתּוֹ׃

כח   תִּתֵּן לָהֶם יִלְקֹטוּן תִּפְתַּח יָדְךָ יִשְׂבְּעוּן טוֹב׃

כט   תַּסְתִּיר פָּנֶיךָ יִבָּהֵלוּן תֹּסֵף רוּחָם יִגְוָעוּן וְאֶל־עֲפָרָם יְשׁוּבוּן׃

ל   תְּשַׁלַּח רוּחֲךָ יִבָּרֵאוּן וּתְחַדֵּשׁ פְּנֵי אֲדָמָה׃

8 The waters rose up the mountains and down the valleys to the place that You prepared for them.

9 You made boundaries to control them so that they would not return to cover the earth.

10 You send out springs of water into the valleys. They run between the mountains.

11 They provide drink for every beast in the field. The wild animals quench their thirst.

12 The birds of heaven live beside them, singing from the branches.

13 You water the mountains from the heavens. The earth is full of the fruit You have made.

14 You make the grass grow for cattle and herbs for people to use, to bring bread from the earth,

15 And wine that gladdens the hearts of man, and oil to make the face shine, and bread that supports man's heart.

16 You water the cedars of Lebanon and the other trees that You planted

17 Where the birds build their nests. The stork makes its nest in the fir trees.

18 The wild goats live in the mountains and the hares live among the rocks.

19 You set the moon to mark the seasons, and the sun knows when to set.

20 You make darkness and it becomes nighttime, when all the wild animals come out.

21 The young lions roar after their prey, and look to God for their food.

22 When the sun rises, they gather to their dens.

23 Man goes to work and labors until evening.

24 Lord, how numerous are Your creations! You created all of them with Your great wisdom. The universe is filled with Your possessions.

25 There is the sea, great and wide, with creeping things beyond number, and creatures large and small.

26 There sail the ships and the Leviathan, which You created to play there.

27 All of them wait for You to provide them with food at the proper time.

28 You give them food and they gather it. You open You hand and they are satisfied with good.

לא יְהִי כְבוֹד יְהוָה לְעוֹלָם יִשְׂמַח יְהוָה בְּמַעֲשָׂיו:

לב הַמַּבִּיט לָאָרֶץ וַתִּרְעָד יִגַּע בֶּהָרִים וְיֶעֱשָׁנוּ:

לג אָשִׁירָה לַיהוָה בְּחַיָּי אֲזַמְּרָה לֵאלֹהַי בְּעוֹדִי:

לד יֶעֱרַב עָלָיו שִׂיחִי אָנֹכִי אֶשְׂמַח בַּיהוָה:

לה יִתַּמּוּ חַטָּאִים מִן־הָאָרֶץ וּרְשָׁעִים עוֹד אֵינָם בָּרֲכִי נַפְשִׁי אֶת־יְהוָה הַלְלוּיָהּ:

פרק קה

א הוֹדוּ לַיהוָה קִרְאוּ בִשְׁמוֹ הוֹדִיעוּ בָעַמִּים עֲלִילוֹתָיו:

ב שִׁירוּ לוֹ זַמְּרוּ־לוֹ שִׂיחוּ בְּכָל־נִפְלְאוֹתָיו:

ג הִתְהַלְלוּ בְּשֵׁם קָדְשׁוֹ יִשְׂמַח לֵב מְבַקְשֵׁי יְהוָה:

ד דִּרְשׁוּ יְהוָה וְעֻזּוֹ בַּקְּשׁוּ פָנָיו תָּמִיד:

ה זִכְרוּ נִפְלְאוֹתָיו אֲשֶׁר עָשָׂה מֹפְתָיו וּמִשְׁפְּטֵי־פִיו:

ו זֶרַע אַבְרָהָם עַבְדּוֹ בְּנֵי יַעֲקֹב בְּחִירָיו:

ז הוּא יְהוָה אֱלֹהֵינוּ בְּכָל־הָאָרֶץ מִשְׁפָּטָיו:

ח זָכַר לְעוֹלָם בְּרִיתוֹ דָּבָר צִוָּה לְאֶלֶף דּוֹר:

ט אֲשֶׁר כָּרַת אֶת־אַבְרָהָם וּשְׁבוּעָתוֹ לְיִשְׂחָק:

י וַיַּעֲמִידֶהָ לְיַעֲקֹב לְחֹק לְיִשְׂרָאֵל בְּרִית עוֹלָם:

יא לֵאמֹר לְךָ אֶתֵּן אֶת־אֶרֶץ כְּנָעַן חֶבֶל נַחֲלַתְכֶם:

יב בִּהְיוֹתָם מְתֵי מִסְפָּר כִּמְעַט וְגָרִים בָּהּ:

29 When You hide Your face, they are afraid; when You withdraw their breath, they die and return to dust.

30 When You send forth Your spirit, they are created, and You renew the surface of the earth.

31 May the glory of the Lord last forever. May the Lord rejoice in His works.

32 When He looks upon the earth, it trembles. When He touches the mountains, they erupt.

33 I will sing to the Lord as long as I live. I will give thanks to my God while I exist.

34 May my prayer be pleasing to Him. I will rejoice in the Lord.

35 May the sinners vanish from the earth, and let the wicked be no more. Bless the Lord, my soul. Hallelujah!

TEHILLIM 105

A song thanking God for His help in the past and in the future

1 Give thanks to the Lord and call upon His name. Make His acts known among the nations.

2 Sing to Him, sing praises to Him and speak about all His miraculous deeds.

3 Glory in His name. May the hearts of those who seek the Lord rejoice.

4 Seek the Lord and His strength. Seek His face always.

5 Remember His miraculous deeds, His wonders and the judgments of His mouth,

6 You, descendants of Avraham, His servant, and you children of Jacob, His chosen ones.

7 He is the Lord our God, and His judgments are over the entire earth.

8 He remembers for all time His covenant and the word that He commanded to a thousand generations,

9 The covenant which He made with Avraham, and His oath to Yitzhak.

10 He established it as a law with Yaakov, an everlasting covenant to Israel,

11 Saying: "I will give you the land of Canaan as an inheritance."

יג וַיִּתְהַלְּכוּ מִגּוֹי אֶל־גּוֹי מִמַּמְלָכָה אֶל־עַם אַחֵר׃

יד לֹא־הִנִּיחַ אָדָם לְעָשְׁקָם וַיּוֹכַח עֲלֵיהֶם מְלָכִים׃

טו אַל־תִּגְּעוּ בִמְשִׁיחָי וְלִנְבִיאַי אַל־תָּרֵעוּ׃

טז וַיִּקְרָא רָעָב עַל־הָאָרֶץ כָּל־מַטֵּה־לֶחֶם שָׁבָר׃

יז שָׁלַח לִפְנֵיהֶם אִישׁ לְעֶבֶד נִמְכַּר יוֹסֵף׃

יח עִנּוּ בַכֶּבֶל רגליו [רַגְלוֹ] בַּרְזֶל בָּאָה נַפְשׁוֹ׃

יט עַד־עֵת בֹּא־דְבָרוֹ אִמְרַת יְהוָה צְרָפָתְהוּ׃

כ שָׁלַח־מֶלֶךְ וַיַּתִּירֵהוּ מֹשֵׁל עַמִּים וַיְפַתְּחֵהוּ׃

כא שָׂמוֹ אָדוֹן לְבֵיתוֹ וּמֹשֵׁל בְּכָל־קִנְיָנוֹ׃

כב לֶאְסֹר שָׂרָיו בְּנַפְשׁוֹ וּזְקֵנָיו יְחַכֵּם׃

כג וַיָּבֹא יִשְׂרָאֵל מִצְרָיִם וְיַעֲקֹב גָּר בְּאֶרֶץ־חָם׃

כד וַיֶּפֶר אֶת־עַמּוֹ מְאֹד וַיַּעֲצִמֵהוּ מִצָּרָיו׃

כה הָפַךְ לִבָּם לִשְׂנֹא עַמּוֹ לְהִתְנַכֵּל בַּעֲבָדָיו׃

כו שָׁלַח מֹשֶׁה עַבְדּוֹ אַהֲרֹן אֲשֶׁר בָּחַר־בּוֹ׃

כז שָׂמוּ־בָם דִּבְרֵי אֹתוֹתָיו וּמֹפְתִים בְּאֶרֶץ חָם׃

כח שָׁלַח חֹשֶׁךְ וַיַּחְשִׁךְ וְלֹא־מָרוּ אֶת־דבריו [דְּבָרוֹ]׃

כט הָפַךְ אֶת־מֵימֵיהֶם לְדָם וַיָּמֶת אֶת־דְּגָתָם׃

ל שָׁרַץ אַרְצָם צְפַרְדְּעִים בְּחַדְרֵי מַלְכֵיהֶם׃

לא אָמַר וַיָּבֹא עָרֹב כִּנִּים בְּכָל־גְּבוּלָם׃

לב נָתַן גִּשְׁמֵיהֶם בָּרָד אֵשׁ לֶהָבוֹת בְּאַרְצָם׃

לג וַיַּךְ גַּפְנָם וּתְאֵנָתָם וַיְשַׁבֵּר עֵץ גְּבוּלָם׃

לד אָמַר וַיָּבֹא אַרְבֶּה וְיֶלֶק וְאֵין מִסְפָּר׃

לה וַיֹּאכַל כָּל־עֵשֶׂב בְּאַרְצָם וַיֹּאכַל פְּרִי אַדְמָתָם׃

12 Then they were only a few people, and only very few people lived there.

13 When they moved from nation to nation, from one kingdom to another people,

14 God allowed no one to harm them and for their sake, He rebuked kings, saying,:

15 "Do not touch My anointed ones or do wrong to My prophets."

16 He called a famine upon the land, and took away all the bread.

17 He sent a man before them, Joseph, who was sold as a slave.

18 His feet were placed in chains and he was put in irons.

19 Until His word was fulfilled, God's own word tested him.

20 The king sent to release him; the ruler of nations set him free.

21 He made him lord of his house and ruler of all he possessed,

22 To imprison princes as he saw fit, and teach his elders wisdom.

23 Then Israel came to Egypt, and Yaakov lived in the land of Ham.

24 God increased His people, and they became too strong for their enemies.

25 He turned their heart to hate His people, to plot against His servants.

26 God sent Moshe, His servant, and Aaron, whom He had chosen.

27 They worked His signs among them, and wondrous deeds in the land of Ham.

28 He sent darkness and it became dark, and they did not rebel against His word.

29 He turned their water into blood and killed their fish.

30 The land swarmed with frogs, including the king's chambers.

31 He brought wild beasts and insects to their land.

32 He turned their rain into hail, and brought fire to their land.

33 It destroyed their vines and fig trees, and shattered the trees within their borders.

34 He spoke and the locusts arrived, and countless beetles,

35 Which ate every herb in their land, devouring the fruit of the earth.

לו   וַיַּךְ כָּל־בְּכוֹר בְּאַרְצָם רֵאשִׁית לְכָל־אוֹנָם:

לז   וַיּוֹצִיאֵם בְּכֶסֶף וְזָהָב וְאֵין בִּשְׁבָטָיו כּוֹשֵׁל:

לח   שָׂמַח מִצְרַיִם בְּצֵאתָם כִּי־נָפַל פַּחְדָּם עֲלֵיהֶם:

לט   פָּרַשׂ עָנָן לְמָסָךְ וְאֵשׁ לְהָאִיר לָיְלָה:

מ   שָׁאַל וַיָּבֵא שְׂלָו וְלֶחֶם שָׁמַיִם יַשְׂבִּיעֵם:

מא   פָּתַח צוּר וַיָּזוּבוּ מָיִם הָלְכוּ בַּצִּיּוֹת נָהָר:

מב   כִּי־זָכַר אֶת־דְּבַר קָדְשׁוֹ אֶת־אַבְרָהָם עַבְדּוֹ:

מג   וַיּוֹצִא עַמּוֹ בְשָׂשׂוֹן בְּרִנָּה אֶת־בְּחִירָיו:

מד   וַיִּתֵּן לָהֶם אַרְצוֹת גּוֹיִם וַעֲמַל לְאֻמִּים יִירָשׁוּ:

מה   בַּעֲבוּר יִשְׁמְרוּ חֻקָּיו וְתוֹרֹתָיו יִנְצֹרוּ הַלְלוּיָהּ:

פרק קו

א   הַלְלוּיָהּ הוֹדוּ לַיהוָה כִּי־טוֹב כִּי לְעוֹלָם חַסְדּוֹ:

ב   מִי יְמַלֵּל גְּבוּרוֹת יְהוָה יַשְׁמִיעַ כָּל־תְּהִלָּתוֹ:

ג   אַשְׁרֵי שֹׁמְרֵי מִשְׁפָּט עֹשֵׂה צְדָקָה בְכָל־עֵת:

ד   זָכְרֵנִי יְהוָה בִּרְצוֹן עַמֶּךָ פָּקְדֵנִי בִּישׁוּעָתֶךָ:

ה   לִרְאוֹת בְּטוֹבַת בְּחִירֶיךָ לִשְׂמֹחַ בְּשִׂמְחַת גּוֹיֶךָ לְהִתְהַלֵּל עִם־נַחֲלָתֶךָ:

ו   חָטָאנוּ עִם־אֲבוֹתֵינוּ הֶעֱוִינוּ הִרְשָׁעְנוּ:

ז   אֲבוֹתֵינוּ בְמִצְרַיִם לֹא־הִשְׂכִּילוּ נִפְלְאוֹתֶיךָ לֹא זָכְרוּ אֶת־רֹב חֲסָדֶיךָ וַיַּמְרוּ עַל־יָם בְּיַם־סוּף:

ח   וַיּוֹשִׁיעֵם לְמַעַן שְׁמוֹ לְהוֹדִיעַ אֶת־גְּבוּרָתוֹ:

ט   וַיִּגְעַר בְּיַם־סוּף וַיֶּחֱרָב וַיּוֹלִיכֵם בַּתְּהֹמוֹת כַּמִּדְבָּר:

36 He struck all their first-born, the first-born of all their strength.

37 God brought them out with gold and silver, and no one among His tribes stumbled.

38 Egypt was glad when Israel left, for they had become afraid of them.

39 He spread a cloud for shelter, and gave them fire for light at night.

40 When they asked, He brought them quail, and satisfied them with bread from heaven.

41 He opened the rock and the waters poured out, making a river in the desert.

42 God remembered His promise to His servant Avraham.

43 He brought out His people with joy, His chosen ones with song.

44 He gave them the lands of the nations, and they took possession of the other nations labor

45 So that they might observe His laws and keep His teachings. Hallelujah!

TEHILLIM 106

*A song describing how the nation's welfare
depends on the behavior of its people*

1 Hallelujah! Give thanks to the Lord, for He is good, and His loving kindness lasts forever.

2 Who can express the Lord's mighty acts or tell all His praise?

3 Happy are they that keep justice and act righteously at all times.

4 Remember me, Lord, when You favor Your people. Grant me Your salvation

5 So that I may witness the prosperity of Your chosen ones and rejoice in the gladness of Your nation, that I may glory with Your inheritance.

6 We and our fathers have sinned. We have committed wrongdoing and we have acted wickedly.

7 Our fathers did not understand Your miracles in Egypt. They did not remember all of Your acts of loving kindness merciful acts, and rebelled at the sea – the Sea of Reeds.

8 Yet He saved them for His name's sake and in order to make known His great might.

י וַיּוֹשִׁיעֵם מִיַּד שׂוֹנֵא וַיִּגְאָלֵם מִיַּד אוֹיֵב׃

יא וַיְכַסּוּ־מַיִם צָרֵיהֶם אֶחָד מֵהֶם לֹא נוֹתָר׃

יב וַיַּאֲמִינוּ בִדְבָרָיו יָשִׁירוּ תְּהִלָּתוֹ׃

יג מִהֲרוּ שָׁכְחוּ מַעֲשָׂיו לֹא־חִכּוּ לַעֲצָתוֹ׃

יד וַיִּתְאַוּוּ תַאֲוָה בַּמִּדְבָּר וַיְנַסּוּ־אֵל בִּישִׁימוֹן׃

טו וַיִּתֵּן לָהֶם שֶׁאֱלָתָם וַיְשַׁלַּח רָזוֹן בְּנַפְשָׁם׃

טז וַיְקַנְאוּ לְמֹשֶׁה בַּמַּחֲנֶה לְאַהֲרֹן קְדוֹשׁ יְהוָה׃

יז תִּפְתַּח־אֶרֶץ וַתִּבְלַע דָּתָן וַתְּכַס עַל־עֲדַת אֲבִירָם׃

יח וַתִּבְעַר־אֵשׁ בַּעֲדָתָם לֶהָבָה תְּלַהֵט רְשָׁעִים׃

יט יַעֲשׂוּ־עֵגֶל בְּחֹרֵב וַיִּשְׁתַּחֲווּ לְמַסֵּכָה׃

כ וַיָּמִירוּ אֶת־כְּבוֹדָם בְּתַבְנִית שׁוֹר אֹכֵל עֵשֶׂב׃

כא שָׁכְחוּ אֵל מוֹשִׁיעָם עֹשֶׂה גְדֹלוֹת בְּמִצְרָיִם׃

כב נִפְלָאוֹת בְּאֶרֶץ חָם נוֹרָאוֹת עַל־יַם־סוּף׃

כג וַיֹּאמֶר לְהַשְׁמִידָם לוּלֵי מֹשֶׁה בְחִירוֹ עָמַד בַּפֶּרֶץ לְפָנָיו לְהָשִׁיב חֲמָתוֹ מֵהַשְׁחִית׃

כד וַיִּמְאֲסוּ בְּאֶרֶץ חֶמְדָּה לֹא־הֶאֱמִינוּ לִדְבָרוֹ׃

כה וַיֵּרָגְנוּ בְאָהֳלֵיהֶם לֹא שָׁמְעוּ בְּקוֹל יְהוָה׃

כו וַיִּשָּׂא יָדוֹ לָהֶם לְהַפִּיל אוֹתָם בַּמִּדְבָּר׃

כז וּלְהַפִּיל זַרְעָם בַּגּוֹיִם וּלְזָרוֹתָם בָּאֲרָצוֹת׃

כח וַיִּצָּמְדוּ לְבַעַל פְּעוֹר וַיֹּאכְלוּ זִבְחֵי מֵתִים׃

כט וַיַּכְעִיסוּ בְּמַעַלְלֵיהֶם וַתִּפְרָץ־בָּם מַגֵּפָה׃

ל וַיַּעֲמֹד פִּינְחָס וַיְפַלֵּל וַתֵּעָצַר הַמַּגֵּפָה׃

לא וַתֵּחָשֶׁב לוֹ לִצְדָקָה לְדֹר וָדֹר עַד־עוֹלָם׃

9 He rebuked the Sea of Reeds, and it became dry. He led His people through the depths as through a wilderness.

10 He saved those who hated them and redeemed them from the enemy's hand.

11 The waters covered all their enemies; not a single one was left.

12 Then they believed His words and sang Him praises.

13 But soon afterwards, they forgot His works and did not wait for His counsel.

14 They desired meat in the wilderness and tested God in the desert.

15 He granted their request, but sent dissatisfaction into their souls.

16 They were jealous of Moshe in the camp, and of Aharon, the holy one of God.

17 The earth opened and swallowed Dathan, and the followers of Aviram.

18 A fire was kindled among them, and flame burned all the wicked.

19 They made a golden calf at Horeb and worshipped a molten image,

20 Exchanging their glory for the likeness of an ox that eats grass.

21 They forgot God their savior and the miracles that He had performed for them in Egypt,

22 Wondrous deeds in the land of Ham and fearsome deeds by the Sea of Reeds.

23 When He decided to destroy them, His chosen one, Moshe, stood in the breach, to turn back His anger from destroying them.

24 They also despised the desirable land and did not believe His word.

25 They muttered in their tents and did not listen to God's voice.

26 Therefore, God swore regarding them that He would bring them down in the wilderness,

27 And that He would cast out their descendants among the nations, and scatter them in the lands.

28 They joined with Baal Peor and ate the sacrifices of the dead.

29 They angered God by their actions, and a plague broke out among them.

30 Then Pinhas rose and acted, and the plague was stopped.

31 This was accounted to him as a righteous act for all generations.

לב וַיַּקְצִיפוּ עַל־מֵי מְרִיבָה וַיֵּרַע לְמֹשֶׁה בַּעֲבוּרָם:

לג כִּי־הִמְרוּ אֶת־רוּחוֹ וַיְבַטֵּא בִּשְׂפָתָיו:

לד לֹא־הִשְׁמִידוּ אֶת־הָעַמִּים אֲשֶׁר אָמַר יְהוָה לָהֶם:

לה וַיִּתְעָרְבוּ בַגּוֹיִם וַיִּלְמְדוּ מַעֲשֵׂיהֶם:

לו וַיַּעַבְדוּ אֶת־עֲצַבֵּיהֶם וַיִּהְיוּ לָהֶם לְמוֹקֵשׁ:

לז וַיִּזְבְּחוּ אֶת־בְּנֵיהֶם וְאֶת־בְּנוֹתֵיהֶם לַשֵּׁדִים:

לח וַיִּשְׁפְּכוּ דָם נָקִי דַּם־בְּנֵיהֶם וּבְנוֹתֵיהֶם אֲשֶׁר זִבְּחוּ לַעֲצַבֵּי כְנַעַן וַתֶּחֱנַף הָאָרֶץ בַּדָּמִים:

לט וַיִּטְמְאוּ בְמַעֲשֵׂיהֶם וַיִּזְנוּ בְּמַעַלְלֵיהֶם:

מ וַיִּחַר־אַף יְהוָה בְּעַמּוֹ וַיְתָעֵב אֶת־נַחֲלָתוֹ:

מא וַיִּתְּנֵם בְּיַד־גּוֹיִם וַיִּמְשְׁלוּ בָהֶם שֹׂנְאֵיהֶם:

מב וַיִּלְחָצוּם אוֹיְבֵיהֶם וַיִּכָּנְעוּ תַּחַת יָדָם:

מג פְּעָמִים רַבּוֹת יַצִּילֵם וְהֵמָּה יַמְרוּ בַעֲצָתָם וַיָּמֹכּוּ בַּעֲוֹנָם:

מד וַיַּרְא בַּצַּר לָהֶם בְּשָׁמְעוֹ אֶת־רִנָּתָם:

מה וַיִּזְכֹּר לָהֶם בְּרִיתוֹ וַיִּנָּחֵם כְּרֹב חסדו [חֲסָדָיו]:

מו וַיִּתֵּן אוֹתָם לְרַחֲמִים לִפְנֵי כָּל־שׁוֹבֵיהֶם:

מז הוֹשִׁיעֵנוּ יְהוָה אֱלֹהֵינוּ וְקַבְּצֵנוּ מִן־הַגּוֹיִם לְהֹדוֹת לְשֵׁם קָדְשֶׁךָ לְהִשְׁתַּבֵּחַ בִּתְהִלָּתֶךָ:

מח בָּרוּךְ־יְהוָה אֱלֹהֵי יִשְׂרָאֵל מִן־הָעוֹלָם וְעַד הָעוֹלָם וְאָמַר כָּל־הָעָם אָמֵן הַלְלוּיָהּ:

32 They also angered Him at the waters of Meribah, causing trouble for Moshe.

33 They embittered his spirit, and his lips spoke rashly.

34 They did not destroy the nations as God had commanded them.

35 Instead they intermixed with these nations and followed their ways.

36 They served their idols, which became a trap for them.

37 And sacrificed their sons and daughters to demons.

38 They shed innocent blood – the blood of their own sons and daughters – whom they sacrificed to the idols of Canaan, and the land became polluted with blood.

39 They became impure by their own acts and went astray through their actions.

40 Then God became angry with His people, and loathed His inheritance.

41 He allowed them to be defeated by the nations, and those who hated them ruled over them.

42 Their enemies oppressed them, and they surrendered to them.

43 Although God rescued them many times, they continued to rebel, and sank low because of their sin.

44 Yet He looked upon their suffering when He heard their cry.

45 He remembered His covenant and relented according to His many kindnesses.

46 He also caused their captors to have mercy upon them.

47 Save us, Lord our God, and gather us from among the nations so that we may give thanks to Your holy name and triumph in Your praise.

48 Blessed be the Lord, the God of Israel forever and ever, and let all the people say "Amen." Hallelujah!

פרק קז

א   הֹדוּ לַיהוָה כִּי־טוֹב כִּי לְעוֹלָם חַסְדּוֹ:

ב   יֹאמְרוּ גְּאוּלֵי יְהוָה אֲשֶׁר גְּאָלָם מִיַּד־צָר:

ג   וּמֵאֲרָצוֹת קִבְּצָם מִמִּזְרָח וּמִמַּעֲרָב מִצָּפוֹן וּמִיָּם:

ד   תָּעוּ בַמִּדְבָּר בִּישִׁימוֹן דָּרֶךְ עִיר מוֹשָׁב לֹא מָצָאוּ:

ה   רְעֵבִים גַּם־צְמֵאִים נַפְשָׁם בָּהֶם תִּתְעַטָּף:

ו   וַיִּצְעֲקוּ אֶל־יְהוָה בַּצַּר לָהֶם מִמְּצוּקוֹתֵיהֶם יַצִּילֵם:

ז   וַיַּדְרִיכֵם בְּדֶרֶךְ יְשָׁרָה לָלֶכֶת אֶל־עִיר מוֹשָׁב:

ח   יוֹדוּ לַיהוָה חַסְדּוֹ וְנִפְלְאוֹתָיו לִבְנֵי אָדָם:

ט   כִּי־הִשְׂבִּיעַ נֶפֶשׁ שֹׁקֵקָה וְנֶפֶשׁ רְעֵבָה מִלֵּא־טוֹב:

י   יֹשְׁבֵי חֹשֶׁךְ וְצַלְמָוֶת אֲסִירֵי עֳנִי וּבַרְזֶל:

יא   כִּי־הִמְרוּ אִמְרֵי־אֵל וַעֲצַת עֶלְיוֹן נָאָצוּ:

יב   וַיַּכְנַע בֶּעָמָל לִבָּם כָּשְׁלוּ וְאֵין עֹזֵר:

יג   וַיִּזְעֲקוּ אֶל־יְהוָה בַּצַּר לָהֶם מִמְּצֻקוֹתֵיהֶם יוֹשִׁיעֵם:

יד   יוֹצִיאֵם מֵחֹשֶׁךְ וְצַלְמָוֶת וּמוֹסְרוֹתֵיהֶם יְנַתֵּק:

טו   יוֹדוּ לַיהוָה חַסְדּוֹ וְנִפְלְאוֹתָיו לִבְנֵי אָדָם:

טז   כִּי־שִׁבַּר דַּלְתוֹת נְחֹשֶׁת וּבְרִיחֵי בַרְזֶל גִּדֵּעַ:

יז   אֱוִלִים מִדֶּרֶךְ פִּשְׁעָם וּמֵעֲוֹנֹתֵיהֶם יִתְעַנּוּ:

יח   כָּל־אֹכֶל תְּתַעֵב נַפְשָׁם וַיַּגִּיעוּ עַד־שַׁעֲרֵי מָוֶת:

יט   וַיִּזְעֲקוּ אֶל־יְהוָה בַּצַּר לָהֶם מִמְּצֻקוֹתֵיהֶם יוֹשִׁיעֵם:

כ   יִשְׁלַח דְּבָרוֹ וְיִרְפָּאֵם וִימַלֵּט מִשְּׁחִיתוֹתָם:

כא   יוֹדוּ לַיהוָה חַסְדּוֹ וְנִפְלְאוֹתָיו לִבְנֵי אָדָם:

TEHILLIM 107

A song about doing loving kindness as God does

1 "Give thanks to the Lord for He is good, and His mercy lasts forever."
2 So say let the Lord's redeemed, whom He has redeemed from the hand of the enemy.
3 He gathered them from the lands, from east and west, from the north and from the sea.
4 They wandered in the wilderness on a desolate path and found no inhabited city.
5 Hungry and thirsty, their souls fainted within them.
6 In their trouble they cried out to the Lord, and He saved them from their distress.
7 He led them on a straight path to an inhabited city.
8 Let them give thanks to the Lord for His loving kindness, and for his wonderful acts to human beings,
9 For he has satisfied the longing soul, and filled the hungry soul with good.
10 Those who sat in darkness and in the shadow of death, bound in suffering and iron –
11 Because they rebelled against the words of God, and scorned the counsel of the Most High –
12 Therefore He humbled their hearts with hard labor; they stumbled and there was no one to help them.
13 In their trouble they cried out to the Lord, and He saved them from their distress.
14 He brought them out of the darkness and the shadow of death, and broke their shackles.
15 Let them give thanks to the Lord for His kindness, and for his wonderful acts to human beings,
16 For He has broken the gates of brass, and cut apart the bonds of iron.
17 Made foolish by their sinful ways, and afflicted by their wrongdoing,
18 Their souls hated all kinds of food, and they drew near to the gates of death.
19 In their trouble they cried out to the Lord, and He saved them from their distress.
20 He sends out His word and heals them, and saves them from destruction.
21 Let them give thanks to the Lord for His loving kindness, and for his wonderful acts to human beings.

כב וַיִּזְבְּחוּ זִבְחֵי תוֹדָה וִיסַפְּרוּ מַעֲשָׂיו בְּרִנָּה:

כג יוֹרְדֵי הַיָּם בָּאֳנִיּוֹת עֹשֵׂי מְלָאכָה בְּמַיִם רַבִּים:

כד הֵמָּה רָאוּ מַעֲשֵׂי יְהֹוָה וְנִפְלְאוֹתָיו בִּמְצוּלָה:

כה וַיֹּאמֶר וַיַּעֲמֵד רוּחַ סְעָרָה וַתְּרוֹמֵם גַּלָּיו:

כו יַעֲלוּ שָׁמַיִם יֵרְדוּ תְהוֹמוֹת נַפְשָׁם בְּרָעָה תִתְמוֹגָג:

כז יָחוֹגּוּ וְיָנוּעוּ כַּשִּׁכּוֹר וְכָל־חָכְמָתָם תִּתְבַּלָּע:

כח וַיִּצְעֲקוּ אֶל־יְהֹוָה בַּצַּר לָהֶם וּמִמְּצוּקֹתֵיהֶם יוֹצִיאֵם:

כט יָקֵם סְעָרָה לִדְמָמָה וַיֶּחֱשׁוּ גַּלֵּיהֶם:

ל וַיִּשְׂמְחוּ כִי־יִשְׁתֹּקוּ וַיַּנְחֵם אֶל־מְחוֹז חֶפְצָם:

לא יוֹדוּ לַיהֹוָה חַסְדּוֹ וְנִפְלְאוֹתָיו לִבְנֵי אָדָם:

לב וִירֹמְמוּהוּ בִּקְהַל־עָם וּבְמוֹשַׁב זְקֵנִים יְהַלְלוּהוּ:

לג יָשֵׂם נְהָרוֹת לְמִדְבָּר וּמֹצָאֵי מַיִם לְצִמָּאוֹן:

לד אֶרֶץ פְּרִי לִמְלֵחָה מֵרָעַת יֹשְׁבֵי בָהּ:

לה יָשֵׂם מִדְבָּר לַאֲגַם־מַיִם וְאֶרֶץ צִיָּה לְמֹצָאֵי מָיִם:

לו וַיּוֹשֶׁב שָׁם רְעֵבִים וַיְכוֹנְנוּ עִיר מוֹשָׁב:

לז וַיִּזְרְעוּ שָׂדוֹת וַיִּטְּעוּ כְרָמִים וַיַּעֲשׂוּ פְּרִי תְבוּאָה:

לח וַיְבָרֲכֵם וַיִּרְבּוּ מְאֹד וּבְהֶמְתָּם לֹא יַמְעִיט:

לט וַיִּמְעֲטוּ וַיָּשֹׁחוּ מֵעֹצֶר רָעָה וְיָגוֹן:

מ שֹׁפֵךְ בּוּז עַל־נְדִיבִים וַיַּתְעֵם בְּתֹהוּ לֹא־דָרֶךְ:

מא וַיְשַׂגֵּב אֶבְיוֹן מֵעוֹנִי וַיָּשֶׂם כַּצֹּאן מִשְׁפָּחוֹת:

מב יִרְאוּ יְשָׁרִים וְיִשְׂמָחוּ וְכָל־עַוְלָה קָפְצָה פִּיהָ:

מג מִי־חָכָם וְיִשְׁמָר־אֵלֶּה וְיִתְבּוֹנְנוּ חַסְדֵי יְהֹוָה:

22 Let them bring offerings of thanksgiving and declare His acts with song.

23 Those who go down to the sea in ships, who do their work on the great seas

24 Have seen the works of the Lord, and His wonders in the deep.

25 He gave command, and raised the stormy wind, which lifted up the waves.

26 They rise to the sky, they sink down in the deep, their soul melts away in evil.

27 They reel and stagger like a drunken man, and all their wisdom is swallowed up.

28 In their trouble they cried out to the Lord, and He saved them from their distress.

29 He calmed the storm, and the waves were stilled.

30 Then they were glad because the waves were still, and He led them safely to their destination.

31 Let them give thanks to the Lord for His kindness, and for his wonderful acts to human beings.

32 Let them exalt Him among the assembled people, and praise him at the meeting of the elders.

33 He turns rivers to desert, and springs of water into dry and thirsty ground.

34 He turns a fruitful land into a salty one because of the evil of its inhabitants.

35 He turns a desert into a lake, and a dry land into springs of water.

36 He caused the hungry to live there, so that they would build cities,

37 To sow fields and plant vineyards, and produce a harvest.

38 He also blessed them so that they multiplied greatly, and did not decrease their cattle.

39 And then their numbers were reduced and they dwindled away through the imposition of evil and sorrow.

40 He pours contempt upon princes and makes them wander in trackless waste places.

41 But he rises up the poor from suffering, and makes His families like a flock.

42 People of integrity see this and rejoice, and all wrongdoing closes its mouth.

43 Let those who are wise consider these things, and meditate upon the loving kindness of God.

פרק קח

א שִׁיר מִזְמוֹר לְדָוִד:

ב נָכוֹן לִבִּי אֱלֹהִים אָשִׁירָה וַאֲזַמְּרָה אַף־כְּבוֹדִי:

ג עוּרָה הַנֵּבֶל וְכִנּוֹר אָעִירָה שָּׁחַר:

ד אוֹדְךָ בָעַמִּים יְהֹוָה וַאֲזַמֶּרְךָ בַּל־אֻמִּים:

ה כִּי־גָדוֹל מֵעַל־שָׁמַיִם חַסְדֶּךָ וְעַד־שְׁחָקִים אֲמִתֶּךָ:

ו רוּמָה עַל־שָׁמַיִם אֱלֹהִים וְעַל כָּל־הָאָרֶץ כְּבוֹדֶךָ:

ז לְמַעַן יֵחָלְצוּן יְדִידֶיךָ הוֹשִׁיעָה יְמִינְךָ וַעֲנֵנִי:

ח אֱלֹהִים דִּבֶּר בְּקָדְשׁוֹ אֶעְלֹזָה אֲחַלְּקָה שְׁכֶם וְעֵמֶק סֻכּוֹת אֲמַדֵּד:

ט לִי גִלְעָד לִי מְנַשֶּׁה וְאֶפְרַיִם מָעוֹז רֹאשִׁי יְהוּדָה מְחֹקְקִי:

י מוֹאָב סִיר רַחְצִי עַל־אֱדוֹם אַשְׁלִיךְ נַעֲלִי עֲלֵי־פְלֶשֶׁת אֶתְרוֹעָע:

יא מִי יֹבִלֵנִי עִיר מִבְצָר מִי נָחַנִי עַד־אֱדוֹם:

יב הֲלֹא־אֱלֹהִים זְנַחְתָּנוּ וְלֹא־תֵצֵא אֱלֹהִים בְּצִבְאֹתֵינוּ:

יג הָבָה־לָּנוּ עֶזְרָת מִצָּר וְשָׁוְא תְּשׁוּעַת אָדָם:

יד בֵּאלֹהִים נַעֲשֶׂה־חָיִל וְהוּא יָבוּס צָרֵינוּ:

פרק קט

א לַמְנַצֵּחַ לְדָוִד מִזְמוֹר אֱלֹהֵי תְהִלָּתִי אַל־תֶּחֱרַשׁ:

ב כִּי פִי רָשָׁע וּפִי־מִרְמָה עָלַי פָּתָחוּ דִּבְּרוּ אִתִּי לְשׁוֹן שָׁקֶר:

ג וְדִבְרֵי שִׂנְאָה סְבָבוּנִי וַיִּלָּחֲמוּנִי חִנָּם:

ד תַּחַת־אַהֲבָתִי יִשְׂטְנוּנִי וַאֲנִי תְפִלָּה:

TEHILLIM 108

A song about God's battle plans

1 A song, a psalm by David.
2 My heart is steadfast, God. I will sing. It is my honor to sing thanksgiving praise.
3 Awake, lyre and harp. I will awake the dawn.
4 I will give thanks to my Lord among the peoples. I will give honor to my Lord among the nations.
5 Your great kindness extends beyond the heavens and Your truth extends to the skies.
6 Be exalted, God, above the heavens, and let Your glory be upon all the earth.
7 So that Your beloved ones may be saved, save with Your right hand, and answer me.
8 God spoke in His holiness, saying that I would be glad; that I would divide Shechem, and measure out the valley of Sukkot.
9 Gilead is Mine, Menashe are Mine. Ephraim is my main fortress. Judah is my lawmaker.
10 Moab is my washbasin. I cast my shoe upon Edom. Over Philistia I will shout.
11 Who will bring me into the fortified city? Who will lead me to Edom?
12 God, have You abandoned us? God, will You not lead our army?
13 Help us against our enemy, for the help of man is worthless.
14 With God's help we shall have the victory, for He will trample our enemies.

TEHILLIM 109

*A song expressing faith in God's protection
against cruel adversaries*

1 For the chief musician, a psalm of David. God of my praise, do not be silent,
2 For the mouth of the wicked and the mouth of deceitful have opened against me. They have spoken to me with a lying tongue.
3 They have surrounded me with words of hatred and fought against me for no reason.

ה וַיָּשִׂימוּ עָלַי רָעָה תַּחַת טוֹבָה וְשִׂנְאָה תַּחַת אַהֲבָתִי:

ו הַפְקֵד עָלָיו רָשָׁע וְשָׂטָן יַעֲמֹד עַל־יְמִינוֹ:

ז בְּהִשָּׁפְטוֹ יֵצֵא רָשָׁע וּתְפִלָּתוֹ תִּהְיֶה לַחֲטָאָה:

ח יִהְיוּ־יָמָיו מְעַטִּים פְּקֻדָּתוֹ יִקַּח אַחֵר:

ט יִהְיוּ־בָנָיו יְתוֹמִים וְאִשְׁתּוֹ אַלְמָנָה:

י וְנוֹעַ יָנוּעוּ בָנָיו וְשִׁאֵלוּ וְדָרְשׁוּ מֵחָרְבוֹתֵיהֶם:

יא יְנַקֵּשׁ נוֹשֶׁה לְכָל־אֲשֶׁר־לוֹ וְיָבֹזּוּ זָרִים יְגִיעוֹ:

יב אַל־יְהִי־לוֹ מֹשֵׁךְ חָסֶד וְאַל־יְהִי חוֹנֵן לִיתוֹמָיו:

יג יְהִי־אַחֲרִיתוֹ לְהַכְרִית בְּדוֹר אַחֵר יִמַּח שְׁמָם:

יד יִזָּכֵר עֲוֹן אֲבֹתָיו אֶל־יְהֹוָה וְחַטַּאת אִמּוֹ אַל־תִּמָּח:

טו יִהְיוּ נֶגֶד־יְהֹוָה תָּמִיד וְיַכְרֵת מֵאֶרֶץ זִכְרָם:

טז יַעַן אֲשֶׁר לֹא זָכַר עֲשׂוֹת חָסֶד וַיִּרְדֹּף אִישׁ־עָנִי וְאֶבְיוֹן וְנִכְאֵה לֵבָב לְמוֹתֵת:

יז וַיֶּאֱהַב קְלָלָה וַתְּבוֹאֵהוּ וְלֹא־חָפֵץ בִּבְרָכָה וַתִּרְחַק מִמֶּנּוּ:

יח וַיִּלְבַּשׁ קְלָלָה כְּמַדּוֹ וַתָּבֹא כַמַּיִם בְּקִרְבּוֹ וְכַשֶּׁמֶן בְּעַצְמוֹתָיו:

יט תְּהִי־לוֹ כְּבֶגֶד יַעְטֶה וּלְמֵזַח תָּמִיד יַחְגְּרֶהָ:

כ זֹאת פְּעֻלַּת שֹׂטְנַי מֵאֵת יְהֹוָה וְהַדֹּבְרִים רָע עַל־נַפְשִׁי:

כא וְאַתָּה יְהֹוִה אֲדֹנָי עֲשֵׂה־אִתִּי לְמַעַן שְׁמֶךָ כִּי־טוֹב חַסְדְּךָ הַצִּילֵנִי:

כב כִּי־עָנִי וְאֶבְיוֹן אָנֹכִי וְלִבִּי חָלַל בְּקִרְבִּי:

כג כְּצֵל־כִּנְטוֹתוֹ נֶהֱלָכְתִּי נִנְעַרְתִּי כָּאַרְבֶּה:

כד בִּרְכַּי כָּשְׁלוּ מִצּוֹם וּבְשָׂרִי כָּחַשׁ מִשָּׁמֶן:

כה וַאֲנִי הָיִיתִי חֶרְפָּה לָהֶם יִרְאוּנִי יְנִיעוּן רֹאשָׁם:

כו עָזְרֵנִי יְהֹוָה אֱלֹהָי הוֹשִׁיעֵנִי כְחַסְדֶּךָ:

4 In return for my love they have become my enemies – yet I
 continually pray.
5 They have given me evil for good, and hatred for my love.
6 "Place a wicked man over him, and let an enemy stand at his right
 hand.
7 Let him be condemned in judgment and turn his prayer to sin.
8 Let his life be short and his position be taken by another.
9 Let his children be orphans and his wife a widow.
10 Let his children be wanderers, and begging, and seek food in the
 ruins.
11 Let the creditor seize all he possesses, and let strangers loot his work.
12 Let no one be kind to him, and let no one be gracious to his
 orphaned children.
13 May his descendants be cut off; in the next generation, may their
 name be blotted out.
14 May the Lord remember the wrongdoing of his ancestors, and may
 the sin of his mother not be erased.
15 May the sins be brought before the Lord, at all times, so that He may
 cut their memory off from the earth
16 Because he did not remember to be kind, but persecuted the poor
 and needy, and was ready to slay the brokenhearted.
17 Since he loved cursing, let it be upon him. Since he didn't desire
 blessing, let it remain far from him.
18 He dressed himself in cursing as in a garment, and it has come inside
 his body like water, and like oil into his bones.
19 "Let this be the garment that he puts on, and the belt that he always
 wears."
20 This is what my enemies, and those who seek the ruin of my soul,
 should receive from the Lord.
21 But You, God, please deal with me for Your name's sake. Save me in
 the goodness of Your kindness.
22 I am poor and needy and my heart is empty within me.
23 I am gone like a lengthening shadow, shaken off like a locust.
24 My knees buckle from fasting, and my flesh has lost its fat.
25 I have become an object of mockery to them. When they see me,
 they shake their heads.
26 Help me, Lord my God. Save me according to Your loving kindness
27 So that they will know that this is the work of Your hand and that
 You, my Lord, have accomplished it.

פרק קי

כז וְיֵדְעוּ כִּי־יָדְךָ זֹּאת אַתָּה יְהוָה עֲשִׂיתָהּ:

כח יְקַלְלוּ־הֵמָּה וְאַתָּה תְבָרֵךְ קָמוּ וַיֵּבֹשׁוּ וְעַבְדְּךָ יִשְׂמָח:

כט יִלְבְּשׁוּ שׂוֹטְנַי כְּלִמָּה וְיַעֲטוּ כַמְעִיל בָּשְׁתָּם:

ל אוֹדֶה יְהוָה מְאֹד בְּפִי וּבְתוֹךְ רַבִּים אֲהַלְלֶנּוּ:

לא כִּי־יַעֲמֹד לִימִין אֶבְיוֹן לְהוֹשִׁיעַ מִשֹּׁפְטֵי נַפְשׁוֹ:

פרק קי

א לְדָוִד מִזְמוֹר נְאֻם יְהוָה לַאדֹנִי שֵׁב לִימִינִי עַד־אָשִׁית אֹיְבֶיךָ הֲדֹם לְרַגְלֶיךָ:

ב מַטֵּה עֻזְּךָ יִשְׁלַח יְהוָה מִצִּיּוֹן רְדֵה בְּקֶרֶב אֹיְבֶיךָ:

ג עַמְּךָ נְדָבֹת בְּיוֹם חֵילֶךָ בְּהַדְרֵי־קֹדֶשׁ מֵרֶחֶם מִשְׁחָר לְךָ טַל יַלְדֻתֶיךָ:

ד נִשְׁבַּע יְהוָה וְלֹא יִנָּחֵם אַתָּה־כֹהֵן לְעוֹלָם עַל־דִּבְרָתִי מַלְכִּי־צֶדֶק:

ה אֲדֹנָי עַל־יְמִינְךָ מָחַץ בְּיוֹם־אַפּוֹ מְלָכִים:

ו יָדִין בַּגּוֹיִם מָלֵא גְוִיּוֹת מָחַץ רֹאשׁ עַל־אֶרֶץ רַבָּה:

ז מִנַּחַל בַּדֶּרֶךְ יִשְׁתֶּה עַל־כֵּן יָרִים רֹאשׁ:

פרק קיא

א הַלְלוּיָהּ אוֹדֶה יְהוָה בְּכָל־לֵבָב בְּסוֹד יְשָׁרִים וְעֵדָה:

ב גְּדֹלִים מַעֲשֵׂי יְהוָה דְּרוּשִׁים לְכָל־חֶפְצֵיהֶם:

ג הוֹד־וְהָדָר פָּעֳלוֹ וְצִדְקָתוֹ עֹמֶדֶת לָעַד:

28 Let them curse while You bless. When they arise against me, they will be put to shame, but Your servant will rejoice.

29 My enemies will be clothed in humiliation, and wear their shame like a coat.

30 I will give great thanks to the Lord with my mouth, and I will praise him among the many

31 Because he stands at the right hand of the needy, to save him from those who would judge his soul.

TEHILLIM 110

A song about God's might in battle

1 A psalm by David. The Lord said to my Master: "Sit at my right side until I turn your enemies into your footstool."

2 The Lord will send the rod of Your strength from Zion. "You will rule over your enemies."

3 Your people mobilize willingly on the day of your battle. In splendid holiness, from Your emergence from the womb, you possessed the dew of your youth.

4 The Lord has sworn and will not retract: "You are a priest forever, as Melchizedek said."

5 The Lord at your right hand will crush kings on the day of His wrath.

6 He will judge the nations filled with corpses; He crushes heads over a mighty land.

7 He will drink from the stream on the road. Therefore, let Israel lift up its head.

TEHILLIM 111

A song of thanks to God for His mercy to Israel

1 Hallelujah! I will give thanks to the Lord with my whole heart at the meetings of the upright, and among the congregation.

2 The works of the Lord are great, sought by those who take delight in them.

3 His work is glory and majesty, and His righteousness lasts forever.

ד זֵכֶר עָשָׂה לְנִפְלְאֹתָיו חַנּוּן וְרַחוּם יְהוָה:

ה טֶרֶף נָתַן לִירֵאָיו יִזְכֹּר לְעוֹלָם בְּרִיתוֹ:

ו כֹּחַ מַעֲשָׂיו הִגִּיד לְעַמּוֹ לָתֵת לָהֶם נַחֲלַת גּוֹיִם:

ז מַעֲשֵׂי יָדָיו אֱמֶת וּמִשְׁפָּט נֶאֱמָנִים כָּל־פִּקּוּדָיו:

ח סְמוּכִים לָעַד לְעוֹלָם עֲשׂוּיִם בֶּאֱמֶת וְיָשָׁר:

ט פְּדוּת שָׁלַח לְעַמּוֹ צִוָּה לְעוֹלָם בְּרִיתוֹ קָדוֹשׁ וְנוֹרָא שְׁמוֹ:

י רֵאשִׁית חָכְמָה יִרְאַת יְהוָה שֵׂכֶל טוֹב לְכָל־עֹשֵׂיהֶם תְּהִלָּתוֹ עֹמֶדֶת לָעַד:

פרק קי"ב

א הַלְלוּיָהּ אַשְׁרֵי־אִישׁ יָרֵא אֶת־יְהוָה בְּמִצְוֺתָיו חָפֵץ מְאֹד:

ב גִּבּוֹר בָּאָרֶץ יִהְיֶה זַרְעוֹ דּוֹר יְשָׁרִים יְבֹרָךְ:

ג הוֹן־וָעֹשֶׁר בְּבֵיתוֹ וְצִדְקָתוֹ עֹמֶדֶת לָעַד:

ד זָרַח בַּחֹשֶׁךְ אוֹר לַיְשָׁרִים חַנּוּן וְרַחוּם וְצַדִּיק:

ה טוֹב אִישׁ חוֹנֵן וּמַלְוֶה יְכַלְכֵּל דְּבָרָיו בְּמִשְׁפָּט:

ו כִּי־לְעוֹלָם לֹא יִמּוֹט לְזֵכֶר עוֹלָם יִהְיֶה צַדִּיק:

ז מִשְּׁמוּעָה רָעָה לֹא יִירָא נָכוֹן לִבּוֹ בָּטֻחַ בַּיהוָה:

ח סָמוּךְ לִבּוֹ לֹא יִירָא עַד אֲשֶׁר־יִרְאֶה בְצָרָיו:

ט פִּזַּר נָתַן לָאֶבְיוֹנִים צִדְקָתוֹ עֹמֶדֶת לָעַד קַרְנוֹ תָּרוּם בְּכָבוֹד:

י רָשָׁע יִרְאֶה וְכָעָס שִׁנָּיו יַחֲרֹק וְנָמָס תַּאֲוַת רְשָׁעִים תֹּאבֵד:

4 He has made a memorial for His marvelous works; the Lord is gracious and merciful.

5 He has given food to those who revere Him. He will bear in mind His covenant, forever.

6 He has declared the power of His works to His people in giving them the heritage of the nations.

7 The works of His hands are truth and justice. All His teachings are sure.

8 They are established for all time; they are performed in truth and integrity.

9 He has sent redemption to His people and commanded His covenant forever; holy and awe-inspiring is His name.

10 The beginning of wisdom is reverence for the Lord is the beginning of wisdom. All who perform His commandments have good understanding; His praise endures forever.

TEHILLIM 112

A song of rejoicing from those who love God

1 Hallelujah. Happy is the man who loves the Lord, who takes great delight in His commandments.

2 His offspring will be mighty upon the earth; the generation of the upright will be blessed.

3 Wealth and prosperity are in his house, and his righteousness lasts forever.

4 For people of integrity God shines a light as in the darkness. He is gracious, compassionate and righteous.

5 A good man is gracious and lends, he conducts his affairs honestly.

6 He will never be swayed. He will be remembered as a righteous man forever.

7 He will never be afraid of bad news; for his heart is firm, trusting in the Lord.

8 His heart is well steadfast. He will not be afraid when he gazes upon his enemies.

9 He has distributed and given to the needy. His righteousness lasts forever. His reputation will be exalted in honor.

10 The wicked will see this and be angry. He will grind his teeth and melt away; the greed of the wicked will perish.

פרק קי"ג

א הַלְלוּיָהּ הַלְלוּ עַבְדֵי יְהוָה הַלְלוּ אֶת־שֵׁם יְהוָה׃

ב יְהִי שֵׁם יְהוָה מְבֹרָךְ מֵעַתָּה וְעַד־עוֹלָם׃

ג מִמִּזְרַח־שֶׁמֶשׁ עַד־מְבוֹאוֹ מְהֻלָּל שֵׁם יְהוָה׃

ד רָם עַל־כָּל־גּוֹיִם יְהוָה עַל הַשָּׁמַיִם כְּבוֹדוֹ׃

ה מִי כַּיהוָה אֱלֹהֵינוּ הַמַּגְבִּיהִי לָשָׁבֶת׃

ו הַמַּשְׁפִּילִי לִרְאוֹת בַּשָּׁמַיִם וּבָאָרֶץ׃

ז מְקִימִי מֵעָפָר דָּל מֵאַשְׁפֹּת יָרִים אֶבְיוֹן׃

ח לְהוֹשִׁיבִי עִם־נְדִיבִים עִם נְדִיבֵי עַמּוֹ׃

ט מוֹשִׁיבִי עֲקֶרֶת הַבַּיִת אֵם־הַבָּנִים שְׂמֵחָה הַלְלוּיָהּ׃

פרק קי"ד

א בְּצֵאת יִשְׂרָאֵל מִמִּצְרָיִם בֵּית יַעֲקֹב מֵעַם לֹעֵז׃

ב הָיְתָה יְהוּדָה לְקָדְשׁוֹ יִשְׂרָאֵל מַמְשְׁלוֹתָיו׃

ג הַיָּם רָאָה וַיָּנֹס הַיַּרְדֵּן יִסֹּב לְאָחוֹר׃

ד הֶהָרִים רָקְדוּ כְאֵילִים גְּבָעוֹת כִּבְנֵי־צֹאן׃

ה מַה־לְּךָ הַיָּם כִּי תָנוּס הַיַּרְדֵּן תִּסֹּב לְאָחוֹר׃

ו הֶהָרִים תִּרְקְדוּ כְאֵילִים גְּבָעוֹת כִּבְנֵי־צֹאן׃

ז מִלִּפְנֵי אָדוֹן חוּלִי אָרֶץ מִלִּפְנֵי אֱלוֹהַּ יַעֲקֹב׃

ח הַהֹפְכִי הַצּוּר אֲגַם־מָיִם חַלָּמִישׁ לְמַעְיְנוֹ־מָיִם׃

TEHILLIM 113

A song about trusting God

1 Hallelujah! Praise, servants of the Lord, praise the name of the Lord.
2 Blessed be the name of the Lord from now and forever.
3 From the rising of the sun to its setting, let the name of the Lord be praised.
4 The Lord is high above all nations. His glory is above the heavens.
5 Who can compare to the Lord our God, who is enthroned on high,
6 Yet stoops down to observe looks down on the heaven and the earth?
7 He raises the poor from the dust, and lifts the needy from the refuse heap;
8 Seating them with nobles, the princes of the people.
9 He returns the barren woman to her home as a happy mother of children. Hallelujah!

TEHILLIM 114

A song of how nature responded to God's freeing Israel from Egypt

1 When Israel came out of Egypt, the children of Jacob from a foreign tongue,
2 Then Judah became His Sanctuary and Israel His kingdom.
3 The sea saw this and fled, and the Jordan River turned backward.
4 The mountains skipped like rams, the hills like young sheep.
5 What troubles you, sea, that you flee, Jordan River, that you turn backward?
6 And you, mountains that skip like rams, and you, hills like young sheep?
7 Tremble, earth, before the Lord, before the God of Jacob,
8 Who turns the rock into a pool of water, and the pebbles into a fountain of water.

פרק קטו

א לֹא לָנוּ יְהוָה לֹא לָנוּ כִּי לְשִׁמְךָ תֵּן כָּבוֹד עַל־חַסְדְּךָ עַל־אֲמִתֶּךָ:

ב לָמָּה יֹאמְרוּ הַגּוֹיִם אַיֵּה־נָא אֱלֹהֵיהֶם:

ג וֵאלֹהֵינוּ בַשָּׁמָיִם כֹּל אֲשֶׁר־חָפֵץ עָשָׂה:

ד עֲצַבֵּיהֶם כֶּסֶף וְזָהָב מַעֲשֵׂה יְדֵי אָדָם:

ה פֶּה־לָהֶם וְלֹא יְדַבֵּרוּ עֵינַיִם לָהֶם וְלֹא יִרְאוּ:

ו אָזְנַיִם לָהֶם וְלֹא יִשְׁמָעוּ אַף לָהֶם וְלֹא יְרִיחוּן:

ז יְדֵיהֶם וְלֹא יְמִישׁוּן רַגְלֵיהֶם וְלֹא יְהַלֵּכוּ לֹא־יֶהְגּוּ בִּגְרוֹנָם:

ח כְּמוֹהֶם יִהְיוּ עֹשֵׂיהֶם כֹּל אֲשֶׁר־בֹּטֵחַ בָּהֶם:

ט יִשְׂרָאֵל בְּטַח בַּיהוָה עֶזְרָם וּמָגִנָּם הוּא:

י בֵּית אַהֲרֹן בִּטְחוּ בַיהוָה עֶזְרָם וּמָגִנָּם הוּא:

יא יִרְאֵי יְהוָה בִּטְחוּ בַיהוָה עֶזְרָם וּמָגִנָּם הוּא:

יב יְהוָה זְכָרָנוּ יְבָרֵךְ יְבָרֵךְ אֶת־בֵּית יִשְׂרָאֵל יְבָרֵךְ אֶת־בֵּית אַהֲרֹן:

יג יְבָרֵךְ יִרְאֵי יְהוָה הַקְּטַנִּים עִם־הַגְּדֹלִים:

יד יֹסֵף יְהוָה עֲלֵיכֶם עֲלֵיכֶם וְעַל־בְּנֵיכֶם:

טו בְּרוּכִים אַתֶּם לַיהוָה עֹשֵׂה שָׁמַיִם וָאָרֶץ:

טז הַשָּׁמַיִם שָׁמַיִם לַיהוָה וְהָאָרֶץ נָתַן לִבְנֵי־אָדָם:

יז לֹא־הַמֵּתִים יְהַלְלוּ־יָהּ וְלֹא כָּל־יֹרְדֵי דוּמָה:

יח וַאֲנַחְנוּ נְבָרֵךְ יָהּ מֵעַתָּה וְעַד־עוֹלָם הַלְלוּיָהּ:

TEHILLIM 115

The singing of the Levites and the choir

1 Not to us, Lord, not to us, but to Your name give glory, for the sake of Your loving kindness and Your truth.

2 Why should the nations say, "Where is your God?"

3 Indeed our God is in the heavens. He does as He wishes.

4 Their idols are made of silver and gold, the work of human hands.

5 They have mouths but do not speak eyes but do not see.

6 They have ears but do not hear. They have noses but do not smell.

7 They have hands but they do not touch anything. They have feet but do not walk. They utter no sound with their throats.

8 Those who make them will become like them, so too everyone who trusts in them.

9 Israel, trust in the Lord; He is their help and their protector.

10 Children of Aaron, trust in the Lord; He is their help and their protector.

11 You who revere the Lord, trust in the Lord; He is their help and their protector.

12 The Lord has remembered us. He will bless – He will bless the house of Israel. He will bless the house of Aharon.

13 He will bless those who revere the Lord, small and great alike.

14 The Lord will increase you and your descendants.

15 You shall be blessed of the Lord, Who made heaven and earth.

16 The heavens are the heavens of the Lord, but He gave the earth to the children of men.

17 The dead do not praise the Lord, nor do those who go down into the grave.

18 But we will bless the Lord from now and forever. Hallelujah!

פרק קטז

א אָהַבְתִּי כִּי־יִשְׁמַע יְהוָה אֶת־קוֹלִי תַּחֲנוּנָי:

ב כִּי־הִטָּה אָזְנוֹ לִי וּבְיָמַי אֶקְרָא:

ג אֲפָפוּנִי חֶבְלֵי־מָוֶת וּמְצָרֵי שְׁאוֹל מְצָאוּנִי צָרָה וְיָגוֹן אֶמְצָא:

ד וּבְשֵׁם־יְהוָה אֶקְרָא אָנָּה יְהוָה מַלְּטָה נַפְשִׁי:

ה חַנּוּן יְהוָה וְצַדִּיק וֵאלֹהֵינוּ מְרַחֵם:

ו שֹׁמֵר פְּתָאיִם יְהוָה דַּלּוֹתִי וְלִי יְהוֹשִׁיעַ:

ז שׁוּבִי נַפְשִׁי לִמְנוּחָיְכִי כִּי יְהוָה גָּמַל עָלָיְכִי:

ח כִּי חִלַּצְתָּ נַפְשִׁי מִמָּוֶת אֶת־עֵינִי מִן־דִּמְעָה אֶת־רַגְלִי מִדֶּחִי:

ט אֶתְהַלֵּךְ לִפְנֵי יְהוָה בְּאַרְצוֹת הַחַיִּים:

י הֶאֱמַנְתִּי כִּי אֲדַבֵּר אֲנִי עָנִיתִי מְאֹד:

יא אֲנִי אָמַרְתִּי בְחָפְזִי כָּל־הָאָדָם כֹּזֵב:

יב מָה־אָשִׁיב לַיהוָה כָּל־תַּגְמוּלוֹהִי עָלָי:

יג כּוֹס־יְשׁוּעוֹת אֶשָּׂא וּבְשֵׁם יְהוָה אֶקְרָא:

יד נְדָרַי לַיהוָה אֲשַׁלֵּם נֶגְדָה־נָּא לְכָל־עַמּוֹ:

טו יָקָר בְּעֵינֵי יְהוָה הַמָּוְתָה לַחֲסִידָיו:

טז אָנָּה יְהוָה כִּי־אֲנִי עַבְדֶּךָ אֲנִי עַבְדְּךָ בֶּן־אֲמָתֶךָ פִּתַּחְתָּ לְמוֹסֵרָי:

יז לְךָ־אֶזְבַּח זֶבַח תּוֹדָה וּבְשֵׁם יְהוָה אֶקְרָא:

יח נְדָרַי לַיהוָה אֲשַׁלֵּם נֶגְדָה־נָּא לְכָל־עַמּוֹ:

יט בְּחַצְרוֹת בֵּית יְהוָה בְּתוֹכֵכִי יְרוּשָׁלָ͏ִם הַלְלוּיָהּ:

TEHILLIM 116

A personal song of thanksgiving to God for His help

1 I love that the Lord hears my voice and my prayers.

2 Because he has turned His ear to me, I will call upon Him all my days.

3 The bonds of death and the narrow confines of the grave overtake me; trouble and sorrow find me

4 But I called upon the name of the Lord: "Please, Lord, save my soul!"

5 The Lord is merciful and just; God is compassionate.

6 God preserves the simple. I was brought low, and He saved me.

7 Return to your rest, my soul, for the Lord has dealt kindly with you.

8 You have saved my soul from death, my eyes from crying and my feet from stumbling.

9 I will walk before the Lord in the land of the living.

10 I trusted even when I said, "I am suffering terribly."

11 I said in my haste: "All men are deceitful."

12 How can I repay the Lord for all the great things he did for me?

13 I will raise the cup of salvation and call upon the name of the Lord.

14 I will fulfill my vows to the Lord in the presence of His people.

15 Even the death of His righteous ones is precious in the Lord's sight.

16 Please, Lord, I am Your servant, I am Your servant, the son of Your handmaid. You have released me from my bonds.

17 I will offer You a thanksgiving sacrifice and call upon the name of the Lord.

18 I will fulfill my vows to the Lord in the presence of His people,

19 In the courts of the Lord's house in Your midst, Jerusalem. Hallelujah!

פרק קי״ז

א הַלְלוּ אֶת־יְהֹוָה כָּל־גּוֹיִם שַׁבְּחוּהוּ כָּל־הָאֻמִּים:

ב כִּי גָבַר עָלֵינוּ חַסְדּוֹ וֶאֱמֶת־יְהֹוָה לְעוֹלָם הַלְלוּיָהּ:

פרק קי״ח

א הוֹדוּ לַיהֹוָה כִּי־טוֹב כִּי לְעוֹלָם חַסְדּוֹ:

ב יֹאמַר־נָא יִשְׂרָאֵל כִּי לְעוֹלָם חַסְדּוֹ:

ג יֹאמְרוּ נָא בֵית־אַהֲרֹן כִּי לְעוֹלָם חַסְדּוֹ:

ד יֹאמְרוּ נָא יִרְאֵי יְהֹוָה כִּי לְעוֹלָם חַסְדּוֹ:

ה מִן־הַמֵּצַר קָרָאתִי יָּהּ עָנָנִי בַמֶּרְחָב יָהּ:

ו יְהֹוָה לִי לֹא אִירָא מַה־יַּעֲשֶׂה לִי אָדָם:

ז יְהֹוָה לִי בְּעֹזְרָי וַאֲנִי אֶרְאֶה בְשֹׂנְאָי:

ח טוֹב לַחֲסוֹת בַּיהֹוָה מִבְּטֹחַ בָּאָדָם:

ט טוֹב לַחֲסוֹת בַּיהֹוָה מִבְּטֹחַ בִּנְדִיבִים:

י כָּל־גּוֹיִם סְבָבוּנִי בְּשֵׁם יְהֹוָה כִּי אֲמִילַם:

יא סַבּוּנִי גַם־סְבָבוּנִי בְּשֵׁם יְהֹוָה כִּי אֲמִילַם:

יב סַבּוּנִי כִדְבוֹרִים דֹּעֲכוּ כְּאֵשׁ קוֹצִים בְּשֵׁם יְהֹוָה כִּי אֲמִילַם:

יג דָּחֹה דְחִיתַנִי לִנְפֹּל וַיהֹוָה עֲזָרָנִי:

יד עָזִּי וְזִמְרָת יָהּ וַיְהִי־לִי לִישׁוּעָה:

טו קוֹל רִנָּה וִישׁוּעָה בְּאָהֳלֵי צַדִּיקִים יְמִין יְהֹוָה עֹשָׂה חָיִל:

טז יְמִין יְהֹוָה רוֹמֵמָה יְמִין יְהֹוָה עֹשָׂה חָיִל:

TEHILLIM 117

A beautiful short song calling for the entire world to love God.

1 Praise the Lord, all you nations! Praise Him, all you peoples!
2 His kindness to us is overwhelming, and the Lord's truth endures for all time. Hallelujah.

TEHILLIM 118

A song of thanks to God from the people

1 Give thanks to the Lord, for He is good. His loving kindness is everlasting.
2 Let Israel now say: "His loving kindness is everlasting."
3 Let the house of Aaron now say: "His loving kindness is everlasting."
4 Let those who revere the Lord say: "His loving kindness is everlasting."
5 From my distress I called out to the Lord. He answered me with His spaciousness.
6 The Lord is with me; I will not be afraid. What can human beings do to me?
7 The Lord is with me and helps me. I will gaze upon those who hate me.
8 It is better to take refuge in the Lord than to trust in human beings.
9 It is better to take refuge in the Lord than to trust in princes.
10 All nations surround me. In the name of the Lord, I will cut them down.
11 They surround me, yes, they surround me entirely – but in the name of the Lord, I will cut them down.
12 They surround me like bees, but they are extinguished like a brush-fire; in the name of the Lord, I will cut them down.
13 You continually attacked me in order to make me fall, but the Lord helped me.
14 The Lord is my strength and my song, and He has become my salvation.
15 The voice of rejoicing and salvation is in the tents of the righteous; the Lord's right hand accomplishes great things.

יז לֹא אָמוּת כִּי־אֶחְיֶה וַאֲסַפֵּר מַעֲשֵׂי יָהּ:

יח יַסֹּר יִסְּרַנִּי יָּהּ וְלַמָּוֶת לֹא נְתָנָנִי:

יט פִּתְחוּ־לִי שַׁעֲרֵי־צֶדֶק אָבֹא־בָם אוֹדֶה יָהּ:

כ זֶה־הַשַּׁעַר לַיהֹוָה צַדִּיקִים יָבֹאוּ בוֹ:

כא אוֹדְךָ כִּי עֲנִיתָנִי וַתְּהִי־לִי לִישׁוּעָה:

כב אֶבֶן מָאֲסוּ הַבּוֹנִים הָיְתָה לְרֹאשׁ פִּנָּה:

כג מֵאֵת יְהֹוָה הָיְתָה זֹּאת הִיא נִפְלָאת בְּעֵינֵינוּ:

כד זֶה־הַיּוֹם עָשָׂה יְהֹוָה נָגִילָה וְנִשְׂמְחָה בוֹ:

כה אָנָּא יְהֹוָה הוֹשִׁיעָה נָּא אָנָּא יְהֹוָה הַצְלִיחָה נָּא:

כו בָּרוּךְ הַבָּא בְּשֵׁם יְהֹוָה בֵּרַכְנוּכֶם מִבֵּית יְהֹוָה:

כז אֵל יְהֹוָה וַיָּאֶר לָנוּ אִסְרוּ־חַג בַּעֲבֹתִים עַד קַרְנוֹת הַמִּזְבֵּחַ:

כח אֵלִי אַתָּה וְאוֹדֶךָּ אֱלֹהַי אֲרוֹמְמֶךָּ:

כט הוֹדוּ לַיהֹוָה כִּי־טוֹב כִּי לְעוֹלָם חַסְדּוֹ:

פרק קיט

א אַשְׁרֵי תְמִימֵי־דָרֶךְ הַהֹלְכִים בְּתוֹרַת יְהֹוָה:

ב אַשְׁרֵי נֹצְרֵי עֵדֹתָיו בְּכָל־לֵב יִדְרְשׁוּהוּ:

ג אַף לֹא־פָעֲלוּ עַוְלָה בִּדְרָכָיו הָלָכוּ:

ד אַתָּה צִוִּיתָה פִקֻּדֶיךָ לִשְׁמֹר מְאֹד:

ה אַחֲלַי יִכֹּנוּ דְרָכָי לִשְׁמֹר חֻקֶּיךָ:

ו אָז לֹא־אֵבוֹשׁ בְּהַבִּיטִי אֶל־כָּל־מִצְוֹתֶיךָ:

ז אוֹדְךָ בְּיֹשֶׁר לֵבָב בְּלָמְדִי מִשְׁפְּטֵי צִדְקֶךָ:

16 The right hand of the Lord is exalted; the right hand of the Lord accomplishes great things.

17 I shall not die, but I live, and I will tell of the Lord's acts.

18 The Lord has made me suffer, but He has not given me up to death.

19 Open the gates of righteousness for me. I will enter them and give thanks to the Lord.

20 This is the gate of the Lord; the righteous will enter it.

21 I will give You thanks for You have helped me, and You have become my salvation.

22 The stone that the builders rejected has become the cornerstone.

23 This is the Lord's doing; it is marvelous to us.

24 This is the day that the Lord has made; we will rejoice and be glad in it.

25 Please, Lord, save us! Please, Lord, make us prosper!

26 Blessed are you who come in the name of the Lord. We bless you from the house of the Lord.

27 The Lord is God and has given us light. Bind the holiday sacrifices with cords until they are brought to the corners of the altar.

28 You are my God and I will give thanks to You. You are my God and I will exalt You.

29 Give thanks to the Lord for He is good. His loving kindness is everlasting.

TEHILLIM 119

*Each verse of this song, which expresses joy of life
and love for God's teachings, contains eight lines
for each letter of the Hebrew alphabet*

Aleph

1 Happy are those who morally upright and follow the teaching of the Lord.

2 Happy are those who observe His commandments and seek Him wholeheartedly.

3 Not only do they do no evil; they walk in His ways.

4 You have commanded Your statutes so that we should observe them carefully.

5 My wish is that my actions were directed to observe Your laws!

ח אֶת־חֻקֶּיךָ אֶשְׁמֹר אַל־תַּעַזְבֵנִי עַד־מְאֹד:

ט בַּמֶּה יְזַכֶּה־נַּעַר אֶת־אָרְחוֹ לִשְׁמֹר כִּדְבָרֶךָ:

י בְּכָל־לִבִּי דְרַשְׁתִּיךָ אַל־תַּשְׁגֵּנִי מִמִּצְוֹתֶיךָ:

יא בְּלִבִּי צָפַנְתִּי אִמְרָתֶךָ לְמַעַן לֹא אֶחֱטָא־לָךְ:

יב בָּרוּךְ אַתָּה יְהוָה לַמְּדֵנִי חֻקֶּיךָ:

יג בִּשְׂפָתַי סִפַּרְתִּי כֹּל מִשְׁפְּטֵי־פִיךָ:

יד בְּדֶרֶךְ עֵדְוֹתֶיךָ שַׂשְׂתִּי כְּעַל כָּל־הוֹן:

טו בְּפִקֻּדֶיךָ אָשִׂיחָה וְאַבִּיטָה אֹרְחֹתֶיךָ:

טז בְּחֻקֹּתֶיךָ אֶשְׁתַּעֲשָׁע לֹא אֶשְׁכַּח דְּבָרֶךָ:

יז גְּמֹל עַל־עַבְדְּךָ אֶחְיֶה וְאֶשְׁמְרָה דְבָרֶךָ:

יח גַּל־עֵינַי וְאַבִּיטָה נִפְלָאוֹת מִתּוֹרָתֶךָ:

יט גֵּר אָנֹכִי בָאָרֶץ אַל־תַּסְתֵּר מִמֶּנִּי מִצְוֹתֶיךָ:

כ גָּרְסָה נַפְשִׁי לְתַאֲבָה אֶל־מִשְׁפָּטֶיךָ בְכָל־עֵת:

כא גָּעַרְתָּ זֵדִים אֲרוּרִים הַשֹּׁגִים מִמִּצְוֹתֶיךָ:

כב גַּל מֵעָלַי חֶרְפָּה וָבוּז כִּי עֵדֹתֶיךָ נָצָרְתִּי:

כג גַּם יָשְׁבוּ שָׂרִים בִּי נִדְבָּרוּ עַבְדְּךָ יָשִׂיחַ בְּחֻקֶּיךָ:

כד גַּם־עֵדֹתֶיךָ שַׁעֲשֻׁעָי אַנְשֵׁי עֲצָתִי:

כה דָּבְקָה לֶעָפָר נַפְשִׁי חַיֵּנִי כִּדְבָרֶךָ:

כו דְּרָכַי סִפַּרְתִּי וַתַּעֲנֵנִי לַמְּדֵנִי חֻקֶּיךָ:

כז דֶּרֶךְ־פִּקּוּדֶיךָ הֲבִינֵנִי וְאָשִׂיחָה בְּנִפְלְאוֹתֶיךָ:

6 Then I would not be ashamed to see all Your commandments.
7 I will give thanks to You with the integrity of my heart when I learn of your righteous laws.
8 I will keep Your laws. Do not completely abandon me.

Bet

9 How should a young man keep his path pure? By taking care to obey Your word.
10 I have sought You with my whole heart. Let me not sin against Your commandments.
11 I have hidden Your word in my heart so that I will not sin against You.
12 Blessed are You, Lord. Teach me Your laws.
13 With my lips I have retold the laws of Your mouth.
14 I have rejoiced in the path of Your laws as much as in all wealth.
15 I will meditate upon Your commandments and look to Your ways.
16 I will take delight in Your laws, and I will not forget Your word.

Gimel

17 Grant abundance to Your servant that I may live and obey Your word.
18 Open my eyes so that I may see wondrous things from Your law.
19 I am a stranger on the earth. Do not hide Your commandments from me.
20 My soul is overcome with yearning for Your laws at all times.
21 You have rebuked the accursed, haughty sinners who deviate from Your commandments.
22 Remove disgrace and scorn from me, for I have kept Your laws.
23 Though rulers should sit and talk against me, I will meditate on Your laws.
24 Your laws are my delight. They are my advisers.

Dalet

25 My soul cleaves to the dust. Revive me according to Your word.
26 I spoke of my ways and You answered me. Teach me Your laws.
27 Help me to understand Your laws so that I may speak about Your marvels.

כח דָּלְפָה נַפְשִׁי מִתּוּגָה קַיְּמֵנִי כִּדְבָרֶךָ:

כט דֶּרֶךְ שֶׁקֶר הָסֵר מִמֶּנִּי וְתוֹרָתְךָ חָנֵּנִי:

ל דֶּרֶךְ אֱמוּנָה בָחָרְתִּי מִשְׁפָּטֶיךָ שִׁוִּיתִי:

לא דָּבַקְתִּי בְעֵדְוֹתֶיךָ יְהֹוָה אַל תְּבִישֵׁנִי:

לב דֶּרֶךְ מִצְוֹתֶיךָ אָרוּץ כִּי תַרְחִיב לִבִּי:

לג הוֹרֵנִי יְהֹוָה דֶּרֶךְ חֻקֶּיךָ וְאֶצְּרֶנָּה עֵקֶב:

לד הֲבִינֵנִי וְאֶצְּרָה תוֹרָתֶךָ וְאֶשְׁמְרֶנָּה בְכָל לֵב:

לה הַדְרִיכֵנִי בִּנְתִיב מִצְוֹתֶיךָ כִּי בוֹ חָפָצְתִּי:

לו הַט לִבִּי אֶל עֵדְוֹתֶיךָ וְאַל אֶל בָּצַע:

לז הַעֲבֵר עֵינַי מֵרְאוֹת שָׁוְא בִּדְרָכֶךָ חַיֵּנִי:

לח הָקֵם לְעַבְדְּךָ אִמְרָתֶךָ אֲשֶׁר לְיִרְאָתֶךָ:

לט הַעֲבֵר חֶרְפָּתִי אֲשֶׁר יָגֹרְתִּי כִּי מִשְׁפָּטֶיךָ טוֹבִים:

מ הִנֵּה תָּאַבְתִּי לְפִקֻּדֶיךָ בְּצִדְקָתְךָ חַיֵּנִי:

מא וִיבֹאֻנִי חֲסָדֶךָ יְהֹוָה תְּשׁוּעָתְךָ כְּאִמְרָתֶךָ:

מב וְאֶעֱנֶה חֹרְפִי דָבָר כִּי בָטַחְתִּי בִּדְבָרֶךָ:

מג וְאַל תַּצֵּל מִפִּי דְבַר אֱמֶת עַד מְאֹד כִּי לְמִשְׁפָּטֶךָ יִחָלְתִּי:

מד וְאֶשְׁמְרָה תוֹרָתְךָ תָמִיד לְעוֹלָם וָעֶד:

מה וְאֶתְהַלְּכָה בָרְחָבָה כִּי פִקֻּדֶיךָ דָרָשְׁתִּי:

מו וַאֲדַבְּרָה בְעֵדֹתֶיךָ נֶגֶד מְלָכִים וְלֹא אֵבוֹשׁ:

מז וְאֶשְׁתַּעֲשַׁע בְּמִצְוֹתֶיךָ אֲשֶׁר אָהָבְתִּי:

מח וְאֶשָּׂא כַפַּי אֶל מִצְוֹתֶיךָ אֲשֶׁר אָהָבְתִּי וְאָשִׂיחָה בְחֻקֶּיךָ:

28 My soul melts away in sorrow. Support me according to Your word.
29 Remove the path of falsehood from me, and graciously grant me Your Torah.
30 I have chosen the path of faithfulness. I have set Your law before me.
31 I follow Your laws closely, Lord. Do not put me to shame.
32 I will run in the way of Your laws, for You have freed my heart.

Heh

33 Lord, teach me the way of Your commandments, and I will keep them consistently.
34 Give me understanding so that I may keep Your law and observe it wholeheartedly.
35 Guide me on the path of Your commandments, for that is what I delight in.
36 Turn my heart to Your laws and not to personal profit.
37 Keep my eyes from seeing vanity, and revive me in Your ways.
38 Fulfill Your promise to Your servant who revere's you.
39 Take away my disgrace, which I dread, for Your laws are good.
40 See, I long for Your commandments; revive me in Your righteousness.

Vav

41 My Lord, send me Your kindness and the salvation that You promised me
42 So that I may have an answer for the one's who taunt me; for I trust in Your word.
43 Do not take Your truth away from me, for my hope is in Your laws.
44 I will keep Your laws always and forever.
45 I will walk in peace because I have sought Your Torah.
46 I will also speak of Your laws to kings and will feel no shame.
47 I will take delight in Your commandments, for I love them.
48 I will lift my hands to Your teachings, which I love, and I will meditate upon Your laws.

מט זְכֹר־דָּבָר לְעַבְדֶּךָ עַל אֲשֶׁר יִחַלְתָּנִי:

נ זֹאת נֶחָמָתִי בְעָנְיִי כִּי אִמְרָתְךָ חִיָּתְנִי:

נא זֵדִים הֱלִיצֻנִי עַד־מְאֹד מִתּוֹרָתְךָ לֹא נָטִיתִי:

נב זָכַרְתִּי מִשְׁפָּטֶיךָ מֵעוֹלָם יְהוָה וָאֶתְנֶחָם:

נג זַלְעָפָה אֲחָזַתְנִי מֵרְשָׁעִים עֹזְבֵי תּוֹרָתֶךָ:

נד זְמִרוֹת הָיוּ־לִי חֻקֶּיךָ בְּבֵית מְגוּרָי:

נה זָכַרְתִּי בַלַּיְלָה שִׁמְךָ יְהוָה וָאֶשְׁמְרָה תּוֹרָתֶךָ:

נו זֹאת הָיְתָה־לִּי כִּי פִקֻּדֶיךָ נָצָרְתִּי:

נז חֶלְקִי יְהוָה אָמַרְתִּי לִשְׁמֹר דְּבָרֶיךָ:

נח חִלִּיתִי פָנֶיךָ בְכָל־לֵב חָנֵּנִי כְּאִמְרָתֶךָ:

נט חִשַּׁבְתִּי דְרָכָי וָאָשִׁיבָה רַגְלַי אֶל־עֵדֹתֶיךָ:

ס חַשְׁתִּי וְלֹא הִתְמַהְמָהְתִּי לִשְׁמֹר מִצְוֹתֶיךָ:

סא חֶבְלֵי רְשָׁעִים עִוְּדֻנִי תּוֹרָתְךָ לֹא שָׁכָחְתִּי:

סב חֲצוֹת־לַיְלָה אָקוּם לְהוֹדוֹת לָךְ עַל מִשְׁפְּטֵי צִדְקֶךָ:

סג חָבֵר אָנִי לְכָל־אֲשֶׁר יְרֵאוּךָ וּלְשֹׁמְרֵי פִּקּוּדֶיךָ:

סד חַסְדְּךָ יְהוָה מָלְאָה הָאָרֶץ חֻקֶּיךָ לַמְּדֵנִי:

סה טוֹב עָשִׂיתָ עִם־עַבְדְּךָ יְהוָה כִּדְבָרֶךָ:

סו טוּב טַעַם וָדַעַת לַמְּדֵנִי כִּי בְמִצְוֹתֶיךָ הֶאֱמָנְתִּי:

סז טֶרֶם אֶעֱנֶה אֲנִי שֹׁגֵג וְעַתָּה אִמְרָתְךָ שָׁמָרְתִּי:

סח טוֹב־אַתָּה וּמֵטִיב לַמְּדֵנִי חֻקֶּיךָ:

סט טָפְלוּ עָלַי שֶׁקֶר זֵדִים אֲנִי בְּכָל־לֵב אֱצֹר פִּקּוּדֶיךָ:

Zayin

49 Remember Your promise to Your servant because You have given me hope.

50 This is my comfort in my suffering: that Your word has revived me.

51 Although arrogant people have ridiculed me terribly, I have not turned away from Your law.

52 I remember Your ordinances of old, Lord, and I take comfort.

53 Terrible fury has seized me because of the wicked people who forsake Your law.

54 Your laws have been my song in my dwelling place.

55 During the night I remember Your name, Lord, and observe Your law.

56 This has been my lot, for I have obeyed Your teachings.

Het

57 My portion is the Lord: I have said that I would keep Your words.

58 I have sought Your presence with all my heart; be kind to me as You have promised.

59 I considered my ways and turned my feet back to Your laws.

60 I hurried, without delay, to observe Your law.

61 Though the ropes of the wicked closed around me, I did not forget Your law.

62 At midnight I will awaken to thank You for Your righteous laws.

63 I am a companion to all who revere You and observe Your laws.

64 The earth, Lord, is full of Your loving kindness; teach me Your laws.

Tet

65 Lord, You have dealt kindly with Your servant, as You promised.

66 Teach me good understanding and wisdom, for I have believed in Your commandments.

67 Before I suffered, I was in error, and now I fulfill Your word.

68 You are good and You do good. Teach me Your laws.

69 Although arrogant people have slandered me, I will keep Your laws with all my heart.

70 Their heart is as thick as fat, but I take delight in Your law.

71 It was good for me to suffer, since I learned Your laws.

ע טָפַשׁ כַּחֵלֶב לִבָּם אֲנִי תּוֹרָתְךָ שִׁעֲשָׁעְתִּי:

עא טוֹב־לִי כִי־עֻנֵּיתִי לְמַעַן אֶלְמַד חֻקֶּיךָ:

עב טוֹב־לִי תוֹרַת פִּיךָ מֵאַלְפֵי זָהָב וָכָסֶף:

עג יָדֶיךָ עָשׂוּנִי וַיְכוֹנְנוּנִי הֲבִינֵנִי וְאֶלְמְדָה מִצְוֹתֶיךָ:

עד יְרֵאֶיךָ יִרְאוּנִי וְיִשְׂמָחוּ כִּי לִדְבָרְךָ יִחָלְתִּי:

עה יָדַעְתִּי יְהוָה כִּי־צֶדֶק מִשְׁפָּטֶיךָ וֶאֱמוּנָה עִנִּיתָנִי:

עו יְהִי־נָא חַסְדְּךָ לְנַחֲמֵנִי כְּאִמְרָתְךָ לְעַבְדֶּךָ:

עז יְבֹאוּנִי רַחֲמֶיךָ וְאֶחְיֶה כִּי תוֹרָתְךָ שַׁעֲשֻׁעָי:

עח יֵבֹשׁוּ זֵדִים כִּי־שֶׁקֶר עִוְּתוּנִי אֲנִי אָשִׂיחַ בְּפִקּוּדֶיךָ:

עט יָשׁוּבוּ־לִי יְרֵאֶיךָ וידעו [וְיֹדְעֵי] עֵדֹתֶיךָ:

פ יְהִי־לִבִּי תָמִים בְּחֻקֶּיךָ לְמַעַן לֹא אֵבוֹשׁ:

פא כָּלְתָה לִתְשׁוּעָתְךָ נַפְשִׁי לִדְבָרְךָ יִחָלְתִּי:

פב כָּלוּ עֵינַי לְאִמְרָתֶךָ לֵאמֹר מָתַי תְּנַחֲמֵנִי:

פג כִּי־הָיִיתִי כְּנֹאד בְּקִיטוֹר חֻקֶּיךָ לֹא שָׁכָחְתִּי:

פד כַּמָּה יְמֵי עַבְדֶּךָ מָתַי תַּעֲשֶׂה בְרֹדְפַי מִשְׁפָּט:

פה כָּרוּ־לִי זֵדִים שִׁיחוֹת אֲשֶׁר לֹא כְתוֹרָתֶךָ:

פו כָּל־מִצְוֹתֶיךָ אֱמוּנָה שֶׁקֶר רְדָפוּנִי עָזְרֵנִי:

פז כִּמְעַט כִּלּוּנִי בָאָרֶץ וַאֲנִי לֹא־עָזַבְתִּי פִקּוּדֶיךָ:

פח כְּחַסְדְּךָ חַיֵּנִי וְאֶשְׁמְרָה עֵדוּת פִּיךָ:

72 The law of Your mouth is better to me than thousands in gold and silver.

Yod

73 Your hands made me and shaped me. Give me understanding so that I may learn Your commandments.

74 Those who revere You will see me and rejoice, for I hoped for Your word.

75 Lord, I know that Your judgments are righteous and believe you justly made me suffer.

76 Please let Your loving kindness comfort me, as You promised Your servant.

77 Let Your compassion come to me so that I may live, for Your teaching is my delight.

78 Let the arrogant ones be put to shame, for they have lied about me – but I will meditate upon Your teachings.

79 Let those who revere You and those who know Your laws return to me.

80 Let my heart keep wholly to Your laws so that I will not be put to shame.

Kaf

81 My soul pines away for Your salvation. I put my hope in Your word.

82 My eyes grow weak pining for Your word, saying: When will You comfort me?

83 Though I have become like a water-pouch dried up in smoke, I will not forgotten Your laws.

84 How many days does your servant have left? When will You judge my enemies?

85 The arrogant have dug pits for me, which is not according to Your law.

86 All Your commandments are based on faithfulness. They pursue me for no reason with lies. Help me.

87 They had almost destroyed me on earth, but for my part, I did not abandon Your law.

88 Revive me according to Your kindness, and I will keep the laws of Your mouth.

פט   לְעוֹלָם יְהוָה דְּבָרְךָ נִצָּב בַּשָּׁמָיִם:

צ   לְדֹר וָדֹר אֱמוּנָתֶךָ כּוֹנַנְתָּ אֶרֶץ וַתַּעֲמֹד:

צא   לְמִשְׁפָּטֶיךָ עָמְדוּ הַיּוֹם כִּי הַכֹּל עֲבָדֶיךָ:

צב   לוּלֵי תוֹרָתְךָ שַׁעֲשֻׁעָי אָז אָבַדְתִּי בְעָנְיִי:

צג   לְעוֹלָם לֹא־אֶשְׁכַּח פִּקּוּדֶיךָ כִּי־בָם חִיִּיתָנִי:

צד   לְךָ־אֲנִי הוֹשִׁיעֵנִי כִּי פִקּוּדֶיךָ דָרָשְׁתִּי:

צה   לִי קִוּוּ רְשָׁעִים לְאַבְּדֵנִי עֵדֹתֶיךָ אֶתְבּוֹנָן:

צו   לְכָל תִּכְלָה רָאִיתִי קֵץ רְחָבָה מִצְוָתְךָ מְאֹד:

צז   מָה־אָהַבְתִּי תוֹרָתֶךָ כָּל־הַיּוֹם הִיא שִׂיחָתִי:

צח   מֵאֹיְבַי תְּחַכְּמֵנִי מִצְוֹתֶךָ כִּי לְעוֹלָם הִיא־לִי:

צט   מִכָּל־מְלַמְּדַי הִשְׂכַּלְתִּי כִּי עֵדְוֹתֶיךָ שִׂיחָה לִי:

ק   מִזְּקֵנִים אֶתְבּוֹנָן כִּי פִקּוּדֶיךָ נָצָרְתִּי:

קא   מִכָּל־אֹרַח רָע כָּלִאתִי רַגְלָי לְמַעַן אֶשְׁמֹר דְּבָרֶךָ:

קב   מִמִּשְׁפָּטֶיךָ לֹא־סָרְתִּי כִּי־אַתָּה הוֹרֵתָנִי:

קג   מַה־נִּמְלְצוּ לְחִכִּי אִמְרָתֶךָ מִדְּבַשׁ לְפִי:

קד   מִפִּקּוּדֶיךָ אֶתְבּוֹנָן עַל־כֵּן שָׂנֵאתִי כָּל־אֹרַח שָׁקֶר:

קה   נֵר־לְרַגְלִי דְבָרֶךָ וְאוֹר לִנְתִיבָתִי:

קו   נִשְׁבַּעְתִּי וָאֲקַיֵּמָה לִשְׁמֹר מִשְׁפְּטֵי צִדְקֶךָ:

קז   נַעֲנֵיתִי עַד־מְאֹד יְהוָה חַיֵּנִי כִדְבָרֶךָ:

קח   נִדְבוֹת פִּי רְצֵה־נָא יְהוָה וּמִשְׁפָּטֶיךָ לַמְּדֵנִי:

קט   נַפְשִׁי בְכַפִּי תָמִיד וְתוֹרָתְךָ לֹא שָׁכָחְתִּי:

Lamed

89 Lord, Your word stands forever in Heaven.

90 Your faithfulness lasts for all generations. You established the earth, and it endures.

91 Everything exists today according to Your laws, for all things are Your servants.

92 If Your Torah had not been my delight, I would have died in my suffering.

93 I will never forget Your laws, for with them You have revived me.

94 I am Yours. Save me, for I have sought out Your laws.

95 The wicked have hoped to destroy me, but I will obey Your laws.

96 I have seen that there is an end to everything, but Your commandments are without bounds.

Mem

97 How greatly do I love Your Torah! I think about it all day long.

98 Your commandments make me wiser than my enemies, for they are always with me.

99 I have learned understanding from all my teachers, for Your laws are my meditation.

100 I have received insights from my elders, and kept your precepts from my youth.

101 I have kept my feet from every evil path so that I might observe Your law.

102 I have not turned away from Your laws, for You have taught me.

103 How sweet are Your words to my palate, sweeter than honey to my mouth.

104 From Your precepts I receive understanding. Therefore I hate every false way.

Nun

105 Your law is a lamp for my feet, a light for my path.

106 I have sworn, and I will fulfill it – to keep your righteous laws.

107 I am suffering very much. Revive me, Lord, according to Your word.

108 Lord, accept the offerings of my mouth, and teach me Your laws.

109 My soul is always in danger, but I have not forgotten Your law.

קי נָתְנוּ רְשָׁעִים פַּח לִי וּמִפִּקּוּדֶיךָ לֹא תָעִיתִי:

קיא נָחַלְתִּי עֵדְוֹתֶיךָ לְעוֹלָם כִּי־שְׂשׂוֹן לִבִּי הֵמָּה:

קיב נָטִיתִי לִבִּי לַעֲשׂוֹת חֻקֶּיךָ לְעוֹלָם עֵקֶב:

קיג סֵעֲפִים שָׂנֵאתִי וְתוֹרָתְךָ אָהָבְתִּי:

קיד סִתְרִי וּמָגִנִּי אָתָּה לִדְבָרְךָ יִחָלְתִּי:

קטו סוּרוּ מִמֶּנִּי מְרֵעִים וְאֶצְּרָה מִצְוֹת אֱלֹהָי:

קטז סָמְכֵנִי כְאִמְרָתְךָ וְאֶחְיֶה וְאַל־תְּבִישֵׁנִי מִשִּׂבְרִי:

קיז סְעָדֵנִי וְאִוָּשֵׁעָה וְאֶשְׁעָה בְחֻקֶּיךָ תָמִיד:

קיח סָלִיתָ כָּל־שׁוֹגִים מֵחֻקֶּיךָ כִּי־שֶׁקֶר תַּרְמִיתָם:

קיט סִגִים הִשְׁבַּתָּ כָל־רִשְׁעֵי־אָרֶץ לָכֵן אָהַבְתִּי עֵדֹתֶיךָ:

קכ סָמַר מִפַּחְדְּךָ בְשָׂרִי וּמִמִּשְׁפָּטֶיךָ יָרֵאתִי:

קכא עָשִׂיתִי מִשְׁפָּט וָצֶדֶק בַּל־תַּנִּיחֵנִי לְעֹשְׁקָי:

קכב עֲרֹב עַבְדְּךָ לְטוֹב אַל־יַעַשְׁקֻנִי זֵדִים:

קכג עֵינַי כָּלוּ לִישׁוּעָתֶךָ וּלְאִמְרַת צִדְקֶךָ:

קכד עֲשֵׂה עִם־עַבְדְּךָ כְחַסְדֶּךָ וְחֻקֶּיךָ לַמְּדֵנִי:

קכה עַבְדְּךָ אָנִי הֲבִינֵנִי וְאֵדְעָה עֵדֹתֶיךָ:

קכו עֵת לַעֲשׂוֹת לַיהוָה הֵפֵרוּ תוֹרָתֶךָ:

קכז עַל־כֵּן אָהַבְתִּי מִצְוֹתֶיךָ מִזָּהָב וּמִפָּז:

קכח עַל־כֵּן כָּל־פִּקּוּדֵי כֹל יִשָּׁרְתִּי כָּל־אֹרַח שֶׁקֶר שָׂנֵאתִי:

110 The wicked have laid a trap for me, yet I remained loyal to Your teachings.

111 I have taken Your Torah as an inheritance forever and it is the happiness of my heart.

112 I have inclined my heart to perform Your laws, forever, at every step.

Samech

113 Those of divided heart I hate, but I love Your Torah.

114 You are my refuge and my shield, and I put my hope in Your word.

115 Go away from me, you who do evil, so that I may keep my Lord's commandments.

116 Support me according to Your word that I may live, and do not put me to shame in my hope.

117 Strengthen me and I will be saved, and I will occupy myself with Your laws always.

118 You have made light of all those who deviate from Your law, for their dishonesty is worthless.

119 You have removed all the wicked from the world like waste. Therefore, I love Your law.

120 My flesh shakes from fear of You, and I am in awe of Your judgments.

Ayin

121 I have done justice and righteousness. Do not leave me to my oppressors.

122 Attest for Your servant for good. Do not let the arrogant harm me.

123 My eyes yearn for Your salvation, and for the word of Your righteousness.

124 Deal with Your servant according to Your loving kindness, and teach me Your laws.

125 I am Your servant. Grant me understanding so that I may know Your laws.

126 It is time for the Lord to act, for they have rejected Your law.

127 Therefore, I have loved Your commandments more than gold or refined gold.

128 Therefore, I know that all Your laws about everything are perfect; I hate every false path.

קכט פְּלָאוֹת עֵדְוֹתֶיךָ עַל־כֵּן נְצָרָתַם נַפְשִׁי:

קל פֵּתַח דְּבָרֶיךָ יָאִיר מֵבִין פְּתָיִים:

קלא פִּי־פָעַרְתִּי וָאֶשְׁאָפָה כִּי לְמִצְוֹתֶיךָ יָאָבְתִּי:

קלב פְּנֵה־אֵלַי וְחָנֵּנִי כְּמִשְׁפָּט לְאֹהֲבֵי שְׁמֶךָ:

קלג פְּעָמַי הָכֵן בְּאִמְרָתֶךָ וְאַל־תַּשְׁלֶט־בִּי כָל־אָוֶן:

קלד פְּדֵנִי מֵעֹשֶׁק אָדָם וְאֶשְׁמְרָה פִּקּוּדֶיךָ:

קלה פָּנֶיךָ הָאֵר בְּעַבְדֶּךָ וְלַמְּדֵנִי אֶת־חֻקֶּיךָ:

קלו פַּלְגֵי־מַיִם יָרְדוּ עֵינָי עַל לֹא־שָׁמְרוּ תוֹרָתֶךָ:

קלז צַדִּיק אַתָּה יְהֹוָה וְיָשָׁר מִשְׁפָּטֶיךָ:

קלח צִוִּיתָ צֶדֶק עֵדֹתֶיךָ וֶאֱמוּנָה מְאֹד:

קלט צִמְּתַתְנִי קִנְאָתִי כִּי־שָׁכְחוּ דְבָרֶיךָ צָרָי:

קמ צְרוּפָה אִמְרָתְךָ מְאֹד וְעַבְדְּךָ אֲהֵבָהּ:

קמא צָעִיר אָנֹכִי וְנִבְזֶה פִּקֻּדֶיךָ לֹא שָׁכָחְתִּי:

קמב צִדְקָתְךָ צֶדֶק לְעוֹלָם וְתוֹרָתְךָ אֱמֶת:

קמג צַר־וּמָצוֹק מְצָאוּנִי מִצְוֹתֶיךָ שַׁעֲשֻׁעָי:

קמד צֶדֶק עֵדְוֹתֶיךָ לְעוֹלָם הֲבִינֵנִי וְאֶחְיֶה:

קמה קָרָאתִי בְכָל־לֵב עֲנֵנִי יְהֹוָה חֻקֶּיךָ אֶצֹּרָה:

קמו קְרָאתִיךָ הוֹשִׁיעֵנִי וְאֶשְׁמְרָה עֵדֹתֶיךָ:

קמז קִדַּמְתִּי בַנֶּשֶׁף וָאֲשַׁוֵּעָה לִדבָרֶיךָ [לִדְבָרְךָ] יִחָלְתִּי:

קמח קִדְּמוּ עֵינַי אַשְׁמֻרוֹת לָשִׂיחַ בְּאִמְרָתֶךָ:

קמט קוֹלִי שִׁמְעָה כְחַסְדֶּךָ יְהֹוָה כְּמִשְׁפָּטֶךָ חַיֵּנִי:

Peh

129 Your testimonies are wonderful. Therefore, my soul cherishes them.

130 Your opening words give light, granting understanding to the simple.

131 I opened my mouth wide and eagerly swallowed them, for I longed for Your commandments.

132 Turn to me and be gracious to me, as is Your way toward those who love Your name.

133 Guide my footsteps according to Your word and do not let sin influence me.

134 Redeem me from the bad acts of human beings, and I will obey Your law.

135 Let Your face shine upon Your servant, and teach me Your laws.

136 Rivers of tears stream from my eyes because they do not keep Your law.

Tzadik

137 Lord, You are righteous and upright in judgment.

138 You have commanded Your testimonies with righteousness and required great faithfulness.

139 My jealousy for You has brought me down, knowing my enemies have forgotten Your words.

140 Your word is exceedingly pure, and Your servant loves it.

141 Though I am young and despised, I have not forgotten Your laws.

142 Your righteousness lasts forever, and Your Torah is truth.

143 Trouble and distress have overcome me, yet Your law is my delight.

144 Your laws are righteous forever. Grant me understanding, and I shall live.

Kuf

145 I have called You with all my heart. Lord, answer me. I will treasure Your laws.

146 I have called to You. Save me, and I will keep Your testimonies.

147 I awoke early at dawn and cried. I placed my hope in Your word.

148 My eyes stayed awake during the night watches so that I might meditate upon Your word.

קנ   קָרְבוּ רֹדְפֵי זִמָּה מִתּוֹרָתְךָ רָחָקוּ:

קנא   קָרוֹב אַתָּה יְהֹוָה וְכָל־מִצְוֺתֶיךָ אֱמֶת:

קנב   קֶדֶם יָדַעְתִּי מֵעֵדֹתֶיךָ כִּי לְעוֹלָם יְסַדְתָּם:

קנג   רְאֵה־עָנְיִי וְחַלְּצֵנִי כִּי־תוֹרָתְךָ לֹא שָׁכָחְתִּי:

קנד   רִיבָה רִיבִי וּגְאָלֵנִי לְאִמְרָתְךָ חַיֵּנִי:

קנה   רָחוֹק מֵרְשָׁעִים יְשׁוּעָה כִּי־חֻקֶּיךָ לֹא דָרָשׁוּ:

קנו   רַחֲמֶיךָ רַבִּים יְהֹוָה כְּמִשְׁפָּטֶיךָ חַיֵּנִי:

קנז   רַבִּים רֹדְפַי וְצָרָי מֵעֵדְוֺתֶיךָ לֹא נָטִיתִי:

קנח   רָאִיתִי בֹגְדִים וָאֶתְקוֹטָטָה אֲשֶׁר אִמְרָתְךָ לֹא שָׁמָרוּ:

קנט   רְאֵה כִּי־פִקּוּדֶיךָ אָהָבְתִּי יְהֹוָה כְּחַסְדְּךָ חַיֵּנִי:

קס   רֹאשׁ־דְּבָרְךָ אֱמֶת וּלְעוֹלָם כָּל־מִשְׁפַּט צִדְקֶךָ:

קסא   שָׂרִים רְדָפוּנִי חִנָּם [וּמִדְּבָרְךָ] וּמדבריך פָּחַד לִבִּי:

קסב   שָׂשׂ אָנֹכִי עַל־אִמְרָתֶךָ כְּמוֹצֵא שָׁלָל רָב:

קסג   שֶׁקֶר שָׂנֵאתִי וַאֲתַעֵבָה תּוֹרָתְךָ אָהָבְתִּי:

קסד   שֶׁבַע בַּיּוֹם הִלַּלְתִּיךָ עַל מִשְׁפְּטֵי צִדְקֶךָ:

קסה   שָׁלוֹם רָב לְאֹהֲבֵי תוֹרָתֶךָ וְאֵין לָמוֹ מִכְשׁוֹל:

קסו   שִׂבַּרְתִּי לִישׁוּעָתְךָ יְהֹוָה וּמִצְוֺתֶיךָ עָשִׂיתִי:

קסז   שָׁמְרָה נַפְשִׁי עֵדֹתֶיךָ וָאֹהֲבֵם מְאֹד:

קסח   שָׁמַרְתִּי פִקּוּדֶיךָ וְעֵדֹתֶיךָ כִּי כָל־דְּרָכַי נֶגְדֶּךָ:

149 Hear my voice, Lord, according to Your loving kindness, and revive me according to Your laws.

150 Those who run after wickedness are approaching. They are far from Your Torah.

151 You are near, God, and all Your commandments are truth.

152 I have learned of the past through the wisdom of your testimonies which are established forever.

Resh

153 See my suffering and rescue me, for I have not forgotten Your law.

154 Fight my battle and redeem me; revive me according to Your word.

155 Salvation is far from the wicked because they do not seek Your laws.

156 Great are Your mercies, Lord. Revive me according to Your laws.

157 Many are my enemies and that hate me, but I have not turned away from Your testimonies.

158 I saw traitors and fought against them because they did not obey Your word.

159 See how I love Your commandments. Lord, revive me according to Your loving kindness.

160 The beginning of Your word is truth, and all Your righteous laws endure forever.

Shin

161 Princes have persecuted me for no reason, yet my heart reveres only Your words.

162 I rejoice as much over Your word as one who obtains great spoil.

163 I hate falsehood and it is despicable, but I love Your Torah.

164 I praise You seven times a day for Your righteous laws.

165 Those who love Your law have great peace, and there is no stumbling for them.

166 I have hoped for Your salvation, Lord, and performed Your commandments.

167 My soul has kept Your laws, and I love them very much.

168 I have observed Your precepts and Your laws because all my ways are before You.

קסט תִּקְרַב רִנָּתִי לְפָנֶיךָ יְהוָה כִּדְבָרְךָ הֲבִינֵנִי:

קע תָּבוֹא תְּחִנָּתִי לְפָנֶיךָ כְּאִמְרָתְךָ הַצִּילֵנִי:

קעא תַּבַּעְנָה שְׂפָתַי תְּהִלָּה כִּי תְלַמְּדֵנִי חֻקֶּיךָ:

קעב תַּעַן לְשׁוֹנִי אִמְרָתֶךָ כִּי כָל־מִצְוֹתֶיךָ צֶּדֶק:

קעג תְּהִי־יָדְךָ לְעָזְרֵנִי כִּי פִקּוּדֶיךָ בָחָרְתִּי:

קעד תָּאַבְתִּי לִישׁוּעָתְךָ יְהוָה וְתוֹרָתְךָ שַׁעֲשֻׁעָי:

קעה תְּחִי־נַפְשִׁי וּתְהַלְלֶךָּ וּמִשְׁפָּטֶךָ יַעֲזְרֻנִי:

קעו תָּעִיתִי כְּשֶׂה אֹבֵד בַּקֵּשׁ עַבְדֶּךָ כִּי מִצְוֹתֶיךָ לֹא שָׁכָחְתִּי:

פרק קכ

א שִׁיר הַמַּעֲלוֹת אֶל־יְהוָה בַּצָּרָתָה לִּי קָרָאתִי וַיַּעֲנֵנִי:

ב יְהוָה הַצִּילָה נַפְשִׁי מִשְּׂפַת־שֶׁקֶר מִלָּשׁוֹן רְמִיָּה:

ג מַה־יִּתֵּן לְךָ וּמַה־יֹּסִיף לָךְ לָשׁוֹן רְמִיָּה:

ד חִצֵּי גִבּוֹר שְׁנוּנִים עִם גַּחֲלֵי רְתָמִים:

ה אוֹיָה־לִי כִּי־גַרְתִּי מֶשֶׁךְ שָׁכַנְתִּי עִם־אָהֳלֵי קֵדָר:

ו רַבַּת שָׁכְנָה־לָּהּ נַפְשִׁי עִם שׂוֹנֵא שָׁלוֹם:

ז אֲנִי־שָׁלוֹם וְכִי אֲדַבֵּר הֵמָּה לַמִּלְחָמָה:

פרק קכא

א שִׁיר לַמַּעֲלוֹת אֶשָּׂא עֵינַי אֶל־הֶהָרִים מֵאַיִן יָבֹא עֶזְרִי:

ב עֶזְרִי מֵעִם יְהוָה עֹשֵׂה שָׁמַיִם וָאָרֶץ:

Tav

169 Let my song come before You, Lord. Grant me understanding according to Your word.

170 Let my plea come before You. Save me according to Your word.

171 My lips give forth praise because You teach me Your laws.

172 My tongue sings of Your word, for all Your commandments are righteous.

173 Let Your hand help me, for I have chosen Your precepts.

174 I have longed for Your salvation, Lord, and Your Torah is my delight.

175 Let my soul live and it will praise You, and let Your laws help me.

176 I have gone astray like a lost sheep. For I am Your servant, please find me for I have not forgotten Your commandments.

TEHILLIM 120

A song about a wandering soul praying for rest

1 A song of Ascents. In my suffering I called to the Lord, and He answered me.

2 Lord, save my soul from lying lips and a false tongue.

3 What advantage will you have, and what gain will you receive, you false tongue?

4 The sharp arrow of the mighty, with burning coals awaits you.

5 Woe to me, that I live with Meshech, that I dwell beside the tents of Kedar!

6 My soul is fed up with living among those who hate peace.

7 I am for peace, but when I speak, they are for war.

TEHILLIM 121

The well-known song of complete trust in God

1 A song of ascents. I will lift up my eyes to the mountains; from where does my help come?

2 My help comes from the Lord who made heaven and earth.

ג אַל־יִתֵּן לַמּוֹט רַגְלֶךָ אַל־יָנוּם שֹׁמְרֶךָ:

ד הִנֵּה לֹא יָנוּם וְלֹא יִישָׁן שׁוֹמֵר יִשְׂרָאֵל:

ה יְהוָה שֹׁמְרֶךָ יְהוָה צִלְּךָ עַל־יַד יְמִינֶךָ:

ו יוֹמָם הַשֶּׁמֶשׁ לֹא־יַכֶּכָּה וְיָרֵחַ בַּלָּיְלָה:

ז יְהוָה יִשְׁמָרְךָ מִכָּל־רָע יִשְׁמֹר אֶת־נַפְשֶׁךָ:

ח יְהוָה יִשְׁמָר־צֵאתְךָ וּבוֹאֶךָ מֵעַתָּה וְעַד־עוֹלָם:

פרק קכב

א שִׁיר הַמַּעֲלוֹת לְדָוִד שָׂמַחְתִּי בְּאֹמְרִים לִי בֵּית יְהוָה נֵלֵךְ:

ב עֹמְדוֹת הָיוּ רַגְלֵינוּ בִּשְׁעָרַיִךְ יְרוּשָׁלָם:

ג יְרוּשָׁלַם הַבְּנוּיָה כְּעִיר שֶׁחֻבְּרָה־לָּהּ יַחְדָּו:

ד שֶׁשָּׁם עָלוּ שְׁבָטִים שִׁבְטֵי־יָהּ עֵדוּת לְיִשְׂרָאֵל לְהֹדוֹת לְשֵׁם יְהוָה:

ה כִּי שָׁמָּה יָשְׁבוּ כִסְאוֹת לְמִשְׁפָּט כִּסְאוֹת לְבֵית דָּוִד:

ו שַׁאֲלוּ שְׁלוֹם יְרוּשָׁלָם יִשְׁלָיוּ אֹהֲבָיִךְ:

ז יְהִי־שָׁלוֹם בְּחֵילֵךְ שַׁלְוָה בְּאַרְמְנוֹתָיִךְ:

ח לְמַעַן־אַחַי וְרֵעָי אֲדַבְּרָה־נָּא שָׁלוֹם בָּךְ:

ט לְמַעַן בֵּית־יְהוָה אֱלֹהֵינוּ אֲבַקְשָׁה טוֹב לָךְ:

פרק קכג

א שִׁיר הַמַּעֲלוֹת אֵלֶיךָ נָשָׂאתִי אֶת־עֵינַי הַיֹּשְׁבִי בַּשָּׁמָיִם:

ב הִנֵּה כְעֵינֵי עֲבָדִים אֶל־יַד אֲדוֹנֵיהֶם כְּעֵינֵי שִׁפְחָה אֶל־יַד גְּבִרְתָּהּ כֵּן
עֵינֵינוּ אֶל־יְהוָה אֱלֹהֵינוּ עַד שֶׁיְּחָנֵּנוּ:

3 He will not allow your foot to stumble. Your Guardian will not sleep.

4 See – the Guardian of Israel neither slumbers nor sleeps.

5 The Lord is your guardian. The Lord is your protection at your right hand.

6 The sun will not harm you during the day nor the moon at night.

7 The Lord will protect you from all evil. He will protect your soul.

8 The Lord shall guard your going out and your coming in from now on and forever.

TEHILLIM 122

A song of rejoicing upon praying in the Sanctuary

1 A song of Ascents by David. I was happy when they said to me: "Come, let us go to the house of the Lord."

2 Our feet were standing within Your gates, Jerusalem –

3 Jerusalem built up, a city connected all together,

4 To which the tribes would go on pilgrimage, the tribes of God – as Israel's testimony to praise the name of the Lord.

5 The thrones of judgment were placed there, the thrones of the house of David.

6 Pray for the well-being of Jerusalem; may those who love Jerusalem be at peace with themselves.

7 May there be peace within your walls and serenity within Your palaces.

8 For the sake of my relatives and my friends, I pray, "May peace be within you."

9 For the sake of the house of the Lord our God, I will seek your good.

TEHILLIM 123

A song of the people asking God for assistance

1 A song of Ascents. I lift up my eyes to You, You Who are enthroned in the heavens.

ג חָנֵּנוּ יְהוָה חָנֵּנוּ כִּי־רַב שָׂבַעְנוּ בוּז׃

ד רַבַּת שָׂבְעָה־לָּהּ נַפְשֵׁנוּ הַלַּעַג הַשַּׁאֲנַנִּים הַבּוּז לִגְאֵיוֹנִים [לִגְאֵי יוֹנִים]׃

פרק קכד

א שִׁיר הַמַּעֲלוֹת לְדָוִד לוּלֵי יְהוָה שֶׁהָיָה לָנוּ יֹאמַר־נָא יִשְׂרָאֵל׃

ב לוּלֵי יְהוָה שֶׁהָיָה לָנוּ בְּקוּם עָלֵינוּ אָדָם׃

ג אֲזַי חַיִּים בְּלָעוּנוּ בַּחֲרוֹת אַפָּם בָּנוּ׃

ד אֲזַי הַמַּיִם שְׁטָפוּנוּ נַחְלָה עָבַר עַל־נַפְשֵׁנוּ׃

ה אֲזַי עָבַר עַל־נַפְשֵׁנוּ הַמַּיִם הַזֵּידוֹנִים׃

ו בָּרוּךְ יְהוָה שֶׁלֹּא נְתָנָנוּ טֶרֶף לְשִׁנֵּיהֶם׃

ז נַפְשֵׁנוּ כְּצִפּוֹר נִמְלְטָה מִפַּח יוֹקְשִׁים הַפַּח נִשְׁבָּר וַאֲנַחְנוּ נִמְלָטְנוּ׃

ח עֶזְרֵנוּ בְּשֵׁם יְהוָה עֹשֵׂה שָׁמַיִם וָאָרֶץ׃

פרק קכה

א שִׁיר הַמַּעֲלוֹת הַבֹּטְחִים בַּיהוָה כְּהַר־צִיּוֹן לֹא־יִמּוֹט לְעוֹלָם יֵשֵׁב׃

ב יְרוּשָׁלַיִם הָרִים סָבִיב לָהּ וַיהוָה סָבִיב לְעַמּוֹ מֵעַתָּה וְעַד־עוֹלָם׃

ג כִּי לֹא יָנוּחַ שֵׁבֶט הָרֶשַׁע עַל גּוֹרַל הַצַּדִּיקִים לְמַעַן לֹא־יִשְׁלְחוּ הַצַּדִּיקִים בְּעַוְלָתָה יְדֵיהֶם׃

ד הֵיטִיבָה יְהוָה לַטּוֹבִים וְלִישָׁרִים בְּלִבּוֹתָם׃

ה וְהַמַּטִּים עֲקַלְקַלּוֹתָם יוֹלִיכֵם יְהוָה אֶת־פֹּעֲלֵי הָאָוֶן שָׁלוֹם עַל־יִשְׂרָאֵל׃

2 Like the eyes of servants to the hand of their master, like the eyes of a handmaiden to the hand of her mistress, so too our eyes look to the Lord our God waiting for Him to favor us.

3 Be gracious to us, Lord; be gracious to us, for we have had more than enough humiliation.

4 We have had enough of the scorn of those who do not care, the contempt of the arrogant.

TEHILLIM 124

A song of thanksgiving

1 A song of Ascents by David. "Had it not been for the Lord who fought for us," let Israel now say,

2 "Had it not been for the Lord who fought for us when men rose up to attack us,

3 They would have swallowed us alive in their anger against us.

4 The waters would have swept us away, the stream would have gone over our soul;

5 The raging waters would have passed over our soul."

6 Blessed be the Lord, who did not give us as food to their teeth.

7 Our souls escaped like a bird that is freed from the trap of the trappers; the trap is broken, and we have escaped.

8 Our help is in the name of the Lord, Who made heaven and earth.

TEHILLIM 125

A song of trust in God

1 A song of Ascents. Those who trust in the Lord are like Mount Zion, which cannot be moved, but lasts forever.

2 As the mountains surround Jerusalem, so the Lord surrounds His people from now and forever.

3 The reign of the wicked will not influence the way of life rest upon the lot of the righteous, therefore the righteous will not set their hands to wrongdoing.

4 Do good, Lord to the good, and to those whose hearts are upright.

5 But as for those who act dishonestly in their wickedness, the Lord will lead them away with those who do evil. Peace be upon Israel.

פרק קכו

א שִׁיר הַמַּעֲלוֹת בְּשׁוּב יְהוָה אֶת־שִׁיבַת צִיּוֹן הָיִינוּ כְּחֹלְמִים:

ב אָז יִמָּלֵא שְׂחוֹק פִּינוּ וּלְשׁוֹנֵנוּ רִנָּה אָז יֹאמְרוּ בַגּוֹיִם הִגְדִּיל יְהוָה לַעֲשׂוֹת עִם־אֵלֶּה:

ג הִגְדִּיל יְהוָה לַעֲשׂוֹת עִמָּנוּ הָיִינוּ שְׂמֵחִים:

ד שׁוּבָה יְהוָה אֶת־שבותנו [שְׁבִיתֵנוּ] כַּאֲפִיקִים בַּנֶּגֶב:

ה הַזֹּרְעִים בְּדִמְעָה בְּרִנָּה יִקְצֹרוּ:

ו הָלוֹךְ יֵלֵךְ וּבָכֹה נֹשֵׂא מֶשֶׁךְ־הַזָּרַע בֹּא־יָבוֹא בְרִנָּה נֹשֵׂא אֲלֻמֹּתָיו:

פרק קכז

א שִׁיר הַמַּעֲלוֹת לִשְׁלֹמֹה אִם־יְהוָה לֹא־יִבְנֶה בַיִת שָׁוְא עָמְלוּ בוֹנָיו בּוֹ אִם־יְהוָה לֹא־יִשְׁמָר־עִיר שָׁוְא שָׁקַד שׁוֹמֵר:

ב שָׁוְא לָכֶם מַשְׁכִּימֵי קוּם מְאַחֲרֵי־שֶׁבֶת אֹכְלֵי לֶחֶם הָעֲצָבִים כֵּן יִתֵּן לִידִידוֹ שֵׁנָא:

ג הִנֵּה נַחֲלַת יְהוָה בָּנִים שָׂכָר פְּרִי הַבָּטֶן:

ד כְּחִצִּים בְּיַד־גִּבּוֹר כֵּן בְּנֵי הַנְּעוּרִים:

ה אַשְׁרֵי הַגֶּבֶר אֲשֶׁר מִלֵּא אֶת־אַשְׁפָּתוֹ מֵהֶם לֹא־יֵבֹשׁוּ כִּי־יְדַבְּרוּ אֶת־אוֹיְבִים בַּשָּׁעַר:

TEHILLIM 126

A prayer for a blessing for the future

1 A song of Ascents. When the Lord brings back the return to Zion, we will feel like dreamers.
2 Our mouths will fill with laughter, and our tongue with song. Among the nations, they will say, "The Lord has done great things for these people."
3 The Lord has done great things for us; we rejoice.
4 End our captivity, Lord, like springs in the desert.
5 Those who sow with tears will reap with joy.
6 Though he go weeping as he carries the sack of seed, he will come back rejoicing, bearing his sheaves.

TEHILLIM 127

A song praying for God's help to rebuild and repopulate the Land of Israel

1 A song of Ascents by Solomon. Unless the Lord builds the house, those who build it labor in vain; unless the Lord watches over the city, the watchman stays awake in vain.
2 In vain you rise early and stay up late to eat the bread of toil; He gives much to His beloved ones even as they sleep.
3 Children are a heritage from the Lord; the fruit of the womb is His reward.
4 As arrows in the hand of a mighty man, so are the children of youth.
5 Happy is the man who has many children; they will not be put to shame when they speak with their enemies at the gate.

פרק קכח

א שִׁיר הַמַּעֲלוֹת אַשְׁרֵי כָּל־יְרֵא יְהוָה הַהֹלֵךְ בִּדְרָכָיו:

ב יְגִיעַ כַּפֶּיךָ כִּי תֹאכֵל אַשְׁרֶיךָ וְטוֹב לָךְ:

ג אֶשְׁתְּךָ כְּגֶפֶן פֹּרִיָּה בְּיַרְכְּתֵי בֵיתֶךָ בָּנֶיךָ כִּשְׁתִלֵי זֵיתִים סָבִיב לְשֻׁלְחָנֶךָ:

ד הִנֵּה כִי־כֵן יְבֹרַךְ גָּבֶר יְרֵא יְהוָה:

ה יְבָרֶכְךָ יְהוָה מִצִּיּוֹן וּרְאֵה בְּטוּב יְרוּשָׁלָ͏ִם כֹּל יְמֵי חַיֶּיךָ:

ו וּרְאֵה־בָנִים לְבָנֶיךָ שָׁלוֹם עַל־יִשְׂרָאֵל:

פרק קכט

א שִׁיר הַמַּעֲלוֹת רַבַּת צְרָרוּנִי מִנְּעוּרַי יֹאמַר־נָא יִשְׂרָאֵל:

ב רַבַּת צְרָרוּנִי מִנְּעוּרָי גַּם לֹא יָכְלוּ־לִי:

ג עַל־גַּבִּי חָרְשׁוּ חֹרְשִׁים הֶאֱרִיכוּ למעניתם [לְמַעֲנִיתָם]:

ד יְהוָה צַדִּיק קִצֵּץ עֲבוֹת רְשָׁעִים:

ה יֵבֹשׁוּ וְיִסֹּגוּ אָחוֹר כֹּל שֹׂנְאֵי צִיּוֹן:

ו יִהְיוּ כַּחֲצִיר גַּגּוֹת שֶׁקַּדְמַת שָׁלַף יָבֵשׁ:

ז שֶׁלֹּא מִלֵּא כַפּוֹ קוֹצֵר וְחִצְנוֹ מְעַמֵּר:

ח וְלֹא אָמְרוּ הָעֹבְרִים בִּרְכַּת יְהוָה אֲלֵיכֶם בֵּרַכְנוּ אֶתְכֶם בְּשֵׁם יְהוָה:

TEHILLIM 128

A song about happy family life according to God's teachings

1 A song of Ascents. Happy are those who love the Lord and follow in His ways.
2 When you eat from the work of your hands, you will be happy and it will be well with you.
3 Your wife will be like a fruitful vine in the innermost parts of your house; Your children will be like olive shoots around your table.
4 See, this is how those who revere the Lord shall be blessed.
5 May the Lord bless you from Zion, and may you see the good of Jerusalem all the days of your life,
6 And may you merit to see your children's children. Peace be upon Israel.

TEHILLIM 129

A song asking for God's blessings

1 A song of Ascents. Although they have tormented me from my youth, let Israel now say:
2 "Although they have tormented me from my youth, yet they have not defeated me.
3 Plowers plowed upon my back, making long furrows.
4 But the Lord is righteous; he has severed the bonds of the wicked."
5 Let all who hate Zion be ashamed and turn backward.
6 May they be like grass on the rooftops, which dries before it springs up,
7 So that which the reaper does not fill his hand, nor the binder of sheaves his arms,
8 Nor do the passersby say: "The Lord's blessing be upon you; we bless you in the name of the Lord."

פרק קל

א שִׁיר הַמַּעֲלוֹת מִמַּעֲמַקִּים קְרָאתִיךָ יְהוָה:

ב אֲדֹנָי שִׁמְעָה בְקוֹלִי תִּהְיֶינָה אָזְנֶיךָ קַשֻּׁבוֹת לְקוֹל תַּחֲנוּנָי:

ג אִם־עֲוֹנוֹת תִּשְׁמָר־יָהּ אֲדֹנָי מִי יַעֲמֹד:

ד כִּי־עִמְּךָ הַסְּלִיחָה לְמַעַן תִּוָּרֵא:

ה קִוִּיתִי יְהוָה קִוְּתָה נַפְשִׁי וְלִדְבָרוֹ הוֹחָלְתִּי:

ו נַפְשִׁי לַאדֹנָי מִשֹּׁמְרִים לַבֹּקֶר שֹׁמְרִים לַבֹּקֶר:

ז יַחֵל יִשְׂרָאֵל אֶל־יְהוָה כִּי־עִם־יְהוָה הַחֶסֶד וְהַרְבֵּה עִמּוֹ פְדוּת:

ח וְהוּא יִפְדֶּה אֶת־יִשְׂרָאֵל מִכֹּל עֲוֹנֹתָיו:

פרק קלא

א שִׁיר הַמַּעֲלוֹת לְדָוִד יְהוָה לֹא־גָבַהּ לִבִּי וְלֹא־רָמוּ עֵינַי וְלֹא־הִלַּכְתִּי בִּגְדֹלוֹת וּבְנִפְלָאוֹת מִמֶּנִּי:

ב אִם־לֹא שִׁוִּיתִי וְדוֹמַמְתִּי נַפְשִׁי כְּגָמֻל עֲלֵי אִמּוֹ כַּגָּמֻל עָלַי נַפְשִׁי:

ג יַחֵל יִשְׂרָאֵל אֶל־יְהוָה מֵעַתָּה וְעַד־עוֹלָם:

פרק קלב

א שִׁיר הַמַּעֲלוֹת זְכוֹר־יְהוָה לְדָוִד אֵת כָּל־עֻנּוֹתוֹ:

ב אֲשֶׁר נִשְׁבַּע לַיהוָה נָדַר לַאֲבִיר יַעֲקֹב:

ג אִם־אָבֹא בְּאֹהֶל בֵּיתִי אִם־אֶעֱלֶה עַל־עֶרֶשׂ יְצוּעָי:

TEHILLIM 130

A song asking forgiveness for personal and national sins

1 A song of Ascents. From the depths I have called to You, Lord.
2 Lord, listen to my voice; let Your ears be attentive to the voice of my pleas.
3 Lord, if You were to keep track of sins, who could stand before you?
4 For with You is forgiveness, so that You may be revered.
5 I wait for the Lord. My soul waits, and I hope for His word.
6 My soul waits only for the Lord; it waits more than watchmen do for the morning – yes, more than those that keep watch for the morning.
7 Israel, hope in the Lord, for with the Lord is loving kindness, and with Him there is abundant redemption.
8 And He will forgive Israel of all its sins.

TEHILLIM 131

A song of Israel's trust in God

1 A song of Ascents by David. Lord, my hearts was not proud, nor were my eyes haughty. I did not deal with things too great and wonderful for me.
2 But I have stilled and quieted my soul like a child weaned by his mother; my soul within me is like a drown child.
3 Israel, hope in the Lord from now and forever.

TEHILLIM 132

A song expressing faith in the fulfillment of God's promise to King David

1 A song of Ascents. Lord, remember all of David's affliction,
2 How he swore to the Lord, vowing to the Mighty One of Jacob:
3 "I will not enter the tent of my home, nor go up to the bed that is spread for me;

ד אִם־אֶתֵּן שְׁנַת לְעֵינָי לְעַפְעַפַּי תְּנוּמָה:

ה עַד־אֶמְצָא מָקוֹם לַיהֹוָה מִשְׁכָּנוֹת לַאֲבִיר יַעֲקֹב:

ו הִנֵּה־שְׁמַעֲנוּהָ בְאֶפְרָתָה מְצָאנוּהָ בִּשְׂדֵי־יָעַר:

ז נָבוֹאָה לְמִשְׁכְּנוֹתָיו נִשְׁתַּחֲוֶה לַהֲדֹם רַגְלָיו:

ח קוּמָה יְהֹוָה לִמְנוּחָתֶךָ אַתָּה וַאֲרוֹן עֻזֶּךָ:

ט כֹּהֲנֶיךָ יִלְבְּשׁוּ־צֶדֶק וַחֲסִידֶיךָ יְרַנֵּנוּ:

י בַּעֲבוּר דָּוִד עַבְדֶּךָ אַל־תָּשֵׁב פְּנֵי מְשִׁיחֶךָ:

יא נִשְׁבַּע יְהֹוָה לְדָוִד אֱמֶת לֹא־יָשׁוּב מִמֶּנָּה מִפְּרִי בִטְנְךָ אָשִׁית לְכִסֵּא־לָךְ:

יב אִם־יִשְׁמְרוּ בָנֶיךָ בְּרִיתִי וְעֵדֹתִי זוֹ אֲלַמְּדֵם גַּם־בְּנֵיהֶם עֲדֵי־עַד יֵשְׁבוּ לְכִסֵּא־לָךְ:

יג כִּי־בָחַר יְהֹוָה בְּצִיּוֹן אִוָּהּ לְמוֹשָׁב לוֹ:

יד זֹאת־מְנוּחָתִי עֲדֵי־עַד פֹּה אֵשֵׁב כִּי אִוִּתִיהָ:

טו צֵידָהּ בָּרֵךְ אֲבָרֵךְ אֶבְיוֹנֶיהָ אַשְׂבִּיעַ לָחֶם:

טז וְכֹהֲנֶיהָ אַלְבִּישׁ יֶשַׁע וַחֲסִידֶיהָ רַנֵּן יְרַנֵּנוּ:

יז שָׁם אַצְמִיחַ קֶרֶן לְדָוִד עָרַכְתִּי נֵר לִמְשִׁיחִי:

יח אוֹיְבָיו אַלְבִּישׁ בֹּשֶׁת וְעָלָיו יָצִיץ נִזְרוֹ:

פרק קלג

א שִׁיר הַמַּעֲלוֹת לְדָוִד הִנֵּה מַה־טּוֹב וּמַה־נָּעִים שֶׁבֶת אַחִים גַּם־יָחַד:

ב כַּשֶּׁמֶן הַטּוֹב עַל־הָרֹאשׁ יֹרֵד עַל־הַזָּקָן זְקַן אַהֲרֹן שֶׁיֹּרֵד עַל־פִּי מִדּוֹתָיו:

ג כְּטַל־חֶרְמוֹן שֶׁיֹּרֵד עַל־הַרְרֵי צִיּוֹן כִּי שָׁם צִוָּה יְהֹוָה אֶת־הַבְּרָכָה חַיִּים עַד־הָעוֹלָם:

4   "Nor will I allow my eyes to sleep or my eyelids to rest,

5   Until I build a house for the Lord, a dwelling place for the Mighty One of Jacob."

6   We heard it was in Efrat; we found it in a forest field.

7   Let us go into His dwelling-place; let us worship at His Sanctuary.

8   Arise, Lord, to Your resting place, You and the ark of Your strength.

9   May Your priests be clothed in righteousness and Your righteous ones shout for joy.

10   For the sake of Your servant David, do not turn away from the face of Your anointed one.

11   The Lord swore to David, and a truth he will not turn back: "From your descendants of I will choose those who sit upon your throne.

12   If your children keep My covenant and My laws, which I shall teach them, then their children, too, shall sit forever upon your throne."

13   The Lord has chosen Zion, desiring it for His dwelling-place:

14   "For this is My resting place for all time. I will dwell here, for I desire it.

15   I will bless her food with abundance, and I will satisfy her poor with bread.

16   I will clothe her priests with salvation and her righteous ones shall shout for joy.

17   There I will raise David's fortunes; there I have arranged a lamp for My anointed one."

18   His enemies I will clothe with shame, but his crown shall shine upon him."

TEHILLIM 133

*A song relating how Jewish unity will strengthen
Jerusalem and the entire country*

1   A song of Ascents by David. See how good and pleasant it is for brothers to live together in unity!

2   It is like the precious oil upon the head, coming down upon the beard, the beard of Aharon, that flows down to the edge of his robes;

3   So like the dew of Hermon that comes down upon the mountains of Zion, for there the Lord commanded the blessing of life forever.

פרק קלד

א שִׁיר הַמַּעֲלוֹת הִנֵּה בָּרֲכוּ אֶת־יְהוָה כָּל־עַבְדֵי יְהוָה הָעֹמְדִים בְּבֵית־יְהוָה בַּלֵּילוֹת:

ב שְׂאוּ־יְדֵכֶם קֹדֶשׁ וּבָרֲכוּ אֶת־יְהוָה:

ג יְבָרֶכְךָ יְהוָה מִצִּיּוֹן עֹשֵׂה שָׁמַיִם וָאָרֶץ:

פרק קלה

א הַלְלוּיָהּ הַלְלוּ אֶת־שֵׁם יְהוָה הַלְלוּ עַבְדֵי יְהוָה:

ב שֶׁעֹמְדִים בְּבֵית יְהוָה בְּחַצְרוֹת בֵּית אֱלֹהֵינוּ:

ג הַלְלוּיָהּ כִּי־טוֹב יְהוָה זַמְּרוּ לִשְׁמוֹ כִּי נָעִים:

ד כִּי־יַעֲקֹב בָּחַר לוֹ יָהּ יִשְׂרָאֵל לִסְגֻלָּתוֹ:

ה כִּי אֲנִי יָדַעְתִּי כִּי־גָדוֹל יְהוָה וַאֲדֹנֵינוּ מִכָּל־אֱלֹהִים:

ו כֹּל אֲשֶׁר־חָפֵץ יְהוָה עָשָׂה בַּשָּׁמַיִם וּבָאָרֶץ בַּיַּמִּים וְכָל־תְּהוֹמוֹת:

ז מַעֲלֶה נְשִׂאִים מִקְצֵה הָאָרֶץ בְּרָקִים לַמָּטָר עָשָׂה מוֹצֵא־רוּחַ מֵאוֹצְרוֹתָיו:

ח שֶׁהִכָּה בְּכוֹרֵי מִצְרָיִם מֵאָדָם עַד־בְּהֵמָה:

ט שָׁלַח אֹתוֹת וּמֹפְתִים בְּתוֹכֵכִי מִצְרָיִם בְּפַרְעֹה וּבְכָל־עֲבָדָיו:

י שֶׁהִכָּה גּוֹיִם רַבִּים וְהָרַג מְלָכִים עֲצוּמִים:

יא לְסִיחוֹן מֶלֶךְ הָאֱמֹרִי וּלְעוֹג מֶלֶךְ הַבָּשָׁן וּלְכֹל מַמְלְכוֹת כְּנָעַן:

יב וְנָתַן אַרְצָם נַחֲלָה נַחֲלָה לְיִשְׂרָאֵל עַמּוֹ:

יג יְהוָה שִׁמְךָ לְעוֹלָם יְהוָה זִכְרְךָ לְדֹר־וָדֹר:

TEHILLIM 134

*The last song of ascents contains the greetings of the worshippers,
the Kohanim and the Levites to each other in the Temple*

1 A song of Ascents. Bless the Lord, all you servants of the Lord, who stand in the house of the Lord during the night.
2 Lift up your hands to the Sanctuary, and bless the Lord.
3 May the Lord, the Creator of heaven and earth, bless you from Zion.

TEHILLIM 135

*A song of thanksgiving to God for His
great acts and His love for Israel*

1 Hallelujah! Praise the name of the Lord. Give praise, you servants of the Lord,
2 You who stand in the house of the Lord, in the courts of the house of our God.
3 Praise the Lord. For the Lord is good; sing praise to His name because it is pleasant.
4 The Lord chose Jacob for Himself and Israel for His treasure.
5 I know that our Lord is great, and our master is above all gods.
6 Our Lord can do as he wishes in heaven, on earth, in the seas and the deepest places.
7 He causes clouds to rise from the ends of the earth. He makes lightning for rain and brings out the wind from his treasures.
8 He struck down the first born of Egypt, both of man and beast.
9 He sent signs and marvels into the midst of you, Egypt, upon Pharaoh and upon all his servants.
10 He struck many nations and killed mighty kings; including,
11 Sihon, the king of the Amorites, and Og, king of Bashan, and all the kingdoms of Canaan,
12 And gave their land as a heritage, a heritage for Israel, His people.
13 Lord, Your name lasts forever; Your remembrance endures for all generations.
14 The Lord will judge His people and have mercy upon His servants.

יד כִּי־יָדִין יְהֹוָה עַמּוֹ וְעַל־עֲבָדָיו יִתְנֶחָם:

טו עֲצַבֵּי הַגּוֹיִם כֶּסֶף וְזָהָב מַעֲשֵׂה יְדֵי אָדָם:

טז פֶּה־לָהֶם וְלֹא יְדַבֵּרוּ עֵינַיִם לָהֶם וְלֹא יִרְאוּ:

יז אָזְנַיִם לָהֶם וְלֹא יַאֲזִינוּ אַף אֵין־יֶשׁ־רוּחַ בְּפִיהֶם:

יח כְּמוֹהֶם יִהְיוּ עֹשֵׂיהֶם כֹּל אֲשֶׁר־בֹּטֵחַ בָּהֶם:

יט בֵּית יִשְׂרָאֵל בָּרְכוּ אֶת־יְהֹוָה בֵּית אַהֲרֹן בָּרְכוּ אֶת־יְהֹוָה:

כ בֵּית הַלֵּוִי בָּרְכוּ אֶת־יְהֹוָה יִרְאֵי יְהֹוָה בָּרְכוּ אֶת־יְהֹוָה:

כא בָּרוּךְ יְהֹוָה מִצִּיּוֹן שֹׁכֵן יְרוּשָׁלָ͏ִם הַלְלוּיָהּ:

פרק קלו

א הוֹדוּ לַיהֹוָה כִּי־טוֹב כִּי לְעוֹלָם חַסְדּוֹ:

ב הוֹדוּ לֵאלֹהֵי הָאֱלֹהִים כִּי לְעוֹלָם חַסְדּוֹ:

ג הוֹדוּ לַאֲדֹנֵי הָאֲדֹנִים כִּי לְעוֹלָם חַסְדּוֹ:

ד לְעֹשֵׂה נִפְלָאוֹת גְּדֹלוֹת לְבַדּוֹ כִּי לְעוֹלָם חַסְדּוֹ:

ה לְעֹשֵׂה הַשָּׁמַיִם בִּתְבוּנָה כִּי לְעוֹלָם חַסְדּוֹ:

ו לְרֹקַע הָאָרֶץ עַל־הַמָּיִם כִּי לְעוֹלָם חַסְדּוֹ:

ז לְעֹשֵׂה אוֹרִים גְּדֹלִים כִּי לְעוֹלָם חַסְדּוֹ:

ח אֶת־הַשֶּׁמֶשׁ לְמֶמְשֶׁלֶת בַּיּוֹם כִּי לְעוֹלָם חַסְדּוֹ:

ט אֶת־הַיָּרֵחַ וְכוֹכָבִים לְמֶמְשְׁלוֹת בַּלָּיְלָה כִּי לְעוֹלָם חַסְדּוֹ:

י לְמַכֵּה מִצְרַיִם בִּבְכוֹרֵיהֶם כִּי לְעוֹלָם חַסְדּוֹ:

יא וַיּוֹצֵא יִשְׂרָאֵל מִתּוֹכָם כִּי לְעוֹלָם חַסְדּוֹ:

יב בְּיָד חֲזָקָה וּבִזְרוֹעַ נְטוּיָה כִּי לְעוֹלָם חַסְדּוֹ:

15 The idols of the nations are made of silver and gold, the work of human hands.

16 They have mouths but do not speak, they have eyes but do not see,

17 They have ears but do not hear, nor is there any breath in their mouths.

18 Those who make them shall become like them – yes, everyone who trusts in them.

19 House of Israel, bless the Lord! House of Aharon, bless the Lord!

20 House of Levi, bless the Lord! You who revere the Lord, bless the Lord!

21 Blessed be the Lord from Zion, Who dwells in Jerusalem. Hallelujah!

TEHILLIM 136

A song of praise to God. Called Hallel Hagadol, the great praise

1 Give thanks to the Lord, for He is good: His loving kindness lasts forever.

2 Give thanks to the God of gods, for His loving kindness lasts forever.

3 Give thanks to the Lord of lords, for His loving kindness lasts forever.

4 To Him Who alone works wonders, for His loving kindness lasts forever.

5 To Him Who made the heavens with understanding, for His loving kindness lasts forever.

6 To Him Who spread the earth above the waters, for His loving kindness lasts forever.

7 To Him Who made the great lights, for His loving kindness lasts forever;

8 The sun to rule by day, for His loving kindness lasts forever,

9 And the moon and the stars to rule at night, for His loving kindness lasts forever.

10 To Him Who struck down Egypt by killing their the first-born, for His loving kindness lasts forever;

11 And brought out Israel from among them, for His loving kindness lasts forever,

כִּי לְעוֹלָם חַסְדּוֹ:	לְגֹזֵר יַם־סוּף לִגְזָרִים	יג
כִּי לְעוֹלָם חַסְדּוֹ:	וְהֶעֱבִיר יִשְׂרָאֵל בְּתוֹכוֹ	יד
כִּי לְעוֹלָם חַסְדּוֹ:	וְנִעֵר פַּרְעֹה וְחֵילוֹ בְיַם־סוּף	טו
כִּי לְעוֹלָם חַסְדּוֹ:	לְמוֹלִיךְ עַמּוֹ בַּמִּדְבָּר	טז
כִּי לְעוֹלָם חַסְדּוֹ:	לְמַכֵּה מְלָכִים גְּדֹלִים	יז
כִּי לְעוֹלָם חַסְדּוֹ:	וַיַּהֲרֹג מְלָכִים אַדִּירִים	יח
כִּי לְעוֹלָם חַסְדּוֹ:	לְסִיחוֹן מֶלֶךְ הָאֱמֹרִי	יט
כִּי לְעוֹלָם חַסְדּוֹ:	וּלְעוֹג מֶלֶךְ הַבָּשָׁן	כ
כִּי לְעוֹלָם חַסְדּוֹ:	וְנָתַן אַרְצָם לְנַחֲלָה	כא
כִּי לְעוֹלָם חַסְדּוֹ:	נַחֲלָה לְיִשְׂרָאֵל עַבְדּוֹ	כב
כִּי לְעוֹלָם חַסְדּוֹ:	שֶׁבְּשִׁפְלֵנוּ זָכַר־לָנוּ	כג
כִּי לְעוֹלָם חַסְדּוֹ:	וַיִּפְרְקֵנוּ מִצָּרֵינוּ	כד
כִּי לְעוֹלָם חַסְדּוֹ:	נֹתֵן לֶחֶם לְכָל־בָּשָׂר	כה
כִּי לְעוֹלָם חַסְדּוֹ:	הוֹדוּ לְאֵל הַשָּׁמָיִם	כו

פרק קלז

א   עַל־נַהֲרוֹת בָּבֶל שָׁם יָשַׁבְנוּ גַּם־בָּכִינוּ בְּזָכְרֵנוּ אֶת־צִיּוֹן:

ב   עַל־עֲרָבִים בְּתוֹכָהּ תָּלִינוּ כִּנֹּרוֹתֵינוּ:

ג   כִּי שָׁם שְׁאֵלוּנוּ שׁוֹבֵינוּ דִּבְרֵי־שִׁיר וְתוֹלָלֵינוּ שִׂמְחָה שִׁירוּ לָנוּ מִשִּׁיר
צִיּוֹן:

12 With a mighty hand and an outstretched arm, for His loving kindness lasts forever.

13 To Him who split the Sea of Reeds, for His loving kindness lasts forever,

14 And passed Israel pass through it, for His loving kindness lasts forever,

15 And shook up Pharaoh and his army into the Sea of Reeds, for His loving kindness lasts forever.

16 To Him Who led His people through the wilderness, for His loving kindness lasts forever.

17 To Him Who struck down great kings, for His loving kindness lasts forever,

18 And killed mighty kings, for His loving kindness lasts forever:

19 Sihon, king of the Amorites and Og, king of Bashan, for His loving kindness lasts forever,

20 And Og king of Bashan for his loving kindness lasts forever,

21 And gave their land as a heritage, for His loving kindness lasts forever,

22 An inheritance for Israel His servant, for His loving kindness lasts forever.

23 He remembered us when we were cast down low, for His loving kindness lasts forever,

24 And freed us from our oppressors, for His loving kindness lasts forever.

25 He gives food to all living things, for His loving kindness lasts forever.

26 Give thanks to the God of heaven, for His loving kindness lasts forever.

TEHILLIM 137

A song of lamentation on seeing the ruins of Jerusalem

1 By the rivers of Babylon, there we sat and wept when we remembered Zion.

2 There we hung our harps upon the willow trees,

3 For there our captors asked us to sing to make them happy and our tormentors asked us mockingly to sing songs of Zion.

4 How shall we sing the Lord's song in a strange land?

ד אֵיךְ נָשִׁיר אֶת־שִׁיר יְהֹוָה עַל אַדְמַת נֵכָר:

ה אִם־אֶשְׁכָּחֵךְ יְרוּשָׁלָ͏ִם תִּשְׁכַּח יְמִינִי:

ו תִּדְבַּק־לְשׁוֹנִי לְחִכִּי אִם־לֹא אֶזְכְּרֵכִי אִם־לֹא אַעֲלֶה אֶת־יְרוּשָׁלַ͏ִם עַל רֹאשׁ שִׂמְחָתִי:

ז זְכֹר יְהֹוָה לִבְנֵי אֱדוֹם אֵת יוֹם יְרוּשָׁלַ͏ִם הָאֹמְרִים עָרוּ עָרוּ עַד הַיְסוֹד בָּהּ:

ח בַּת־בָּבֶל הַשְּׁדוּדָה אַשְׁרֵי שֶׁיְשַׁלֶּם־לָךְ אֶת־גְּמוּלֵךְ שֶׁגָּמַלְתְּ לָנוּ:

ט אַשְׁרֵי שֶׁיֹּאחֵז וְנִפֵּץ אֶת־עֹלָלַיִךְ אֶל־הַסָּלַע:

פרק קלח

א לְדָוִד אוֹדְךָ בְכָל־לִבִּי נֶגֶד אֱלֹהִים אֲזַמְּרֶךָּ:

ב אֶשְׁתַּחֲוֶה אֶל־הֵיכַל קָדְשְׁךָ וְאוֹדֶה אֶת־שְׁמֶךָ עַל־חַסְדְּךָ וְעַל־אֲמִתֶּךָ כִּי־הִגְדַּלְתָּ עַל־כָּל־שִׁמְךָ אִמְרָתֶךָ:

ג בְּיוֹם קָרָאתִי וַתַּעֲנֵנִי תַּרְהִבֵנִי בְנַפְשִׁי עֹז:

ד יוֹדוּךָ יְהֹוָה כָּל־מַלְכֵי־אָרֶץ כִּי שָׁמְעוּ אִמְרֵי־פִיךָ:

ה וְיָשִׁירוּ בְּדַרְכֵי יְהֹוָה כִּי גָדוֹל כְּבוֹד יְהֹוָה:

ו כִּי־רָם יְהֹוָה וְשָׁפָל יִרְאֶה וְגָבֹהַּ מִמֶּרְחָק יְיֵדָע:

ז אִם־אֵלֵךְ בְּקֶרֶב צָרָה תְּחַיֵּנִי עַל אַף אֹיְבַי תִּשְׁלַח יָדֶךָ וְתוֹשִׁיעֵנִי יְמִינֶךָ:

ח יְהֹוָה יִגְמֹר בַּעֲדִי יְהֹוָה חַסְדְּךָ לְעוֹלָם מַעֲשֵׂי יָדֶיךָ אַל־תֶּרֶף:

5 If I forget you, Jerusalem, may my right hand forget how to function.

6 May my tongue stick to the roof of my mouth, if I don't remember you, if I don't put Jerusalem above my greatest joy.

7 Remember, Lord, that the day of Jerusalem, when the children of Edom said, "Destroy it, destroy it to its very foundation!"

8 Daughter of Babylon, you are destroyed, for happy is the one who repays you for what you did to us.

9 Happy we will be when Babylon is punished.

TEHILLIM 138

A song of overwhelming gratitude to God

1 By David. I will give You thanks with my whole heart. In the presence of the mighty I will sing praises to You.

2 I will bow down toward Your holy Sanctuary and give thanks to Your name for Your loving kindness and Your truth, for You have increased Your Your promise far beyond Your name.

3 On the day that I called, You answered me, and You inspired me with courage.

4 All the kings of the earth gave You thanks, Lord, for they heard the words of Your mouth.

5 They will sing of the Lord's ways, for the glory of the Lord is great.

6 Though the Lord is exalted, he sees the humble. Though lofty, He makes himself known from afar.

7 Though I walk in the midst of trouble, You revive me; You stretch out Your hand against the fury of my enemies, and Your right hand saves me.

8 The Lord will accomplish for me. Your loving kindness, Lord, lasts forever; do not abandon the work of Your own hands.

פרק קלט

א לַמְנַצֵּחַ לְדָוִד מִזְמוֹר יְהוָה חֲקַרְתַּנִי וַתֵּדָע:

ב אַתָּה יָדַעְתָּ שִׁבְתִּי וְקוּמִי בַּנְתָּה לְרֵעִי מֵרָחוֹק:

ג אָרְחִי וְרִבְעִי זֵרִיתָ וְכָל־דְּרָכַי הִסְכַּנְתָּה:

ד כִּי אֵין מִלָּה בִּלְשׁוֹנִי הֵן יְהוָה יָדַעְתָּ כֻלָּהּ:

ה אָחוֹר וָקֶדֶם צַרְתָּנִי וַתָּשֶׁת עָלַי כַּפֶּכָה:

ו פְּלִאיָה [פְּלִיאָה] דַעַת מִמֶּנִּי נִשְׂגְּבָה לֹא־אוּכַל לָהּ:

ז אָנָה אֵלֵךְ מֵרוּחֶךָ וְאָנָה מִפָּנֶיךָ אֶבְרָח:

ח אִם־אֶסַּק שָׁמַיִם שָׁם אָתָּה וְאַצִּיעָה שְּׁאוֹל הִנֶּךָּ:

ט אֶשָּׂא כַנְפֵי־שָׁחַר אֶשְׁכְּנָה בְּאַחֲרִית יָם:

י גַּם־שָׁם יָדְךָ תַנְחֵנִי וְתֹאחֲזֵנִי יְמִינֶךָ:

יא וָאֹמַר אַךְ־חֹשֶׁךְ יְשׁוּפֵנִי וְלַיְלָה אוֹר בַּעֲדֵנִי:

יב גַּם־חֹשֶׁךְ לֹא־יַחְשִׁיךְ מִמֶּךָ וְלַיְלָה כַּיּוֹם יָאִיר כַּחֲשֵׁיכָה כָּאוֹרָה:

יג כִּי־אַתָּה קָנִיתָ כִלְיֹתָי תְּסֻכֵּנִי בְּבֶטֶן אִמִּי:

יד אוֹדְךָ עַל כִּי נוֹרָאוֹת נִפְלֵיתִי נִפְלָאִים מַעֲשֶׂיךָ וְנַפְשִׁי יֹדַעַת מְאֹד:

טו לֹא־נִכְחַד עָצְמִי מִמֶּךָּ אֲשֶׁר־עֻשֵּׂיתִי בַסֵּתֶר רֻקַּמְתִּי בְּתַחְתִּיּוֹת אָרֶץ:

טז גָּלְמִי רָאוּ עֵינֶיךָ וְעַל־סִפְרְךָ כֻּלָּם יִכָּתֵבוּ יָמִים יֻצָּרוּ ולא [וְלוֹ] אֶחָד בָּהֶם:

יז וְלִי מַה־יָּקְרוּ רֵעֶיךָ אֵל מֶה עָצְמוּ רָאשֵׁיהֶם:

יח אֶסְפְּרֵם מֵחוֹל יִרְבּוּן הֱקִיצֹתִי וְעוֹדִי עִמָּךְ:

יט אִם־תִּקְטֹל אֱלוֹהַּ רָשָׁע וְאַנְשֵׁי דָמִים סוּרוּ מֶנִּי:

כ אֲשֶׁר יֹאמְרֻךָ לִמְזִמָּה נָשֻׂא לַשָּׁוְא עָרֶיךָ:

TEHILLIM 139

A song about a close and personal relationship to God

1 For the chief musician, a psalm by David. Lord, You have investigated me, so You know me.

2 You know when I stand up and when I sit down, and You understand my thoughts from far away.

3 You measure my paths and my lying down, and You are familiar with all my ways.

4 For there is not a word upon my tongue but You, Lord, know it entirely.

5 From back and front You surround me, and placed Your hand upon me.

6 Such knowledge is too wondrous for me, too high. I cannot understand.

7 Where will I go from Your spirit? Where will I flee from Your presence?

8 If I go up to heaven, You are there; if I make my bed in the netherworld, behold, You are there.

9 If I take the wings of the morning and dwell in the outermost part of the sea,

10 Even there Your hand would lead me, and Your right hand would hold me.

11 If I were to say: "Surely darkness shall surround me", and the night would become light around me,"

12 Even the darkness is not too dark for You, but the night shines like the day; the darkness is like the light.

13 For You created my mind; You fashioned me in my mother's womb.

14 I will give You thanks, for I am marvelously and wondrously made; wonderful are your works, and my soul knows this very well.

15 My body was not hidden from You when I was made in the safety of my mothers womb, and woven together in the depths of the earth.

16 Your eyes saw me yet unformed, and all of it was written in Your book – when the days were created, when none of them existed yet.

17 How precious are Your thoughts to me, God! How overwhelming their numbers!

18 If I were to count them, they number more than the sand; if I were to reach their end, still I would be with You.

כא הֲלוֹא־מְשַׂנְאֶיךָ יְהוָה אֶשְׂנָא וּבִתְקוֹמְמֶיךָ אֶתְקוֹטָט:

כב תַּכְלִית שִׂנְאָה שְׂנֵאתִים לְאוֹיְבִים הָיוּ לִי:

כג חָקְרֵנִי אֵל וְדַע לְבָבִי בְּחָנֵנִי וְדַע שַׂרְעַפָּי:

כד וּרְאֵה אִם־דֶּרֶךְ־עֹצֶב בִּי וּנְחֵנִי בְּדֶרֶךְ עוֹלָם:

פרק קמא

א לַמְנַצֵּחַ מִזְמוֹר לְדָוִד:

ב חַלְּצֵנִי יְהוָה מֵאָדָם רָע מֵאִישׁ חֲמָסִים תִּנְצְרֵנִי:

ג אֲשֶׁר חָשְׁבוּ רָעוֹת בְּלֵב כָּל־יוֹם יָגוּרוּ מִלְחָמוֹת:

ד שָׁנְנוּ לְשׁוֹנָם כְּמוֹ־נָחָשׁ חֲמַת עַכְשׁוּב תַּחַת שְׂפָתֵימוֹ סֶלָה:

ה שָׁמְרֵנִי יְהוָה מִידֵי רָשָׁע מֵאִישׁ חֲמָסִים תִּנְצְרֵנִי אֲשֶׁר חָשְׁבוּ לִדְחוֹת פְּעָמָי:

ו טָמְנוּ גֵאִים פַּח־לִי וַחֲבָלִים פָּרְשׂוּ רֶשֶׁת לְיַד מַעְגָּל מֹקְשִׁים שָׁתוּ־לִי סֶלָה:

ז אָמַרְתִּי לַיהוָה אֵלִי אָתָּה הַאֲזִינָה יְהוָה קוֹל תַּחֲנוּנָי:

ח יְהוִה אֲדֹנָי עֹז יְשׁוּעָתִי סַכֹּתָה לְרֹאשִׁי בְּיוֹם נָשֶׁק:

ט אַל־תִּתֵּן יְהוָה מַאֲוַיֵּי רָשָׁע זְמָמוֹ אַל־תָּפֵק יָרוּמוּ סֶלָה:

י רֹאשׁ מְסִבָּי עֲמַל שְׂפָתֵימוֹ יכסומו [יְכַסֵּמוֹ]:

יא ימיטו [יִמּוֹטוּ] עֲלֵיהֶם גֶּחָלִים בָּאֵשׁ יַפִּלֵם בְּמַהֲמֹרוֹת בַּל־יָקוּמוּ:

יב אִישׁ לָשׁוֹן בַּל־יִכּוֹן בָּאָרֶץ אִישׁ־חָמָס רָע יְצוּדֶנּוּ לְמַדְחֵפֹת:

19 If only You would slay the wicked, God. Go away from me, men of blood,

20 Who rebel wickedly against You and take Your name in vain.

21 Do I not hate, Lord, those who hate you? Do I not fight those who rise up against You?

22 I utterly hate them! I count them my enemies.

23 Investigate me, God, and know my heart. Test me, and know my thoughts,

24 And see whether there is any idolatrous thing in me; lead me in the everlasting path.

TEHILLIM 140

A song about the suffering of the righteous and a prayer for help

1 For the chief musician, a Psalm by David.

2 Save me, Lord, from the evil man; preserve me from the violent man

3 Who plan evil deeds in their heart and stir up wars every day.

4 They have sharpened their tongue like a serpent; the venom of vipers is beneath their lips. Selah.

5 Guard me, Lord, from the hands of the wicked. Preserve me from the violent man who plans to make me stumble.

6 The proud have set a trap for me, and spread a net by the roadside; they have set traps for me. Selah.

7 I have said to the Lord, "You are my God." Listen, Lord, to the voice of my pleas.

8 God, Lord, the strength of my salvation, You have protected me on the day of battle,

9 Do not grant, Lord, the wishes of the wicked. Do not let their plan succeed, so that they may be raised high. Selah.

10 May the evil leaders who surround me be covered with the deception of the evil of their own lips.

11 Let burning coals fall upon them. Let them be thrown into the fire, into pits from which they never rise up again.

12 A slanderer will not be established on earth. The man of violence and evil will be hunted, and pushed aside.

13 I know that the Lord will support the cause of the poor and give justice to the needy.

יג יָדַעַת [יָדַעְתִּי] כִּי־יַעֲשֶׂה יְהוָה דִּין עָנִי מִשְׁפַּט אֶבְיֹנִים:

יד אַךְ צַדִּיקִים יוֹדוּ לִשְׁמֶךָ יֵשְׁבוּ יְשָׁרִים אֶת־פָּנֶיךָ:

פרק קמא

א מִזְמוֹר לְדָוִד יְהוָה קְרָאתִיךָ חוּשָׁה לִּי הַאֲזִינָה קוֹלִי בְּקָרְאִי־לָךְ:

ב תִּכּוֹן תְּפִלָּתִי קְטֹרֶת לְפָנֶיךָ מַשְׂאַת כַּפַּי מִנְחַת־עָרֶב:

ג שִׁיתָה יְהוָה שָׁמְרָה לְפִי נִצְּרָה עַל־דַּל שְׂפָתָי:

ד אַל־תַּט לִבִּי לְדָבָר רָע לְהִתְעוֹלֵל עֲלִלוֹת בְּרֶשַׁע אֶת־אִישִׁים פֹּעֲלֵי־אָוֶן וּבַל־אֶלְחַם בְּמַנְעַמֵּיהֶם:

ה יֶהֶלְמֵנִי־צַדִּיק חֶסֶד וְיוֹכִיחֵנִי שֶׁמֶן רֹאשׁ אַל־יָנִי רֹאשִׁי כִּי־עוֹד וּתְפִלָּתִי בְּרָעוֹתֵיהֶם:

ו נִשְׁמְטוּ בִידֵי־סֶלַע שֹׁפְטֵיהֶם וְשָׁמְעוּ אֲמָרַי כִּי נָעֵמוּ:

ז כְּמוֹ פֹלֵחַ וּבֹקֵעַ בָּאָרֶץ נִפְזְרוּ עֲצָמֵינוּ לְפִי שְׁאוֹל:

ח כִּי אֵלֶיךָ יְהוִה אֲדֹנָי עֵינָי בְּכָה חָסִיתִי אַל־תְּעַר נַפְשִׁי:

ט שָׁמְרֵנִי מִידֵי־פַח יָקְשׁוּ לִי וּמֹקְשׁוֹת פֹּעֲלֵי אָוֶן:

י יִפְּלוּ בְמַכְמֹרָיו רְשָׁעִים יַחַד אָנֹכִי עַד־אֶעֱבוֹר:

פרק קמב

א מַשְׂכִּיל לְדָוִד בִּהְיוֹתוֹ בַמְּעָרָה תְפִלָּה:

ב קוֹלִי אֶל־יְהוָה אֶזְעָק קוֹלִי אֶל־יְהוָה אֶתְחַנָּן:

ג אֶשְׁפֹּךְ לְפָנָיו שִׂיחִי צָרָתִי לְפָנָיו אַגִּיד:

14 Surely the righteous will give thanks to Your name; people of integrity will dwell in Your presence.

TEHILLIM 141

A song describing how the righteous suffer, yet continue to do good

1 A psalm of David. Lord, I have called to You. Hurry to help me. Listen to my voice when I call to You.
2 May my prayer be before You like incense, the lifting of my hands to You like the evening offering.
3 Set a guard, Lord, at my mouth; keep watch at the door of my lips.
4 Let my heart not turn toward any evil thing, or be involved with immoral men who commit sins; and let me not enjoy what they call pleasure.
5 May the righteous people strike me with kindness, and rebuke me. Let my head never refuse precious oil, for I continue to pray not to be part their wickedness.
6 Their judges are cast down by the rock; they then hear that my words are sweet.
7 As when the earth is dug and broken up, so our bones are scattered at the mouth of the grave.
8 My eyes are lifted to You, God. I have taken refuge in You; do not let my soul slip way.
9 Guard me from the trap that they have set for me, and from the snare of the immoral sinners.
10 May the wicked fall into their own nets, while I escape.

TEHILLIM 142

A personal song for help from danger

1 An instructor of David, when he was in the cave, a prayer.
2 With my voice I cry out to the Lord. With my prayers I make my plea to the Lord.
3 I pour out my heart to Him. I tell Him my troubles.
4 When my spirit surrounds me – You know my path – as I go on my way, they have laid a trap for me.

ד בְּהִתְעַטֵּף עָלַי רוּחִי וְאַתָּה יָדַעְתָּ נְתִיבָתִי בְּאֹרַח־זוּ אֲהַלֵּךְ טָמְנוּ פַח לִי:

ה הַבֵּיט יָמִין וּרְאֵה וְאֵין־לִי מַכִּיר אָבַד מָנוֹס מִמֶּנִּי אֵין דּוֹרֵשׁ לְנַפְשִׁי:

ו זָעַקְתִּי אֵלֶיךָ יְהֹוָה אָמַרְתִּי אַתָּה מַחְסִי חֶלְקִי בְּאֶרֶץ הַחַיִּים:

ז הַקְשִׁיבָה אֶל־רִנָּתִי כִּי־דַלּוֹתִי מְאֹד הַצִּילֵנִי מֵרֹדְפַי כִּי אָמְצוּ מִמֶּנִּי:

ח הוֹצִיאָה מִמַּסְגֵּר נַפְשִׁי לְהוֹדוֹת אֶת־שְׁמֶךָ בִּי יַכְתִּרוּ צַדִּיקִים כִּי תִגְמֹל עָלָי:

פרק קמג

א מִזְמוֹר לְדָוִד יְהֹוָה שְׁמַע תְּפִלָּתִי הַאֲזִינָה אֶל־תַּחֲנוּנַי בֶּאֱמֻנָתְךָ עֲנֵנִי בְּצִדְקָתֶךָ:

ב וְאַל־תָּבוֹא בְמִשְׁפָּט אֶת־עַבְדֶּךָ כִּי לֹא־יִצְדַּק לְפָנֶיךָ כָל־חָי:

ג כִּי רָדַף אוֹיֵב נַפְשִׁי דִּכָּא לָאָרֶץ חַיָּתִי הוֹשִׁיבַנִי בְמַחֲשַׁכִּים כְּמֵתֵי עוֹלָם:

ד וַתִּתְעַטֵּף עָלַי רוּחִי בְּתוֹכִי יִשְׁתּוֹמֵם לִבִּי:

ה זָכַרְתִּי יָמִים מִקֶּדֶם הָגִיתִי בְכָל־פָּעֳלֶךָ בְּמַעֲשֵׂה יָדֶיךָ אֲשׂוֹחֵחַ:

ו פֵּרַשְׂתִּי יָדַי אֵלֶיךָ נַפְשִׁי כְּאֶרֶץ־עֲיֵפָה לְךָ סֶלָה:

ז מַהֵר עֲנֵנִי יְהֹוָה כָּלְתָה רוּחִי אַל־תַּסְתֵּר פָּנֶיךָ מִמֶּנִּי וְנִמְשַׁלְתִּי עִם־יֹרְדֵי בוֹר:

ח הַשְׁמִיעֵנִי בַבֹּקֶר חַסְדֶּךָ כִּי־בְךָ בָטָחְתִּי הוֹדִיעֵנִי דֶּרֶךְ־זוּ אֵלֵךְ כִּי־אֵלֶיךָ נָשָׂאתִי נַפְשִׁי:

ט הַצִּילֵנִי מֵאֹיְבַי יְהֹוָה אֵלֶיךָ כִּסִּתִי:

י לַמְּדֵנִי לַעֲשׂוֹת רְצוֹנֶךָ כִּי־אַתָּה אֱלוֹהָי רוּחֲךָ טוֹבָה תַּנְחֵנִי בְּאֶרֶץ מִישׁוֹר:

יא לְמַעַן־שִׁמְךָ יְהֹוָה תְּחַיֵּנִי בְּצִדְקָתְךָ תוֹצִיא מִצָּרָה נַפְשִׁי:

יב וּבְחַסְדְּךָ תַּצְמִית אֹיְבָי וְהַאֲבַדְתָּ כָּל־צֹרֲרֵי נַפְשִׁי כִּי אֲנִי עַבְדֶּךָ:

5 Look to my right and see: there is no one who knows me. I have nowhere to flee. No one cares for my soul.

6 I have cried out to You, Lord. I have said: "You are my refuge, my portion in the land of the living."

7 Hear my cry, for I am very needy; save me from those who pursue me, for they are too strong for me.

8 Bring my soul out of prison so that I may give thanks to Your name. The righteous will crown themselves because of me, for You have been good to me.

TEHILLIM 143

A personal song to God to hear his servant's prayer

1 A psalm by David. Lord, hear my prayer. Listen to my pleas. Answer me in Your faithfulness and in Your righteousness.

2 Do not enter into judgment with Your servant, for no living person can be justified before You.

3 The enemy has pursued my soul; he has crushed my life down to the ground; he made me live in darkness like the dead of the world.

4 My spirit surrounds me; my heart is stunned inside me.

5 I remember the ancient days; I meditate on all Your works; I consider the work of Your hands.

6 I spread out my hands to You; my soul longs for You like dry land. Selah.

7 Answer me quickly, Lord, for my spirit fails. Do not hide Your face from me, so that I will not become like those who go down into the pit.

8 Let me hear Your loving kindness in the morning, for I trust in You. Teach me the path in which I should walk, for to You I have lifted up my soul.

9 Save me from my enemies, Lord. I hide myself in You.

10 Teach me to do Your will, for You are my God. Let Your good spirit lead me to level ground.

11 For Your name's sake, Lord, revive me. In Your righteousness, bring my soul out of trouble.

12 And in Your loving kindness, cut off my enemies, and destroy all who opress my soul, for I am Your servant.

פרק קמד

א לְדָוִד בָּרוּךְ יְהוָה צוּרִי הַמְלַמֵּד יָדַי לַקְרָב אֶצְבְּעוֹתַי לַמִּלְחָמָה:

ב חַסְדִּי וּמְצוּדָתִי מִשְׂגַּבִּי וּמְפַלְטִי לִי מָגִנִּי וּבוֹ חָסִיתִי הָרוֹדֵד עַמִּי תַחְתָּי:

ג יְהוָה מָה־אָדָם וַתֵּדָעֵהוּ בֶּן־אֱנוֹשׁ וַתְּחַשְּׁבֵהוּ:

ד אָדָם לַהֶבֶל דָּמָה יָמָיו כְּצֵל עוֹבֵר:

ה יְהוָה הַט־שָׁמֶיךָ וְתֵרֵד גַּע בֶּהָרִים וְיֶעֱשָׁנוּ:

ו בְּרוֹק בָּרָק וּתְפִיצֵם שְׁלַח חִצֶּיךָ וּתְהֻמֵּם:

ז שְׁלַח יָדֶיךָ מִמָּרוֹם פְּצֵנִי וְהַצִּילֵנִי מִמַּיִם רַבִּים מִיַּד בְּנֵי נֵכָר:

ח אֲשֶׁר פִּיהֶם דִּבֶּר־שָׁוְא וִימִינָם יְמִין שָׁקֶר:

ט אֱלֹהִים שִׁיר חָדָשׁ אָשִׁירָה לָּךְ בְּנֵבֶל עָשׂוֹר אֲזַמְּרָה־לָּךְ:

י הַנּוֹתֵן תְּשׁוּעָה לַמְּלָכִים הַפּוֹצֶה אֶת־דָּוִד עַבְדּוֹ מֵחֶרֶב רָעָה:

יא פְּצֵנִי וְהַצִּילֵנִי מִיַּד בְּנֵי־נֵכָר אֲשֶׁר פִּיהֶם דִּבֶּר־שָׁוְא וִימִינָם יְמִין שָׁקֶר:

יב אֲשֶׁר בָּנֵינוּ כִּנְטִעִים מְגֻדָּלִים בִּנְעוּרֵיהֶם בְּנוֹתֵינוּ כְזָוִיֹּת מְחֻטָּבוֹת תַּבְנִית הֵיכָל:

יג מְזָוֵינוּ מְלֵאִים מְפִיקִים מִזַּן אֶל־זַן צֹאונֵנוּ מַאֲלִיפוֹת מְרֻבָּבוֹת בְּחוּצוֹתֵינוּ:

יד אַלּוּפֵינוּ מְסֻבָּלִים אֵין פֶּרֶץ וְאֵין יוֹצֵאת וְאֵין צְוָחָה בִּרְחֹבֹתֵינוּ:

טו אַשְׁרֵי הָעָם שֶׁכָּכָה לּוֹ אַשְׁרֵי הָעָם שֶׁיְהוָה אֱלֹהָיו:

TEHILLIM 144

A song of thanksgiving to God for preparing man to work successfully

1 By David. Blessed be the Lord, my Rock, who trains my hands for war and my fingers how to fight.

2 My loving kindness and my fortress, my high tower and my rescuer; my shield, in whom I take refuge, who makes my people my subjects.

3 Lord, what is man that You should be aware of him, Or the son of man that You should take note of him?

4 Man is like a breath; his days are like a shadow that passes away.

5 My Lord, incline Your heavens and come down. Touch the mountains and they will vanish like smoke.

6 Send out lightning to scatter them. Send out Your arrows and frighten them.

7 Stretch out Your hands from high. Rescue me and save me from the multitude of waters, from the hands of strangers

8 Whose mouth speaks falsehood, and whose right hand is a right hand of lies.

9 God, I will sing a new song to You, and with the ten-stringed lyre I will sing praises to You,

10 Who gives salvation to a king, who rescues Your servant David from the evil sword.

11 Rescue me and save me from the hand of strangers, whose mouth speaks falsehood, and whose right hand is a right hand of lies.

12 So that our sons are like plants nurtured in their youth; our daughters are like supporting pillars of a palace.

13 Our storehouses are full of every kind of food; our sheep increase by the thousands and ten thousands in our fields.

14 Our leaders carry the burden, there is no worry in the city and the walls are secure and protected.

15 Happy is the nation who lives in this way. Happy is the nation whose God is the Lord.

פרק קמה

א   תְּהִלָּה לְדָוִד אֲרוֹמִמְךָ אֱלוֹהַי הַמֶּלֶךְ וַאֲבָרְכָה שִׁמְךָ לְעוֹלָם וָעֶד:

ב   בְּכָל־יוֹם אֲבָרְכֶךָּ וַאֲהַלְלָה שִׁמְךָ לְעוֹלָם וָעֶד:

ג   גָּדוֹל יְהוָה וּמְהֻלָּל מְאֹד וְלִגְדֻלָּתוֹ אֵין חֵקֶר:

ד   דּוֹר לְדוֹר יְשַׁבַּח מַעֲשֶׂיךָ וּגְבוּרֹתֶיךָ יַגִּידוּ:

ה   הֲדַר כְּבוֹד הוֹדֶךָ וְדִבְרֵי נִפְלְאֹתֶיךָ אָשִׂיחָה:

ו   וֶעֱזוּז נוֹרְאֹתֶיךָ יֹאמֵרוּ וגדולתיך [וּגְדוּלָּתְךָ] אֲסַפְּרֶנָּה:

ז   זֵכֶר רַב־טוּבְךָ יַבִּיעוּ וְצִדְקָתְךָ יְרַנֵּנוּ:

ח   חַנּוּן וְרַחוּם יְהוָה אֶרֶךְ אַפַּיִם וּגְדָל־חָסֶד:

ט   טוֹב־יְהוָה לַכֹּל וְרַחֲמָיו עַל־כָּל־מַעֲשָׂיו:

י   יוֹדוּךָ יְהוָה כָּל־מַעֲשֶׂיךָ וַחֲסִידֶיךָ יְבָרְכוּכָה:

יא   כְּבוֹד מַלְכוּתְךָ יֹאמֵרוּ וּגְבוּרָתְךָ יְדַבֵּרוּ:

יב   לְהוֹדִיעַ לִבְנֵי הָאָדָם גְּבוּרֹתָיו וּכְבוֹד הֲדַר מַלְכוּתוֹ:

יג   מַלְכוּתְךָ מַלְכוּת כָּל־עֹלָמִים וּמֶמְשַׁלְתְּךָ בְּכָל־דּוֹר וָדוֹר:

יד   סוֹמֵךְ יְהוָה לְכָל־הַנֹּפְלִים וְזוֹקֵף לְכָל־הַכְּפוּפִים:

טו   עֵינֵי כֹל אֵלֶיךָ יְשַׂבֵּרוּ וְאַתָּה נוֹתֵן־לָהֶם אֶת־אָכְלָם בְּעִתּוֹ:

טז   פּוֹתֵחַ אֶת־יָדֶךָ וּמַשְׂבִּיעַ לְכָל־חַי רָצוֹן:

יז   צַדִּיק יְהוָה בְּכָל־דְּרָכָיו וְחָסִיד בְּכָל־מַעֲשָׂיו:

יח   קָרוֹב יְהוָה לְכָל־קֹרְאָיו לְכֹל אֲשֶׁר יִקְרָאֻהוּ בֶאֱמֶת:

יט   רְצוֹן־יְרֵאָיו יַעֲשֶׂה וְאֶת־שַׁוְעָתָם יִשְׁמַע וְיוֹשִׁיעֵם:

כ   שׁוֹמֵר יְהוָה אֶת־כָּל־אֹהֲבָיו וְאֵת כָּל־הָרְשָׁעִים יַשְׁמִיד:

כא   תְּהִלַּת יְהוָה יְדַבֶּר־פִּי וִיבָרֵךְ כָּל־בָּשָׂר שֵׁם קָדְשׁוֹ לְעוֹלָם וָעֶד:

TEHILLIM 145

A song thanking God for His providing hand to everyone

1 A song of praise by David. I will exalt You, my God, my Lord, and I will bless Your name forever and ever.

2 Each day I will bless you, and I will sing to Your name forever and ever.

3 The Lord is great and abundantly to be praised. His greatness is beyond all knowledge.

4 Each generation will praise Your greatness to the next, and speak of Your mighty acts.

5 I will declare the glorious splendor of Your majesty and of Your marvelous works.

6 People will speak of the power of Your awesome acts, and I will tell of Your greatness.

7 They will make mention of Your great goodness, and will sing of Your righteousness.

8 The Lord is gracious and compassionate, slow to anger and abundant in loving kindness.

9 The Lord is good to all, and His mercy is upon all His works.

10 All Your works will praise You, Lord, and Your faithful ones will bless You.

11 They will speak about the honor due Your kingdom and talk of Your power.

12 To reveal Your mighty acts to human beings, and the glory of Your kingdom's majesty.

13 Your kingdom is a kingdom for all times, and Your rule endures forever.

14 The Lord supports all who fall, and straightens all who are bowed down.

15 The eyes of all await You, and You give them their food at the proper time.

16 You open Your hand and satisfy the desire every living thing with favor.

17 The Lord is righteous in all His ways, and gracious in all His deeds.

18 The Lord is near to all who call upon Him, to all who call upon Him in truth.

19 He will fulfill the desire of those who revere Him. He will hear their cry and save them.

20 The Lord protects all who love Him, but will destroy all the wicked.

21 My mouth will speak the praise of the Lord, and let every living being bless His holy name forever and ever.

פרק קמו

א הַלְלוּיָהּ הַלְלִי נַפְשִׁי אֶת־יְהֹוָה:

ב אֲהַלְלָה יְהֹוָה בְּחַיָּי אֲזַמְּרָה לֵאלֹהַי בְּעוֹדִי:

ג אַל־תִּבְטְחוּ בִנְדִיבִים בְּבֶן־אָדָם שֶׁאֵין לוֹ תְשׁוּעָה:

ד תֵּצֵא רוּחוֹ יָשֻׁב לְאַדְמָתוֹ בַּיּוֹם הַהוּא אָבְדוּ עֶשְׁתֹּנֹתָיו:

ה אַשְׁרֵי שֶׁאֵל יַעֲקֹב בְּעֶזְרוֹ שִׂבְרוֹ עַל־יְהֹוָה אֱלֹהָיו:

ו עֹשֶׂה שָׁמַיִם וָאָרֶץ אֶת־הַיָּם וְאֶת־כָּל־אֲשֶׁר־בָּם הַשֹּׁמֵר אֱמֶת לְעוֹלָם:

ז עֹשֶׂה מִשְׁפָּט לַעֲשׁוּקִים נֹתֵן לֶחֶם לָרְעֵבִים יְהֹוָה מַתִּיר אֲסוּרִים:

ח יְהֹוָה פֹּקֵחַ עִוְרִים יְהֹוָה זֹקֵף כְּפוּפִים יְהֹוָה אֹהֵב צַדִּיקִים:

ט יְהֹוָה שֹׁמֵר אֶת־גֵּרִים יָתוֹם וְאַלְמָנָה יְעוֹדֵד וְדֶרֶךְ רְשָׁעִים יְעַוֵּת:

י יִמְלֹךְ יְהֹוָה לְעוֹלָם אֱלֹהַיִךְ צִיּוֹן לְדֹר וָדֹר הַלְלוּיָהּ:

פרק קמז

א הַלְלוּיָהּ כִּי־טוֹב זַמְּרָה אֱלֹהֵינוּ כִּי־נָעִים נָאוָה תְהִלָּה:

ב בּוֹנֵה יְרוּשָׁלַ͏ִם יְהֹוָה נִדְחֵי יִשְׂרָאֵל יְכַנֵּס:

ג הָרֹפֵא לִשְׁבוּרֵי לֵב וּמְחַבֵּשׁ לְעַצְּבוֹתָם:

ד מוֹנֶה מִסְפָּר לַכּוֹכָבִים לְכֻלָּם שֵׁמוֹת יִקְרָא:

ה גָּדוֹל אֲדוֹנֵינוּ וְרַב־כֹּחַ לִתְבוּנָתוֹ אֵין מִסְפָּר:

ו מְעוֹדֵד עֲנָוִים יְהֹוָה מַשְׁפִּיל רְשָׁעִים עֲדֵי־אָרֶץ:

ז עֱנוּ לַיהֹוָה בְּתוֹדָה זַמְּרוּ לֵאלֹהֵינוּ בְכִנּוֹר:

TEHILLIM 146

A song to God, our deliverer

1 Hallelujah! Give thanks to the Lord, my soul.

2 I will praise the Lord while I live. I will sing praises to my God while I exist.

3 Do not put your trust in princes, nor in the son of man, who has no ability to help.

4 His breath leaves him, he returns to his dust; on that same day his plans are lost.

5 Happy is he whose help is the God of Jacob, whose hope is in the Lord his God,

6 Who made heaven and earth, the sea and all that they contain, who keeps truth forever;

7 Who grants justice to the oppressed, Who gives bread to the hungry. The Lord frees the prisoners.

8 The Lord opens the eyes of the blind. The Lord raises up those who are bowed down. The Lord loves the righteous.

9 The Lord protects strangers. The Lord supports orphans and widows, but prevents the way of the wicked.

10 The Lord will reign forever, he is Your God, Zion, from generation to generations. Hallelujah!

TEHILLIM 147

A song of praise to God for the creation and maintenance of the world

1 Hallelujah! Truly, it is good to sing praises to our God, and His praise is pleasant.

2 The Lord builds Jerusalem and gathers together the scattered of Israel.

3 He heals the broken-hearted and binds up their wounds.

4 He numbers the stars and gives them their names.

5 Our Lord is great and full of power. His understanding is boundless.

6 The Lord supports the humble. He brings the wicked down to the ground.

7 Sing to the Lord with thanksgiving and sing upon the harp to our God.

ח הַמְכַסֶּה שָׁמַיִם בְּעָבִים הַמֵּכִין לָאָרֶץ מָטָר הַמַּצְמִיחַ הָרִים חָצִיר:

ט נוֹתֵן לִבְהֵמָה לַחְמָהּ לִבְנֵי עֹרֵב אֲשֶׁר יִקְרָאוּ:

י לֹא בִגְבוּרַת הַסּוּס יֶחְפָּץ לֹא־בְשׁוֹקֵי הָאִישׁ יִרְצֶה:

יא רוֹצֶה יְהוָה אֶת־יְרֵאָיו אֶת־הַמְיַחֲלִים לְחַסְדּוֹ:

יב שַׁבְּחִי יְרוּשָׁלַ ם אֶת־יְהוָה הַלְלִי אֱלֹהַיִךְ צִיּוֹן:

יג כִּי־חִזַּק בְּרִיחֵי שְׁעָרָיִךְ בֵּרַךְ בָּנַיִךְ בְּקִרְבֵּךְ:

יד הַשָּׂם גְּבוּלֵךְ שָׁלוֹם חֵלֶב חִטִּים יַשְׂבִּיעֵךְ:

טו הַשֹּׁלֵחַ אִמְרָתוֹ אָרֶץ עַד־מְהֵרָה יָרוּץ דְּבָרוֹ:

טז הַנֹּתֵן שֶׁלֶג כַּצָּמֶר כְּפוֹר כָּאֵפֶר יְפַזֵּר:

יז מַשְׁלִיךְ קַרְחוֹ כְפִתִּים לִפְנֵי קָרָתוֹ מִי יַעֲמֹד:

יח יִשְׁלַח דְּבָרוֹ וְיַמְסֵם יַשֵּׁב רוּחוֹ יִזְּלוּ־מָיִם:

יט מַגִּיד דברו [דְּבָרָיו] לְיַעֲקֹב חֻקָּיו וּמִשְׁפָּטָיו לְיִשְׂרָאֵל:

כ לֹא עָשָׂה כֵן לְכָל־גּוֹי וּמִשְׁפָּטִים בַּל־יְדָעוּם הַלְלוּיָהּ:

פרק קמח

א הַלְלוּיָהּ הַלְלוּ אֶת־יְהוָה מִן־הַשָּׁמַיִם הַלְלוּהוּ בַּמְּרוֹמִים:

ב הַלְלוּהוּ כָל־מַלְאָכָיו הַלְלוּהוּ כָּל־צבאו [צְבָאָיו]:

ג הַלְלוּהוּ שֶׁמֶשׁ וְיָרֵחַ הַלְלוּהוּ כָּל־כּוֹכְבֵי אוֹר:

ד הַלְלוּהוּ שְׁמֵי הַשָּׁמָיִם וְהַמַּיִם אֲשֶׁר מֵעַל הַשָּׁמָיִם:

ה יְהַלְלוּ אֶת־שֵׁם יְהוָה כִּי הוּא צִוָּה וְנִבְרָאוּ:

ו וַיַּעֲמִידֵם לָעַד לְעוֹלָם חָק־נָתַן וְלֹא יַעֲבוֹר:

ז הַלְלוּ אֶת־יְהוָה מִן־הָאָרֶץ תַּנִּינִים וְכָל־תְּהֹמוֹת:

8 He covers the heavens with clouds. He prepares rain for the earth. He makes the mountains sprout with grass.

9 He gives food to the animals and to the young ravens that call.

10 He takes no delight in the strength of the horse, nor pleasure in the stamina of man.

11 The Lord takes pleasure in those who revere Him and in those who wait for His loving kindness.

12 Jerusalem, give glory to the Lord! Praise your God, Zion,

13 For he has strengthened the bars of your gates and blessed your children among you.

14 He makes your borders peaceful. He gives you the best of the wheat in abundance.

15 He sends out His commandment upon earth; His words spread swiftly.

16 He gives snow easily; He brings the cold and ash everywhere.

17 He throws down His ice like crumbs. Who can withstand His cold?

18 He sends forth His word and melts them; He orders His wind to blow, and the waters flow.

19 He relays His word to Jacob, His statutes and laws to Israel.

20 He has not done so for any nation, nor have they known His laws. Hallelujah!

TEHILLIM 148

*A song to all of creation to thank God
following Israel's return to its land*

1 Hallelujah! Praise the Lord from the heavens. Praise Him in the heights.

2 Praise Him, all you angels. Praise Him, all his hosts.

3 Praise Him, sun and moon. Praise Him, all you stars of light.

4 Praise Him, you heavens of heavens, and you waters that are above the heavens.

5 Let them praise the name of the Lord, for He commanded and they were created.

6 He set them in place forever and ever. He made a decree that will never be broken.

7 Praise the Lord from the earth, you sea creatures, and all the depths,

ח אֵשׁ וּבָרָד שֶׁלֶג וְקִיטוֹר רוּחַ סְעָרָה עֹשָׂה דְבָרוֹ:

ט הֶהָרִים וְכָל־גְּבָעוֹת עֵץ פְּרִי וְכָל־אֲרָזִים:

י הַחַיָּה וְכָל־בְּהֵמָה רֶמֶשׂ וְצִפּוֹר כָּנָף:

יא מַלְכֵי־אֶרֶץ וְכָל־לְאֻמִּים שָׂרִים וְכָל־שֹׁפְטֵי אָרֶץ:

יב בַּחוּרִים וְגַם־בְּתוּלוֹת זְקֵנִים עִם־נְעָרִים:

יג יְהַלְלוּ אֶת־שֵׁם יְהוָה כִּי־נִשְׂגָּב שְׁמוֹ לְבַדּוֹ הוֹדוֹ עַל־אֶרֶץ וְשָׁמָיִם:

יד וַיָּרֶם קֶרֶן לְעַמּוֹ תְּהִלָּה לְכָל־חֲסִידָיו לִבְנֵי יִשְׂרָאֵל עַם־קְרֹבוֹ הַלְלוּיָהּ:

פרק קמט

א הַלְלוּיָהּ שִׁירוּ לַיהוָה שִׁיר חָדָשׁ תְּהִלָּתוֹ בִּקְהַל חֲסִידִים:

ב יִשְׂמַח יִשְׂרָאֵל בְּעֹשָׂיו בְּנֵי־צִיּוֹן יָגִילוּ בְמַלְכָּם:

ג יְהַלְלוּ שְׁמוֹ בְמָחוֹל בְּתֹף וְכִנּוֹר יְזַמְּרוּ־לוֹ:

ד כִּי־רוֹצֶה יְהוָה בְּעַמּוֹ יְפָאֵר עֲנָוִים בִּישׁוּעָה:

ה יַעְלְזוּ חֲסִידִים בְּכָבוֹד יְרַנְּנוּ עַל־מִשְׁכְּבוֹתָם:

ו רוֹמְמוֹת אֵל בִּגְרוֹנָם וְחֶרֶב פִּיפִיּוֹת בְּיָדָם:

ז לַעֲשׂוֹת נְקָמָה בַּגּוֹיִם תּוֹכֵחֹת בַּל־אֻמִּים:

ח לֶאְסֹר מַלְכֵיהֶם בְּזִקִּים וְנִכְבְּדֵיהֶם בְּכַבְלֵי בַרְזֶל:

ט לַעֲשׂוֹת בָּהֶם מִשְׁפָּט כָּתוּב הָדָר הוּא לְכָל־חֲסִידָיו הַלְלוּיָהּ:

8 Fire and hail, snow and vapor, storm wind fulfill His command;

9 Mountains and all hills, fruit trees and all cedars,

10 Beasts and all cattle, creeping things and winged birds,

11 Kings of the earth and all nations, princes and all the judges of the earth,

12 Young men and maidens too, old men and youths –

13 They will praise the name of the Lord, for His name alone is lifted high; His glory is above the earth and heaven.

14 He has raised the fortunes of His people. This is for the glory all His faithful ones, the children of Israel, a nation close to Him. Hallelujah!

TEHILLIM 149

A song of Israel's happiness with their God

1 Hallelujah! Sing to the Lord a new song, and praise him in the assembly of the holy ones.

2 May Israel rejoice in its Maker; let the children of Zion rejoice in their King.

3 Let them praise His name in the dance; let them sing praises to Him with drum and harp.

4 The Lord takes pleasure in His people. He adorns the humble with Salvation.

5 Let the holy ones rejoice in glory. Let them sing joyfully upon their beds.

6 Let high praise of God be in their throats, and a double-edged sword in their hand,

7 To exact vengeance from the nations, and rebuke the peoples,

8 To bind their kings with chains and their nobles with iron shackles;

9 To execute the written sentence upon them. He is the glory of all His faithful. Hallelujah!

פרק קנ

א   הַלְלוּיָהּ הַלְלוּ־אֵל בְּקָדְשׁוֹ הַלְלוּהוּ בִּרְקִיעַ עֻזּוֹ:

ב   הַלְלוּהוּ בִגְבוּרֹתָיו הַלְלוּהוּ כְּרֹב גֻּדְלוֹ:

ג   הַלְלוּהוּ בְּתֵקַע שׁוֹפָר הַלְלוּהוּ בְּנֵבֶל וְכִנּוֹר:

ד   הַלְלוּהוּ בְתֹף וּמָחוֹל הַלְלוּהוּ בְּמִנִּים וְעוּגָב:

ה   הַלְלוּהוּ בְצִלְצְלֵי־שָׁמַע הַלְלוּהוּ בְּצִלְצְלֵי תְרוּעָה:

ו   כֹּל הַנְּשָׁמָה תְּהַלֵּל יָהּ הַלְלוּיָהּ:

TEHILLIM 150

Israel's message to the world is a beautiful song of praise to God

1 Hallelujah! Praise God in His sanctuary; praise Him in the heavens of His power.
2 Praise Him according to His mighty deeds. Praise Him according to His abundant greatness.
3 Praise Him with Shofar blasts; praise Him with lyre and harp.
4 Praise Him with drum and dance; praise Him with stringed instruments and flute.
5 Praise him with the crashing cymbals; praise Him with resounding cymbals.
6 Let everything that breathes praise the Lord. Hallelujah!

GLOSSARY

(In order of appearance in the Book of Psalms)

Absalom (3:1): son of King David; became heir after assassinating Amnon. When he led a rebellion against his father and was subsequently killed by his cousin Joab, the commander-in-chief of the army, King David mourned him

Selah (3:3): a term denoting a closing thought of enduring significance; it is our obligation to bless and thank Hashem forever. The term appears seventy-one times in the Book of Psalms

nehiloth (5:1): wind instruments, possibly flutes

Netherworld (6:6): *Sheol* in Hebrew; the afterlife for sinners, or the grave itself

gittith (8:1): either a musical instrument or a particular melody

Zion (9:12): refers to Eretz Yisrael, but sometimes refers to the city Jerusalem i.e. Har Zion

Jacob (14:7): son of Isaac and grandson of Abraham; the father of the twelve founding tribes of the nation of Israel; third of the three patriarchs of the Jewish people

Cherub (18:11): winged creatures that guard the entrance to the Garden of Eden. The cover of the Ark in the Holy of Holies contained the sculpted likenesses of two cherubs facing each other

Meal-offering (20:4): an offering to God comprised of fine flour

Burnt offering (20:4): an animal offering that is completely burned on the altar. In this psalm, the offering is made before going to battle

Bashan (22:13): a region of the Land of Israel located on the eastern side of the Jordan River; conquered by Moses

Cedars of Lebanon (29:5): cedar trees native to the mountains of Lebanon

Sirion (29:6): an ancient name of Mount Lebanon

Kadesh (29:8): a desert region in the south of Israel

Avimelech (34:1): king of the Philistines

Aha (35:21): a mocking, contemptuous exclamation; a moment of understanding after struggling to understand

Yedutun (39:1): conductor of the Temple choir, who was a leviate or possibly instructions to him

Sons of Korach (42:1): Korach's descendants, who may have composed and sung songs in the Temple choir

Jordan (42:7): region on the eastern side of the Jordan River

Hermon (42:7): mountain range in Israel's northern region and in Lebanon and Syria

Mizar (42:7): hill grouped together with the mountains of Jordan and the Hermon mountain range

Myrrh, aloes, and cassia (45:9): spices used to prepare anointing oils and perfumes.

Ophir (45:10): land known for its fine gold and wealth, perhaps India

Tyre (45:13): city in Lebanon

alamoth (46:1) possibly musical instruments

Mount Zion (48:3): mountain in Jerusalem on which the three patriarchs of the Jewish people worshipped and upon which the Beit ha-Mikdash was built

Tarshish (48:8): a port city in Southern Spain

Judah (48:12): fourth-born son of Jacob by Leah; also the name of the tribe and its traditional region in the land of Israel. Here, the name refers to cities in the southern part of Judah's territory

Asaph (50:1): musician of the Beit ha-Mikdash whose name appears in connection with twelve psalms

Nathan (51:2): prophet who spoke to King David about Batsheva's concern over the succession of Solomon, her son by David, after David's impending death

Batsheva (51:2): originally the wife of Uriah the Hittite, an officer in King David's army, she later became the wife of King David and the mother of his successor, Solomon

Hyssop (51:9): herb traditionally used for purification

Doeg the Edomite (52:2): servant of King Saul

Acimelech (52:2): High Priest in King Saul's time who lived in the city of Nov

Saul (52:2): man of the tribe of Benjamin; first king of the Israelites

machalath (53:1): instructions to the leader, on a musical instrument

Ziphites (54:2): people from the barren area of Ziph in the Judean Desert

Philistines (56:1): hostile nation on Israel's southern coast

Gath (56:1): Philistine city

Aram-Naharayim (60:2): region in Syria

Aram-Zobah (60:2): region in Syria; ally of Aram Naharayim

Joab (60:2): commander-in-chief of King David's army

Edom (60:2): traditionally, Esau's descendants, who lived on the eastern side of the Jordan River

Valley of Salt (60:2): place near the Dead Sea where King David won a military victory

Shechem (60:8): city in Samaria that Jacob gave to his son Joseph

Succoth (60:8): region on the eastern side of the Jordan River

Gilead (60:9): region on the eastern side of the Jordan River that was conquered by Moses and given to the tribes of Reuven, Gad and half of Manasseh.

Manasseh (60:9): elder son of Joseph and brother of Ephraim; also the tribe of Manasseh

Ephraim (60:9): younger son of Joseph and brother of Manasseh; also the tribe of Ephraim

Moab (60:10): hostile nation that lived on the east side of the Jordan River

Philistia (60:10): region on the southern coast of Israel, home of the Philistines

Sinai (68:9): mountain at which God gave the Torah to Israel

Zalmon (68:15): mountain near Shechem

Benjamin (68:28): Jacob's youngest son and the second son of Rachel; also the tribe of Benjamin

Zevulun (68:28) Jacob's sixth son by Leah and the tenth-born of his children; also the tribe of Zebulun

Naphtali (68:28): Jacob's second son by Bilhah and the sixth-born of his children; also the tribe of Naphtali

Sheba (72:10): rich region in southeastern Arabia

Seba (72:10): possibly a region in Ethiopia

Leviathan (74:14): large sea creatures

Shalem (76:3): ancient name for Jerusalem

Manna (78:24): miraculous food that God provided to the Israelites every day during their forty-year sojourn in the desert

Zoan (78:43): region of Goshen in Egypt, where the people of Israel lived during the famine in Canaan

Cham (78:51): second of Noah's three sons

Shilo (78:60): city in Samaria where the Holy Ark was kept before the Temple was constructed

Meribah (81:8): place where God gave the Israelites water from a rock

Ishmaelites (83:7): descendants of Ishmael, son of Abraham and Hagar

Hagrites (83:7): hostile nation lived on the eastern side of the Jordan River

Gebal – (83:8): region on the eastern side of the Jordan River, north of Edom

Ammon (83:8): hostile nation descended from Lot

Amalek (83:8): traditional enemy of Israel who Jews are commanded to destroy

Assyria (83:9): hostile nation to the north of Israel

descendents of Lot (83:9): Moab and Ammon, nations descended from Lot's two sons who bore those names

Midian (83:10): hostile nation located on the eastern side of the Jordan River

Sisera (83:10): general from Hatzor in the north who attacked Israel during the time of the judge Deborah

Jabin (83:10): king of Hatzor

Kishon (83:10): river where the battle between the Israelites and Sisera's forces took place, resulting in a rout of the enemy forces and Sisera's death

En-dor (83:11): town on the River Kishon where the battle took place

Oreb (83:12): prince of Midian

Zeeb (83:12): prince of Midian

Zebah (83:12): prince of Midian

Zalmunna (83:12): prince of Midian

Babylon (87:4): nation that destroyed the first Temple and Jerusalem in 586 B.C.E.

Mahalath le-annoth (88:1): A song with musical accompaniment regarding one who is sick with love for Hashem

Heiman the Ezrahite (88:1): musical conductor in the Temple

Ethan the Ezrahite (89:1): musical conductor in the Temple

Mount Tabor (89:13): mountain in Israel known since ancient times for its beauty

Moses (99:6): youngest child of Amram and Yocheved; brother of Miriam and Aaron; prophet and leader of the Jewish people

Aaron (99:6): elder brother of Moses and younger brother of Miriam; first High Priest of the Israelite nation

Shmuel (99:6): prophet and leader in the time of the Judges; anointed Saul and afterwards David as kings

Halleluya (104:35): Hebrew exclamation: "Praise God!" Possibly used to call the people to join the singing in the Temple

Canaan (105:11): name of the land that God promised to the Jewish people

Joseph (105:17): the twelfth-born child of Jacob and first-born son of Rachel who became viceroy in Egypt and saved the region – together with his family, saved the Jewish nation – from famine

Dathan and Aviram (106:17): prominent members of Korach's rebellion against Moses and Aaron; died with Korach in the desert

Horeb (106:19): another name for Mount Sinai

Baal-peor (106:28): idol worshipped in Moab

Pinhas (106:30): son of Elazar and grandson of Aaron. During the Israelites' sojourn in the wilderness, he stopped a plague by killing Zimri, prince of the tribe of Simeon, and Cozbi, daughter of the Midianite prince Zur, in the midst of illicit relations

Ascents (120:1): Song of Ascents. Psalms sung by the Levites in the Temple as they stood upon the fifteen steps between the Women's Court and the Court of the Israelites. Refers specifically to Psalms 120–134 inclusive

Meshech (120:5): Gentile nation to which King David, before becoming king, may have fled for safety

Kedar (120:5): Gentile nation, nomadic nation

Solomon (127:1): son of David and Bathsheba; succeeded his father to the Israelite throne; the Temple was built during his reign

Ephrat (132:6): area on the road to Hebron

Pharaoh (135:9): king of Egypt

Sihon (135:11): king of the Amorites; defeated in battle by Moses

Amorites (135:11): hostile nation

Og (135:11): brother of Sihon and king of Bashan; also defeated in battle by Moses

ABOUT THE TRANSLATOR

Dr. ABRAHAM RAND OBM, also known as ABE, was born in 1935 to his parents MOSHE and ESTHER RAND. He grew up and went to school in Passaic, New Jersey. He graduated from Seton Hall University and then proceeded to Howard University for his DDS degree, followed by Oral Surgery specialty training at Boston University. He married DINA (Daryl) SIMON in 1962 and they settled in Monsey New York. They had 6 children whilst living in the USA.

In 1979 they fulfilled their lifelong dream and love for Israel and decided to make Aliyah. They moved to Israel where they had another two children. One of his first achievements in Israel, together with a group of friends, was founding the Neve Aliza community in Ginot Shomron as well as having a part in establishing the Young Israel shul there.

Despite the fact that he did not benefit from a yeshiva education, his life revolved around Torah and Judaism. He was always interested in learning, and sought to compensate for what he had missed in his early life. He regularly attended many shiurim including Daf Hayomi. He always woke up early to start his day with a shiur and davening, and went to sleep late after many hours of work and Torah study. He utilized every spare moment of his time, including that spent travelling to and from work, learning from a sefer that he always carried in his bag. He would never omit telling a dvar Torah on any family occasion or gathering, whether on a tiyul, hike or even to a pizza store. He was also involved in many chesed and voluntary endeavors including Zaka, Magen David Adom and the Police. He used his time to serve G-d with love and joy, and influenced those around him to do the same – as was quoted on his matzaiva – עבדו את ה' בשמחה (serve Hashem in joy). He fulfilled the pasuk "ואהבת לרעך כמוך" (You should love your neighbor as yourself) with everyone around him, young and old alike. He had the greatest respect for Rabbonim and talmidei chachamim. His relationship "בין אדם לחברו" (between man and his fellow man) was particularly apparent and he always had a good word for everyone.

He composed this translation of Sefer Tehillim, completing it shortly before he passed away on 13 August 2009 – 23 Av 5769. He is survived by his wife DINA, his 8 children, 34 grandchildren and 3 great grandchildren, *bli ayin hora*, as well as his brothers LEON and SAM and sister SANDY. He was predeceased by his brother JACK OBM.

~: May his Memory be blessed – יהי זכרו ברוך :~

——— **לעילוי נשמת** ———

ר' אברהם בן ר' משה אהרן הלוי רנד ז"ל
נלב"ע כ"ג אב תשס"ט

ת.נ.צ.ב.ה

ר' משה אהרן בן ר' אברהם הלוי רנד ז"ל
נלב"ע ב' שבט תשל"ז

ת.נ.צ.ב.ה

חיה אסתר בת ר' אליעזר הלוי ז"ל
נלב"ע כ"ה שבט תשל"א

ת.נ.צ.ב.ה

ר' יעקב יוסף בן ר' משה אהרן הלוי ז"ל
נלב"ע כ"ז אדר תשנ"א

ת.נ.צ.ב.ה

Dedicated by:
Dr. Leon Rand
Dr. Samuel & Mrs. Debra Rand, Children, Grandchildren & Great Grandchildren.
Mr. Yosef & Mrs. Sandy Avrahami, Children & Grandchildren.

——— **לעילוי נשמת** ———

ר' דוד בן ר' אברהם הלוי ז"ל
נלב"ע ו' סיון תשמ"א

ת.נ.צ.ב.ה

גיטל בת ר' משה ז"ל
נלב"ע כ"ז כסלו תש"ל

ת.נ.צ.ב.ה